AF669221

Readings in Educational Psychology

Dr. S.B. Kakkar

Published by
ATLANTIC
PUBLISHERS & DISTRIBUTORS (P) LTD
7/22, Ansari Road, Darya Ganj, New Delhi-110002
Phones : +91-11-40775252, 40775214, 23273880, 23275880
Fax : +91-11-23285873
Web : www.atlanticbooks.com
E-mail : orders@atlanticbooks.com

Printed & bound in India by Atlantic Print Services

Preface

A student has to go through his textbook in order to pass a course. Again, a textbook is a tool to be employed for teaching. It makes generous use of the outcomes of research studies – compiling, synthesising and interpreting them for students within the framework of a general design. A well-planned text can do this job successfully, but it cannot go intensively into the details of individual psychological research, nor can it convey the flavour of the primary sources. To get the feel of the ways in which hypotheses are formulated and tested, of the methods by which the design is carried out, of the conclusions that can and cannot be drawn from the data, and, above all, of the tentativeness of our understanding, the students need to go directly to the original sources.

Perhaps the academic ideal is to direct students to the library to collect primary materials from journals and other periodical literature. But in these days of increasing enrolments and frequent paucity of funds to keep library acquisitions proportionate to increases in the student body, a different strategy is warranted. Also, students often need help in understanding what they find in original sources and in relating it to what they read and discuss in classes.

It is these considerations that have led to the present collection of READINGS IN EDUCATIONAL PSYCHOLOGY in each of the 11 divisions in this book, the author has selected 5 to 10 papers that document, expand, or illuminate specific points brought out in most educational psychology textbooks. The selections are original reports of research the findings of which are either of theoretical interest or are applicable to practical problems of education. The readings have been chosen to meet the specific teaching purposes of post-graduate students of psychology, education and other social sciences who have not only to go through the courses of research but have to produce a research dissertation firstly at the post-graduate level and later at the M.Phil. and Ph.D. levels. It is felt that this book would be serving them best by giving them a sampling of great variety and range, both in assumptions and methodology, that characterize educational research and writing.

The selection of readings was demanding. Only the articles designed to foster intellectual and personal growth, that are within the technical competence of the student now in the field, have been included. instead of presenting an array of articles dealing with a potpourri of current issues confronting education and psychology, the author decided to focus on areas which are of crucial importance in the field of educational psychology, the basic theme of this volume. Some of the studies are on perplexing problems of education which are too critical to avoid and through which we can bring particular attention to the most important challenges in our educational system. It is hoped that the ideas conveyed through the readings will continue to find relevance with those who are concerned about such issues.

The present volume is based on the work and experience of the author in teaching post-graduate, M.Phil. and Ph.D. classes for over three decades. It is a fairly judicious selection from his research papers that found place in university, national and international research journals. The focus has been on the post-graduate students whose knowledge of statistics is modest. Articles presenting extensive tables and elaborate statistical analysis have been excluded. The student readers are expected to understand elementary statistical concepts: correlation, various measures of central tendency and dispersion, and the simpler ways of expressing confidence limits, besides elementary concepts of variance analysis, normal distribution, and testing of experimental hypotheses.

The need for a volume of readings for students of educational psychology and research is especially acute at this time. The number of students for courses in these subjects has multiplied greatly, and the interests and reading range of these students are much wider than they were years ago. Moreover, suitable supplementary readings are not to be had in most libraries, or, if they are catalogued, they are difficult to locate. The present compilation of the research material may be found extremely convenient in correlating the basic text with. It is very much in harmony with the new trends in current educational psychology.

The book may be of immense use to the teachers and students of psychology, education and other social sciences, as also to university and college libraries which serve as book banks for all those who need guidance in fundamental concepts and research.

Acknowledgements are gratefully made to the numerous publishers and editors who found place for the research papers included in this volume in their esteemed journals.

January, 1993 **S.B. Kakkar**

Contents

I. EARLY CHILDHOOD

1. BEHAVIOUR PROBLEMS AMONG SCHOOL CHILDREN

"As soon as I start teaching, children in the back rows talk and whisper", "many children have no manners", "boys do not know how to address their teachers", "if you ask a child why he makes noise he shifts the blame on to his classmate", are some of the reactions which teacher-trainees (of Govt. Training College, Jullundur) undergoing six weeks' school practice showed when they were asked: "Why can't some of you control your classes, are there some problem children in your class"? The writer was provoked to ask this question after he met the trainees in an interval following his day-long observations of their lessons in which he, to his dismay, had found a number of classroom-indiscipline cases. To study these cases in an organised way with a view to eradicating them in so far as the teacher-trainees could help, the present investigation was undertaken.

The behaviour problems of one type or another are experienced by every teacher no matter whether he is experienced or inexperienced, young or old, male or female. These problems interfere with the teacher's teaching plans and the learner's learning activities. They seriously block children's full development and annoy teachers, parents and children alike. Guidance Counsellor can aid the teacher in dealing with such problems.

Method

Ninety-five teacher-trainees (of Govt. Training College, Jullundur Session 1963-64) teaching in 8 local high schools (classes 6th to 9th, age-group 11-14) situated in diverse socio-economic sectors of Jullundur city were asked to write down three behaviour problems on paper slips, which pupils showed in their classes, and which they, the trainees, found most annoying. The teachers ranged in age from 20 to 37 years, 63 of them were males and 32 were females.

Findings

A cursory look over the slips containing three problems each showed that the age and sex seemed to bear no direct relation to the type of problems. The same types of problems were mentioned by almost all age-groups among both male and female teachers. It was, therefore, found not necessary to count the problems age-wise or sex-wise. Analysis revealed only 272 problems, as some of the teachers mentioned in actual fact two, not three, problems.

These problems duly categorised are presented in the following table:

Category	*Per cent of the Problems*	
Talking, whispering, gossiping	25	
Whistling, chattering, pinching or disturbing others.	8	
Attention-getting devices like too much hand-raising, speaking when not asked etc.	14	
Changing seats, running within classroom, unnecessary movements, gestures or other physical activity.	5	
Bad manners of talking or addressing others, abusing.	7	(Each of these problems were less than 1 percent to not more than 2.5 per cent of the total number of problems.)
Inattention, showing no interest, being dumb	18	
Other types of behaviour like disobedience, dirty dress and demeanour, carelessness, mutual jealously, trying to outdo others and the like.	23	

Discussion

Talking, inattention and attention-getting, in that order, accounted for the largest number of problems while disturbing others, bad-manners and physical activities in order of decreasing frequency came next. Lastly, a wide variety of other behaviour problems, mentioned by an insignificantly small number of teachers, were also reported.

To suggest remedies for all or any of these behaviour problems which annoy teachers is not within the scope of this paper. All the same, the belief that teachers with the help of guidance counsellor must study children's behaviour in order to understand it and must possess insight to deal with it has certainly withstood the shocks of all contrary arguments. The teachers must have certain qualities of head and heart as well as a proper cultivation of their own minds to be able to prevent the incidence of a behaviour problem or to deal with it when necessary.

Children show a variety of behaviour problems into which teachers can gain insight by acquiring knowledge of dynamics of behaviour in a classroom and by having adequate self-understanding and self-acceptance in order that they can willingly accept different kinds of children and interpret their behaviour without getting upset or unhinged. Emotional expression of children and its concomitant behaviour have to be accepted by teachers.

Tradition and orthodoxy have a great impact on teachers who assume that: classrooms should be quiet, children should be glued to their seats and be respectful to their teachers, they should be all-attentive and calm, and they should mind their own business. Such teachers are alarmed most by behaviour problems however slight and unwitting.

Post-training education through seminars, discussion groups etc. to help teachers develop a better understanding of themselves and of children would be immensely useful. To help children solve their problems, teachers need to have insight into the problems of boys and girls. But if teachers have many unsolved problems of their own, they are naturally unable to help children. Teachers are to know and to help children understand why they behave as they do. In fact, both teachers and children know much more than they practice regarding the latter's behaviour problems.

Certain reasons compel a child to behave in a manner which the teacher dislikes. The understanding and competent teacher finds out the reasons which provide worthwhile clues for solving the problem. The not-so-competent teacher is unable to find the reasons and is consequently unable to solve the problem. He looks at the child's behaviour from his own point of view and does not see all sides of a situation and its significance for the child. His own anxiety and predispositions confound his judgment.

Teacher need not consider himself as a custodian of approved behaviour whose task is to mould children to his own pattern. He is just to help children express their feelings in constructive and acceptable ways–feelings which arise within and which clamour for expression. He must be able to understand himself and his pupils, as this understanding influences his reactions to pupils and goes a long way toward developing likeable behaviour patterns in them.

2. ASPIRATION LEVELS OF CHILDREN

Hoppe (16) was perhaps the first researcher who, having approached aspiration level experimentally, suggested that the experience of success or failure in a task depends not upon some absolute score, but it is related to whether or not an individuals expected, or projected goals were reached.* Subsequently, varying amounts of experimental attention have been paid to this parameter of performance. Aspiration level, experimentally, is a score advanced by the individual prior to attempting some tasks in which he may or may not have had previous experience.

Motor-manipulative tasks have been utilised when objectively evaluating aspiration level, chiefly because such tasks yield exact performance scores. Frank (10,11) used 'quoit throwing' and 'pushing a ball up a groove with a stick' as popular tasks. Others used various clerical tasks involving figure cancellation and the like. Still others used more vigorous motor activities. Smith (22) employed football playing time as a performance criterion, while Clark and Clark (5) used a grip-strength task.

The nature and amount of past experience in the task is one variable influencing accuracy and level of aspiration. Clark (5), Gould (13,14) and Clark (6) found that individuals with high aspiration levels perform best. Conversely, those with a background of failure usually have low aspirations or underestimate their performance potential. A second result of failure in a given activity is for the individual to redirect his energies and to formulate high aspirations in a secondary area (25). Frank (11) found that an individual who has enjoyed past success tends

* He called aspiration level "a person's expectations, goals or claims on his future achievement." His definition implies social interaction, because in predicting achievement one must usually refer to some real or imagined norms which may only be constructed with awareness of other scores.

to form a strong self-concept of his potential which he tends to maintain. On the other hand, an individual who has met repeated failure will be more easily shaken by subsequent failure and will usually overact, showing a marked drop in aspiration level in subsequent trials. However, with increased incidence of failure, aspiration does not continue to decrease proportionally, the rate of decrease in aspiration levels off (18, 23) . That the relative strength of the individual's needs [(i) to keep aspiration level high in order to better past performance, (ii) to make aspiration approximate level of future performance and (iii) to avoid failure] is reflected by his aspiration level was found by Clark (10, 11).

Another variable found to be influencing both the level and the accuracy of an individual's aspiration is the nature of the task. Using a hand-steadiness test and another resembling shuffleboard, Gould (13) found a tendency to overestimate performance on motor tasks more than on other tasks emphasising perceptual factors. This tendency may be owing to cultural expectations relative to physical activity. Cratty (7) reports that performance of tasks having known proficiency limits has been found to produce greater feelings of failure when success is not achieved than of tasks whose top scores are not known.

Maturity of the subjects was also found to be affecting accuracy and level of aspiration. Anderson and Brandt (3) found that ten-year-old set unreasonably high goals in a cancellation task. Allport (1) suggested that children are more susceptible to the social implications of a task than are adults, and hence the children's unduly high aspiration levels.

Another group of factors influencing aspiration level of children and adolescents, as revealed in the studies of Rosen and D'Andrade (19), Little and Cohen (17), is the nature of parental training, parents' performance standards, and parents' personal aspirations.

That social factors influence aspiration level was found by Ex (8) whose study suggests that individuals in groups tend to seek higher goals and to expect better performance when they feel "good" about the person or persons with whom they are performing. Gould (14) found that individuals from better socio-economic backgrounds were less likely to fluctuate in their estimations of projected performance than were members of low-income groups. Cratty (7) suggests that the less favoured group are more subject to social and economic stress than are those with economic advantages. Women, having less pressure placed upon them to "get ahead", Find goal-setting situations less stressful than men; thus, they are less likely to show marked differences between actual and estimated scores and to overact to success and to failure (4, 24, 26). That males shift oftener and less accurately in estimates of successive performances has been shown by Burner and Rotter (4). Group pressure usually raises an individual's aspiration (11) and thus generally leads to inaccuracy between absolute performance and aspirations, especially on the part of immature performers (3). Frank (11) points out that social pressures cause aspiration to deviate from past experience, to become irregular and less reasonable when social stimulations like competition accompany performance situation.

Personality traits such as social adjustment, confidence, adaptability and self-concept were yet other variables found to be affecting aspiration level (11,14,12, 20,15).

Fales (9) observed rudimentary aspirations in two-and-three-year-olds according to whether they accepted or refused help with putting on their warps. Anderson (2) found that maturity of level of aspiration, by adult standards, increased with age.

The Present Study

The present study, unlike most of the previous ones in which the method employed did not seem to permit observation and quantification of children's reactions to various unfamiliar tasks, is aimed at devising a method of standardising children's behaviour in a variety of goal-striving situations, facilitating observation and making possible the comparison of choices and performances from task to task and child to child. That the task could make certain predictions relative to modifiability of aspiration behaviour under standard conditions, and that it should possess consistency for individual subjects were also kept in view while devising the tasks to be used. In the test situations used, the levels of difficulty were fixed for the child in terms of "how many other children can attain" each level, the most difficult being possible for "only a very few children." This is similar to the procedure used by Anderson and Brandt (3) and Sears and Levin (21). The experimenter's reaction to the child's choices was kept equally friendly no matter whether the choices were high or low.

The hypotheses were that children will generally choose such levels of difficulty as would lead to maximum achievement, that in the friendly and non-evaluative interaction with the experimenter the child will feel free to choose tasks which are more likely to bring success, and that, in the degree to which children choose to attempt achievement at more difficult levels, there may be individual differences.

Method

The tasks chosen were comprehensible, absorbing and challenging to the children, yet not the ones with which they had prior experience. Instructions were simple. The tasks were such that success and failure were apparent at the conclusion of each performance and were perceived by a child as a direct outcome of his own behaviour. The concept of a graduated order of difficulty, in each task, was meant to be learned and utilized from task to task. This was accomplished by maintaining five levels of difficulty in each of the four tasks arranged for the experiment. Each level was given a characteristic colour which was the same for every task *i.e.*, yellow coloured materials were the easiest level of each separate task and blue always the most difficult. Besides, the child indicated his choice of level by picking out a cube of the colour corresponding to the level from the five cubes of colours representing different levels. These cubes were common to all the tasks.

Four tasks were arranged, each task having five levels of difficulty. The levels were shown by colours *i.e.*, yellow being the easiest, then white, violet, brown and blue which was the hardest. The five levels of difficulty were marked by the same colours for each of the four tasks.

Fifteen seven and eight-year-old children (nine boys and six girls) served as subjects of this study. They were of the Junior Model School, Patiala and they belonged to middle-class, mostly professional families.

Task 1. Catching balloons. Five rubber balloons were fastened below thick steel strings hanging vertically down a horizontal rod in the ceiling. They stood in a row, six inches apart. The easiest to reach (yellow) was just within fingertip reach of the child, and each was hung about three inches higher than the preceding so that the blue was the highest and most difficult for the child to reach. Since the children chosen for the experiment were of about equal height, making any adjustment in the heights of the balloons was not considered necessary. The child was asked to choose the colour of the ball which he would like to catch on his jump.

Task 2. Standing jump. Five circles were painted on the floor, yellow closest to the starting point and blue farthest from it. The child had to reach the colour of his choice by one jump while standing at the same point.

Task 3. Recalling. Objects such as a pen, notebook, inkpot, glasses, watch, bottle etc., were hidden beneath each of the five painted steel hats. The child chose a hat by naming the colour and the experimenter lifted it. The child saw the objects until he told that he was ready, and then the hat was replaced. The child then tried to recall the objects from memory. Levels of difficulty were varied by the number of objects under each hat, starting with five objects under the yellow hat and increasing by one for each colour. To enable the child to repeat a level of difficulty, several series of objects were used.

Task 4. Drawings. Drawings made on cards in the appropriate colours were reproduced by the children on blank paper with the condition that they were not to repeat a line nor to lift their pencils after having once started drawing from a point. The intricacy of the drawings increased with each level of difficulty. Several series of drawings were used so that when a child repeated any given level of difficulty, he could be given another drawing of the same level and colour. The children were to reproduce each of the five drawings in two minutes.

All the tasks were laid out in a room. The order of tasks in the first session stood as given above. The child was taken into the room where the experimenter pointing to the first task instructed: "You have a number of games to play here. Some parts of every game are easy, and some are hard. Violet is moderate hard. Some of you can do it and some can't. Now the brown is harder. Not many children can do it. Blue is hardest of all. Very few children can do it. Yellow is the easiest. White is next harder but not as hard as the violet. Hope you understand. Which one are you going to try? You may tell this by picking out a cube of the colour corresponding to your choice." After the child's performance, the experimenter said in a casual way, "You chose brown, and you got (or did not get) brown. Which are you going to choose next? You may choose brown again, or white, or violet, or yellow, or blue". The instructions about the levels of difficulty were repeated many times during each task until it was certain that the child comprehended the whole procedure. There were five trials in each task. In the second session, five days later, the child was given freedom to choose tasks in the order he wished. The directions about the colours and the mode of making choices were the same as in the first session. The child's choices, whether he succeeded or failed, his comments and gestures were recorded.

Results

As is evident from Table 1, more of easy and less of difficult choices were made by the children in the first session. The preponderance of easy choices is even more significant in the second session. That their colour choices do not show chance value (20 per cent) for each colour dispels the possible doubt that the children were behaving randomly and ascertains the belief that they really reached to the experimental situation.

The percentages of all choices (yellow and white) at the easier levels of the tasks and those (brown and blue) at the harder levels, as shown in the last two rows of Table I, demonstrate that in the second session, there was a marked mean shift of colour choices towards the easier end of the series, and correlatively away from the harder levels. This finding tends to verify the hypothesis that the children's choices will change in the direction that ensures more frequent success, in a situation that is non-evaluative and non-rewarding.

Table 1
Total Choice for Colours

	Session 1		*Session 2*		σ *diff*	*t*	*r*
	*N**	%	*N**	%			
Yellow (Easy)	85	30.03	113	38.43			
White	70	24.73	83	28.23			
Violet	52	18.37	47	15.98			
Brown	46	16.25	30	10.24			
Blue (Hard)	30	10.60	21	7.14			
Yellow and White	155	54.76	196	66.66	4.50	2.64**	.67***
Brown and Blue	76	26.85	51	17.38	3.54	2.67**	.58***

** $p < .05$ *** $p < .01$

* The total possible number of responses per session for all the 15 subjects was 300. The total number of choices in this table is less than 300 because subjects occasionally declined to make all the 20 choices scheduled in a session.

Table 2 shows the choices (upward, downward and at the same level) after success (when the child has already achieved his previously stated choice). There was a significantly greater proportion of successes in the second session than in the first. These successes are followed by setting a lower goal or rechoosing the same goal. Correlatively, lesser successes in the second session were followed by setting of a higher goal, although in both sessions a higher choice after success was the most frequent response to reaching the previously set goal. The average number of successes in the second session was 76.89 per cent of all the trials, as against 71.03 per cent in the first session, showing thereby that the changes in goal setting after success actually resulted in reaching a greater number of goals. This finding goes to prove the hypothesis that with increasing experience, the children would choose such levels of difficulty as would lead to maximum achievement of goal.

Table 2

Choices After Success (for achievement of goals)

	Session 1		*Session 2*		σ *diff*	*t*	*r*
	N	%*	*N*	%*			
Up	113	64.54	101	48.01	4.07	4.06**	.61**
Down	45	24.72	65	28.62	1.72	2.27***	.78**
Same	19	10.84	46	18.54	3.45	2.24***	.35 =
Success	214	71.03	253	76.89	2.49	2.39***	.67**

*** $p < .05$ = not significant ** $p < .01$

* Percentage of each kind of response after success for each subject was calculated with the denominator equal to total number of successes minus the number of tasks which yielded successful responses.

Since the child desires, after continuing experience in the level of aspiration situation, to set goals which he is most likely to reach, the most adaptive response to failure is to set a lower goal for the next trial. Such is the most common response to failure in both sessions as is seen in Table 3. The increase, though non-significant, in the proportion of failures, from one session to the other, followed by setting of a lower goal, was in the expected direction. Similarly, there was a non-significant decrease in the proportion of failures followed by setting of a still higher goal. The small, though again insignificant, increase in the second session in rechoosing the same goal after failure goes against the hypothesis that the child will maximise successes. Both rechoosing and setting a higher goal, however, were rarely made.

Table 3
Choices After Failure

	Session 1		*Session 2*		σ *diff*	*t*	*r*
	N	%**	*N*	%**			
Up	16	24.00	11	18.15	4.15	1.40	.28
Down	41	64.25	33	67.07	6.12	.46	.02
Same	7	12.12	8	16.82	4.29	1.09	.30
Failures	80	28.92	64	20.64	3.00	2.76*	.70***

* $p < .05$ *** $< .01$

* Percentage of each kind of response after failure for each subject was calculated with the denominator equal to the number of failures minus the number of tasks whose responses led to unsuccessful responses.

In the present experiment, there was no external reward for reaching the stated goal. The pressures, if any, to choose the more difficult levels were intrinsic to the child rather than attached to adult approval offered by the experimenter. When such pressures could be relaxed through social interaction in the permissive situation of this experiment, the child was free to try for the "same" achievement at more likely levels.

r's of .67 and .58 (Table 1) show that the children tended to be consistent from session to session in the proportion of easy and difficult tasks they chose. r's of .61 and .78 (Table 2) tell that they were consistent in their responses after success as to the proportion of trials in which they went up or down. They're between the percentage of trials following success in which they chose the same level in the two sessions is .35 (Table 2), which, though positive, is insignificant. These children, then, tended to show consistent responses in the levels of difficulty which they chose, as also in the nature of their choices succeeding successful trials.

The choices after failure, however, do not show consistency from session to session (Table 3). Firstly, this may be due to lower reliability of the failure scores, possibly owing to the fact that there were considerably fewer of them than of the success trials. Secondly, this may be attributable to the finding that behaviour after punishment or failure is more variable than behaviour after reward. This finding is similar to Sears' (20) who found that children who often met failure in school had more widely variable discrepancy scores in level of aspiration situations than children who had often achieved success?

Interestingly enough, though the group means for colour choices and responses following successful trials changed in a predictable manner, the individual children tended to retain their relative positions within the group, as shown by the r's. This typifies a consistency in behaviour over the two sessions.

Summary

Fifteen seven and eight-year-old children were observed in two sessions of a level of aspiration experiment in which four separate tasks (each task graded into five levels of difficulty) were given. The study revealed that the children did discriminate, in the first session, among the levels of difficulty and tended to choose the easier levels of the tasks in a bid to achieve success, that the children's choices of the levels of difficulty and their choices after success changed in the second session in the direction which seemed to promise success, that they tended to be individually consistent from session to session in proportion of choices at given levels of difficulty and in their responses to successful achievement at the level chosen, and that there was no such consistency in their responses to failure in achieving a previously set level.

References

1. Allport, F.H., "Influence of Group upon Association and Thought," J. Exp. Psychol., 1920, 3,159-182.
2. Anderson, C. "The Development of a Level of Aspiration in Young Children." Unpublished Doctor's Dissertation. State Univ. of Iowa (1940).
3. Anderson, Harold H., and Brandt, H.F. "Study of Motivation Involving Self-Announced Goals of Fifth Grade Children of the Concept of Level of Aspiration." J. Soc. Psychol., 1939,10, 209-232.
4. Bruner E.M. and Rotter, J.B. "A Level-of-Aspiration Study among the Ramah Navaho." J. Personal, 1947,16,69-77.
5. Clark, H.H., and Clark, D.H. "Relationships Between Level of Aspiration and Selected Physical Factors of Boys aged Nine Years." Res. Quart., 1961,32,12-19.
6. Clark, H.H., and Stratton, Stephen. "A Level of Aspiration Test Based on the Grip Strength Efforts of Nine-Year-Old Boys." Child Dev. 1962, 33, 897-905.
7. Cratty, Bryant J. "Social Dimensions of Physical Activity." Prentice-Hall, INC., 20- 25.

8. Ex, J. "The Nature of Contact Between Cooperating Persons and Their Expectancy Concerning the Level of Their Common Achievement." Acta Psychol., 1959,16,99-107.
9. Fales, E. "Genesis of Levels of Aspiration in Children from One and One-Half to Three Years of Age." Reported in Lewin et. al (6).
10. Frank, Jerome D. "Some Psychological Determinants of the Level of Aspiration." Amer. J. Psychol., 1937,45, 285-298.
11. Frank, J.D., "Recent Studies of the Level of Aspiration." Psychol. Bull., 1941,38, 218-226.
12. Gardener, John W. "Level of Aspiration." J. Exp. Psychol., 1939, 25, 601-621.
13. Gould, Rosalind. "An Experimental Analysis of Level of Aspiration." Genet. Psychol. Monog., 1939, 21,1-115.
14. Gould, Rosalind. "Some Sociological Determinants of Goal Striving." J. Soc. Psychol., N.Y. Macmillan, 1941,13, 461-473.
15. Gruen, E.W. "Level of Aspiration in Relation to Personality Factors in Adolescents." Child Dev., 1945,16,181-188.
16. Hoppe, F. "Erfolg and Misserforg." Psych. Forsch., 1930,14, 1-62.
17. Little, Sue W., and Cohen, L.D. "Goal Setting Behaviour of Asthmatic Children and of Their Mothers for Them." J. Personal., 1950,19, 376-389.
18. Rao, K.U. "The Effects of Stress on Level of Aspiration Behaviour." Unpubl. Ph.D. Thesis, Univ. of London, 1954.
19. Rosen, Bernard C., and D. Andrade Roy. "The Psycho-Social Origins of Achievement Motivation." Sociometry, 1959, 22,185-218.
20. Sears, Pauline S. "Levels of Aspiration in Academically Successful and Unsuccessful Children." J. Abnorm and Soc. Psychol., 1940, 35, 489-536.
21. Sears, Pauline S., and Levin Harry. "Levels of Aspiration in Pre-School Children." Readings in Educ. Psycho. Noll & Noll, McMillan Co., 1962, 20, 231-238.
22. Smith, C.H. "Influence of Athletic Success and Failure on the level of Aspiration." Res. Quart., 1949, 20,196.
23. Staisel, I.M., and Cohen, B.D. "The Effects of Two Degrees of Failures on Level of Aspiration and Performance" J. Abnorm and Soc. Psychol. 1951,46,79-82.
24. Sumner, F.C., and Johnson, E.E. "Sex differences in Levels of Aspiration and in Self Estimates of Performance in a Classroom situation." J. Psychol., 1949,27,483-90.
25. Thompson, Merril. "A Comparison of Physical Achievement of Anglo-and Spanish-American Boys in Junior High School." Res. Quart., 1942,13, 341-46.
26. Walter, L.M. and Marzole, S.S. "The Relation of Sex, Age, and School Achievement to Levels of Aspiration." J. Educ. Psychol., 1959, 42, 285-292.

3. ALTRUISTIC INTERESTS OF SCHOOL CHILDREN

(Mr. Kakkar presents here his study of altruistic interests of school children. The results tend to confirm that with increasing class level, there is increasing development of feelings of sympathy and concern for fellow beings everywhere. This study indicates a good angle of studying pupils. Researchers have studied in the past the intelligence, achievement, attitudes of school children but a study of altruistic interests and other such factors demands greater attention. -Editors)

Rogers and Long (1966) in an exploratory study of the development of social sensitivity in elementary school children found that children at all levels expressed considerable concern for people in far off places with the greatest growth occurring between grades two and four. Research dealing with adult feelings of sympathy and concern for human beings wherever they may live (1950) seems to indicate that many adult Americans are relatively unconcerned about human misery, tragedy, etc., that occurs at any considerable physical distance from them. Lembo (1967) verified the assumption that no group differences, with respect to altruistic attitudes, exist in a culture where both "looking out for yourself" and "helping others" are valued. His study also suggested that the foundation and direction of development of altruistic attitudes may be substantially formed before adolescence.

The purpose of this study is to measure the degree to which children in grades three, five and seven demonstrate feelings of sympathy and concern for people in a series of physical locations progressing from near too far. The study may reveal the extent of children's willingness to go out from themselves–to be altruistic–to offer help to people in distress wherever they may be.

Procedure

The population studied consisted of 150 children attending an elementary school located in a largely middle-class suburb of Jullundur. Thirty children of class III and 60 each of class V and VII were included in the study.

Children were asked to imagine that they had ten rupees to give away to the needy. The needy were indicated in a 27-item paired comparisons "who shall we help?" test. They were classified into three categories, *i.e.,* our state, our nation and our world. There were three items in each category and each item was compared with every other item on the test. In each case the child was asked to decide to whom he would prefer to give his ten rupees. If he wished to help the needy nearby (our state) who, for example, were displaced because of an earthquake, he was to write ₹ 10 in column 1. If he wished to help the needy in adjoining state (our country) who, for example, were without homes because of bombardment by enemy planes, he was to write ₹ 10 in column 2. If, however, he wished to do his bit for the people of another country (the world) who owing to famine conditions were on the brink of starvation, he was to write ₹ 10 in column 3. The test was given in two sessions of approximately forty minutes each.

All the children of class III were tested and then retested twenty days later in an effort to determine the reliability of the instrument. A high degree of consistency was found, showing that the instrument is reasonably reliable (Table 1). Ten days following the test administration, an informal discussion was held with the children of class III to ascertain their reasons for giving away their money as they did; the children of classes V and VII wrote a short paragraph in which they were asked to tell to whom they gave most of their money and why they did so. The children's responses revealed that they were, in fact, concerned about people and their problems rather than merely expressing an interest in the things strange or foreign (Tables 2, 3).

Results and Discussion

Children of class III demonstrated a significant concern for people in other parts of the world. When choosing between their state *versus* the world, and their nation *versus* the world, they showed that, felt that they despite physical distance, the people afar would need their financial help to a greater degree than would people near home (Table 4).

Children in classes V and VII are even more emphatic in their desire to help people in need who are far from home (Tables 5,6).

Table 1

Consistency of the Responses of Class III Children to help others, on Re-test Following 20 Days' Interval

Similar responses	604	83%
Different responses	125	17%
Total	729	
Subjects	27*	

* Responses of 3 children being vague or incomplete were excluded.

Table 2
Responses, in Terms of "Shall give most to .....", of Class V Children

	Reason	Number	Per cent
my own state....		3	5
because they are our own people	3		
the nation....		7	12
because all countrymen are our flesh and blood	2		
because we must keep our country united the world..	5	45	75
because it is our human duty	6		
because all people are one	5		
because they are poor and yet growing	30		
because we can win their sympathy that way	4		
Vague or incomplete responses....		5	8
Subjects		60	100

Table 3
Responses, in Terms of "Shall give most to....," of Class VII Children

	Reason	Number	Per cent
my own state....		3	5
because we must help our own people	3		
the nation.....		4	7
because we must help all Indians	4		
the world....		48	80
because all countries are interdependent	7		
because we can get their sympathy only then	4		
because we must help them stand on their own legs	37		
Vague or incomplete responses		5	8
Subjects		60	100

Table 4
Responses, in Terms of help to State, Nation or World, of Class III Children

	Total	Number	Per cent	Critical ratio
State *Vs* Nation	250	140-110	56-44	1.89*
State *Vs* World	250	102-148	41-59	2.80**
Nation *Vs* World	250	90-160	36-64	4.26**

* Significant at .05 level.
** Significant at .01 level.

Table 5
Responses, in Terms of help to State, Nation or World, of Class V Children

	Total	Number	Per cent	Critical ratio
State *Vs* Nation	500	205-295	41-59	3.98*
State *Vs* World	500	110-390	22-78	11.52**
Nation *Vs* World	500	90-410	18-82	13.18**

* Significant at .05 level. ** Significant at .01 level.

Table 6
Responses, in Terms of help to State, Nation or World, of Class VII Children

	Total	Number	Per cent	Critical ratio
State *Vs* Nation	500	220-280	44-56	2.67*
State *Vs* World	500	120-380	24-76	10.80**
Nation *Vs* World	500	115-385	23-77	10.67**

* Significant at .05 level. ** Significant at .01 level.

The greatest growth in concern for people farther away seems to occur between classes III and V. There is apparently little change between classes V and VII (Table 7,8).

Table 7
Responses (in Terms of help to People of the State, Nation or World) of Class III Children *Vs* Responses of Class V Children

	Class III per cents	Class V per cents	Chi[1] square
State *Vs* Nation	56-44	41-59	3.84*
State *Vs* World	41-59	22-78	8.84**
Nation *Vs* World	36-64	18-82	7.74

* Significant at .05 level. ** Significant at .01 level.

Table 8
Responses (in Terms of help to People of the State, Nation or World) of Class V Children *Vs* Responses of Class VII Children

	Class V per cents	Class VII per cents	Chi[1] square
State *Vs* Nation	41-59	44-56	2.56
State *Vs* World	22-78	24-76	0.72
Nation *Vs* World	18-82	23-77	0.64

1. pp. 228-30, Psychological Statistics by Quinn McNemar, John Wiley and Sons, INC.

Children of classes V and VII seemed keen to help other countries largely because they perceive the other countries as "poor". Similarly, they (like the children of class III) saw little existing need in either their own state or in India.

Altruistic interest in the distressed or the needy, wherever they may be, has been clearly expressed by the children of all the three classes.

Benevolence which, as a value of Indian high school students, college students and teachers, has been demonstrated to be exceeding that of comparable American and Japanese population Kakkar (67), and which is the off shoot of India's culture, may be equally inherent in Indian children as well and may have contributed to the formation of altruistic interests unfolded by this study.

The results tend to confirm that with increasing class level there is increasing development of feelings of sympathy and concern for fellow beings everywhere. Whereas such altruistic interests seem to be slightly extending towards the people of one's own country, these are found to be much more inclined towards the people of other countries.

One of the desirable aims of modern education is to develop altruistic interests in the learners. This aim seems to be met if the altruistic feelings and the growth in such feelings, as manifested in this study, are somehow proved to be exclusively related to or to be solely caused by educational experiences. Other studies, involving rigorous controls and wider samples as well as better techniques, may provide such proof. Whether growth in such feelings continues as children grow into adulthood is another question suggested by this study.

Summary

The study, in a bid to estimate the degree of 150 children's (classes III, V and VII) feelings of concern for people in far off places when forced to choose between helping people of other countries and people closer to home on a "who shall we help" test, revealed that children at all of the class levels tested expressed considerable concern for people in far off places with the greatest growth occurring between classes three and five. Most of the children at all class levels perceived other countries, shown in distress, as "poor" needing financial help. That children have altruistic interests seems obvious.

References

1. Kakkar, S.B. "A Cross-Cultural Study of Values." The Research Bull. (Arts), Punjab University No. LV (1) 1967, 1-17.
2. Lembo, John M. "Altruistic Attitudes Among Catholic Lay and Religious Female College I Students." The Journal of Educational Research, Vol. 61, No. 2, October 1967, 71-74.
3. Rogers, Vincent R. and Elizabeth Long. "An Exploratory Study of the Development of Social Sensitivity in Elementary School Children." The Journal of Edu. Research, Vol. 59, No. 9, May-June 1966, 392-394.
4. Sorokin Pitirim A. "Altruistic Love." Boston: Beacon Press, 1950, p. 5.

4. EXPERIMENTAL EXTINCTION OF TANTRUM BEHAVIOUR

Abstract

Tantrum behaviour in a school going child has been treated on the basis of learning principles. The treatment did not involve aversive punishment. Reinforcement sustaining the tantrum behaviour was eventually found to be extinguished. Spontaneous recovery of the tantrum and subsequent extinction techniques adopted attest the validity of applying learning principles to treatment of the present problem.

Williams (1938) in his experiments on rats found that the greater the number of reinforcements during acquisition the slower is the extinction. Razran (1939) studied conditioned salivary responses in humans and illustrated that the more complex the conditioned stimulus (CS) the slower is the extinction. Rohrer (1947) manipulating massing and distribution of extinction trials on several groups of rats arrived at the empirically derived generalisation that extinction is more rapid with massed extinction trials. Mowrer and Jones (1943) in their experiment on three groups of rats verified the hypothesis that the greater the work required of the organism in making the response, the faster is the extinction. Estes (1944) using a Skinner-box situation concluded that there is little evidence to show that punishment at the time of response hastens extinction. Again Ellson (1938) using rats in the same situation found that if a spontaneous recovery takes place as a function of time, the longer the interval the greater is the number of trials required for the second extinction. Williams (1959) succeeded in the extinction of tyrant-like tantrum behaviour of a 21 months' old male child by eliminating reinforcement. And when the response recovered after one week it took him nearly the same time to extinguish it by the same method.

Procedure

This paper reports the successful treatment of a tantrum behaviour in a female child by the removal of reinforcement. The subject (S) was about 28 months' old. Being the only and the first child, she had always received special care and attention of her parents. She had adequate weight and vigour, was quite healthy and active. She enforced some of her wishes, especially when leaving for the nursery school every morning, by unleashing tantrum behaviour to control the actions of her parents.

The parent (father or mother) dropped S in the school early morning. If the parent left the school gate after leaving the S there, S would scream and fuss until the parent returned to the gate. As a result, the parent was unable to leave the school until after S went to her class where the teacher took over. Thus, the parent was spending about 15 to 20 minutes each morning just waiting in the school until S went to her class.

After medical reassurance regarding S's physical condition, the parents were advised to remove the reinforcement of this tantrum behaviour. Consistent with the learning principle that, in general, behaviour that is not reinforced will be extinguished, the parent left S at the school gate in a leisurely and relaxed manner and after exchanging a pleasantry or two drove off without looking back. S screamed and raged, but the parent did not return to the gate as she did before the experiment. The duration of screaming and crying for each day was obtained from the school watchman who stood on duty at the gate.

Results and Discussion

The results were drawn in graph (not presented here) and analysed. It was seen that S continued crying for 40 minutes the first time she was left at the school gate in the first extinction series. She cried less the next time she was left there. By the ninth time, S no longer whimpered or cried when the parent left the school gate. Rather, she smiled as they left. The parents heard the happy sounds she made while briskly trotting towards her class.

About six days later, S screamed and fussed after her aunt left her at the school gate, probably reflecting spontaneous recovery of the tantrum behaviour. The aunt then reinforced the tantrum behaviour by returning to the gate and remaining there until S joined her class. Thus, it became necessary to extinguish this behaviour a second time.

The second extinction series reached zero by the seventh day, but the third extinction series following the second spontaneous recovery, which occurred ten days after the previous extinction, reached zero by the eleventh day. No further tantrums at the time S was left at the school gate were reported during the next one and a half years. Perhaps three successive extinctions eliminated the S's response from her repertoire of responses, though this does not stand established for want of observational records of S's behaviour in the subsequent years.

The treatment in this experiment did not involve aversive punishment. All that was done was to remove reinforcement. Extinction of the tantrum behaviour then followed.

Besides replicating Williams' (1959) findings, the experiment tends to suggest that some of the findings, concerning the rate of extinction, the shape of extinction curves, spontaneous recovery and successive extinctions, that experiments on relatively simple organisms like those of rats' yield, may be equally applicable to humans who are neurologically more complex, on whom experimenter's control is rather loose and whose behaviour is easily shaped by cultural and environmental forces.

References

1. Ellson, D.C. (1938)—Quantitative Studies of the Interaction of Simple Habits: 1 Recovery from Specific and Generalised Effects of Extinction. *Journal of Experimental Psychology*, 23, 339-358.
2. Estes, W.K. (1944) — An Experimental Study of Punishment. *Psychological Monographs*, 57, No. 263.
3. Mower, O.H. and Jones, Helen, M. (1943)—Extinction and Behaviour Variability as Functions of Effortfulness of Task. *Journal of Experimental Psychology*, 33, 369-386.
4. Razran, G.H.S. (1939) — Studies in Configural Conditioning: VI. Comparative Extinction and Forgetting of Pattern and Single-Stimulus Conditioning. *Journal of Experimented Psychology*. 24, 432-438.
5. Rohrer, J.H. (1947) — Experimental Extinction as a Function of the Distribution of Extinction Trials and Response Strength. *Journal of Experimental Psychology*, 37,473-493.
6. Williams, Carl, D. (1959) — The Elimination of Tantrum Behaviour by Extinction Procedures. *Journal of Abnormal & Social Psychology*, 59, 269.

7. Williams, S.B. (1938) — Resistance to Extinction as a Function of the Number of Reinforcements. *Journal of Experimental Psychology,* 23, 506-522.

5. BEHAVIOUR PROBLEMS OF CHILDREN AS VIEWED BY FATHERS

Ellis and Miller(1), Hunter (2), Mitchell (3), Porter (4), Rivlin (5), Schrupp and Gjerde (6), Sparks (7), Stendler (8), Stouffer (9), and Thomas Mangan and David Shafer (10) are some of the researchers who studied the rating of behaviour of children by different adult groups.

The author here reports a study of children in seventh and eighth grades by securing parents' opinions concerning the seriousness of behaviour.

Procedure

A list of 47 types of behaviour was framed, using the list compiled by Wickman (11) as a guide. Three types of behaviour, namely, hetero-sexual behaviour, masturbation and enuresis, of Wickman's list were omitted for the fear that most of the Indian parents might not like to say anything on these or that they might feel affronted when asked to express their opinion on these types of behaviour.

The author personally contacted 120 fathers whose children were in grades seventh to eighth of six Government Schools of Patiala. A total of 156 children were involved, male and female in equal number. On meeting a father, the author asked him to give his views on the seriousness of different types of behaviour. He was given a list of the 47 types of behaviour with four columns for choice *i.e.* very acute, acute, not acute, ordinary. The categories of choice and the types of behaviour were explained to him, where necessary.

The results were correlated with similar results yielded by Wickman's study. These were also correlated with the results that Porter (4) obtained from his study and that Thomas Mangan and David Shafer (10) got from theirs. The list of behaviour problems as ranked in different studies is appended at the end.

Results and Discussion

Fathers tend to acquire the attitudes of children toward certain behavioural types. There was a +.82 correlation with the children.

Introjection may be the mechanism responsible for this finding, though a replication on fathers and their own children would be necessary before generalising this statement.

Fathers also tend to acquire the attitudes of teachers towards certain behavioural types. There was a +.59 correlation with the traditional teachers. This may be explained by the fact that teachers are father surrogates in many ways and hence may come to possess several attitudes, including that toward behaviour problems, similar to fathers. A lesser correlation, +.39, with the modern teachers may be owing to the more liberal and considerably diverse views (on children's behaviour problems) that the modern teachers possess.

It may be further observed that father's attitudes on the seriousness of certain types of behaviour are similar to those of college students. There was a +.47 correlation with college seniors. College seniors tend to attain maturity of views proximal to parents' and hence perhaps this correlation.

Fathers' views on certain behavioural types are quite different from, in some cases even reverse of school students. There was a –.27 correlation with high school students. This finding may be explained by the possibility that high school students lack the maturity and right thinking that parents often have, owing to the onset of adolescence and its stresses and strains especially in our culture. The conflicts and confusions caused by this stage of development, which the society does not recognise as such, tend to hinder the child from developing adult attitudes and values and hence perhaps this discrepancy.

Fathers' views on behaviour problems tend to be considerably different from, and in many cases even reverse of, mental hygienists. There was a –.04 correlation with the mental hygienists. Mental hygienists, being fully aware of cause-effect relationship in behaviour problems and believing as they do that such problems may arise because of several factors external to the child over most of which the child has no control, tend to judge the seriousness of a behaviour problem on the basis of the complexity and seriousness of its cause and not from the adult point of view, which parents and teachers often cherish and which is, not unsoften, moralistic and symptomatic of social standards of conduct. Consequently, their views may be diametrically opposite to, and in most cases very much different from those of fathers and hence the said correlation.

References

1. Ellis, D.B., and Miller, L.W. "Teachers' Attitudes and Behaviour Problems", *Journal of Educational Psychology,* Oct. 1936, pp. 501-511.
2. Hunter, E.C. "Changes in Teachers' Attitudes Toward Children's Behaviour Over the Last Thirty Years", *Mental Hygiene,* III, Jan. 1957, pp. 3-11.
3. Mitchell, John C. "A Study of Teachers' and Mental Hygienists' Ratings of Certain Behaviour Problems of Children". *Journal of Education Research,* XXXVII, December, 1942, pp. 292-307.
4. Porter, Robert M. "Student Attitudes Toward Child Behaviour Problems". *Journal of Educational Research,* May 1954, pp. 349-352.
5. Rivlin, Harry N. "*Educating for Adjustment*", New York, Appleton-Century-Crofts, 1936, pp. 254.
6. Schrupp, Manfred H., and Gjerde, Clayton M. "Teacher Growth in Attitudes Toward Behaviour Problems of Children". *Journal of Educational Psychology,* XLIV, April, 1953, pp. 203-214.
7. Sparks, J.N. "Teachers' Attitudes Toward the Behaviour Problems of Children". *Journal of Educational Psychology,* XLIII, May, 1952, pp. 284-291.
8. Stendler, Celia B. "How Well do Elementary School Teachers Understand Child Behaviour?" *Journal of Educational Psychology,* XL, December, 1949, pp. 489-498.
9. Stouffer, George AW., Jr. "Behaviour Problems of Children as Viewed by Teachers and Mental Hygienists". *Mental Hygiene,* XXXVI, April, 1952, pp. 271-285.
10. Thomas Mangan and David Shafer. "Behaviour Problems of Children as Viewed by Children in the Fifth Through Eighth Grades". *Journal of Educational Research,* Vol. 56, No. 2, Oct. 1962, pp. 104-106.
11. Wickman, E.K. "Children's Behaviour and Teachers' Attitudes". New York: *The Commonwealth Fund, Division of Publications,* 1928.

BEHAVIOUR PROBLEMS AND THEIR RANKS

Ranking by different adult groups	R_1	R_2	R_3	R_4	R_5	R_6	R_7
1. Stealing	1	1	1	1	8	0	1
2. Skipping school	5	2	4	3	17	6	17
3. Cheating	11	3	7	15	24	1	3
4. Destroying school material	10	4	8	6	21	0	2
5. Temper tantrum	2	5	11	11	15	9	12
6. Lying	6	6	3	8	19	3	4

7. Obscene material	3	7	2	13	32	4	7
8. Swearing	24	8.5	13	37	45	2.5	15
9. Smoking	14	8.5	16	34	46	24.5	32
10. Disobedience	13	10	9	9	38	10	9
11. Defiance	4	11	5	5	29	6	5
12. Lack of interest	17	12	12	19	23	2	19
13. Impoliteness	9	13	14	20	40	4	13
14. Thoughtlessness	15	14.5	35	42	36	29.5	42
15. Bullying	18	14.5	6	2	5	9.5	6
16. Imaginative lying (fantasy)	12	16.5	39	46	37	10.5	35
17. Resentful	8	16.5	26	10	7	9.5	20
18. Unreliable	19	18	10	7	20	11	10
19. Shabby in appearance	16	19	31	39	30	9	37
20. Easily discouraged	7	20	20	21	14	1	11
21. Selfishness	20	21	21	16	25	8	18
22. Inattention	23	22.5	23	25	28	14.5	36
23. Quarrelsomeness	40	22.5	24	17	26	1.5	14
24. Domineering	45	24	30	18	16	8	22
25. Inquisitiveness	25	25.5	41	44	41	13.5	44
26. Silliness	22	25.5	36	27	35	3.5	40
27. Suspiciousness	27	27	34	32	4	14	28
28. Careless in work	30	28	22	31	39	14	33
29. Overcritical	29	29	42	29	13	8	21
30. Stubbornness	28	30	29	35	34	10	39
31. Disorderliness	38	32.5	18	26	42	9.5	23
32. Interrupting	36	32.5	40	45	44	1.5	45
33. Sullenness (Gloominess)	33	32.5	32	27	22	2.5	29
34. Laziness	34	32.5	15	29	33	17.5	26
35. Suggestible	47	35	25	22	12	13	27
36. Tardiness	39	36	27	41	43	6	43
37. Tattling (Idle Talk)	32	37	43	43	31	12	30
38. Coward	35	38	28	28	18	0	31
39. Dreaminess	44	39	38	36	10	4	38
40. Unsocial	46	40.5	37	12	1	8.5	16
41. Unhappy	41	40.5	19	4	2	22.5	8
42. Whispering	31	42	44	47	47	4	46
43. Sensitiveness	26	43	45	30	9	1	41
44. Fearfulness	37	44	33	23	3	13	24
45. Nervousness	42	45	17	14	11	9	25

46. Restlessness	43	46	46	40	27	1	47
47. Shyness	21	47	47	32	6	0	34

KEY:

R_1 ... The Author's
R_2 ... Thomas' and David's Children
R_3 ... Wickman's Traditional Teachers
R_4 ... Wickman's Modern Teachers
R_5 ... Wickman's Mental Hygienists
R_6 ... Porter's High School Seniors
R_7 ... Porter's College Seniors

CORRELATIONS: using Spearman's formula:

With the Thomas' and David's Children	+.82
With the Wickman's Traditional Teachers	+.59
With the Wickman's Modern Teachers	+.39
With the Wickman's Mental Hygienists	–.04
With the Porter's High School Seniors	–.27
With the Porter's College Seniors	+.47

All correlations except the negative ones are significant at .01 level.

6. A PSYCHOLOGICAL STUDY OF COMMON AVERSIONS

"I hate the sight of a boy chewing his nails". "The fumes emitted by a kerosene stove are intolerable". "A woman brandishing a rod is very annoying". "It pains me to see things in the room lying helter skelter", are some of the expressions indicating irritants which many of us experience in day-to-day life. Men and women irrespective of their ages, levels of education or culture, are known to have irritants or aversions of one kind or another. Different things, sights, sounds, smells or situations exasperate different individuals depending upon their past experiences or inherent dislikes.

The present study is an attempt to gauge the nature and extent of common aversions and to classify them in a few relevant areas.

Method

The sample consisted of 1056 persons of both sexes, varying in age from 12 to 45 years, representing wide ranges of intelligence, educational level, economic and social status, physical characteristics, religion, and locality (all belonging to Jullundur). The persons were asked to write down five aversions which they experienced in daily life. They were given a few examples of the types mentioned in para 1 above. The data were collected in groups of 10 to 30 persons at a time from amongst school students, college students, teachers, office-workers, and professionals. Though no time limit was fixed, no group took more than 20 to 30 minutes to record the aversions. They were told not to mention their names, so that they could express themselves without any fear of ridicule or rebuff. The only identifying particulars they were required to give were sex and occupation.

Findings

The subjects mentioned 318 common aversions amongst a total of 4910 collected from the total sample. An aversion was categorised as common when it was mentioned by ten or more persons. Some persons were found to have recorded only 3 or 4 aversions, while some others wrote ambiguous statements which were discarded.

These 318 aversions were classified into six areas with most of them falling into the area "human behaviour". The six areas and the percentages of aversions in each area are as follows:

Nature and characteristics of human behaviour	56.0
Dress and manner of dress	16.9
Inanimate things, situations and objects	12.8
Physical characteristics of people	6.3
Etiquette, social manners	4.8
Ethics of conduct	3.2
	100.0

A few typical aversions are listed below. In each case the average aversion score is shown for both males and females. The range is from 1.12 to 36.0.

Aversion	*Male*	*Female*
1. The odour of nightsoil	25.0	22.3
2. A person sneezing in my face	23.2	24.0
3. To have to get off the road to pass people who are occupying the whole road?	22.0	19.4
4. To see or hear a child being maltreated by a person	27.2	28.4
5. A person telling me how to walk or talk	22.5	17.0
6. To see a woman smoking or drinking	15.9	17.5
7. To be held very close by someone speaking directly into my ears	9.6	14.8

8.	To find my things in disarray when I enter the room	11.7	10.4
9.	To see an old woman in high make-up	9.4	3.0

Discussion

Whereas some of the aversions are concrete and matter of fact, some are strong enough to be classed as cases of anger; others are matters of offence to taste; still others include an element of fear, pity or compassion.

A great many of the aversions seem to be there in people of all places, religions and nationalities. These existed scores of years ago and persist today. Some of them are characteristic of custom, standards, taboos or conventions of community. Though a few of them seem to be universal, being basic human aversions, most of them are peculiar to the cultural setting.

Aversions tend to arouse emotions of fear, anger, disgust and the like and lead one to adjustment in normal situations of life. These make civilised living possible as persons avert certain repulsive things or acts and through their display of aversion discourage the doer from betraying what may be commonly averted. At the same time, aversions are too mild to cause any violent alarm or emotional upset as is caused by unusual situations or by the involved way in which we look upon those situations. A little dislike, discomfort, distress or even fillings of bodily upset are all those aversions may amount to. Even at worst therefore these need not lead to any displeasure.

II. THE ADOLESCENCE

7. INTERESTS AND PROBLEMS OF ADOLESCENTS

Adolescents, their interests and problems, have been intriguing parents, teachers and counsellors for scores of years. A number of studies in a bid to identify and quantify those interests and problems revealed interesting facts. Symonds' (2, 3) survey of problems and interests' of 1641 adolescents, and its repetition (1) twenty-two years later with 1165 adolescents disclosed that the problems and interests of adolescents are, in most cases, the same today as before; and that the changes, though there, have neither been many nor drastic.

Present Study, Its Method and Procedure

The present study was made on 360 adolescents (boys and girls in equal number) drawn randomly from high schools of Jullundur, a town which is above average on the socio-economic, industrial, educational and urbanity levels of the state. The sample represented in general the socio-economic dispersal of the communities from which they were drawn.

The method used was ranking of twelve items chosen and then phrased, from adolescents' discussions of issues, parents' general complaints against their adolescent boys and girls, and teachers' experiences with their young wards. The adolescents in this sample were asked to rank these items, considering these as their personal problems and reflecting their own experience with these. Later they were asked to rerun the same items in order of their interest, considering the items as topics they would like to read about or discuss.

The ranks given to a series of items are systematically affected by the order in which the items are first presented. Each ranking made removes a degree of freedom and relates to the choices already made and those still to be made. The resulting rank orders may not be a true scale of values. This limitation and its consequent errors were prevented by presenting the items in reverse order to half the subjects of each sex.

The purpose of the study is to isolate the problems which concern the young people and to estimate the extent of their concern for different problems.

The hypothesis is that the adolescents all over present similar problems and interests, with variations motivated by different socio-economic and cultural structures.

Results

The results are given in Tables 1 and 2 below:

Table 1
Ranking of Items Considered as Problems

Problem	Boys		Girls	
	Mean Rank	Rank	Mean Rank	Rank
Personal Appearance	6.6	6	6.0	5
Money, Material Comforts	6.0	3	5.9	3.5
Personal, Moral Traits	5.4	2	5.7	2
* Home, Family Relationships	8.3	9	7.2	7
* Adjustment with others	7.8	8	6.4	6
* Philosophy of Life	6.4	5	8.0	8
Health	9.2	10	9.7	11
Studies, Learning	4.6	1	5.3	1
Recreation	10.9	12	10.2	12
Love, Marriage	9.4	11	8.8	9
* Conflicts, indecision	7.2	7	5.9	3.5
* Manners, etiquette	6.2	4	9.0	10

* Sex difference significant at .01 level.

Table 2
Ranking of Items Considered as Interests

Interest	Boys		Girls	
	Mean Rank	Rank	Mean Rank	Rank
* Personal Appearance	7.1	7	5.3	1
* Money, Material Comforts	6.3	4	9.1	8

* Personal, Moral Traits	7.7	8	9.5	10
Home, Family Relationships	6.7	6	6.4	3
*Adjustment with others	5.8	3	5.9	2
* Philosophy of Life	65	5	6.7	4
* Health	5.4	2	7.8	7
Studies, Learning	9.2	11	10.6	12
* Recreation	4.7	1	7.6	6
* Love, Marriage	8.1	9	7.1	5
* Conflicts, indecision	9.6	12	9.3	9
Manners, etiquette	8.3	10	10.2	11

* Significant at .01 level.

How do young people separated by sex difference compare in the ordering of their problems and interests? Boys and girls rank their problems almost similarly; the similarity of their rank order is expressed by a correlation value of +.75 (significant at .01 level). Their ranking of interests is slightly less similar, as is evident from the correlation value of +.50 (significant at .05 level).

As problems (Table 1), three items change three ranks or more across sex (Philosophy of life, Conflicts, Manners). As interests (Table 2), three items change five ranks or more across sex (Personal appearance, health, recreation). Evidently the sex differences are more in interests than in problems. In problems, five items significantly differentiated the sexes at the .01 level of certainty. This index of significance refers to the difference between mean ranks, interpreted in terms of the errors of these means. It does not represent shift in rank order. In interests, as many as nine items satisfy the .01 level.

Poor or negative correlation between problems and interests both in case of boys (–0.42) and girls (–.26) denotes wide disparity between what annoys the adolescents and what enchants them.

Item choices show that a number of items are relatively high as sources of problems.

Personal, moral traits are high as a problem to both boys and girls (ranks 2,2 respectively). These are of somewhat greater interest to boys than to girls (rank 8 as compared with rank 10).

Studies are perhaps highest as a problem to both boys and girls (ranks 1,1 respectively), though the item ranked very low in interest value to both the sexes.

Money is equally high as a problem to the adolescents of each sex (ranks 3,3.5); but it is of considerably greater interest to boys than to girls (rank 4 as compared with rank 8).

Manners come next in position as problem, especially among boys (rank 4 as against girls' rank 10); but as items of interest, they shrink very low among both boys and girls (ranks 10,11 respectively).

Philosophy of life and personal appearance are the ranks standing next in a descending order of their problem value as well as interest value among boys. To girls, the two items have problem values which are widely different from their values as interests.

Of moderate concern as problems are the following items: Conflicts to boys and girls, though for the latter these appear in the top five ranks. Conflicts, likewise, move down significantly ($p = .01$) in rank of interest to both boys and girls, though for the former these touch the lowest rank. Adjustment with others is likewise ranked higher as a problem by girls than by boys, though both rank this item considerably higher on the list of interests, girls even more considerably so (rank 2 compared with rank 3). Home, down somewhat as a problem, more so for boys than girls (rank 9 compared with rank 7), moves up sharply as an interest for both, though more so for girls than boys (rank 3 compared with rank 6).

Health as a problem is down sharply for both the sexes (ranks 10, 11 for boys and girls respectively); but as an interest it touched a new high for boys (rank 2) and a moderate rank for girls (rank 7). Love and marriage, ranked low as a problem by boys has risen to a slightly higher rank as a problem for girls. Both sexes give it a higher interest rating, girls giving considerably higher than boys (rank 5 compared with rank 9). Both problem and interest values of love and marriage are statistically significant, highly so for girls.

Of least concern as a problem for both the sexes is recreation. On the interest list, astonishingly enough, this item shoots up to the top rank for boys and to about median rank for girls. Interest value of recreation is highly significant especially for boys.

Discussion

Indian adolescents obviously have problems and interests similar to those of the American adolescents of Minnesota study (1) or of

Symonds' study (2,3). Adolescents whether in India or America tend to accord almost or nearly similar ranks to most of the problems, especially those of most concern (studies, personal and moral traits, money) and the ones of least concern (recreation, health, love and marriage) to adolescents. Their ranking of the items as interests (especially recreation, manners, health, personal appearance, home and family relationships, studies, philosophy of life) also reflects identical observation. Differences, though slight in most cases and considerable in the rest, between the ranks, accorded to both problems and interests, by Indian and American adolescents, may be attributed to differences in the cultural and socio-economic structures of the two countries to which the adolescents in this study and their counterparts in Symonds' (3) or Minnesota (1) study belong. The hypothesis of this study thus stands verified.

Ten years period [since the latter American study (1) was made in 1957] and geographic differences also change the circumstances and hence to some extent the findings of the two studies.

In both studies, the samples represented different socio-economic structures of society and different geographic areas without any close control through a stratification procedure. The comparability of samples, as has been utilised here, is therefore questionable. The investigator appreciates this limitation of the present study. Comparability of the present Indian sample with the then American sample is also not indubitable across the long time intervals, in which social and cultural changes, among the Indian adolescents, possibly of the type their American counterparts represented (and had imbibed in them) ten or more years ago have occurred; this phenomenon of the changes might have contributed toward bringing the then American adolescent and the present Indian adolescent at par with each other especially in the matter of evaluating their problems and interests. Thus, even when stratification by some socio-economic index is attempted, comparing the samples drawn from two different eras may be of little avail, because changing conditions may themselves affect the index.

Supposing for a moment, however, that the time interval between the two studies, having brought the American and Indian adolescents at par in the realm of problems and interests, has nullified the influence of "changing conditions", the fact of differences in the social and economic structures of the communities represented in the two samples stares the investigator in the face. It may therefore be reiterated that it is these differences which may have, at best, caused differences in the relative emphasis of these problems and interests by American and Indian adolescents.

Looking at the specific ranking accorded to items in this study, some observations may be noteworthy, particularly in the face of the findings yielded by Minnesota study (1).

Philosophy of life, to boys, has the same significance as a problem as it has as an interest. To girls it is not so much of a problem, though they betray in it interest even greater than boys'. Over-protection to the extent of chaperoning the adolescent girls and their relatively greater dependence on parents than boys on the Indian scene seem to make the girls' lives too cozy to afford thinking on questions of ultimate reality or of principles of knowledge and existence. These questions of abstract nature present them no problem. Hence perhaps the girls' low ranking of the philosophy of life as a problem. American girls embrace their

Indian counterparts in this matter, though probably for different reasons; affluence coupled with peace and plenty may explain their low ranking of this problem.

The lack of concern with love and marriage, both as a problem and as an interest, symbolizes sex adjustment and the low rankings of it may be owing to sex-repression in our society, as also in American or other civilised societies. Similar ranking of it by American adolescents confirms the shift in their social trends in recent years or since 1957; American youth now marry younger and show an earlier interest in social relations, love, and marriage as their culture seems to recognise more openly now than twenty years ago the love, sex and marriage problems of youth. This is a trend which the Indian society already cherishes since ages.

Money is ranked high by both American and Indian groups in the problem list. Dependence on parents and lack of freedom to negotiate money among Indian adolescents, while abundance of needs among the American group, warranting the necessity of earning money in the society which wants its youth to be independent and self-earning too soon, may account for this equal problem significance of money.

American adolescents rank money as a problem and as an interest a little higher than their Indian counterparts. Material values obtaining in American culture as against not-so-material outlook in Indian culture may explain this difference. Money drops to a lower rank in interest value from its rank in problem value both for American and Indian groups. This may again be attributed to not-so-material philosophy of Indians, as against American affluence where money may be too plentifully available to be considered as of a special interest.

Low significance of personal appearance as a problem and as an interest to both American and Indian boys, and the highest significance this item obtains as an interest for American and Indian girls, show that personal appearance as an issue in adolescence is common, in this case equally intense too, for all adolescents, be they Indian, American or others. Similar point can be made about adjustment with others [getting along with other people in the American studies (1,3)]. This is not much of a problem for the Indian and American adolescents but has risen to a much higher rank in interest value for the said individuals.

Identical rankings of conflicts, indecision (Indian sample) and Mental Hygiene (American sample) both as problems and as interests may also be similarly explained as inevitable concomitants of adolescence. The low ranks accorded to this issue were discussed by Symonds (2) thus: "Mental health is no concern of healthy, growing adolescents. The crest of life is before them. Their failures and thwarting have not yet turned them back upon themselves." But this was the position three decades ago in America and this is the position today in India. The changed cultural ethos in today's America must have made difference in the significance attached to such issues in adolescence.

Greater concern of Indian adolescents than their American counterparts for personal and moral traits as a problem signifies greater emphasis on purity, morality, and chastity in daily life as preached in India's spiritual and idealistic philosophy. America's pragmatic philosophy perhaps does not lay so much stress upon the said values, though it should not be understood that Americans regard these values as of less importance. As an interest, this item drops to a new and much lower rank both for Indians and Americans, showing thereby that adolescents all over, owing perhaps to hard realities of sheer adolescence, have more imperious interests than the one for personal and moral traits.

Home and family relationships are as much a problem and an interest to Indian as to American boys and girls. Low rankings of this item as a problem by both American and Indian groups and still lower rankings of it as an interest indicate the identity of home and family set-up *vis-a-vis* adolescent members in the then American (1957) homes and today's Indian homes.

Health which often passes for physical health is today a trivial problem risen to a somewhat higher rank in interest value both for American and Indian youth. It receives less attention in schools and popular press and hence the decline in its rankings.

Studies and recreation which as problem are ranked highest and lowest respectively achieve reverse ranks (lowest and highest respectively) in interest value from both American and Indian groups. This further confirms that these items are just adolescent trends applicable to all boys and girls, no matter what country they belong to.

Slightly lower rankings by American as compared to Indian adolescents of manners as a problem may be due to the fact that an increase in informality and casualness in dress and day-to-day behaviour characteristic of American way of life may reflect itself in decreased concern with manners and etiquette.

Whereas some of the adolescents' problems and interests as revealed by this study are what may be expected—significance of money as a problem, much interest in recreation, much concern over studies as a problem but lack of interest in it, greater interest of girls than boys in personal appearance etc. – we need to attend to the adolescents' relative unconcern with health, manners, studies and conflicts.

Summary

A study made on 360 adolescents (boys and girls in equal number), who were asked to rank 12 items on a list as problems and rerank them as interests, gave out that problems and interests of Indian adolescents are similar or somewhat similar to those of their American counterparts both in their (items') nature and extent, and that the slight variations may be attributed to differences in the two countries' socio-economic and cultural structures. As problems, studies, personal and moral traits, and money ranked highest, while love and marriage, health and recreation ranked lowest both for Indian boys and girls. As interests, recreation, health, adjustment with others, and money ranked highest, while conflicts, studies, and manners ranked lowest for boys; for girls, personal appearance, adjustment with others, and home ranked highest, while manners, studies and personal, moral traits ranked lowest.

The findings of this study in many ways concur with those of Minnesota study (1) conducted under the auspices of the Institute of Child Development, University of Minnesota. The findings have been compared to those of Minnesota study and the commonalities and divergences between the problems and interests of American and Indian adolescents laid bare.

References

1. Society for Research in Child Development, Inc. "Child Development", 30:453-59 (Dec., 1959). (Minnesota Study)
2. Symonds, P.M., "life Interests and Problems of Adolescents." Sch. Rev. 44:506-18 (1936).
3. Symonds, P.M., ''Sex differences in the Life Problems and Interests of Adolescents." Sch. and Soc. 43:751-52 (1936).

8. A STUDY OF PROBLEMS OF YOUTH

Procedure

To help the youth adjust better to their problems, there is the need of bringing the problems of the individual into the open and in appraising the major concerns of the group. To obtain a broad perspective of the problem world of candidates seeking appointment as officers is the main purpose of this study.

A total of 54 such candidates filled up the Adult Form of the Mooney Problem Checklist. The candidates belong to an average socio-economic stratum of a business-*cum*-residential locality of Jullundur town, have an age-range of 21 to 32 years and represent a fairly random sample of the youth seeking jobs of good status and high salary. The educational level varies from Intermediate to Graduate and Post-graduate degrees.

The Adult Form of Mooney Problem Checklist consists of 288 problems divided into nine areas running horizontally across the page in groupings of six items. The nine areas are Health, Economic Security, Self-improvement, Personality, Home and Family, Courtship, Sex, Religion and Occupation. The candidates were instructed to underline the problems troubling them, and then to circle those troubling them most. The usual precautions were taken to ensure valid responses. On page 5 of the checklist they were to list their severe problems not covered in the list.

The problems marked by at least 18 per cent of the group, and the problems-of-most-concern marked by at least 9 per cent of them are tabulated. Only those severe problems were tabulated which 3 or more per cent of them mentioned.

Results

1. (*Tables 1, 2, 3*): As many as 44 problems are troubling 18.5 per cent to 50 per cent of the group. Maximum number of candidates want to improve dependence on others. Next in number come those (in descending order of frequency) who want worthwhile discussions with people, who take things too seriously, who want to read worthwhile books more, who want a more pleasing personality, who need money for education or training, whose parents sacrifice too much for them, who lack modern conveniences in homes, and who avoid ones they don't like. Least number of them need information about sex, try to forget an unpleasant experience, wish they had a better educational background, wonder if there is life after death, and need financial assistance.

2. (*Tables 4, 5, 6*): 9.2 to 33.3 per cent of the group are troubled most by as many as 33 problems. Most of them, however, regard these problems (in descending order of frequency) as of too much concern: disliking financial dependence on others, wanting worthwhile discussions with people, wanting to improve culturally, parents sacrificing too much for them, dissatisfied with their present jobs, taking things too seriously, wanting a more pleasing personality, needing a job, needing money for education or training, wanting very much to travel. Least of them want to be more popular, want more chance for self-expression, want to have a systematic savings plan, are disappointed in love affairs, and want love or affection.

3. A few of the candidates are troubled most by such problems as are not the problems of most of them *i.e.* needing a philosophy of life, needing part-time work, not having enough money for necessities, and wanting to break a bad habit.

4. (*Table 7*): Severe problems (not posed in the checklist) of wanting to improve intellectual horizon and wanting to get a job of high status. Those perplexed by the riddle of the universe, and those worried about corruption and dishonesty in people came next, while least of all the candidates stated to be dissatisfied with some bosom friends and depressed due to many failures.

5. (*Table 8*): A very large percentage of the group suffer from status of self-improvement, personality, and economic security, while much less have problems of boy-girl relations area. The average number of problems per individual is maximum in personality area and minimum in the area of sex-relations.

6. The problems troubling them most are also in the areas of personality, self-improvement, and economic security, while much less are troubled most by sex-problems. The average number of problems-of-most-concern per individual is maximum in the area of self-improvement and minimum in the areas of religion and occupation.

7. The largest number of individuals seem to have no problem in the sex area, while those having no problem in the areas of personality and self-improvement are very few.

8. Problems of health do not exist as problems for the largest number, while a few only are lucky to have no personality problem as the one troubling them most.

9. (*Tables 9, 10*): The most insistent areas of problems are self-improvement and personality while those of problems-of-most-concern are personality, self-improvement and economic security. Personality problems are thus most vital.

10. The least insistent are the problems in the area of sex. As problems-of-most-concern problems of religion are least insistent.

Conclusions

The purpose of this study is not to attempt to hint how these problems can be solved, as that can be done only by experts. It is, however, hoped that administrators, guidance workers, and guardians of these candidates, by knowing what their main problems are, can mobilise their efforts to meet these problems. The checklist also enables the individual to articulate those problems of which he is only diffusely conscious; this way he can reform his self-concept and attempt to meet his problems more squarely and realistically.

The fact that most problems exist for most individuals and a few only for the rest indicates that there are more likenesses than differences amongst individuals. Educators would do well to emphasize the likenesses rather than differences while attempting to meet the problems and hence the vital need of meeting those problems first which exist most.

Limitations

1. A larger sample would make the study more fruitful and interesting.

2. If variables like age, marital status, interest patterns and educational level are controlled, the differences in problems and areas in relation to one or more factors would be more significant.

3. For validation, the results need to be corresponded with actual behaviours as judged by other criteria.

Table 1
Problems Marked by At Least 18 Per cent of the Sample

Sl. No.	*Problem*	*Per cent frequency*
1.	Wanting to improve myself culturally	50.0
2.	Disliking financial dependence upon others	50.0
3.	Wanting worthwhile discussions with people	40.7
4.	Taking things too seriously	38.8
5.	Wanting to read worthwhile books more	38.8
6.	Wanting a more pleasing personality	37.0
7.	Needing money for education or training	33.3
8.	Parents sacrificing too much for me	33.3
9.	Lacking modern conveniences in my home	29.6
10.	Avoiding someone I don't like	29.6
11.	Wanting very much to travel	29.6
12.	Wanting to be more popular	29.6
13.	Wanting to improve my manners or etiquette	27.7
14.	Wanting more chances for self-expression	27.7
15.	Dissatisfied with my present job	27.7
16.	Not reaching the goal I've set for myself	25.9
17.	Wanting to develop a hobby	24.0
18.	Not finding a suitable life partner	24.0
19.	Not mixing with the opposite sex	24.0
20.	Finding it hard to talk before a group	24.0
21.	Wanting to improve my mind	24.0
22.	Needing more exercise	24.0
23.	Not going to place of worship often enough	24.0
24.	Not having a systematic saving plan	24.0
25.	Poor prospects of advancement in my present job	24.0
26.	Lacking skill in sports or games	22.2

27.	Differing from my family in religious beliefs	22.2
28.	Needing a job	22.2
29.	Working too hard	22.2
30.	Wanting love and affection	20.3
31.	Wanting more personal freedom	20.3
32.	Disliking certain persons	20.3
33.	Little chance to enjoy art or music	20.0
34.	Not enough time for recreation	20.3
35.	Lacking leadership ability	18.5
36.	Being timid or shy	18.5
37.	Worried about a member of family	18.5
38.	Not being as efficient as I should like	18.5
39.	Worry how I impress people	18.5
40.	Needing financial assistance	18.5
41.	Wondering if there is life after death	18.5
42.	Wishing I had a better educational background	18.5
43.	Trying to forget an unpleasant experience	18.5
44.	*Needing information about sex*	*18.5*

Table 2
Ten Problems Marked Most

1. Wanting to improve myself culturally
2. Disliking financial dependence upon others
3. Wanting worthwhile discussions with people
4. Taking things too seriously
5. Wanting a more pleasing personality
6. Wanting to read worthwhile books more.
7. Needing money for education or training
8. Parents sacrificing too much for me
9. Lacking modern conveniences in my home
10. Avoiding someone I don't like.

Table 3
Five Problems Marked Least

1. Needing information about sex
2. Trying to forget an unpleasant experience
3. Wishing I had a better educational background
4. Wondering if there is life after death
5. Needing financial assistance

Table 4
Problems-of-Most-Concern Marked by At Least 9% of the Sample

Sl. No.	*Problems*	*Per cent frequency*
1.	Disliking financial dependence on others	33.3
2.	Wanting worthwhile discussion with people	20.3
3.	Wanting to improve myself culturally	18.5
4.	Parents sacrificing too much for me	18.5
5.	Dissatisfied with my present job	16.6
6.	Taking things too seriously	16.6
7.	Wanting a more pleasing personality	14.8
8.	Needing a job	14.8
9.	Needing money for education or training	14.8
10.	Wanting very much to travel	14.8
11.	Lacking modern conveniences in my home	12.9
12.	Wanting to improve manners or etiquette	12.9
13.	Needing more exercise	12.9
14.	Wanting more personal freedom	12.9
15.	Wanting to develop a hobby	11.1
16.	Not finding a suitable life partner	11.1
17.	Needing part-time work	11.1
18.	Wanting to improve my mind	11.1
19.	Wishing I had a better educational background	11.1
20.	Wanting to read worthwhile books more	11.1
21.	Wanting to break a bad habit	11.1
22.	Poor prospect of advancement in my present job	11.1
23.	Worried about a member of my family	9.2
24.	Needing a philosophy of life	9.2
25.	Differing from family in religious beliefs	9.2
26.	Not mixing with opposite sex	9.2
27.	Needing financial assistance	9.2
28.	Not having enough money for necessities	9.2
29.	Wanting love and affection	9.2
30.	Disappointed in love affair	9.2
31.	Not having a systematic saving plan	9.2
32.	Wanting more chance for self-expression	9.2
33.	Wanting to be more popular	9.2

Table 5
Ten Problems-of-Most-Concern Marked Most

1. Disliking financial dependence on others
2. Wanting worthwhile discussion with people
3. Wanting to improve myself culturally
4. Parents sacrificing too much for me
5. Dissatisfied with my present job
6. Taking things too seriously
7. Wanting more pleasing personality
8. Needing a job
9. Needing money for education or training
10. Wanting very much to travel

Table 6
Five Problems-of-Most-Concern Marked Least

1. Wanting to be more popular
2. Wanting more chance for self-expression
3. Not having a systematic saving plan
4. Disappointed in a love affair
5. Wanting love & affection

Table 7
Some Severe Problems Not Posed in the Checklist

Sl. No.	Problems	Per cent of the sample
1.	Wanting to improve my intellectual horizon	9.2
2.	Wanting to get a job of high salary or status	9.2
3.	Worried about corruption and dishonesty in people	5.5
4.	Perplexed by the riddle of the universe	5.5
5.	Dissatisfied with some bosom friend	3.7
6.	Depressed due to many failures	3.7

Table 8

Total Frequency of Problems Area wise

Sl. No.	Problem Area	Total No. of problems marked	No. of Individuals who marked these	Average No. of problems-per individual	Problems-of-most-concern marked	No. of Individuals who marked these	Average No. of problems-of-most-concern per individual	No. of Individuals who showed havingno-problem-of-most concern	No. of individuals having no problem at all
1.	Personality	364	50	7.2	189	42	2.8	8	4
2.	Self-improvement	322	51	6.3	112	36	3.1	15	3
3.	Economic security	211	47	4.2	100	33	3.0	14	7
4.	Home and family	142	39	3.6	50	20	2.5	19	15
5.	Religion	104	37	2.8	28	18	1.5	19	17
6.	Health	92	36	2.5	30	16	1.8	20	18
7.	Occupation	90	33	2.7	37	22	1.6	11	21
8.	Courtship	71	27	2.6	29	15	1.9	12	27
9.	Sex	50	21	2.3	17	9	1.9	12	33

Table 9
Problem Areas

Serial No. in Descending Order of Frequency	(Problem Area)
1.	Self-improvement
2.	Personality
3.	Economic security
4.	Home and family
5.	Religion
6.	Health
7.	Occupation
8.	Courtship
9.	Sex

Table 10
Areas of Problems-of-Most-Concern

Sl. No. in Descending Order of Frequency	Area of problem-of-most-concern
1.	Personality
2.	Occupation
3.	Sex
4.	Courtship
5.	Economic security
6.	Self-improvement
7.	Religion
8.	Home and family
9.	Health

9. A SEARCH INTO THE ADJUSTMENT PROBLEMS OF STUDENTS

One of the vital functions of the school is to assist its students in adjusting themselves to their problems. This function can legitimately start after having probed into those problems which hinder the students from adjusting to the demands of day-to-day life.

Sample—In this study an attempt was made to survey the problems of girl students of a local higher secondary school for girls. The three classes 9th, 10th and 11th formed part of the sample which comprised 70 students chosen at random from each class. The school was located in a business-*cum*-residential locality of the town and has about an equal number of different communities. The sample was on the whole representative of just average socio-economic stratum.

Procedure-A new approach to elicit their problems was made. The students were instructed to write out on a piece of paper only one problem which according to them was their biggest and most insistent problem in so far as it jeopardised their adjustment in home and school. No suggestion or direction of any kind, as is characteristic of a questionnaire, inventory, or checklist, was given. The usual test situation, which encourages inhibition, was avoided in that an informal student-investigator-relationship was created by talking to the students on student-welfare activities for about half-an-hour preceding the actual study. The students were told not to write their names or any other identification mark on the scrap of paper on which they had to write their problem in any language they preferred; this gave them freedom to express themselves in any manner they liked. There was no time limit though the students handed over their scraps of paper within about 15 minutes. This procedure was adhered to in respect of the students of all the three classes which met separately on different occasions.

Results

A quantitative analysis of the problems thus revealed is given below. Problems mentioned by less than two per cent of the students were not accounted for in any of the tables. Percentage connotes the number (per cent) of students who wrote the same problem on their pieces of paper, the total number of students in each class being 70.

Table 1
Problems Common to the Students of 9th, 10th & 11th Classes

Sl. No.	*Problems*	*Percentage of 9th class*	*Percentage of 10th class*	*Percentage of 11th class*	Total *Percentage having this problem*
1.	Cannot keep my mind on studies	9	14	2	8.3
2.	Trouble with Mathematics	10	3	2	5.0
3.	Too much emotional attachment with a school mate	3	4	10	5.7
4.	Unable to stick to time schedule for study	2	10	5	5.7
5.	Not interested in certain subjects especially Economics, Social Studies	4	4	8	5.3
6.	Trouble with English	2	2	12	5.3
7.	Getting low marks in scholastic achievement	2	7	3	4.0
8.	Not knowing how to be popular	5	2	3	3.0
	Percentage having Adjustment Problems	37	46	44	42.3

Table 2
Problems Common to the Students of 10th & 11th Classes

Sl. No.	*Problems*	*Percentage of*	
		10th class	*11th class*
1.	Afraid of examination, tests, etc.	4	9
2.	Not knowing how much time to allocate to the study of each subject	4	9
3,	Lacking self-control	7	5
4.	Poor height	4	5
5.	Too little time to study mostly due to domestic chores	3	5
6.	Not knowing how to seek teacher's help in studies	3	5

Table 3
Problems Common to the Students of 9th & 10th Classes

Sl. No.	*Problems*	*Percentage of*	
		9th class	*10th class*
1.	Noisy classes or noisy house environments	3	11
2.	Wanting to have beautifully designed clothes for different occasions	6	4
3.	Wanting to know 'What is God'; 'What is life', etc.	6	4

Table 4
Problems Characteristic of 9th Class Students Only

Sl. No.	*Problems*	*Percentage*
1.	Teachers not doing full justice to their job	8
2.	How to choose good friends	8
3.	Wanting to be a leader in some fields	7
4.	Afraid of coming on the stage	7
5.	Not permitted to read stories, fiction, etc.	5
6.	Wanting to serve my country	5

Interpretation

1. Table 1 shows that as many as eight problems are common to the students of all the three classes. This is expected when all the students belong to the secondary level and when all of them are adolescents. Most of these problems are presented by the school situation. It is, therefore, up to school to help the students solve their problems. It is always possible for the school to identify many of the specific problems troubling the student; as such, it should be easier for the school to help solve these problems.

10th and 11th class students have more adjustment problems than 9th class students. Tenth class students find it more difficult to keep their minds on their studies and to stick to study-schedules; they are also more concerned over getting low marks in scholastic achievement. Eleventh class students have more trouble with English and are getting more and more bored with certain subjects especially Economics, Social Studies and the like; emotional attachments with school mates are also more frequent in their case. Ninth class students show considerable inability to keep their minds on their studies and have greater difficulty with Mathematics.

The greatest problem of: (i) 9th class students is trouble with Mathematics, (ii) 10th class students is inability to keep their minds on their studies and (iii) 11th class students is trouble with English.

'Inability to keep their minds on studies' is the problem faced by the maximum number of students in the total sample.

Some of the problems are not directly school problems, or some of the school problems may have been caused by factors outside the school, but these should be of interest to counsellors and other experts.

2. Table 2 shows that as many as six problems, other than those shown in Table 1, are common to the students of 10th and 11th classes. Again, most of these problems are the ones presented by the school situation. Of these problems, "Fear of test' and 'Not knowing how much time to allocate to the study of each subject' are the greatest problems of 11th class students, while 'Lack of self-control' is the greatest problem of the 10th class students. Both the groups are generally concerned about their poor height.

3. Table 3 indicates that three problems, other than those given in the other two tables, are common to the students of 9th and 10th classes, but those problems mostly are not school problems. Whereas 'Noisy classroom or noisy environment of home' are the greatest problem for the 10th class students, 'Wanting to have beautiful clothes and the anxiety 'to know the occult' are the greatest problems of 9th class students.

4. Some of the problems revealed in the study, as listed in Table 4, are the distinct problems of 9th class students and are not at all shared by their juniors or seniors. Eight per cent of students of 9th class find that 'Their teachers are not doing full justice' and the same percentage of students do not know 'How to choose good friends'; seven per cent of them 'Want to be leaders in some fields' and are 'afraid of coming on the stage'; five per cent of them are concerned about the fact that they are 'Not permitted to read stories' and the same 'want to serve their country'.

5. The problems discovered through the study are in these areas: academic, vocational, emotional, social relations, home, physical development and abstract.

The purpose of this short study is not to suggest how the school can help its students solve their problems, as that can be done only by experts in the field. Nevertheless, it is believed that school teachers, counsellors and administrators, after knowing what the main problems of higher secondary students are, can articulate their problems. Though there are more likenesses than differences in the problems of the three groups, and these at any rate should be dealt with first, yet special attention should be given to some of the more acute problems of 9th class students as these problems become all the more imperious owing to the onset of puberty.

10. PROBLEMS OF HIGH SCHOOL BOYS

That students need guidance and counselling in the High school especially, in regard to their adjustment to schoolwork and their personal adjustment, is being increasingly felt. As many students with significant problems leave school by the age of fifteen or sixteen years, guidance workers and teachers can exert the most widely-disseminated influence during the early years of puberty. In most cases guidance given at this stage may forestall any future maladjustment.

Kuhlen (1), in a rather ingenious study of the school-drop-out problem, stressed the need of reducing the sources of psychological conflict and strain evoked by the school environment.

Morris (2) in an attempt to establish needs as a basis for future planning found the maximum number of problems in the area of "Adjustment to Schoolwork," minimum in "Morals and Religion" and "Home and Family." Garret (3) listed "help in teen-age problems" to be the most frequently occurring problem area of high school girls. Abel (4) found that in a school where adequate counselling facilities were provided the dropout rate was much less than the expected drop-out frequency. Mooney (5) found "vocational and educational future," "finances and employment," and "school adjustment" as the chief problem areas of high school students. Abel and Ruby (6) identifying problems of adolescent girls listed "Adjustment to schoolwork", "Social Psychological relations," and "Personal psychological relations" as the areas of greatest concern, and "Home and Family", "Curriculum and Teaching Procedure," and "Morals and Religion" as those of least concern.

The present study assumes that adequate counselling by teacher or the guidance worker requires the awareness of the type of problems encountered by high school students. If problems are identified and effective counselling given during the high school years, the number of dropouts could be reduced and proper adjustment of students who remain in school ensured.

Method

Two hundred boys (100 each from tenth and eleventh grades) from four higher secondary schools of Jullundur were asked to check "Troublesome" and "Very Troublesome" problems on the Mooney Problem Checklist (7). It was felt that these cases comprised a reasonable cross-section of tenth and eleventh class boys in Jullundur.

The checklist identifies eleven problem areas, each with 30 problems, thus making it convenient to delineate groups of problems as well as specific problems. The data were analysed in accordance with the total number of problems checked in each of the eleven areas. Problems checked by 25 per cent or more of the boys were considered common enough to justify further investigation.

Findings

A Chi square test revealed a value of .431 indicating no significant difference in the number of problems checked by the boys of the tenth and eleventh grades. Consequently the two groups were treated as one homogeneous group.

A total of 7931 problems were checked by the 200 boys. These are shown area-wise in Table 1. It may be of interest to note that the areas of greatest concern in descending order are "Adjustment to schoolwork" (ASW), Personal Psychological Relations" (PPR), "Finances, Living Conditions and Employment "(FLE), and "Social Psychological Relations" (SPR). The areas of least concern in ascending order are "Morals and Religion" (MR), "Courtship, Sex and Marriage," (CSM), "Home and Family" (HF), and "Curriculum and Teaching Procedure" (CTP).

Whereas Mooney (5) found an average of 25 problems in a group of ninth grade boys and girls, Garrison and Cunningham (8) arrived at the average of 36.3 for girls and 30.6 for boys, Abel and Ruby (6) got the mean number of 48.6 among the girls of ninth and tenth grades, and the present study yields an average of 39.6 which is higher than that found in earlier studies except the study of Abel and Ruby (6).

The ranks of problem areas in this study are almost similar to those presented by Morris (2), and Abel and Ruby (6). Both of them found that the maximum number of problems was in the area of "Adjustment to Schoolwork," and the least in "Morals and Religion" and "Home and Family." On the other hand, Mooney's (5) findings reveal marked differences in the order of problem-clusters.

A rank order correlation between Mooney's 10 problem areas (which did not then include CTP) and like areas in the present study yields a significant (.05 level) Rho of .64, that between Abel-and-Ruby's 11 problem areas and like areas in the present study gives a significant (.01 level) Rho of .80, while that between Mooney's and Abel-and Ruby's like areas comes to a non-significant Rho of .30. A to comparison of these data is shown in Table 1.

In a striking contrast to Mooney's findings, SPR and FVE are fourth and seventh in importance as against Mooney's seventh and first. CSM is tenth in importance compared to Abel-and-Ruby's sixth. ASW and PPR remain as important and high-ranking areas, while MR and HF tend to be low in the order of importance. HPD stands as a middle category. FLE in this study is nearer in rank to Mooney's than to Abel-and-Ruby's. In SRA the three studies present ranks close to each other.

Forty-four problems were checked by 25 per cent or more of the boys. These problems in order of frequency are shown in Table 2. Three problems were checked by more than 50 per cent of the sample and 24 problems were considered troublesome by over 33 per cent of the boys.

Discussion

Concentration in the area of ASW is revealed by the analysis of the total number of problems checked and of the 44 problems checked by 25 per cent or more of the boys. "Adjustment to Schoolwork" is thus the hallmark of the boys' problem world. Problems involving Personal-psychological relations, Social-psychological relations, Social and recreational activities, those involving economic and employment conditions (PPR, SPR, FLE, SRA), also rank much above the average in both sets of tabulations. These are the problems which the 10th and 11th grade boys are able to identify and are willing to regard as being distressing.

It may be inferred from the above finding that the teacher or counselor should attend to these problem areas with a view to assisting the boys in meeting their problems and also in preventing their occurrence. Group discussions, individual counselling and guidance to parents may be some of the means likely to prove effective in this matter. The specific problems shown in Table 2 warrant the need of providing more concrete help, since these are the problems which trouble at least one-fourth of the boys in the sample and may for that matter trouble other tenth and eleventh grade boys.

It seems fairly reasonable and convincing to believe that as the student gets guidance in more important problems revealed in this study, he may feel confident enough to perceive and recognize many other vague and subtle problems which, unassisted, he fails to spell out and which generally elude his conscious vigilance.

Summary

A random sample of 200 boys of 10th and 11th grades of higher secondary schools was administered. Mooney Problem Checklists to find out the number of times each of the 330 problems was checked and the frequency of times problems in each of the eleven areas were checked. The average number of problems checked was 39.6. The most troublesome areas were ASW, PPR, FLE and SPR, while the least troublesome were MR, CSM, HF, and CTP. A rank order correlation between the order of problem areas in Mooney's findings and the order of those in the present study came out to be a significant Rho of .64, suggesting that the order of problem areas has not undergone a notable change.

References

1. Kuhlen, R.G. "The Psychology of Adolescent Development" (N.Y. Harper and Bros. 1952).
2. Morris, GA "How Five Schools made Plans based on Pupil Needs" (Clearing House XXIX, 1954), p. 131-4.
3. Garret, L.D. "Attitudes of Senior High School Girls toward Home Economics", L (1958), p. 92-96.
4. Abel, H. "The Relativity of Social Class and Sex to Social Need Satisfaction". Syracuse Univ. Ph.D. Dissert. N.Y. 58.

5. Mooney, R.L. "Surveying High School Students' Problems by means of Problem Checklist" Educ. Res. Bull. XXI (1942), p. 57-60.
6. Abel, H., and Ruby G. "Identifying Problems of Adolescent Girls". J. of Ed. Res. 1965 May-June.
7. Mooney, R.L. and Gordon, L.V., "The Mooney Problem Checklists". Manual, N.Y. The Psych. Corp. 1950.
8. Garrison, K.C. and Cunningham, B. W. Jr., "Personal Problems of Ninth Grade Pupils". School Review, LX (1952), pp. 30-33.

Table 1
Area-wise Distribution of Problems and Comparison of Problem Areas

Problem Areas	*No. of Problems Checked*	*Rank in Present Study*	*Rank in Abel & Ruby's Study*	*Rank in Mooney's Study*
Adjustment to Schoolwork.... ASW	1012	1	1	3
Personal Psychological Relations.,..PPR	941	2	3	4
Finances, Living conditions and Employment....FLE	924	3	5	2
Social Psychological Relations....SPR	847	4	2	7
Social & Recreational Activities...SRA	798	5	4	6
Health & Physical Development...HPD	702	6	7	5
The Future: Vocational and Educational...FVE	688	7	8	1
Curriculum & Teaching Procedure...CTP	592	8	10	*
Home & Family... HF	562	9	11	8
Courtship, Sex & Marriage ...CSM	469	10	6	9
Morals & Religion ....MR	396	11	9	10
Total:	**7931**			

Table 2
Problems Checked Most Frequently by Tenth and Eleventh Grade Boys

	Number & Statement of Problem		*No. of Times Checked*	*Per cent*	*Problem** Area*
1.	321	Getting low grades	112	56	ASW
2.	63	Family worried about money	110	55	FLE
3.	241	Wanting to be more popular	104	52	SPR
4.	301	Too many personal problems	96	48	PPR
5.	233	Wanting to improve myself culturally	96	48	SRA
6.	76	Wanting a more pleasing personality	92	46	SPR
7.	234	Wanting to improve my appearance	92	46	SRA
8.	159	Can't keep my mind on studies	84	42	ASW
9.	50	Not spending enough time in studies	84	42	ASW
10.	9	Having to ask parents for money	80	40	FLE
11.	227	Not having certain conveniences at home	80	40	FLE
12.	170	Not very attractive physically	78	39	HPD
13.	137	Trouble making up my mind about things	78	39	PPR
14.	41	Unable to enter desired vocation	78	39	FVE
15.	45	Wanting advice on what to do after high school	76	38	FVE
16.	30	Worrying	76	38	PPR
17.	139	Too easily discouraged	76	38	PPR
18.	250	Lacking self-confidence	76	38	PPR
19.	101	Not really interested in books	76	38	ASW
20.	248	Having bad luck	76	38	PPR
21.	174	Having no place to entertain friends	72	36	FLE

22.	227	Not having certain conveniences at home	70	35	FLE
23.	255	Lacking self-control	70	35	MR
24.	193	Failing in so many things I try to do	66	33	PPR
25.	166	Poor complexion or skin trouble	62	31	HPD
26.	180	Too little social Life	60	30	SRA
27.	79	Too easily led by other people	60	30	SPR
28.	194	Can't see the value of most things I do	56	28	PPR
29.	134	Getting embarrassed too easily	56	28	SPR
30.	211	Trouble with Mathematics	56	28	ASW
31.	108	So often feel restless in classes	56	28	CTP
32.	216	Classes too dull	56	28	CTP
33.	27	Taking some things too seriously	54	27	PPR
34.	138	Afraid of making mistakes	54	27	PPR
35.	62	Too little money for recreation	53	26.5	FLE
36.	117	Wanting to buy more of my own things	53	26.5	FLE
37.	158	Not interested in some subjects	52	26	ASW
38.	75	Embarrassed by talk about sex	52	26	CSM
39.	29	Getting excited too easily	51	25.5	PPR
40.	269	Worrying about grades	51	25.5	ASW
41.	113	Not getting enough sleep	51	25.5	HPD
42.	102	Unable to express myself in words	50	25	ASW
43.	39	Parents not understanding me	50	25	HF
44.	32	Not living up to my ideal	50	25	MR

* Not in Mooney's original checklist.

** Latter designation elaborated in Table 1.

11. A STUDY OF ADOLESCENTS' HAPPINESS

Whereas problems, behaviour difficulties, and distress of adolescents have been studied a great deal by psychologists and educators, much less attention seems to have been paid towards the study of pleasures and happiness that the adolescent enjoy. One can detect in adolescents' lives a number of joyous occasions.

Each period of growth adds to the possibilities of life and opens a new vista for richer satisfactions and ample enjoyment. When adolescence does not bring undue stresses and strains in its wake and when things go well, the adolescent experiences joy, as when he achieves success in his ventures, when his ambitions are realized, when he is granted privileges, when he is appreciated for his maturity, when he is given responsibilities he longs for, when he loves or is loved by others.

Method

Some of the outstanding pleasures and occasions for happiness that adolescents have in their lives are described in the table below. The data was drawn from short accounts the youngsters wrote when asked to describe "the happiest incident of your life." The youngsters varied in their age from 7 to 17 years, they were boys and girls in the local primary, middle and higher secondary schools and represented below average, average and above average socio-economic strata of Jullundur town. From the accounts they gave, matters or moments of happiness were sifted and collected into many different piles each containing occasions or matters of happiness falling in one category. The pile containing infrequent categories such as gardening, art and painting, workshop and many other activities mentioned by only a few was discarded. This left 8 broad categories of happiness.

Results

The table includes both young children and adolescents to show age differences in matters of happiness. A glance over the figures indicates:

1. As children grow older, they give less attention to holidays and days of festivity. Boys do so much quicker than girls.

2. Adolescents in the middle and late teens mention incidents relating to personal benefits or pleasures more than younger children do.

3. Boys mention sports and going to places of recreation more than girls.

4. Girls mention companionship and social intermixture more than boys.

5. Getting gifts and prizes becomes less pleasure some as adolescents enter late teens.

6. Sports, both for boys and girls, are consistently pleasure-giving right till late teens.

7. School, on some occasions, is a place of joy more for boys than for girls.

8. Talks and sermons become more meaningful and pleasure-giving as the children grow older. In the late teens girls give greater attention to these than boys.

9. On the whole, the occasions of happiness mentioned by girls are a little more than those mentioned by boys.

10. Why the incidents described by the children were regarded by them as being especially joyous is not indicated. A deeper probe to seek this would have made the data more meaningful and interesting.

References

1. Tanner, J.M., 1955 Growth at Adolescence. Springfield IPP., C.C.T.
2. Symonds, P.M., 1942 Adolescent Fantasy, N.Y., C.U.P.
3. Jones, H.E., 1943 Development in Adolescence, N.Y., Appleton Century.
4. Hollingworth, L.S., 1928 Psychology of the Adolescent, N.Y., D.A.C.
5. Cole, L., 1959 Psychology of Adolescence 5th Ed., N.Y., Rinehart & Co.

Table showing frequency of categorised responses when children described "Happiest incident of my life"

Categories of Happiness	*Percentage of children giving one or more responses in each category*							
	Age group 7-9		*Age group 9-12*		*Age group 12-14*		*Age group 14-17*	
	Boys	Girls	Boys	Girls	Boys	Girls	Boys	Girls
	N. 106	63	86	60	74	49	70	42
Holidays, marriage or other festive occasions, birthdays, going out for dinners, fair, festivals, etc.	45.6	46.8	37.2	43.5	8.3	12.4	0.8	7.5
Sports, games, trekking, cycling, Travelling, shopping, etc.	15.4	12.3	13.2	8.7	16.5	8.4	17.2	13.8

Going out for recreation to parks, restaurants, cinemas, friends' houses	8.9	8.0	9.2	10.5	9.2	12.7	28.3	5.6
Getting toys, articles, sweetmeats, gifts, artwork, photos, prizes, certificates, etc.	7.6	7.0	9.5	6.6	10.0	3.8	5.0	2.6
Making friends, being with a particular friend or relative, return home of parents, receiving guests and relatives	6.8	14.6	7.3	14.8	9.5	20.4	7.8	16.8
School incidents like result day, tea, hockey match with another school, sports day, celebration, drama etc.	3.5	3.2	5.2	4.2	13.0	10.7	6.8	5.3
Self-incidents like success, excelling others, making a mark in studies or games, distinctions, etc.	2.2	2.0	2.7	1.7	4.4	4.0	13.2	15.1
Enjoying talks or sermons, visits to temples etc.	0.8	1.0	2.9	2.8	2.0	2.4	7.2	9.0

12. A STUDY OF DELINQUENT BEHAVIOUR

Adolescents at times commit offences which either border on delinquency or are delinquent acts from a legal or social viewpoint. Such cases of delinquent behaviour do not come to light, if the defaulter, coming from some well-to-do and influential family, is not intercepted by the police or a vigilant social set-up. They, however, come to public or legal notice, if a young thief, pickpocket, or sexual offender comes of a lower socio-economic status–partly because of the inherent belief that the high can do no wrong and partly because of the knowledge that many adolescents do belong to a poor socio-economic background, such background being a formidable causative to delinquency. The present study attempts to peep into delinquent behaviour with a view to revealing one, or in some cases more than one, dominant or all-pervasive determinants of delinquency.

Sample

Only 20 cases, 4 each from five local High Schools, were taken up for study. All of them were adolescent boys of the age range 9 to 14 and were labelled as delinquents by at least three teachers of their own school. They were so labelled, because of repeated acts of stealing, destroying school property, incessant wandering, truancy and telling lies.

Method

The method employed was case study supplemented by observation of and interview with the boys and their teachers/ parents from time to time during a protracted period of one to three years; 7 of the boys were studied during the first year, 5 in the second year and the remaining 8 in the third year. The findings of the 20 cases are given in paras 5,6,7 below.

The case study involved collection of details about: the boys' health (vision, hearing, speech, height-weight ratio, general physical condition); mental level (verbal and non-verbal intelligence); educational background (reading ability, achievement in different subjects, ability to apply learnt principles, attitude toward learning, promotions and failures, kind and number of schools attended, teachers' opinions about him); home and family background (parents, siblings, his family position, economic status and cultural background of family, relations, home, undue lenience or strictness of parents, inability to exercise proper control, whether over-occupied/unemployed/bickering parents); and social history (leisure-time interests, sports, gang activities if any, unusual sex behaviour, adventures, friends, his unusual social experiences, why shy or aggressively social).

Findings

A critical and probing study of the details of the cases, with an eye on cause-and-effect relationships, was then made. The following results were arrived at:

(1) 5 delinquents out of the 20 possess below average intelligence. This shows that, as a group, delinquents compared with non-delinquents have lower average intelligence.

(2) Most of them (76 per cent) have a record of difficulties in early childhood. These difficulties are severe illness, accidents, being impulsive, lack of self-control, extreme depression, being too submissive, snobbishness, suspicion, being unduly defiant or hostile or destructive, vanity, being stubborn and over-suggestibility. The parents remarked that in early childhood one or more of these difficulties were so often experienced by the children, resulting in unpleasant situations. This indicates that cause for delinquency may be traced to early life.

(3) There is a distinct difference, broadly speaking, between "gang" delinquency of 4 adolescents (belonging to a lower-class community having its own traditions, values and a long-established integrity) and actually competitive and rebellious behaviour of 6 others (belonging to the lower-middle class in an area where there is a conflict between the lower middle class and the upper middle class and where the lower-middle class people deliberately violate upper middle class norms). The former being fatal in their attitudes tend to believe it is futile to work towards a goal while the latter being smart tend to outwit or dupe others. This indicates that culture is one of the generators of delinquency.

(4) Each of the adolescents shows delinquent behaviour which is distinct and unique of him. This is in spite of the fact that a number of them belong to one or another culture. This shows that delinquency is an outgrowth of personal predicaments which may occur in any culture.

(5) As many as 12 boys either steal things or destroy property at school and valuable works of art at home or attack other boys. All these delinquent acts just appear to be the vehicles of expressing the underlying motives and are quite incidental The underlying motives, when diagnosed, were found to include the need to satisfy hunger (as expressed in stealing fruits from shops), need to conform to the group (as expressed in stealing money when others possess pocket money), need to act out hostile impulses (as expressed in attacking others), need to do something or be somebody (as

expressed in trying to show off or to get attention through breaking things to pieces) and the like. Meeting a need or solving a problem or getting out of a personal predicament is another determinant of delinquency. Not what a delinquent does, but why he does it, is therefore important.

(6) Four of the delinquents indulge in lying, temper tantrums, and blind adventures. Severe disturbance and personality disorders seem to be at the back of their behaviour. Symptoms of depression and psychasthenia were evidence of it. These boys violated no rules or laws but were openly expressing their aggressive impulses, emotional turmoil and distress (as shown in telling lies when provoked emotionally and resorting to futile ventures out of bad temper). Emotional maladjustment is another cause of delinquency.

(7) Truancy and vagrancy are the bane of the remaining 4 boys' acts of delinquency. These two acts were found to be the inevitable response of frustration at school or home. At home, overcrowding, discomfort, others' attitudes which reminded them of their inferior status, and parents' betrayal that they were unwanted children caused frustration. At school, disapproval, punishment, ridicule, inability to pace up with the class owing to poor verbal intelligence, failure, loss of self-respect piled up their frustration. Running away from the school is just a means of expressing their resentment against the school. Two of them damaged school and home articles to give vent to their rage against teachers and parents. Frustration is yet another cause of delinquency.

Other causes of delinquency may be revealed through the study of more delinquents. This small, though intensive study, brings to surface only a cross-section of delinquent behaviour which is rich both in variety and detail.

References

1. Glueck, S. and Glueck, E., 1940: 'Unraveling Juvenile Delinquency'. Cambridge, Mass, H.U.P.
2. Heely, W., and A.F. Bronner, 1936: 'New Light on Delinquency and its Treatment'. New Haven, Conn: Y.U.P.
3. Kvaraceus, W.C., 1945: 'Juvenile Delinquency and the School'. Yonkers, N.Y.W.B.C.
4. Merrill, M.A., 1947: 'The Problems of Child Delinquency'. Boston: H.M.

5. Wattenberg, W.W. 1955: 'The Adolescent Years'. New York, Harcourt, Brace.
6. Tanner, J.M., 1955: 'Growth at Adolescent'. Springfield, III., C.C.T.
7. Good, Carter, V. and Scates, Douglas E: "Methods of Research", Inc. A.C.C.

13. NEED OF EDUCATIONAL GUIDANCE: A STUDY

"Rama is intelligent, but his marks in various subjects are too low to merit a pass;" "My son has failed in his tests though he is above the average in intelligence;" "School teachers seem to nurse a grudge against my bright child, since they have given him poor marks"–these are some of the reactions of parents when they're not unintelligent lads or daughters happen to drop in their grades or achieve poor credits in their tests. Such reactions seem to be a logical outcome of the belief that intelligence and scholastic achievement go together, or that the more intelligent a child is, the greater is his achievement. That this belief is erroneous and that factors other than intelligence may influence scholastic achievement is the *hypothesis* of this small study.

It is these 'other factors' "which may" obviously cause such disparities between intelligence and achievement. What are these factors, how can their influence be eliminated or reduced, and how should the teacher-counsellor or guidance worker set about his task of educational guidance–are the questions which need to be answered.

Sample

Sixteen students (11 boys and 5 girls) of the 9th and 10th classes (age-group 13-15) of the Junior Model School attached to the Government Training College, Jullundur, formed the sample. All the students belong to an above-average stratum of the social and economic life of the town.

Procedure

The Lorge-Throndike Intelligence Test (Level 5. Form A, Non-verbal Battery) was used to measure intelligence. It is made up of figure analogies, figure classifications and number series, the three tests requiring 27 minutes' working time in all. Thirty minutes before they started working were used in distributing the test-booklets and answer-sheets, filling in the information blanks, and reading the directions. To ensure that the students understood what they were supposed to do, directions were explained, and examples illustrated. The answer sheets were scored by hand by means of the rights-key and the raw scores read against the students' CA (Chronological Age) on the table of norms to find their I.Q. (Intelligence Quotient).

The aggregate of the students' marks in English, Mathematics, Social Studies, General Science, Hindi, Panjabi, and Agricultural/ Sewing in their most recent examination were taken to be the achievement scores.

The two scores were correlated through the Rank-Difference Method.

Data -

	Achievement Scores			*Intelligence Test Raw Scores*	
Sl. No.	*Score*	*Rank*	*Sl. No.*	*Score*	*Rank*
1	400	6	1	85	15
2	410	5	2	98	12
3	350	11	3	87	14
4	417	4	4	99	11
5	280	16	5	89	13
6	371	10	6	107	8
7	496	2	7	105	9
8	324	12	8	109	4.5
9	296	15	9	80	16
10	317	14	10	110	3
11	378	8	11	132	1
12	374	9	12	113	2
13	382	7	13	108	6.5
14	320	13	14	108	6.5
15	508	1	15	103	10
16	418	3	16	109	4.5

Correlation coefficient calculated through Rank-Difference Method = .04

Note – The intelligence test scores as above are just raw scores meant to indicate the student's scholastic aptitude as compared to his achievement and as compared to others' scholastic aptitude. Those are not to be understood as I. Q.'s which can be measured through tests standardised on comparable and representative samples only.

Findings

1. *The Poor Correlation*–Coefficient suggests that factors other than intelligence have influenced scholastic achievement. Such factors may be preparation for the examination, study-habits, parental guidance, teaching methods, work-sense, need of special attention in some subjects, etc. Differences in the adequacy of these factors, together with differences in intelligence, may lead to differences in achievement. But, whereas differences in intelligence would lead to correspondingly proportionate differences in achievement, 'other factors,' when not controlled, would tilt the balance of correlation. Since none of these 'other factors' was controlled in the experiment, the capacity of intelligence to bear high positive relationship with achievement was tremendously cut down, and hence a low coefficient.
2. The following cases who rank disproportionately higher in intelligence than in achievement need to be studied by the teacher-counsellor in greater detail to detect the incidence of 'other factors' and to provide the necessary educational guidance.

Sl. No.	Rank in Achievement	Rank in I.T. Score
8	12	4.5
10	14	3
11	8	1
12	9	2
14	13	65

3. The following cases rank disproportionately higher in achievement than in intelligence. "Other factors" may have played a considerable part in their achievement, which is therefore creditable.

Sl. No.	Rank in Achievement	Rank in I.T. Score
1	6	15
2	5	12
4	4	11
7	2	9
15	1	10

The following cases alone seem to fulfil the belief that intelligence and achievement are somewhat correlated, since the 'r' calculated through Rank-Difference Method comes to 0.27.

Sl. No.	Rank in Achievement	Rank in I.T. Score
3	11	14
5	16	13
6	10	8
9	15	16
13	7	6.5
16	3	4.5

But the 'r' here too is too low to confirm that achievement bears the same directional relationship to intelligence. Obviously 'other factors' have intervened.

Conclusions and Limitations

1. Except for measuring intelligence for its own sake, for which intelligence tests standardised on our own population-samples are needed, Lorge-Thorndike Non-verbal Intelligence Tests are highly useful for a classroom teacher. The areas of such usefulness may be organising classroom groups on the basis of ability level, identifying intellectually gifted and slow-learning children, forming working groups for some projects, setting standards of pupils' achievement and educational guidance.
2. Even though the non-verbal test used in the experiment is culture-free, I.T. scores yielded by it may not be truly representative of the sample under study. As such, those scores may not result in ranks which a more suitable intelligence test would have yielded. To that extent therefore the relationship between intelligence and achievement may get vitiated.
3. Thus the hypothesis that factors other than intelligence may influence achievement, for the better or the worse of certain children is proved. Educational guidance is the vital need in the case of those children, in the present study, in whose case 'other factors' got the better of intelligence. Consequently, a suggestion has been made to the school headmistress to study these cases closely with a view to determine the 'what' and 'why' of such factors as may have interfered with the children's scholastic achievement so that they could be given the necessary guidance as soon as possible.
4. The results however need to be verified through an experiment on a bigger sample.

III. LEARNING AND ITS PHENOMENA

14. LEARNING EXPERIENCES IN CLASSROOMS

Abstract

This paper highlights five most frequent and five least frequent learning experiences provided in 45 classrooms, as reported by each of the 45 class teachers, each teacher's principal, a fellow teacher, and a trained observer. Presence of a learning experience was accepted only when it was indicated by at least three of the four reporters. The learning experiences were those listed as criteria for evaluating elementary classroom learning experiences by at least 12 of the 16 headmasters chosen to frame such criteria.

How does your school compare with these 45 classrooms? Are the experiences reported as most frequent present in your school? Are those listed as least frequent also provided in your school? Perhaps the answer "yes" to these two questions determines that your school may be better than the schools studied for this paper.

Learning experiences which, together with evaluation procedures, are the instruments or the means related to the purpose of instruction make educational programme meaningful and worthwhile. Education is possible only because the child learns, and the child learns when a learning experience is provided to him. The quality of the learning experience of course determines the quality of learning. Hence the importance of examining the nature and degree of learning experiences that our classrooms provide.

Procedure

Fifteen learning experiences found commonly in 12 (75 per cent) forms from amongst the 16 that the headmasters filled formed a checklist which was used to determine the presence or absence of learning experiences in classrooms. The 16 headmasters chosen to provide the infrastructure to the checklist were those who had the minimum experience of teaching elementary classes for six years and heading elementary schools for ten years. Besides, each of them was fully conversant, as was ascertained by the author before undertaking this study, with the concept of learning experiences and with the intrinsic interdependence of the trinity-educational purposes, learning experiences and evaluation techniques. Each headmaster was asked to pen down on a blank form 20 criteria that he considered essential for evaluating elementary classroom learning experiences. While framing the checklist, presented below, every effort was made to preserve the wording and exact connotation of the learning experiences mentioned in the forms.

Teacher Activities – A Checklist

The following activities/behaviours may be present or absent in your classroom. Indicate presence by a check in the presence column or absence by a check in the absence column. Your comments, if any, may be briefly given in the column at the right of the page.

In this classroom the teacher:

		Presence	*Absence*
1.	Chooses learning experiences together with pupils.		
2.	Provides the programme that is related to actual situations in the child's life.		
3.	Encourage pupils to work in a group.		
4.	Provides opportunities for social experiences.		
5.	Exhorts pupils to participate in the classroom activity.		
6.	Encourages pupils to accommodate the ideas of others.		
7.	Gives opportunity for assuming leadership.		
8.	Works along with pupils, acting as a democratic leader.		

9. Provides opportunities for educational trips, community projects and study of social problems.
10. Helps pupils identify their special interests.
11. Gives opportunities for arousing pupils' creative abilities.
12. Creates situations that foster self-discipline and exemplary behaviour.
13. Provides opportunities for frequent evaluation.
14. Gives increasing opportunities for application of learnt material.
15. Creates situations that during the adventure and thrill of learning.

Forty-five teachers drawn from ten elementary schools of Punjab who showed keen interest in the present study formed the subjects. Each teacher, his principal and his fellow teacher were asked to mark the checklist. Earlier it was ensured that each principal was in a position to have observed the teacher's classroom behaviour over a period of time. The fellow-teachers, on the other hand, were oriented, by the investigator, with the nature of the checklist and the method to mark it; they were told not to sign the checklists so that their identity is not disclosed. The investigator (herein called observer) marked the experiences for which there was evidence in two classroom visits.

Each of these persons was to mark the presence or absence of each experience using this question as a criterion: Is provision of this learning experience a typical reaction in most situations for this teacher? The teachers marked the checklist on the basis of recall, the principals on the basis of observation and recall and the fellow teachers and observer on observation alone. All were to mark the lists independently.

The checklist was in the possession of each principal for one month as he wanted to use the items as observation points prior to his marking the list. Most of the teachers marked the list soon after receiving it and returned it within ten days, while the fellow teachers who marked it after two observations, each lasting for half an hour on different days in a teacher's classroom, kept it for a longer period of time. The observer marked the list after two observations of 20 to 30 minutes on different days in each teacher's classroom. He marked only those experiences for which specific evidence was available in the two visits.

Having ascertained the competence of different reporters for the task in hand, no assumption was made that the judgement of one group was more reliable than that of another though differences in judgement owing to certain unspecified reasons cannot be altogether ruled out. However, the fact that there were as many as four reporters, that the evidence was taken into consideration only when as many as 3 (75 per cent) reporters dittoed it, that the reporters were keenly interested in the study, and that the reporters were fully conscious of the purpose of the study acted as reasonable safeguards against most of the errors which could contaminate the data or render the results unreliable.

The learning experiences reported 'present' were analysed for the following two patterns: (1) The most frequent experiences (those reported present for 80 to 100 per cent of the teachers by the teachers themselves, their principals, and their fellow teachers), and (2) the least frequent experiences (those reported present for 40 to 60 per cent of the teachers by the teachers themselves, their principals, and their fellow teachers).

The five experiences reported most commonly by the observer and by a composite of three of the four reporters were termed as the most frequent experiences, while the five reported as least often by each of the four reporters and by a composite of three of the four reporters were taken to be the least frequent experiences.

Findings

The data were analysed for three reporter-agreement. The five learning experiences reported as most frequently present and the five learning experiences reported as least frequently present are presented in Tables 1 and 2 respectively.

Table 1

The five most frequent experiences found among the experiences reported 'present' by at least three of the four reporters

Most Frequent experiences	*Per cent of Teachers Providing*
Provides opportunities for social experiences	95
Exhorts pupils to participate in the classroom activity	92
Encourages pupils to work in a group	90

Gives opportunity for assuming leadership	85
Works along with pupils, acting as a democratic leader	81

Table 2

The five least frequent experiences found among the experiences reported 'present' by at least three of the four reporters

Least Frequent experiences	*Per cent of Teachers Providing*
Provides the programme that is related to actual situations in the child's life	41
Provides opportunities for frequent evaluation	48
Gives increasing opportunities for application of learnt material	52
Helps pupils identify their special interests	55
Provides opportunities for educational trips, community projects and study of social problems	58

All the five most frequently present experiences seek to make the school programme fruitful by training the child for social life, instructing him in group behaviour, strengthening learning through social participation, and developing leadership qualities. Again, the five experiences reported least frequently present aim at making the school programme productive by promoting application of knowledge, helping realise special interests, providing life-centred school fare and encouraging the study of community problems.

Summary and Implications

All of the most frequent learning experiences seek some form of individual or group participation. This may be an encouraging as well as a satisfying situation, since these experiences are all related to important democratic values. Children in a democracy should be functioning in environments in which individuals are respected, have dignity, make their own choices and decisions, assume and discharge responsibilities, act as leaders and have opportunities to work in close cooperation with others.

Whatever can be done in the school to afford practice in democratic living will provide the most valuable aid to developing the kind of personality that is needed in an enviably social and democratic order. Democracy is, in fact, much more than a political technique; it is a moral and personality problem as well. What the school can do towards encouraging practice in democratic procedures counts far more than the making of good citizens. It is a means of fostering wholesome mental health. Sharing responsibility, pooling opinions, taking part in cooperative activities and capitalising on individual potentialities are opportunities for practising the basic elements of democracy. One cannot work in groups without developing respect for the talents and wisdom of others. Anyone who joins in such work will learn the true connotation of equality and will appreciate the outcome of cooperative endeavour. Just as equality, justice and freedom are basic elements in the concept of democracy, so too are these attributes basic to the realisation of the need for companionship that the school can best develop through relevant learning experiences.

Again, all of the least frequent experiences represent an area that needs to be bolstered in our schools. All these experiences are closely related to the provision of a meaningful programme.

If children are to achieve real understanding through the development of accurate concepts, they must have first-hand experiences related to their own lives. Cooperative evaluation is as important as cooperative planning (reported as a common learning experience), if children are to grow in learning to work together for improvement. Through opportunities for community projects and study of community problems, children gain increasing insight into the community needs and into the significance of service to others.

In fact, the least frequent experiences represent an area that seems to have been cold-shouldered in our schools. These and some other learning experiences such as opportunities to choose, plan, be creative, accommodate the ideas of others, and to enjoy the thrill of learning seem to have been made a short shrift of. These are the experiences through which children can develop some of the important meanings and concepts essential to real learning and to an understanding of human relations and the processes of healthy social living. From activities such as these, children experience and enjoy life in a democracy.

Helping children to identify their special interests and abilities is a learning experience that leads to an appreciation of the individual. Such an understanding is not only basic to fostering mental health in school, but it is also a fundamental of effective education. Democracy lends conviction to the belief that there are extraordinary possibilities in ordinary people, and that if we throw wide the doors of opportunity so that all boys and girls can bring out the best that is in them, we shall get amazing results.

Effective discipline is the self-discipline that a learning experience in the classroom may develop by providing certain situations. It is this discipline which prepares one for significant participation in democratic processes. This discipline not only is a means to the more complete fulfilment of the individual, which in turn has a salutary influence on mental health, it is basic to the functioning of the theory upon which our social and political life is based. This democratic discipline tends to capitalize on individual assets and thus provides a means of stimulating growth towards independence and self-direction. Also, it lessens the chances of generating habits and tensions which are harmful to mental health.

Faith in the superiority of the democratic ideal over any other known social principle as a guide to the good life suggests that it is the most valuable cultural possession of democratic groups. As such, this ideal must become a part and parcel of the thought and practice of the young. Our classrooms alone can help children achieve this ideal by providing well-planned and objective-based learning experiences. Besides, suitable learning experiences will lead us to realise the aims of education that the cataclysmic social change in the present space era has cascaded and crystallised.

References

1. Baruch, Dorothy W. "New Ways in Discipline." McGraw-Hill Book Company, INC., 1949.
2. Bloom, B.S. "Evaluation in Secondary Schools." The All India Council of Secondary Education, New Delhi, 1958.
3. Hymes, James, L. Jr. "Teachers Listen. The Children Speak." New York Committee on Mental Hygiene of the State Charities Aid Association, New York, 1949.
4. Newlon, Jesse H. "Education for Democracy in our Time." McGraw-Hill Book Company, Inc., 1939.
5. Rummell, Frances V. "What are Good Teachers Like." School Life, Vol. 30, June, 1948.
6. Schneideman, Rose. "Democratic Education in Practice." Harper and Brothers, New York, 1945.

7. Thut, I.N., and J.R. Gerberich. "Foundations of Method for Secondary Schools." McGraw-Hill Book Company, INC., 1949.
8. Witty, P.A. and C.E. Skinner. "Mental Hygiene in Modern Education." Rinehart and Company, INC., 1939-

15. OVERLEARNING AND RETENTION

Conscientious students preparing for essay-type examinations in our country tend to overlearn in a bid to ensure retention and subsequent recall. If, for instance, they are memorizing a poem, they go over it more times than is necessary to just reproduce it once correctly. The current belief among such students is that practising an act to an extent greater than that necessary just to learn it leads to great retention. It is of course implied that this will happen only if they work attentively and purposefully. Does overlearning really improve retention? If it does, will a given amount of overlearning improve retention by the same amount? Will the value of a given amount of overlearning be the same after different intervals had elapsed between the original learning and recall?

Kruegar (4), using for learning and overlearning a list of 12 nouns and testing retention at prescribed intervals, found that overlearning may improve retention, but further and further overlearning may lead to diminishing returns in the amount of retention.

Garrett (3) in studies of rote memory shows that overlearning increases retention (recall scores) when the time devoted to study is $1\frac{1}{2}$ or 2 or more times that needed for bare registration. Boring, Longfeld and Weld (1) are of the opinion that practice, long after one thinks he 'knows all about it', is necessary to prevent the learnt skill from breaking up. Ebbinghaus (2) found that, at least up to 64 readings, all repetitions seemed equally effective; but beyond this he suspected diminishing returns.

To answer the questions in para 1 above, a carefully controlled experiment was undertaken by the writer.

Method

Fifteen B.Ed. students of the State College of Education, Patiala, chosen randomly from 50 students, who showed average scholastic achievement were used in the experiment. The material to be learnt consisted of lists of 10 non-sense words, each having one vowel in the middle (*i.e.* SOP, XUE, TEY, KAQ etc.).

Each list was shown visually, in a series, and always in the same order through a tachistoscope. Each word was exposed for 3 seconds. 'Anticipation' method was employed for learning. This method was preferred because it permits better control of the subject's behaviour than other methods. The subject tries to anticipate each word in the list by saying it aloud when he sees the word which precedes it in the series. In the first trial he just looks at the window of the tachistoscope and pronounces each word as it appears there; he can't yet anticipate the words because all the words are strange to him. On all later trials, however, he tries to anticipate by giving the second word in the series when the first word appears, the third word when the second appears, so on and so forth. Each successive word serves to him, as a cue or stimulus for pronouncing the next word in the series. The subject was considered to have learnt the list when he could correctly anticipate each word in it during a single presentation. This was called 100 per cent learning.

Overlearning implied 150 per cent learning when the subjects were given $1\frac{1}{2}$ times the number of trials which they took to just learn the list. It implied 200 per cent learning when they were given twice the number of originals trials.

Retention was tested at five different intervals (after the learning was completed) *i.e.* 2,5,9,14 and 20 days. Each list was tested for recall once only; if the interval was 9 days, the list recalled then was one which had not been tested previously.

Two steps were involved in the retention test. Firstly, the subject recalled each word of the list once by the anticipation method. The number of words correctly anticipated and the percentage which this number was of the 10 words originally learnt, formed the subject's recall score (columns 3,4 of Table 1). Secondly, the subject was then given a sufficient number of exposures of the list until he could relearn it at the 100 per cent level; this was stopped at the moment the subject could anticipate correctly every word of the list during one single exposure. The number of trials required for this relearning was then compared with the number a subject took for the original learning. The formula.

$$(1 - \frac{\text{Number of trials for relearning}}{\text{Number of trials for original learning}}) \times 100$$

yielded the saving score (column 5 of Table 1).

Three degrees of learning (of which two were degrees of overlearning) were used for each of the five intervals of retention test. Thus, there were 15 different experimental conditions of learning. Different groups of subjects (each group consisting of 3 students) were used for the different intervals. Each group was, however, tested for all of the three degrees of learning for any one interval. A different list of almost equal difficulty for each learning-retention record was learnt by every subject, though different subjects could use the same lists. Thus, the total number of lists learnt, and hence the total number of individual retention scores obtained, was 15 for each of the 15 experimental conditions.

Results

1. The findings given in Table 1 are highly suggestive. All the differences between the various retention scores when statistically treated (by computing critical ratio) were found reliable.
2. Fifty per cent overlearning (*i.e.* 150 per cent learning) is superior, in all the cases, to bare learning (100 per cent learning), as the retention score yielded by both methods of measuring retention was higher for every interval.
   Fifty per cent overlearning was at any rate worthwhile, because it always gave at least 50 per cent, in many cases even much more, better retention. After nine days, for instance, it produced a recall score more than ten times higher than the score for 100 per cent learning and a saving score more than 16 times higher.
3. Positive correlation exists between the length of the time interval and the value of the overlearning, in the case of the value of the 50 per cent overlearning for all intervals. For example, after a two-day interval, 50 per cent overlearning was over 100 percent superior to 100 per cent learning by the saving method; after 5 days, it was nearly 900 per cent superior; and after 20 days, over 1500 per cent.
4. One Hundred per cent overlearning (200 percent learning) is superior to 50 per cent overlearning (150 per cent learning), as its retention score at every interval by both the recall and the saving method was higher. But because 200 per cent learning warrants one-third (or $33\frac{1}{3}$ per cent)

more repetitions than does 150 per cent learning, to prove itself proportionately superior to the latter it must give $33\frac{1}{3}$ per cent better retention. A glance at the table shows that in most conditions it did not have this value. By the recall method, 200 per cent learning was found a little more than one-third superior to 150 per cent learning at only one of the intervals, but less than one-third superior at the other four. By the saving method, it does not cause as much as $33\frac{1}{3}$ per cent better retention at any interval.

5. No consistent relationship was found between the length of the time interval and the value of overlearning, in the case of 100 per cent overlearning; by the saving method, it was found 28 per cent superior after 2 days, 9 per cent superior after 9 days, and 22 per cent superior after 20 days.

Discussion

With the increase in the degree of learning from 100 to 150 per cent, the corresponding increase in retention for the two-day interval was the same or more, and this ratio rose rapidly as the length of the interval between learning and recall was increased.

When, however, the degree of learning was extended from 150 per cent to 200 per cent, the corresponding increase in retention was mostly less, and the variation in proportion was not found consistent with the length of the interval.

Table 1

The learning and over-learning scores for different degree of learning after different intervals*

Length of interval (days)	Degree of learning (per cent)	Average number of words recalled	Average per cent of the list recalled	Average per cent saved
2	100	1.23	12.30	11.20
	150	2.72	27.20	25.02
	200	3.58	35.80	32.12
5	100	0.33	3.30	2.50
	150	2.13	21.30	24.75
	200	2.78	27.80	32.10
9	100	0.13	1.30	1.53
	150	1.38	13.80	22.47

	200	1.83	18.30	24.10
14	100	0.03	0.30	0.90
	150	0.63	6.30	18.60
	200	0.98	9.80	23.60
20	100	0.00	0.00	1.14
	150	0.33	3.30	18.20
	200	0.43	4.30	22.35

It is evident that some overlearning, say 50 per cent, is conducive to added retention (for intervals of 2 to 20 days), and the longer the interval, the greater is the retention. Further increases of overlearning, however, for most intervals do not lead to proportionate increases in retention. All in all, overlearning to the tune of 50 per cent alone, and no more than this, may be generally recommended for all learners. Overlearning, whatever its degree, may produce some improvement in retention, but improvement is not likely to be proportional to the amount of extra-learning involved. Law of diminishing returns perhaps operates here as much as it does in economics.

The findings of this study, to a large extent, echo those of Krueger's (4) and Ebbinghaus's (2) experiments, except in matters of the amount of recall scores and the degree of variation in scores which may be explained by the fact that the samples, the nature of words used and the conditions of experiment in this study were different from those of the two other studies.

References

1. Boring, E.G., Longfeld, H.S., and Weld, H.P., *Foundations of Psychology*, John Wiley & Sons, INC., 1968., pp. 169.
2. Ebbinghaus, H. Memory (Trans, by H.A. Ruger and C.E. Bussenius) New York: Teachers College, Columbia University, 1913.
3. Garrett, Henry E., *General Psychology*, American Book Co., 1961, pp. 299-300.
4. Krueger, W.C.F. The Effect of Overlearning on Retention. *Journal of Experimental Psychology*, 1929, Vol. 12, pp. 71-78.

16. INTERRUPTION AND RECALL

Lewin (1935) says that it is due to completion tendency that the child begs to be allowed to finish his game even though he

* The average number of trials required for the bare learning varied from 6.25 to 6.75 repetitions for the different lists. This very small variation shows that the lists were nearly equal in difficulty level.

appears to be thoroughly exhausted, or that the bridge players unanimously insist on finishing the rubber even though it is long past midnight. His "completion tendency" goes beyond the state of the individual; it includes also influences stemming from the nature of the situation with which the individual is dealing, and the possible organisations of this situation for this individual. If a certain activity has been started, but a strong obstacle to its completion is encountered, then according to Lewin a "tension" is created which continues to exist after the overt activity has been interrupted. Does this tension manifest itself in any way? Zeigarnik (1927) answered in the affirmative on the basis of her experimental results saying that individuals tend to remember uncompleted tasks better than they do completed ones, at least over brief periods. Rosenzweig (1943), testing this viewpoint experimentally, found that whether uncompleted tasks would be better remembered or completed ones would depend on the adoption of a particular attitude towards the task. His experiment revealed that individuals whose attitude was task-orientated, when interrupted in work, remembered the uncompleted tasks better than the completed ones, but that the individuals whose attitude was ego-orientated showed the opposite tendency. Lewis and Franklin (1944), Glixman (1949) who performed several experiments on the problem corroborate and extend Rosenzweig's findings.

The present experiment was aimed at testing the influence on recall of the "nature of task" in the event of interruption during the performance of the task. The nature of task for this experiment meant whether the task in question was predominantly motor (often termed "motor" here) or predominantly mental (often termed "mental" here). The hypothesis was that "motor" tasks are remembered more than "mental" tasks when the individual is interrupted during the performance of the task.

Subjects and Procedure

Eighteen tasks were presented to 16 college students, males and females in equal numbers, who were chosen at random from the terminal-year class appearing in the first-degree examination. The class was a well-shuffled group of 176 students coming of below-average to above-average socio-economic strata of the State's urban communities and was representative of identical population in the State. The students who were matched for age, weight, memory span, general scholastic achievement and intelligence formed the sample.

The tasks were presented one after another during a single session. The tasks which differed considerably both in nature and in difficulty were:

(a) naming 20 cities of India, writing 10 sentences of 6 words each, consecutively paging a large pile (n-150) of papers, multiplying 2,593 by 997, putting a dot in each small square of a graph sheet, writting a favourite poem, filling a page with crosses, rewinding a thread ball, cutting a paper sheet into 40 pieces.

(b) counting backwards from 79 to 19, crossing all as from a page, punching holes in a sheet of paper, stringing beads on a thread, encircling all four-lettered words in a page, reading a story, putting tablets one by one in a bottle, sweeping a floor, writing names of 15 Indian girls beginning with letter R.

An attempt was made to so set up the tasks and to so match the groups that a reasonably clear test of whether or not the motor-mental dimension was effective in producing differential retention could be obtained. Specific tasks were used, fairly comparable units of measurement were kept, the degree of original learning was equated, and the retention measured–all this in the same spirit.

All these tasks could be completed in 2 to 4 minutes. The tasks finishable in almost the same time were chosen and the (a) and (b) tasks rotated through both "interrupted" and "completed" conditions with a view to equating the degree of learning of the tasks before making retention comparisons after performing them for certain time intervals. It was to achieve the same purpose that the number of "motor" and "mental" tasks was kept almost equal in the above two sets of tasks and the tasks chosen were such that the "motor" tasks represented almost complete motor involvement and the "mental" tasks almost complete mental or verbal involvement. To ensure that there was no original learning of the tasks, the subjects were asked whether they had previously, at least in the recallable past, done any of those tasks or performed this or a similar experiment. None of the subjects was found to have done so. In this way, the tasks were, as far as possible, balanced for the "interruption" and "completion" conditions.

The Ss were permitted to finish one-half, given in (a) above, of the total number of tasks presented. They were interrupted in the performance of each of the remaining half, given in (b) above, of the tasks by the sudden introduction of a new task. The tasks, thus, interrupted remained permanently unfinished, *i.e.* the subject was never allowed to resume them. The tasks to be completed and those to be interrupted were so mixed up and presented in such random sequence that the subjects could never guess whether or not they would be permitted to complete the task which they were about to undertake. The subjects were not told whether they would be interrupted. After they were interrupted, they were not told why they were interrupted. They, at least ostensibly, undertook every task with the understanding that they would complete it. They never suspected that the interruptions were a necessary accompaniment of the experiment.

The tasks to be interrupted were generally interrupted at the time when the subjects were found to be most absorbed in them. This time was usually near the end when the subjects were close to completion (nine-tenths of the task completed). A few of the tasks, however, were interrupted either at the time they were half-completed (half of the task completed) or soon after the task was started (one-tenth of the task completed).

Thus the point at which a given task was interrupted was controlled by limiting the duration of a task's exposure to the time by which the subject could complete 9/10, $\frac{1}{2}$2 or 1/10 of the task; the actual exposure times for the three kinds of interrupted tasks came to be 2′-3′.50″, 1-2′, and 15″-30″ respectively. To control the possibility that some of the tasks would be more interesting or easier to remember and, therefore, more memorable than other tasks, the tasks which were completed by half of the subjects were interrupted for the other half, and *vice versa*. Thus this step worked as a safeguard against the possibility of interruption variable getting confused with the differential ease of remembering different tasks. This also kept the ordinal positions of the two types of tasks balanced.

The work products of each task, both completed and uncompleted, were removed from the scene as soon as the task had been performed. This was done to remove from the subject's visual field everything that might aid him in the subsequent test of recall.

The experiment was made individually with each of the 16 subjects at different times during the course of 3 days. This made the controlling of the point of interruption (measurable exposure time) possible. The individual experimentation was preferred so as to shut out all distractions and to keep the working conditions constant for every task, so that effective exposure times, which would normally vary for the varied tasks, could be kept as constant as possible. Each subject was subjected to a recall test immediately after he or she finished the experiment. The experimenter asked the subject to list, during recall, the tasks which he or she had been doing during the experiment. Each subject in a list named as many of the tasks as he or she could remember. The experimenter later classified the listed tasks of each subject with respect to their completeness or incompleteness. In this way, he was able to find out whether either of these two types of tasks was better remembered. Then he examined each task, whether completed or interrupted, with respect to its nature with a view to tracing relationship, if any, between the nature of the task and its recall possibility. Whether the nature of the task tends to affect the recall of interrupted tasks or that of completed ones or that of both and the extent to which such effort goes were also examined.

Results

1. Table I gives the number of tasks (interrupted as well as completed) recalled and the number not recalled by each subject. Memory for interrupted tasks under the conditions of this experiment was obviously more effective than memory for completed tasks, as is evident from the fact that 75 per cent of the subjects remembered more interrupted tasks and less completed ones and of the tasks which 75 per cent of the subjects could not recall, the completed ones were more than the interrupted ones.

Table 1
Showing for each of the 16 subjects

(i) The number of interrupted tasks remembered.
(ii) The number of completed tasks remembered.
(iii) The number of interrupted tasks not remembered, and
(iv) The number of completed tasks not remembered.

Serial No. of Subjects	*Number of tasks remembered*		*Number of tasks not remembered*	
	Interrupted tasks	*Completed tasks*	*Interrupted tasks*	*Completed tasks*
1	8	5	1	4
2	9	5	0	4
3	7	6	2	3
4	7	5	2	4
5	9	4	0	5
6	8	4	1	5
7	9	4	0	5
8	7	7	2	2
9	8	4	1	5
10	9	3	0	6
11	8	3	1	6
12	7	4	2	5
13	8	8	1	1
14	7	7	2	2
15	6	8	3	1
16	9	3	0	6

2. Table 2 gives the number of subjects who remembered more interrupted tasks than the completed ones, the number who remembered as many interrupted tasks as the completed tasks, and the number who remembered more completed tasks than the interrupted ones.
3. Table 3 gives the number of subjects who failed to remember more completed tasks than the interrupted ones, the number who remembered both types of tasks equally well, and the number who could not remember more interrupted tasks than the completed ones. Besides what is shown in Table 1, *i.e.* that the tasks subjected to interruption are recalled more than the tasks allowed to be completed, Tables 2 and 3 show that the number of subjects who remembered more interrupted tasks was three times the combined number of

subjects who remembered more completed tasks, and those who remembered an equal number of both types of tasks.

Table 2

Showing –

(i) The number of subjects remembering more interrupted tasks than completed ones;

(ii) The number of subjects remembering as many interrupted tasks as completed ones; and

(iii) The number of subjects remembering more completed tasks than interrupted ones

	Number of Subjects Remembering		
N	(1) More Interrupted Tasks	(2) Both Types of Tasks Equally	(3) More Completed Tasks
16	12	3	1

Table 3

Showing –

(i) The number of subjects not remembering more completed tasks than interrupted ones;

(ii) The number of subjects not remembering as many completed tasks as interrupted ones; and

(iii) The number of subjects remembering more interrupted tasks than completed ones.

	Number of Subjects Remembering		
N	(1) More Interrupted Tasks	(2) Both Types of Tasks Equally	(3) More Completed Tasks
16	12	3	1

4. The degree of the preference in recall for interrupted tasks has been expressed by the ratio "Average RI/Average RC" (4) where RI is the average number of interrupted tasks recalled by all the subjects and RC is the average number of completed tasks recalled by all the subjects. The value of this ratio for the present sample comes to 1.58, as against Zeigarnik's 1.6 (6) in a similar experiment.
5. A comparison of the frequency of recall of the three kinds of tasks, *i.e.* tasks interrupted before they were half-completed, the tasks interrupted when they were just half-completed and those which were interrupted at the time they were just near completion, shows that tasks which had been stopped

when they were nearly completed were remembered far more frequently than were the tasks interrupted soon after they were started. On the average, 85 per cent of the tasks cut off near the end of their course were recalled, 72 per cent of the tasks interrupted in the middle were recalled, and only 45 per cent of the tasks left soon after they were started were remembered.

6. A strong resistance to interruption and an insistent tendency to resume an interrupted task after finishing a task which they were permitted to complete were noticed in all the subjects. None of them demanded to repeat a completed task, howsoever interesting the task might have been.
7. An analysis of the results showed that the frequency of recall varied greatly for different tasks. As is shown in Table 4, as many as 10 of the 18 tasks were remembered by all the 16 subjects. These tasks were: putting a dot in each small square of a graph sheet, filling a page with crosses, rewinding a thread-ball, cutting a paper sheet into 40 pieces, crossing all a's from a page, punching holes in a sheet of paper, stringing beads on a thread, encircling all four-lettered words in a page, putting tablets one by one in a bottle, and sweeping a floor. Of these, more tasks (the last six) happen to be those which were interrupted and less (the first four) happen to be those which were allowed to be completed, thereby confirming the findings at (1) and (2) above.

A close examination of the nature of these ten tasks reveals that they are predominantly motor tasks; these tasks include (i) almost all the "motor" tasks from among the tasks which were allowed to be completed, and (ii) all the "motor" tasks of the lot which were interrupted. No matter whether they were completed or interrupted, they were recalled most frequently by all the subjects though, in these, the tasks interrupted were greater in number than those which were completed. These tasks were remembered more than four times as often as a few other tasks (*e.g.* consecutively paging a large pile of papers, counting backwards from 79 to 19) which were recalled by only about 25

---

* These tasks are obviously not as predominantly motor as the task's mentioned in the first instance. There is perhaps a considerable amount of "mental" component in them.

per cent of the subjects. Of the latter two tasks, the one mentioned first is a completed task while the second is an interrupted one. * The two tasks recalled least frequently are: writing a favourite poem (completed), writing names of 15 Indian girls beginning with letter R (interrupted). These tasks are more "mental" than "motor" in nature.

The four tasks which could not be recalled by any of the subjects are: naming 20 cities of India, writing 10 sentences of 6 words each, multiplying 2,593 by 997, and reading a story. Almost all of them are predominantly "mental". That the first 3 of these tasks happened to be those which were completed and the last one happens to be that which was interrupted, once again confirms that the memory for completed tasks is less than that for interrupted task.

The findings regarding the recall frequency of different tasks, as detailed above, tend to indicate that:

(i) tasks more "motor" than "mental" are remembered, no matter whether they are interrupted or allowed to be completed;
(ii) tasks more "motor" than "mental" are recalled in the event of interruption during their performance;
(iii) the tasks which are more "motor" than "mental" may be recalled less frequently than those which are mostly "motor";
(iv) the tasks which are about as much "motor" as "mental" may be equally recalled to a fair extent;
(v) the tasks which are more "mental" than "motor" may be recalled least frequently; and
(vi) some of the predominantly "mental" tasks, especially those which were allowed to be completed and never interrupted, may not be remembered at all.

On the whole, it seems that the nature of the tasks, *i.e.*, in this experiment its being "motor" or "mental", tends to affect the recall of tasks irrespective of whether the tasks are interrupted or allowed to be completed. The fact that the tasks used under the two conditions were counter-balanced, as far as possible, provides a greater grist to this significant finding.

Table 4

Showing —

(i) The number of tasks remembered by all;
(ii) The number of tasks remembered by some;
(iii) The number of tasks remembered by a few; and
(iv) The number of tasks remembered by none.

Type of Tasks	1 Number of Tasks Remembered by All	2 Number of Tasks Remembered by some	3 Number of tasks remembered by a few	4 Number of tasks not remembered by any
Interrupted	6	1	1	1
Completed	4	1	1	3
Total	10	2	2	4

8. Table 5 shows the effects of interruption on recall-ability which varies considerably for different tasks. Thus it was seen those six tasks (rewinding a thread-ball, filling a page with crosses, punching holes in a sheet of paper, crossing all a's from a page, encircling all four-lettered words in a page, and counting backwards from 79 to 19) were remembered, on the average, more than twice as often when interrupted as when completed; eight other tasks were remembered equally often, whether they had been interrupted or completed; and whereas a few tasks (multiplying 2593 by 997, stringing beads on a thread, writing a favourite poem and cutting a paper in 40 pieces) were remembered a little more frequently when they had been completed than when they had been interrupted Obviously, most of the tasks which are predominantly 'motor' were remembered more often, whether interrupted or completed, than those which are relatively less "motor" as also those which are predominantly "mental". Again, interruption tends to affect the "motor" tasks more than it affect the "mental" ones.

Table 5
Showing the effects of Interruption on Recall-ability

Total Number of Tasks	The number of Tasks remembered more than twice, when they were interrupted, than when they were completed	The number of Tasks remembered equally often whether they were interrupted or completed	The number of Tasks remembered a little more frequently when they were completed than when they were interrupted
18	6	8	4

Discussion

The most significant finding of the present experiment is the more frequent recall of the "motor" than that of the "mental" tasks, suggesting thereby that the nature of a task affects its subsequent recall. It appears that the greater the "motor" component in a task, the greater may be an individual's ability to recall it. Conversely, the greater the "mental" than the "motor" component in a task, the less may be an individual's ability to recall it. This holds good especially if the recall test is given as soon as work on the series of tasks ceases, as is the case in this experiment. This finding may not be ruled out even when an interval, more or less, is interposed between the time at which the work ceases and the time the recall test is given, though the present experiment did not attempt to verify this possibility.

Why are "motor" tasks more memorable than "mental" ones? The explanation may lie in the fact that, in the learning of "motor" tasks, certain native connections are largely drawn upon, that the motions involved in the learning of these tasks are not far removed from movements that are perfectly natural to all of us, and that each such movement is learnt to an enormous degree. On the other hand, "mental" tasks warrant learning that has to be acquired to a much greater degree, and the multiplicity of bonds involved in the learning of mental activities precludes the overlearning of any of these. Perhaps that is why motor skills once learnt are so permanent, while languages and knowledge, in general, are so fugitive; and similarly, the losses in manual habits are much less than those in verbal ones. Native connections available in the case of the learning of "motor" tasks provide facility in learning which, in turn, fosters tenacity in retention — facility in learning and tenacity in retention, on the whole, are positively correlated. This advantage is perhaps denied to the learning of "mental" tasks. These very reasons explain the other findings at 7 in results. The "motor" component of a task tends to make the task more easily recallable, whereas the "mental" component tends to retard its possibility of recall. This may also be explained by the evidence (Buxton, 1940), which shows that it is difficult to produce interference between motor tasks, whereas the retention of verbal materials can be markedly depressed by making us learn other conflicting material.

That nothing learnt is ever completely forgotten, because traces are left behind which, immediately after learning, or even after a very long interval, facilitate relearning, explains why the memory of mental activities, skills or knowledges is not altogether effaced or why we do recall, though to a relatively small degree, some mental tasks also.

The finding that "motor" tasks alone from the two lots of tasks (those interrupted and those completed) were recalled most frequently again clearly suggests that "motor" tasks may be more memorable, whether they are interrupted or allowed to be completed, or that the nature of the task may affect its subsequent recall, irrespective of whether it is subjected to interruption or not.

The finding that, of the interrupted tasks recalled, more were "motor" or more "motor" than "mental" and less were "mental" or more "mental" than "motor" tasks seem to suggest that, in the event of interruption during the performance of a task, the tasks which are "motor" or more "motor" than "mental" are recalled more frequently than those which are "mental" or more "mental" than "motor".

The reasons, as discussed in para 2 (of discussion) earlier, which tend to render "motor" tasks more memorable, explain what the findings in the two preceding paragraphs suggest.

The second finding of this experiment, though less significant, is the replication of Zeigarnik's main result, *i.e.* incompleted activities are recalled more frequently than completed ones, and this finding was shown very consistently and markedly by all the subjects. This result, as in Zeigarnik's experiment, found further support in the observation that when the subjects listed the tasks they could recall, interrupted or unfinished items were placed in the beginning of these lists far more frequently than were the completed ones. The special edge that the recall of interrupted tasks showed over that of completed ones is particularly significant in the light of the fact that a longer time was generally spent on the completed than on the uncompleted tasks.

Zeigarnik's finding that the tasks which require "final activity" (in such tasks, the achievement of the goal demands the fitting together of all the part activities into their proper relationships to one another and to the goal) are more favoured by interruption than the tasks involving continuous activity (in such tasks, the part-activities have no organic relation either to one another or to the goal but merely follow one another in a series) does not seem to withstand the results of this experiment. The task like writing a favourite poem, in her experiment, was according to her, remembered more than three times as often when it was interrupted as when it was completed, because it required "final activity". As it happened, this task chanced to be included as one of the tasks in the present experiment as well.* Here, it, when interrupted, was recalled least often. Again Zeigarnik's tasks, involving "continuous activity", like stringing beads, which were not readily recalled as a result of interruption (in her experiment) were recalled most frequently in the present experiment. Similarly, several other tasks here which can be called as the tasks requiring "final activity" and those requiring "continuous activity" (according to Zeigarnik's classification) were not favoured or disfavoured by interruption as they were in her experiment. In the tasks favoured by interruption, the common element found by the present investigator was "motor activity" and not Zeigarnik's "final activity", as the tasks involving "final activity" were not always recalled, readily or even least frequently, unless they involved "motor activity", and also because almost all the tasks requiring "motor activity" were most frequently recalled as a result of interruption. "Motor activity", and not the "final activity", involved in a task seems to account for its recall.

As in Zeigarnik's experiment, the tasks, in the present case, which had been cut off towards the middle or towards the end of their performance, were more frequently recalled than tasks which had been interrupted soon after they were started. This is because when we have made ample progress in a task and the goal

* A few of the tasks were common to this and Zeigarnik's experiment.

is at hand, the urge to complete the task is much stronger than it is when we have just started. The said difference in recall could also be explained in terms of exposure time which happened to be more or less dependent upon the stage of interruption.

This study corroborates the results of Zeigarnik's (6), Rosenzweig's (5), and Lewis and Franklin's (3), in reporting closely similar "Average RI/Average RC" ratios.

In the finding that the unfinished tasks were remembered with far greater frequency than the completed ones, the present study gets even with Zeigarnik's. But the explanation offered by her in terms of Lewin's theory of tensions (that if the performance of the task is interrupted, the tense-system which is set up when the task is presented, favours the recall of uncompleted tasks) does not find much support from the present investigation. The nature of the task seems to be a more plausible determinant of recall. This contention is supported by the finding that only certain tasks (which are predominantly "motor" in nature) out of the tasks which were left unfinished, and not all the unfinished tasks, were recalled. The hypotheses that interruption produces an emotional shock which of itself increases the attention value of the task and accounts for the more frequent recall of it, and that the interrupted tasks become noteworthy to the subjects because they think they would be asked to resume them later, were tested, in the manner Zeigarnik did, and ruled out as other possible explanations of the finding.

The findings of Rosenzweig (5) and of Lewis and Franklin (3), which point to an additional motivation factor called ego-enhancement that may influence recall, and which suggest the existence of a third factor called ego-defensive motive that leads to the forgetting of experiences associated with failure, as shown by Glixman (1), were not tested by the present investigator.

Inferential experimental evidence, which establishes that motor skills are retained much better than vertical skills, seems to coincide with the main findings of the present study which, though somewhat wanting in the envisagement of more sophisticated experimental manipulation, did yield conclusions that seem to support the hypothesis.

Perhaps a serious limitation of this experiment is the failure, which appears to be somewhat imminent at the present stage of knowledge and experimental technique, to isolate any of the other dimensions on which the tasks in question may vary. In spite of whatever formal experimental manipulation of the "motor mental" variable that the investigator attempted, many such factors, as the degree of meaningfulness of a task, the degree of motor or mental involvement in each task, the degree of a task's auxiliary nature for different subjects, were neither separated from the experimental variable nor equated. Consequently, the observed differences in retention could not be wholly attributed to purely "motor-mental" variable. In fact, it may not be sufficient to evaluate the motor dimension with regard to its effectiveness in producing differences in retention; we have to consider other potential factors as well. Whether or not the degree of motor involvement is an effective variable in and of itself needs to be verified through further research involving a more precise manipulation of several related variables.

References

1. Buxton, C.E. Retroaction and Gains in Motor Learning: III. Evaluation of Results. *J. Gen. Psychol*. 1940, 22, 309-320.
2. Glixman, A.F. Recall of Completed and Incompleted Activities Under Varying Degrees of Stress. *Journal of Experimental Psychology*, 1949, Vol. 39, pp. 281-295.
3. Lewin, K. A *Dynamic Theory of Personality*. New York: McGraw-Hill Book Company, 1935.
4. Lewis, H.B., and M. Franklin. (1) An Experimental Study of the Role of the Ego on Work.(2) The Significance of Task-Orientation in Work. *Journal of Experimental Psychology*, 1944, Vol. 34, pp. 192-215.
5. Marrow, A.J. Goal Tensions and Recall. *Journal of General Psychology*, 1938, Vol. 19, pp. 3-35, 37-64.
6. Rosenzweig, S. An Experimental Study of 'Repression' With Special Reference to Need-Persisted and Ego-Defensive Reactions to Frustration. *Journal of Experimental Psychology*, 1943, Vol. 32, pp. 64-74.
7. Zeigarnik, B. Uber das Behai ten Von Erledigten and Unerledigten Handlungen. *Psychologische*. Forschung, 1927, Vol. 9, pp. 1-85.

17. A STUDY OF RETROACTIVE INHIBITION

Abstract

An experiment conducted on two boys and two girls of the higher secondary class (11th year of school) with the purpose of estimating the degree of retroactive inhibition following equivalent intervals of sleep and waking substantiated earlier finding that sleep condition excels waking condition in that the former inhibits much less than the latter. The author[1]*, however, observes that sleep is not much of a safeguard against forgetting owing to the possibilities of usually unknown stimuli disturbing the otherwise activity-less sleep and factors other than retroactive inhibition influencing both retention and recall. – Ed.*

Forgetting caused by activities intervening between the original learning and the test of retention has been termed as retroactive inhibition. That such inhibition does exist was first demonstrated by two German Psychologists, Muller and Pilzecker (7), in 1900. Incidentally enough, this finding remained obscure by default for a number of years until 1924 when Jenkins and Dalenbach (8), using sleep and waking as the activities intervening between the learning and recall, proved that the inhibitory effect of sleep is much less than that of waking. Their experiment consisted of an intensive study of two college students in that the subjects learned lists of nonsense syllables presented through an exposure apparatus and recalled them after prescribed intervals. Ebbinghaus (1) found three times as much forgetting after 24 hours as after 15 hours. Jenkins and Dallenbach (4) attributed so much increase in forgetting (24 hours after learning) to sleep which in Ebbinghaus' experiment occupied a larger proportion of the 15-hour intervals than it did of the 24-hour ones. Similar result, *i.e.*, forgetting during sleep is much less than that during waking, was obtained by Van Ormer (10), Graves (3), and Newman (8).

Present Experiment

The purpose of the present experiment is to compare the inhibitory effects of sleep and waking across the sex variable. More precisely, the experiment attempts to compare the amount of forgetting which occurs during sleep and that during waking, and to see whether such retroactive inhibition varies from one sex to another.

Method

Four students, two boys and two girls, of the higher secondary class (11th year of school) acted as subjects. They were bereft of

1. Dr. S.B. Kakkar is in the Department of Psychology, State College of Education, Patiala (Punjab).

any experience in psychological experimentation and were not apprised of the purpose of this experiment. The subjects spoke English which alone was their medium of instruction ever since their entry into school. They knew Hindi and Panjabi languages which were just two of their school subjects.

The material to be learned was lists of nonsense syllables (three lettered, CVC=consonant-vowel-consonant type). Each of the syllables chosen was nonsense in English and when pronounced was actually not word (or almost word) in any other language (Hindi or Panjabi) that they spoke or knew. This was done to ensure that the association values and pronounceability of the syllables could not cause any difference in the learning and retention of lists. There were ten syllables in each list. The syllables were exposed to the subjects visually through a tachistoscope, always in the same order, so that each syllable appeared separately for a five-second period and the subject pronounced it aloud as soon as he saw it. After the whole list was thus presented once, the subject recalled as many of the syllables as he could in the same order. The list was then exposed again, and again he recalled as much of it as he could. This procedure was adopted for each of the four subjects until he could recall the whole list once from the beginning to end in correct order. The list was then taken to be originally learned. The number of trials it took for each subject to learn the lists ranged from 5 to 11, the change within this range occurring with different lists and with the two different conditions. The subjects were advised not to use any other devise for remembering the syllables.

The retention test constituted the recall that the subject was required to make after a prescribed interval of time. The number of syllables recalled from the list already learned by him was noted. The lengths of the prescribed intervals were different on different occasions and for different lists. These were 1, 3, and 9 hours. Each subject learned five lists for each of the three intervals, and for both the sleeping and the waking conditions. The total number of lists learned and recalled by all the subjects was 120, containing in all 300 different syllables. The experiment started oh 10th September and ended on 20th October. The learning and recall were performed, and the performance recorded on almost every day and night during this period.

The activities which intervened between the learning and the retention test were sleep and waking in case of each of the three intervals, for each of the five different lists in respect of each of the four subjects. The two conditions, waking and sleeping, to which each subject was exposed daily for testing and the three intervals which intervened in each case followed one another right from the start of the experiment to the end of it, thus ensuring the counterbalancing of the order of training. The improved facility at the task, following gradual learning, even if occurring, must have therefore, benefitted all the subjects; hence the differences in results caused on this account may be ruled out. The lists, when waking was the intervening activity, were learned between 7 A.M. and 9 A.M., almost in the midst of and as a part of a subject's waking activities; this learning was followed by the usual routine of attendance in the classroom, eating, gossiping, playing with others, going home, etc. For retention tests of this learning, the subject was asked to report back to the investigator at a certain later hour for the recall. The lists, when sleep formed the intervening activity, were learned between 10 P.M. and 12 P.M., almost a trifle before the subject got ready for bed; this learning was immediately followed by sleep to which the subject went in a room adjoining the investigator's place of work. For retention tests of this learning, the subject was awakened by an alarm clock during the night at the appropriate time or early the next morning and called upon to recall the list. He was not told beforehand how soon he would be asked to recall the list again. This was done lest the knowledge of the degree of interval before recall might have influenced his attitude on going to sleep. The subject was found rarely awake before the alarm, during these night or early morning recalls. The subjects were told not to revise the lists during the waking or the sleep intervals, in all the cases. Extremely busy schedule of work in the waking interval and the immediate onset of sleep in the sleep interval, which invariably followed learning as observed by the experimenter every time, ensured that there would have been no rehearsal of the learnt material.

Results

The results are shown in the following table and figure. The average number of syllables recalled is given for all the three intervals and for both waking and sleeping conditions. Since there were ten syllables in every list, a recall score of eight, for instance, shows that the subject remembered 80 per cent of the list or, conversely, that 20 per cent is the degree of retroactive inhibition.

Table 1
The average number of syllables recalled by each subject after different intervals of waking or sleep

Subjects		INTERVALS 1 hour		3 hours		9 hours		Average for all intervals	
		Waking	Sleep	Waking	Sleep	Waking	Sleep	Waking	Sleep
BOYS	A	5.3	8.0	2.9	6.5	1.0	6.8	3.0	7.1
	B	5.2	8.2	2.6	6.7	1.4	7.0	3.1	7.3
GIRLS	C	5.0	8.3	3.2	6.2	1.6	6.4	3.3	7.0
	D	4.9	8.1	2.7	6.4	1.1	6.5	2.9	7.0

It is evident that for all the four subjects, retention after an interval of sleep was far superior to retention after an equivalent interval of waking. For instance, subject 'A' after a 3-hour sleep interval recalled 6.5 syllables, but after 3-hour waking interval recalled only 2.9 syllables–even less than half as many. This difference in favour of the sleep condition persisted for all the intervals and the degree of this difference increased as the lengths of the intervals increased. A glance at the table shows that the sex differences in retroactive inhibition for both the waking and sleep conditions were negligible. Perhaps these differences between male and female subjects were not distinguishable with a small number of subjects as in this experiment.

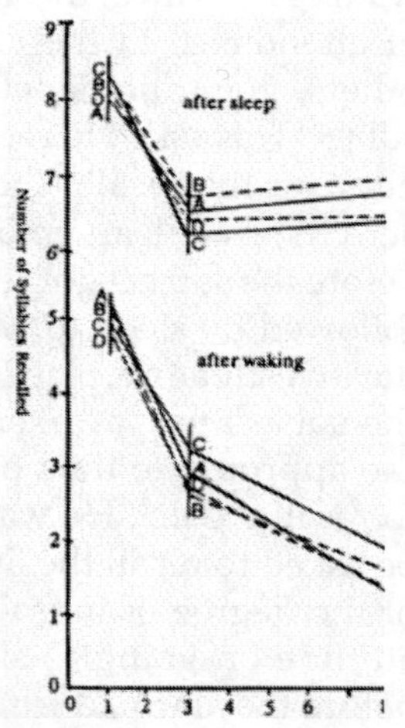

Fig 1. Retention after waking and after sleep

That forgetting is more rapid immediately after learning and is comparatively slow in the later stages holds good in case of both the sleep and waking conditions, as is clear from the table, which shows that subject 'A' recalled only 8 of the 10 syllables after 1 hour interval and as many as 6.8 after 9-hour interval of sleep; again he recalled just 5.3 of the 10 syllables after 1-hour interval and 1 after 9-hour interval of waking. The rate of forgetting tends to diminish as the intervals grow.

As is clear from the figure, there was no decline in recall ability of any subject during the sleep condition after the three-hour interval, for the subjects recalled as many syllables after 9 hours as they did after 3 hours. But during the waking condition the recall ability gradually declined as the interval grew longer, so that the recall after the nine-hour interval was much less than it was after one or three-hour interval. More precisely, it may be said that after the nine-hour interval, the retention was reduced to hardly 10 or 11 per cent of the list originally learned or that about 90 per cent of the syllables were forgotten.

As the number of repetitions required for learning at night was hardly different from the number required for learning during the day, it was presumed that there was nearly no difference in the difficulty of learning the lists under the night and daytime conditions and hence the later retention was not affected on this account.

Conclusions

The experiment, performed intensively though on a limited sample, corroborates the earlier finding (3,4,8,10) that the inhibitory effects of sleep far exceed those of waking. This experiment, in addition, illustrates that the said finding may be as true of males as of females.

Discussion

Oblivescence during sleep has been found to be much less than that during waking, if the time intervals between learning and recall are identical. This may be so because during sleep most activities of the organism, at least all activities of the conscious work-a-day life, are at a minimum, so that the reactions which can interfere with or inhibit the recall of what was originally learned are few and far between. On the other hand, during waking the number and variety of activities or responses of an individual are so many that the reactions which can inhibit the recall are bound to occur, even if the interval between learning and recall is very short. Interval between learning and recall, whether during waking or during sleep, serves as an incubation period, somewhat equivalent to Thorndike's period of disuse, which may consolidate learning or strengthen retention. But the incubation period of sleep may be more conducive to general retentiveness than that of waking activity, because in the former period the organism is so restful, relaxed and activity-less that numerous psychophysical difficulties, interfering associations, bad habits of attention, and useless bonds tend to fade out. Hence the superiority of sleep to waking for retention.

Sleep, however, should not be understood as a panacea against forgetfulness. If it were a panacea or if retroactive inhibition were the only cause of forgetfulness, sleep (which is commonly believed to be dispossessed of any activity likely to inhibit retention) would cause no forgetfulness at all and would preserve the learnt material *ipso facto*. The present experiment, as also the reviewed studies, fail to affirm this assumption. Some material, may be considerably small, was forgotten even after sleep. This reveals that retroactive inhibition is not the only cause of forgetting, and/or that even in sleep some activity may be present. The subjects in this experiment did not always fall asleep immediately on completing the learning. Some mental activity likely to exert inhibitory effect might have preceded the actual sleep. The resulting forgetfulness might also have been contributed to by various reactions, occurring even during the sleeping condition, such as different postural adjustments and dreaming, and by the constant vegetative activities of the body such as digestion, circulation, respiration, and glandular functioning.

That sleep is only a trifle superior for retention was also illustrated by Newman (8), who, using "sense" material instead of nonsense syllables in his experiment, found that for recall of essential items sleep condition was only slightly more effective than waking condition, though it was significantly effective for recall of non-essential items. This is what may be expected, because material that is more meaningful, more related and organised is less likely to be forgotten (2,5,6,9,11). Meaningful material, being less susceptible to retroactive inhibition, or being more resistant to interference from normal daily activities, learning of it need not be followed by sleep. Guarding it from the danger of retroactive inhibition is of little consequence. Sleep would improve its retention very little compared with the effect that can be expected if it were meaningless material like nonsense syllables. This finding may be of ominous significance and happy relief to the student community who have almost always to learn meaningful material and who are not always able to let their learning be followed by sleep. Those who regard sleep as a 'talisman' to achieve the results of all learning, especially of the 'sense' material, also need to expect no more than an insignificant little from the enchanting charm of sleep.

Since sound and dreamless sleep is almost devoid of any interfering reactions, retention after it may be far superior to retention after the sleep, which is dreamful, disturbed and wakeful. Future research may confirm this hypothesis, as also may throw light on the possibility that activities of the unconscious–which has its play in sleep far greater than that in waking, when the strong and active conscious has slammed the door on the unconscious-may also cause retroactive inhibition similar to or different from the one caused by activities of the conscious which is predominant in waking life. Sleep, during which the door to the mind is left ajar for the obscurantist revelry of the unconscious and its agent provocateurs–the desires, forebodings, unreleased tensions, unsatisfied and remote wishes, latent urges, residue of the day and other stimuli of the morbid or psychopathic type–to sneak in and cause the rampage, may also exert inhibitory effect which of course would be much less than the inhibitory effect exerted by waking condition, the enormously increasing activities of which lead to open exasperation of the already interfering processes.

The finding of this experiment that the forgetting is more rapid in the period immediately following learning than in the later stages warrants the need of reviewing what has been learnt, soon after learning.

The present experiment, as also the previous studies, clearly establish that the nature of an individuals activities, during a given time interval, not the mere lapse of time, greatly influences his ability to recall the learnt matter. How different activities, other than sleep and waking conditions, cause different amounts of influence on his ability to recall and what causes the least or the maximum inhibitory effect are the issues for the future researchers to investigate into.

References

1. Ebbinghaus, H. Uber das Gedachtnis: *Untersuchungen Zur Experimentallen Psychologie*, pp. 85-109, 1885.
2. English, H.B., E.L. Welborn; and C.D. Killian: Studies in Substance Memorization *Journal of General Psychology*, 1934, Vol. II, pp. 233-260.
3. Graves, EA.: The Effect of Sleep Upon Retention, *Journal of Experimental Psychology*, 1936, Vol.19, pp. 316-322.

4. Jenkins, J.G., and K.M. Dallenbach. Obliviscence During Sleep and Waking, *American Journal of Psychology*, 1924, Vol. 35, pp. 605-612.
5. Judd, C.H.: The Relation of Special Training to General Intelligence, *Edu. Review* 1908, Vol. 36, pp. 28-42.
6. Katona, George, *Organizing and Memorizing*. Columbia University Press, N.Y. 1940, pp. 165-192, 283-287.
7. Muller, G.E., and A. Pilzecker: Experimentalle Beitrage Zur Lehre Vom Gedachtnis, *zeitschrift fur Psychologie and Physiologie der Sinnesorgane*, Erganzungsband, 1,1900.
8. Newman, E.M. Forgetting of Meaningful Material During Sleep and Waking. *American Journal of Psychology*, 1939, Vol. 52, pp. 65-71.
9. Ruger, H.A. The Psychology of Efficiency, *Archives of Psychology*, 1910, No. 15.
10. Van Ormer, E.B. Retention After Intervals of Sleep and Waking. *Archives of Psychology*, 1932, No. 137.
11. Whitely, P.L., and J.A. McGeoch. The Curve of Retention in Poetry, *Journal of Educational Psychology*, 1928, Vol. 19, pp. 471-479.

18. A STUDY OF STUDENT'S POOR PROGRESS IN Schoolwork

Teachers are often asked the questions: "Why do students not do so well in school?", "Why is students' progress in schoolwork so poor?" Parents as well as administrators seek cogent answers to such questions.

Procedure

In an attempt to answer such questions, 456 students–152 each from 5th, 7th and 9th classes of a local school–were asked to write on a piece of paper ONE factor which is responsible "for making them do not so well in their schoolwork." This was a more or less direct approach toward the probe of a student's frame of mind *vis-a-vis* schoolwork. Three successive classes were covered to determine whether there were significant differences in student responses according to class in school. The school chosen represented different geographical and socio-economic regions of Jullundur. In each case the enquiry was made personally. Students were instructed not to write their names on their chits.

All charts were mixed up and then sorted into three broad categories. The categories were made and defined after an initial perusal of almost all responses. First category contained a heap of all responses relating to something which the teacher did, responses pertaining to the student himself were put in the second category, while those which showed other reasons including conditions of study, want of recognition, sports and various other minor factors mentioned by a few only were put in the third category.

Responses in each category were inspected a second time to ensure their placing in proper categories. Each of the three categories was then refined to heap out responses in different sub-categories. Lastly each heap of a sub-category was broken up according to class level.

Results

1. Of the 456 responses, approximately 30 per cent related to the teacher, 41 per cent related to the student, and 29 per cent related to other factors of different types. Table 1 describes the class-wise percentage of responses.

   The Table indicates that (i) no single category monopolises responses *i.e.* factors conducive to less-than-expected progress in schoolwork fall in many categories; (ii) students in higher classes seem to place greater dependence upon the teacher for being able to show good progress in schoolwork than students in the earlier classes. This fact is probably opposite to what should have been expected.
2. Table 2 describes in greater detail the responses in each of the sub-categories related to the general head of teacher.

   From these figures, and from several other responses given by negligibly few students in this category, it appears that students of 7th and 9th classes feel more concerned than those of 5th class when the teacher fails to come up to their expectations or when they think that the teacher is responsible for their poor performance in school.
3. Table 3 amplifies responses related to the student himself. From these and other responses (which being few and far between did not find place here), it is apparent that students' feelings and moods contribute a good deal toward their readiness to perform well in schoolwork and that their

worries and idiosyncrasies play an important role in their school life. Moreover, it would appear that older students are more concerned about the worthwhileness of school programme than younger students.

4. In Table 4 are described the students' responses included in the category related to "other reasons". Here those factors exist which, strictly speaking, neither pertain to the teacher nor to the student himself. Nevertheless, these factors have been stated to be influencing adversely the students' performance in schoolwork.

Discussion

No single factor can explain why students do not do so well in schoolwork. There are perhaps many factors which influence the student's performance. This may imply that student's motivational patterns are complex and varying.

There are students who seem to respond positively to recognition and approval, others to marks in subjects, others to kind word and liberty, and still others to several other factors as such the teacher must continuously study his students to find as to what motivates them to do well in school. The teacher, in fact, has to select and devise his instructional techniques to suit each child's distinct requirements. The art of teaching lies in discovering and utilising new methods for each educand. "Individualising of education" must be achieved not simply bandied about.

A glance over the data indicates that five factors cover more than half of the total responses: disliking the teacher and the subject, want of marks and other forms of recognition, students' feelings, no facilities for study, lack of interest in the subject. Teacher's understanding of a pupil, his individual attention and above all his dynamic personality can go a long way toward eliminating the negative influence of these factors.

Table 1
Percentage of responses category-wise

Category	5th class	7th class	9th class
Teacher	25	32	34
Student	46	36	40
Other reasons	29	32	26
Total	100	100	100

Table 2
Percentage of responses pertaining to teacher

Response	5th class	7th class	9th class
Subject not presented vividly	6	7	6
Dislike for teacher	4	5	3
Aversion toward subject	4	4	5
Lesson not interesting	3	4	7
Teacher gives no assignment	4	2	1
Teacher disinterested in student	1	2	4
No discipline in class	0	3	2
Teacher not fair or impartial	2	3	3
Too strict teacher	1	2	3
Total	25	32	34

Table 3
Percentage of responses pertaining to Student

Response	5th class	7th class	9th class
No time to study	3	2	2
Do not feel like working	14	12	10
Poor study habits	5	3	2
Feel scared in class	3	2	0
Worrying about other things	1	2	1
I don't understand lessons	3	1	0
I don't think it worthwhile	4	8	14
I do not try to	4	5	5
I can do it very well, but I don't feel fine	9	1	6
Total	46	36	40

Table 4
Percentage of responses related to other reasons

Response	5th class	7th class	9th class
Not getting good marks	11	11	13
Pressure of parents/teachers	4	6	6
No appreciation from others	2	4	4
Rigid discipline	2	1	0
No facilities for study	7	5	2
Minor factors like boring stuff, sports activities, teachers' absence, and the like	3	5	1
Total	29	32	26

Since younger students show less dependence upon teachers than older students in the matter of getting incentives for doing well in schoolwork, our education seems to be getting more and more teacher-centred as the students advance to higher classes. This certainly does not speak well of our education. Teachers would do well to explore reasons for this sad state of affairs. Higher classes should, instead, gradually give added self-dependence and more personal initiative and maturity.

19. A PROBE INTO DIFFERENT METHODS OF STUDY

Different methods of study are suggested to school and college students for learning and retention of learnt material. There has been no agreement on what remains as the most effective method. The present study attempts to compare listening, listening with note taking, reading, or reading with note taking. It was conducted on both college and high school students. A survey test on similar though different school and college populations was later used to check initial results.

Method

The study involved 50 students from the lowest achievement quartile of the first year class of a local college, and 50 students from the highest achievement quartile of the tenth class of a local high school. As the studies used the same research design and virtually the same materials, and as all students participated in all methods of study and used all materials, a number of interesting comparisons were possible without equating the groups. The survey test used to check on reading and study skills used 50 typical first year college students and 50 tenth class students of a college and a high school respectively in a different part of the state of see if the performance of the students in a different setting would agree with that of those in the first setting. The four groups studied were all above average in intelligence, though average and below average students were included in each group.

Material

Four exercises were used in the study and in the survey test. All of the exercises were alike in average sentence length, average syllable count in a hundred words, number of major ideas presented, abstraction level of ideas, number of words in the article, and format.

Procedure

An exercise was presented every week to each of the four classes. The method of presentation used was different every time, using the methods on a rotational basis. Three methods of study were used by the college and school groups; two of the methods were common to both the groups. The time allowed was kept constant at five minutes. Immediately after every presentation, comprehension was tested. This was immediate recall. The following week a retest of the same material was given. This was delayed recall. Then a new exercise was presented by a different method and comprehension tested. After another week, again, there was a delayed recall of the material from the previous week, another exercise was presented and comprehension checked. This procedure was continued until all the exercises by the three methods (used on college and school groups) had been presented. Finally, a test of 20 multiple choice items, five on each of the four exercises, was given to all the students. On college students, unaided recall with blank outlines was used in the weekly tests, but, on the high school students, aided recall tests of multiple-choice items were employed.

No inferential thinking was warranted in the learning. Scoring was dons by idea count. Organisational patterning was observed for confusion in relationships, but no discredits were given for faulty organizational patterns.

Treatment of Data

The scores of the students for each specific method of presentation formed the basic data. Means, standard deviations, and sigma's of the means were computed and critical ratios determined to check the significance of differences. This was done on both the immediate recall and delayed recall tests, by sex and by total groups, and again on the final multiple-choice test. Thus, all the methods were tested for effectiveness of delayed *versus* immediate recall, for effectiveness with boys versus girls, and for effect of recency on recall of learnt material.

Findings

(a) The college students were studied, using listening *versus* listening with notetaking *versus* reading method of study. The group averaged 105 in I.Q. on the Lorge Thorndike Intelligence

Test Non-Verbal Level 5 (1), 17.5 years of age and had as many boys as girls in the group. Only such relationships as were found to be significant at .01 per cent level were considered. Fisher's T tables were used to determine the level of significance after critical ratios were computed. The following findings emerged:

1. On immediate recall, reading was superior to listening with notetaking. On such recall, differences between listening and listening with notetaking or between reading and listening were not significant.
2. On delayed recall, reading was superior to listening and to listening with notetaking. On such recall, no significant difference was found between listening and listening with notetaking.

   Thus reading as a method of study seems to be more effective than listening or listening with notetaking, while listening and listening with notetaking do not seem to differ from each other in effectiveness.
3. Comparing immediate and delayed recall on specific methods, immediate recall was significantly superior to delayed recall on listening as also on listening with notetaking.
4. Reading was superior to listening or listening with notetaking in that there was practically no loss of learning on delayed recall tests given after one week in the case of reading, while there was 20 to 50 per cent loss in the case of the other two methods.
5. The boys were superior to the girls in immediate recall following both listening and listening with notetaking. No significant sex differences appeared in immediate recall following reading. In delayed recall, exactly similar result followed.
6. Recency of learning influenced recall with the most recently presented material being best remembered and the scores decreasing with longer time intervals in the recall. The maximum loss occurred on material learned more than three weeks earlier.
7. Those who recalled in organised structures tended to score higher both on immediate and delayed recall.
8. Students scored significantly higher on multiple-choice tests which stimulated recall (70 per cent) than on unaided

outline recall (45 per cent). Thus, the type of test given makes a difference so far as recall is concerned.

9. No sex differences were found among those who recalled in organised structures or among those who did not.

(b) The school students were studied, using listening *versus* reading *versus* reading with notetaking. The group averaged 115 I.Q. on Lorge Thorndike Intelligence Test Non-verbal Level 5 (1), 15.2 years of age, and was equally divided as to sex. These were the results:

1. On immediate recall, all the three methods appeared to be equally effective.
2. On delayed recall, reading and reading with notetaking were equally effective, though superior to listening.
3. In the case of boys, reading and reading with notetaking gave the best learning and maximum delayed recall.
4. In the case of girls, reading with notetaking gave the best results.
5. On reading with notetaking, the number of items answered correctly on delayed recall after one week was 6.5 per cent greater than that on immediate call.
6. Recency of learning affected recall favourably.

(c) Using the same reading and test materials for a survey of study skills of 50 college students and 50 school students of a different place (Chandigarh), the mean scores were within .7 of the mean scores made by the experimental college group (a) and within .6 of the mean scores made by the experimental school group (b). This was true on both immediate and delayed recall tests.

Discussion

Certain conditions in the study do not seem to permit any generalisation while interpreting results. Firstly, the materials used were somewhat easy, of about eighth grade difficulty, and the results obtained might not hold good when difficult materials under other conditions are used. Secondly, the close proximity of test means on the first and the second group of students (both college and school groups) was obtained on tests of only twenty items. Brevity of the tests might have led to this proximity which probably would disappear if the tests were longer.

Thirdly, the emergence of relationship between organization and better recall may be illusory because the curve of a student who recalled more items was apt to appear better organised than that of the student who recalled lesser items. Fourthly, other factors like familiarity with test materials, will to do well on the tests, confidence and the like, which were not controlled, might have affected the results.

References

1. Thorndike, Robert L., and Irving Lorge. "The Lorge-Thorndike Intelligence Tests, Level 5." Houghton Mifflin Coy. Boston (1957).

20. THE EFFECT OF PRIVACY IN TAKING DICTATION TESTS

Educators often contend that a person to be tested should be seated in a quiet room alone, relatively free from any distraction so that test performance can be as efficient as possible. This is so even though standard textbooks on testing (1,2,3,5) do not give any direct evidence to support this contention. Kirchner (7) in a study found that female job applicants tested alone had in typing tests typed more letters and committed lesser errors than the ones (exactly similar group) tested in groups of five or more. Earlier, Hovey (6), experimenting on college sophomores on the Army Alpha test, found that distinct distractors like balls, buzzers, spotlights, music and others did not significantly reduce test scores of the experimental group. Again, Smith (8) noticed no appreciable effects from such distractors as a 100-decibel noise on performance on number and name checking and on a paper form board test. Fendrick (4), however, did find a deterioration in reading efficiency of students exposed to distraction by phonograph records.

It is difficult to test individuals in a quiet room alone from others in an educational setting, because time and space limitations in education usually make group testing easier and more feasible, even though this may be disadvantageous to the average pupil.

With a view, therefore, to study the effect of privacy or lack of it on students taking tests, the following experiment was conducted using ninety boys of grade 8 of Multipurpose Higher Secondary School, Patiala (session 1968-69), controlled for age (13 to 14 years), socio-economic status (high above average), and intelligence (100 to 115 I.Q. on Lorge Thorndike Non-verbal Form A level 4). The sample was randomly chosen from a total of 270 boys of the said grade who, earlier, had been named for having lined up in the said control range.

Method

A dictation test was planned as the basis for comparison. This test produces a low sound (caused by humming of students and movement of pens) which can distract individuals leading to decrease in writting efficiency. It can, on the other hand, make individuals know, from seeing others' rate of writting, whether or not another person is writting faster or slower which, because of competition-motive, could increase writting efficiency. To ascertain what actually does occur, this study was undertaken.

Forty-five students, each seated alone in a room, were tested individually, while the other forty-five were tested in groups of five or more. The dictation test was the same for all. It comprised of a 300-word page from the prescribed prose textbook of the ninth grade (which none of them had read before) to be dictated at a uniform speed of fifty words per minute. That the students could write at this speed, the optimum loudness of the dictating voice which should be adequately audible, the intonation and punctuation with which the passage should be dictated, and the pronunciation of the one who dictates were ascertained earlier through trial experiments followed by two rehearsals. The five teachers assigned to the task of conducting the test were trained in all these aspects so as to ensure uniformity of procedures. The dictation was given for five minutes at a stretch after which the scripts were collected. No word was spoken more than once while dictating. The test for all the boys was over in one and a half hours (each of the five teachers tested a group at one time-there were 5,7,9,11,13 students in groups A, B, C, D, E respectively–and thus finished the group testing of forty-five students in five minutes). Each of the five teachers then tested one student each in every five minutes, thus finishing the individual testing of another forty-five students in forty-five minutes. Forty minutes passed in preliminaries in between the testing sessions which were held in a continuous period the same day. The groups or individuals relieved after earlier testing sessions were restrained from meeting those due for testing in the succeeding sessions.

Scoring was done in terms of the number of words written per minute and the number of errors made. Each wrong spelling constituted an error and so did each word omitted. Other errors of written expression such as wrong punctuation, faulty capitalization, etc., were not taken notice of. Results of the study follow (See Table 1).

Findings

It is evident from Table 1 that in terms of speed (number of words written per minute) the students tested alone had an advantage. They,

Table 1
Comparison of Ninety Boys of Grade Eight Tested Alone or in Groups on a Dictation Test

Group	N	Writing speed (words per minute) M	SD	No. of errors in writing	SD
Boys (tested alone)	45	48.65	6.17	4.50	3.60
Boys (tested in groups)	45	43.75	8.38	5.00	4.20
Mean difference		4.90		.50	
Significance		6.32*		.68**	

* $p < .01$. ** Not Significant.

on the average, wrote almost five words per minute faster. This was a concrete difference which was statistically also significant. The individually tested students also made slightly fewer errors, on the average, though the mean difference was not statistically significant. That there was a greater variation or spread in the performance of the students who were tested in groups than that in the performance of those tested individually was of some interest. The differences in the performances of individuals tested earlier and those tested later in the case of individual testing, and the bigger groups in the case of group testing, were too negligible to be taken note of.

The results of this limited study tend to suggest that there is a possible disadvantage to students who are tested in a group situation, especially when the group situation brings in noise or other distractors. The general belief that it is better to test subjects individually than in a group, to ensure efficient performance, stands verified from these results. It is, of course, yet to be investigated whether or not testing in a group, when the group setting is made free from noise, other distractors and elements which can jeopardise an individual's efficiency, would mean a detriment of performance for those tested in it.

References

1. Anastasi, A. (1961): *Psychological Testing* (2nd Edition). New York, Macmillan.
2. Cronbach, L.J. (I960): *Essentials of Psychological Testing* (2nd Ed.) New York, Harper.
3. Ebel, Robert, S.L. (1965): *Measuring Educational Achievement.* N.Y., Prentice-Hall International.
4. Fendrick, P. (1937): The Influence of Music Distraction Upon Reading Efficiency. *Journal of Ed. Psy.*, 31, 264-71.
5. Freeman, Frank, S. (1962): "*Psychological Testing.*" I.N.C. Holt, Rinehart and Winston.
6. Hovey, H.B. (1928): "Effects of General Distraction on the Higher Thought Processes." *Amer. Jl. of Psy.*, 40, 585-591.
7. Kirchner, Wayne, K. (1966): "A Note on the Effect of Privacy in Taking Typing Tests." *Jl. of Apply. Psy.*, 50, 5, 373-74.
8. Smith, K.R., (1951): "Intermittent Loud Noise and Mental Performance." *Science*, 114, 132-133.

21. SEX DIFFERENCES IN RETAINING QUANTITATIVE MATERIAL

That men differ from women in the retention of information, both qualitative and quantitative, is an admitted fact. Whereas men are superior to women in tests on arithmetic reasoning and spatial relations, women excel on tasks requiring verbal ability and memory (1, 5). However, some (1, 5) hold that female superiority in recall does not stand if the material is more interesting to the males. This statement does appeal, but there has been very little research designed to investigate the reasons behind it. In fact, there has been far more research relating to motivational factors in perception than that relating to motivational factors in memory. Research on the latter point would be of interest to educators who teach subject matter to students, who vary widely in their interest in the content of courses.

The present study had its origin in the observation during interviews held to determine the interest of students in the subjects (Arts or Science), on admission to the higher secondary class. Boys did consistently better than girls on questions involving estimations of distance, size, or numbers. Even fairly intelligent females were found ignorant of the population of India or the distance from Delhi to Berlin or the height of Pisa Tower. They seemed to be unable to retain this information, even though they must have been exposed to it a number of times.

Such sex differences are not unknown to researchers and educators. Weber (6) wrote: "Mention mathematics to a woman and she freezes into a condescending attitude of tolerance–she knows it exists, she uses it when she must, but it certainly has very little to do with her own delightfully imaginative and delicate world of interests." This debility, however, seems more fundamental than simply a reflection of hostility to mathematics. Schilder (3) states that we remember only what we can and will use in the present situation. If this is so, then investigations into the retention of information may reveal some basic attitudes regarding what type of information, women believe, is useful.

The present study aims to determine whether sex differences in recall of quantitative material pertaining to numbers, sizes, and distances, observed in students seeking admission to certain subject groups at higher school level, appear in other samples.

Procedure

Experiment 1

Two populations of Ss were sampled. The first consisted of graduating students in a liberal arts college and the second of patients (who were at least graduates) in a hospital. The students, 75 males and 40 females, all between 17 and 24 years old, were matched for intelligence (Lorge-Thorndike Intelligence Test Level 5 Form B Non-Verbal); there was no significant difference between the mean IQ of males, 93.5, and that of females, 94.7. The patients included 80 men and 45 women, all between 18 and 35 years old, undergoing treatment in surgery and general diseases wards of an urban hospital, matched for intelligence (above test) in that there was no significant sex difference in mean IQ of males – 86.5 and that of females – 85.8.

The samples were tested by an examiner who requested them to answer the following questions:

1. What is the population of Punjab State?
2. What is the population of Patiala (The town to which all the subjects belonged)?
3. How far is it from Patiala to Delhi?
4. How many teaspoons are there in a tablespoon?

5. What is the height of the Qutab Minar?
6. How many pints make a gallon of milk?

The responses to the questions are presented in Table 1. It is evident that there are large differences in regard to estimating the population, distance and height (with males excelling) and in recalling capacity (with females excelling).

Table 1
Percentage of Correct Responses to Quantitative Items

Item	Male patients N = 80	Female patients N = 45	*P*	Male students N = 75	Female students N = 40	*P*
Population (Punjab)	52	24	.01	76	50	.01
Population (Town)	63	20	.001	79	43	.01
Distance	72	23	.001	86	66	.05
Capacity (Pints)	12	62	.001	16	58	.001
Height	48	23	.01	58	39	.05
Capacity (Teaspoons)	25	58	.01	38	76	.01

All *P* values are based on chi-square tests.

Experiment 2

In the previous experiment where a classification of Ss by sex is used, it may be hazardous to regard the sex differences as genuine until more diverse groups are sampled. So it seemed in order to replicate the study with a fresh sample of 200 university students (120 male students and 80 female students doing M.A./M.SC.).

Table 2
Percentage of Correct Responses to Quantitative Items

Item	Male students N = 120	Female students N = 80	*P*
Population (Punjab)	75	45	.01
Population (Town)	82	52	.01
Distance	64	30	.01
Capacity (Teaspoons)	32	70	.01
Size (Height)	62	30	.01
Capacity (Pints)	72	78	ns

The procedure followed was the same as in the previous experiment. The results, presented in Table 2, support the sex differences revealed before. The males do far better on numbers, that is, population, distance and height items, while the females excel in recalling capacity (teaspoons) though in one capacity item (pints in a gallon) there is no sex difference.

Experiment 3

One snag that could subsist in the above two experiments was that the exposure of the Ss to the information that was requested was not controlled. Hence, it was thought necessary to present an altogether new material to a group of subjects to see if the sex differences revealed earlier in remembering quantitative material endure.

Two brief paragraphs were constructed, each containing both quantitative and non-quantitative material. Care was taken to ensure that the material was "new" to the Ss, so that any differences could not be attributed to any previous exposure. Hence, the "facts" presented were fabricated and for the most part incorrect. The paragraphs were as below:

(a) The British King, Henry the Second, invaded Paris with an army of 15,000 soldiers and airmen. This city of 1,700,000 in a country of 256 million people is one of the most beautiful ports in South-East Europe. The commander of the Army was George Bushel.

(b) This place was the scene of a bloody battle in Egypt. This country of 1,26,000 square miles is one of the richest tea-producing centres on the continent. More than 1,250,000 tons of tea is shipped every month. The other important exports are cotton, orange, coffee, and copper.

The Ss in this experiment were 90 girls and 65 boys (already graduates or postgraduates) undergoing one-year teacher training for becoming high school teachers. There were no sex differences in intelligence [difference in mean IQ's of boys (95.69) and girls (96.20) being non-significant]. The Ss were told that a paragraph would be read to them. When the examiner asked them to begin, they would write down all they remembered of it. The direction to begin writing followed several seconds after the reading of each paragraph.

In scoring the recall data, the paragraphs were divided into "sense units". For example, /the British King/Henry the Second/ invaded Paris/ with an army/of 10,060 soldiers and airmen/......etc., this yielded a total of 25 non-quantitative units and 5 quantitative units. A quantitative unit was scored as correct if the number was recalled correctly, regardless of whether the unit (miles, tons, etc.)

was accurate. All information as to the sex of the respondents was removed when the scoring was done by the writer. Thirty of the protocols were also scored independently by another researcher. The coefficient of agreement between the scorers was .86 for the non-quantitative scores and .97 for the quantitative scores.

The results presented in Table 3 confirm the prediction that boys

Table 3
Average Number of Items Remembered (Teacher Trainees)

	Non-quantitative items				*Quantitative Items*			
	Average number remembered	*SD*	*t*	*p*	*Average number remembered*	*SD*	*t*	*p (one tail)*
Males N = 65	12.45	.65			1.21	.28		
			.19	ns			1.74	ns
Females (N = 90)	12.25	.51			.70	.14		

excel in recalling quantitative items and that on non-quantitative items there are no sex differences. The average number of quantitative items recalled by the boys was 1.46 ± .20, while that by the girls was .82 ± .16. This difference is significant by 't' test at beyond .05 level. An analysis of the data on recall of digited numbers revealed no sex difference in the recall of six and seven digits.

It may be noted that the level of significance of difference in respect of quantitative items in Table 3 is not adequate, so it was, decided to repeat the procedure on a fresh sample. The paragraphs were read to 130 students (45 boys and 85 girls) in commerce classes (at the graduate level). The procedure was identical to that used in the case of teacher trainees. The results shown in Table 4 indicate that the females do slightly better than the males in recalling the non-quantitative material, but the males do significantly better than the female in recalling quantitative material. When the two samples (teacher trainees and commerce students) are pooled, a chi-square test shows that the sex difference in recalling the quantitative items is significantly beyond the .01 level ($x^2 = 6.02$, p < .01).

Table 4
Average Number of Items Remembered (Commerce Students)

	Non-quantitative items				*Quantitative Items*			
	Average number remembered	*SD*	*t*	*p*	*Average number remembered*	*SD*	*t*	*p*
Males N = 45	14.40	.34			1.60	.68		
			.76	ns			1.79	.05
Females (N = 85)	14.82	.29			1.00	.35		

Discussion

The results of Experiments 1 and 2 confirm the predication that female Ss would be poorer than male Ss on retention of quantitative material (numbers, distance, height). It may be noted, however, that the items designated as "quantitative items" did not involve computation, judgement, or even analytic reasoning. Questions on the population of Punjab State, or the distance from Patiala to Delhi, or the height of the Qutab Minar do not in fact constitute a test in estimating number or distance or height. No one has "seen" the population of Punjab and few Ss will attempt to find the answer by dividing the country's population by a set percentage, nor has anyone measured the distance between Patiala and Delhi or the height of the Qutab Minar. These items involve simply the retention of a word or number of figure that one has seen and heard many times.

One might explain these results on the basis of greater familiarity of the male Ss with population, distance and height judgements and of the female Ss with teaspoons and pints. Yet this does not provide the whole answer, for it is evident that both men and women have been exposed to all these items a number of times, surely enough for learning. We all know the people who can tell the number of feet in a mile but are unable to remember the number of pints in a gallon. Such forgetting is in fact highly selective as was shown by Levine and Murphy (2).

Experiment 3, which shows that this difference appears with new material, proves that the difference cannot be attributed solely to a difference in previous contact with the information. This may have implications for the teaching of mathematics and other subjects to female students. Evidently the poorer performance of female students on tests of mathematics is more fundamental than a distance for computation or calculation. Further research will determine the extent of this debility.

The present research indicates that this deficiency in women is not directly related to an antipathy to all numbers; the females excelled in recalling the number of teaspoons in a tablespoon and pints in a gallon. In Experiment 3, although the males surpassed the females in recalling the quantitative material from the paragraphs, there was no difference in the recall of six and seven digits. This result parallels the negligible sex differences in recall of digits mentioned by Lewis Madison Terman (4). Perhaps this indicates that many women may be unable to retain large number (thousands or above). An analysis made of the type of errors in recalling the numbers from the paragraphs showed that 36 per cent of these errors were owing to the incorrect placement of the significant figures. For instance, some Ss wrote "1500" or "150,000" instead of "15,000"; or "26,000", "26,00,000," or "1,026,00" instead of "126,000". This type of error constituted 42 per cent of the incorrect responses by females and 31 per cent of the incorrect responses by males. This difference is not significant, which shows that these are percentages of the incorrect responses given by all Ss. That is, it does not include Ss who did not write any figure or who wrote the correct figure. However, it does indicate that there is need for research on the types of numbers that can be handled by men and women. If women can remember seven digits but cannot remember five or six digited numbers, it is worthwhile to examine the psychological characteristics of numbers qua numbers, instead of numbers as un-related series of digits. Interest, possibly determined by environmental factors in which men and women live and work, may partly explain the differences in retention of material.

Summary

The study aimed at determining whether differences seen between male and female students, seeking admission to certain subject groups at high school level, in the retention of quantitative material exist in other population samples. The Ss tested included 125 hospital patients, 115 college students, and 200 university students. They were asked to recall quantitative material such as population, distance, height, and capacity. The results showed that the males were better on population, distance, and height items while the females were better on capacity items (number of pints in a gallon or number of teaspoons in a tablespoon). Again, the males were better able to retain new quantitative material in a test of immediate recall. In remembering non-quantitative material in digit and span test, no sex differences appeared. Further research into selective retention is warranted.

References

1. Anastasi, A. and Foley, J.P. *Differential Psychology,* N.Y.: MacMillan, 1949.
2. Lewine, J.M. and Murphy, G. The Learning and Forgetting of Controversial Material, *J. Abnorm, Soc. Psychol.* 1943, 38, 507-517.
3. Schilder, P. In D. Rapaport (Ed.), *Organization and Pathology of Thought*, N.Y.: Columbia University Press, 1951.
4. Terman, L.M. *Psychological Sex Differences,* In L. Carmichael (Ed.), *Manual of Child Psychology,* N.Y.: Wiley, 1946.
5. Tyler, L.E. *The Psychology of Human Differences,* N.Y.: Appleton-Century-Crofts, 1947.
6. Weber, Naomi. Science in Books, *Saturday Review of Literature,* November 2, 1957, p. 43.

IV. Intelligence and its Correlates

22. THE VALUE OF INTELLIGENCE TESTS

Some of the questions often posed by teachers, parents and laymen in regard to the value of intelligence tests are: Do intelligence tests really reveal how bright or dull people are? Can we, with the help of intelligence tests, sort out students according to their mental abilities? Do tests of mental ability help us in predicting an individual's performance in the home or school? Can we draw upon intelligence tests to detect backwardness or talent? The writer conducted the following study to seek answers to these questions.

The Study

The subjects of study were 45 M.Ed. scholars (26 males and 19 females) of the Government Training College for Teachers, Jullundur. They were selected from the college's four one-year sessions ending with the year 1965. These subjects were either college lecturers or school principals with at least five years' teaching experience. They were in the age-range of 24-31 years. Each of them had a Master's degree in the Arts besides a degree in Education, and had completed his M.Ed. course. All of them belonged to the average or above-average socio-economic class in the Punjab. Having qualified in the subject of Mental Measurement and Evaluation as a part of their M.Ed. course, they had acquired some experience, though brief, in the field of mental testing in schools.

In a personal interview each of the subjects was asked the following seven questions, in the order in which they appear below. Each person's categorical reply in one of the four terms, *i.e.* 'to a large extent', 'to a reasonable extent', 'help a little', 'don't help at all' was noted in respect of each question, and his general reactions regarding intelligence tests were recorded.

1. How far do intelligence tests help in classifying students according to mental ability?
2. How far do intelligence tests help in understanding the students' level of scholastic achievement?
3. To what extent do intelligence tests reveal how bright or dull young people are?
4. How far do intelligence tests help in diagnosing backwardness?
5. How far do intelligence tests help to classify students in different subject-groups in the higher secondary classes?
6. To what extent do intelligence tests help in predicting an individual's fitness for a vocation?
7. To what extent do intelligence tests help us in predicting an individual's ability to adjust to new environments?

Results and Discussion

The responses are summed up as below on the four-point scale as per cents of subjects favouring a particular degree to which intelligence tests help in each case.

Table 1
Showing percentage of subjects favouring different values of intelligence tests

Question No.	To a large extent	To a reasonable extent	Help a little	Don't help at all
1	81	13	6	0
2	19	22	54	5
3	70	22	8	0
4	68	23	9	0
5	34	38	21	7
6	12	42	34	12
7	31	36	14	19

As we see, the help that intelligence tests given in classifying students according to mental status scored the highest percentages. This is what was to be expected. Kornhauser (1945) also found that as a method of quickly sorting people in terms of mental ability the tests are really useful.

The help that these tests given in knowing how bright young people are or diagnosing backwardness comes next in the degree of favourableness.

That intelligence tests help in classifying students for different subject groups and in predicting their ability to adjust to new environments has been favoured by a large number of the subjects.

That intelligence tests help in predicting an individual's fitness for a vocation has been favoured least of all, by only half the subjects. And a few favoured these tests in understanding achievement level.

Obviously, intelligence tests help most in classification, in identifying a bright or dull child and in diagnosing backwardness, while they help least in predicting an individual's future vocational role and in understanding the level of achievement. This is what may be expected because I.Q., which intelligence tests must reveal, is what is needed most in matters where these tests tend to help most, and several other factors which lie beyond the scope of what intelligence tests can measure are involved in matters where these tests are found to help least.

Most of the experts are unanimous in saying that as a method of quickly sorting people in terms of general intelligence, their ability to learn and their mental alertness, the tests are really useful. They also agree that, by and large, people with high scores in these tests have better intellectual ability that those with an average score, and that the latter have better ability than those with low test scores. The findings of the present study reveal somewhat similar opinions. The tests are not only good at classification in schools; they are believed to classify men much more accurately than other techniques even in the armed forces, in business and in industry.

General Reactions Regarding Intelligence Tests

1. Those of the subjects who said that intelligence tests do not help at all expressed their opinions in various ways. Reactions that 10 per cent or more of the subjects gave are recorded below:
   (i) These tests are cranky questions made up by crank psychologists.
   (ii) There are very funny questions in these tests. How can these measure one's mental ability?

(iii) Intelligence cannot be measured by a few queer and outlandish questions in the tests.

(iv) Different situations in life have to be met with the help of different kinds of ability. These bookish and routine tests can neither create those situations nor measure the various abilities.

(v) Intelligence tests have ruined many promising careers.

(vi) Intelligence tests give a very distorted picture of one's brains.

2. Fifteen per cent of the subjects who sized up the usefulness of the tests for one purpose or another expressed their opinions as follows:

(i) Cheating, previous familiarity with the tests or errors in the testing procedures may make people get higher scores than they deserve.

(ii) Illness, either physical or psychological, emotional disturbance, lack of good education, and failure to put in deliberate effort to do one's best in the test, may give people lower scores than they deserve.

(iii) Intelligence tests are not supposed to measure the brains we are born with. Both heredity and after-birth acquisition determine one's performance in the test.

(iv) Only experts who have specialised in tests and their use can bring about satisfactory results.

(v) I.Q. tests cannot measure anything beyond how bright one is and how good one is in learning and abstract thinking. They cannot indicate one's knowledge, efficiency at a test or whether one would be successful in work.

Conclusions

By and large, the subjects' verdict goes in favour of intelligence tests. The tests are not without flaws. They are not as foolproof as we would like them to be. But they do help in measuring abilities required for scholastic attainment, industry, the defence forces, and the various professions. If used along with other tests and interpreted and applied in the light of other facts about an individual, intelligence tests are an effective tool in the hands of experts.

The much publicised observation of the layman that intelligence tests have no value whatever and that they should be scrapped is not supported by what is revealed in this or other studies.

References

E.G. Boring, H.S. Longfeld and H.P. Weld, *Foundations of Psychology* (Asia Publishing House, 1961), Chap. 18.

J.F. Dashiell, *Fundamentals of General Psychology* (Houghton Mifflin, 1946), Chap. 5.

Arthur W. Kornhauser, *Psychological Tests in Business and Psychology of Labour Management* (Columbia, 1945).

A.W. Kornhauser, 'Are Intelligence Tests Worth While?', *The American Magazine*, July 1945.

N.L. Munn, *Psychology* (Houghton Mifflin, 1946), Chap. 23.

Theodore C. Ruch, *Psychology and Life* (Whitman, Chicago, 1946), Chap. 6.

R.S. Woodworth and D.G. Marquis, *Psychology* (Methuen, 1946), Chap. 2.

23. STABILITY OF IQ SCORES

Estimated true (E.T.) changes in IQ from grades three to seventh and again to eleventh, of 95 boys and 75 girls, who were administered Large Thorndike Intelligence Tests, verbal and non-verbal, revealed that (1) E.T. non-verbal changes were two to three times as great as E.T. verbal changes for both boys and girls and (2) both verbal and non-verbal IQ scores tend to rise, (3) grades three, seventh, and eleventh verbal IQ scores correlated more highly with each other than did grades three, seventh, and eleventh non-verbal IQ scores. There was no significant product-moment correlation between E.T. verbal and E.T. non-verbal IQ change scores. –*Editors*

The Present Study

In a quest for stability of IQ scores, the Large Thorndike Intelligence Tests, verbal and non-verbal, were administered to the residual group of 95 boys and 75 girls of eleventh grade, who were amongst the 112 boys and 94 girls subjected to these tests in their seventh grade and amongst the 135 boys and 115 girls who had started with these tests in their third grade. An interval of four to five years had thus elapsed when each successive test administration was made. The sample consisted of the entire class of third grade in the first instance, and was of moderately better than average socio-economic status, as determined by Kuppuswami's Socio-Economic Status scale[2]. Estimated true changes in the IQ scores using McNemar's method[3] were computed. Table 1 shows the means of the IQ scores and the estimated true changes over the four-to-five-year period.

Table 1

Mean of I.Q. Scores and the Estimated true changes over the Four-to-Five-Year Period

	Grade 3 Mean Verbal IQ	Grade 7 Mean Verbal IQ	Estimated True Verbal IQ Change from grade 3 to grade 7	Grade 11 Mean Verbal IQ	Estimated True Verbal IQ Change from grade 7 to grade 11	Grade 3 Mean Non-Verbal IQ	Grade 7 Mean Non-Verbal IQ	Estimated True Non-Verbal Change from grade 3 to grade 7	Grade 11 Mean Non-Verbal IQ	Estimated True Non-Verbal Change from grade 7 to grade 11
Boys	98.5	103.2	3.34	108.8	4.24	96.2	108.8	11.24	115.95	7.25
Girls	97.8	100.5	2.85	104.7	4.85	93.5	102.7	9.38	109.8	7.12

Discussion

Table 1 shows a mean estimated true measure for boys of 3.34 verbal IQ points and 11.24 non-verbal IQ points. These changes (gains) are significant beyond the .01 level. It may be interesting to note that the non-verbal increase is more than three times that of the verbal change. For girls, the estimated true gains from grade three to grade seven are 2.85 verbal IQ points and 9.38 non-verbal IQ points. These gains are also significant beyond .01 level, and again the non-verbal gain is more than three times the verbal gain.

The estimated true gain in verbal IQ points from grade 7 to grade 11 for both boys and girls is only a little more than that from grade 3 to grade 7, while the estimated true increase in non-verbal IQ points, from grade 7 to grade 11 for both boys and girls is considerably less than that from grade 3 to grade 7. Again the non-verbal gain from grade 7 to grade 11, in respect of both boys and girls, is about twice that of the verbal gain.

Table 2

MEANS OF THE CORRELATIONS BETWEEN GRADES THREE, SEVENTH AND ELEVENTH LORGE-THORNDIKE IQ SCORES

	Boys	Girls	
Verbal	.637	.793	Difference significant at .005
Non-Verbal	.545	.686	Difference significant at .045

All these results indicate that non-verbal IQ scores are more unstable while verbal IQ scores are more stable.

Greater instability of the non-verbal IQ is evident from Table 2 where the mean of the correlations between grade 3 IQ, grade 7 IQ and grade 11 IQ is shown to be greater for verbal scores than non-verbal scores–the difference for girls is significant at .025 level, whereas for boys the difference, though not significant at a conventional level, produced an extreme area EA (1) of .195. Besides, the differences between these stability coefficients (boys *Vs.* girls) indicate that both verbal and non-verbal IQ scores are more stable in the case of girls than boys over the eight year experimental period. The significance levels are found to be .003 for the verbal scores, and .039 for the non-verbal.

A chance, though possibly important, finding was the apparent lack of Linear correlation between estimated true verbal and non-verbal IQ changes for boys (r=.083) and girls (r = .098). This means that although the relationship between verbal and non-verbal IQ scores was found to be of the usual order of around .5, estimated true changes in these series were found to be uncorrelated.

Conclusions

The administration of Lorge-Thorndike tests, verbal and non-verbal, at grade levels 3, 7 and 11 revealed that non-verbal scores are relatively more unstable than verbal scores, that boys' scores are more unstable than girls' scores, that gains in both boys' and girls', verbal or non-verbal, scores are much less between grade 7 and grade 11 than between grade 3 and grade 7, that verbal and non-verbal change scores are apparently independent, and that verbal and non-verbal IQ scores have differential tendency to rise, at least over the eight-year period covered by the present experiment.

References

1. Blommers P., and Lindquist, E.F. "Elementary Statistical Methods", Boston: Houghton-Mifflin Company, 1960, p. 312.
2. Kuppuswami, B. "Socio-Economic Status Scale-Urban." Agra Psychological Research Cell, 1976.
3. McNemar, Q, "Psychological Statistics", New York: Wiley and Sons, 1955.

24. SOME CORRELATES OF RAVEN PROGRESSIVE MATRICES

A review (1958) of the literature on the Raven test shows several studies relating the measure to the Stanford-Binet, the Wechsler-Ballavue, the WISC, and group tests. On the other hand, there are almost no studies relating the test to specific abilities except those measured by Wechsler subtests, or to assess its utility with children.

Again, low correlations of the Raven with the Binet, but slightly higher correlations with performance measures than with verbal measures, have appeared in the review. The literature also detracts somewhat from the claim that the Raven is a pure measure of g.

The Present Study

In a bid to delineate some correlates of the Raven Progressive Matrices (1947), this test along with SRA Primary Mental Abilities Test (PMA) and Goodenough Draw-a-Man (D-a-M) Test was administered individually to 110 Primary School children, 60 boys and 50 girls aged 7-1 to 8-1 selected at random from an urban public school of Punjab State. It took about a month to accomplish all testing.

Table-1 shows means and standard deviations for the three tests. Reference to test norms shows that our group is fairly close to typical performance for its age (7-8) on all measures. It is at the 8-year level on Raven's norms. Table-2 gives the product-moment intercorrelations of the measures. As the correlations calculated separately by sex showed no marked or consistent patterns of differences, these were not taken into cognizance.

Only a weak relationship between the Raven and any of Thurston's (1953) factors measured in comparable group of children emerged. In fact, the Thurston factors inter-correlate for the most part more substantially than does the Raven with any of them. Studies relating the Raven to the WISC show marked discrepancies in results among primary school children. The Raven tends to correlate more substantially with Arithmetic, Block Design and Vocabulary than with Object Assembly, Coding, Mazes, and Comprehension.

Raven's reliability (odd-even split-half corrected) with primary school children in the present study is .416. This is bound to attenuate the relationship that Table-2 presents.

While planning for this study, it appeared that for primary school children some of the original expressions in Raven's Manual had to be modified slightly. Some changes, consistently applied, induced quicker understanding of the task. For instance, the question, "Is that the right one to go in here", aimed at directing attention and ensuring a more careful examination of the materials, actually may shake self-confidence, a baneful effect which then lasts throughout the testing sessions. Probably the directions need to be extensively modified and in some cases, replaced by expressions that are more productive in terms of better understanding and accurate performance.

As the test is graduated in difficulty and the range of difficulty is enormous, there was waning of interest and zeal after some time, especially in the B series. In fact, the test was found difficult by seven-to-eight-year-olds, especially those in the average reaches of intelligence and below. This may be due to cultural differences between Indian children and the British subjects on whom the test was standardised. In spite of the high flexibility and non-verbal nature of the test, an element of newness that a population, other than that on which a test is standardised, confronts is bound to reduce the former's score to a degree.

Table 1
Means and Standard Deviation of Scores on the Raven, The Thurstone PMA, and the Draw-A-Man Tests

	Boys	(N-60)	Girls	(N=50)	Total	(N=110)
	X	SD	X	SD	X	SD
Raven	15.04	4.5	15.26	4.2	15.16	4.3
Primary Mental Abilities:						
Verbal Meaning	24.94	8.2	26.95	7.9	26.51	7.4
Perceptual Speed	8.35	7.4	10.14	1.5	9.40	7.1
Quantitative	9.95	6.6	10.21	6.9	10.10	6.8
Motor	19.52	7.9	22.11	9.1	20.81	8.4
Space	9.15	5.2	12.01	4.8	10.56	5.1
D-a-M	10.56	6.1	13.16	5.6	11.88	5.9

Table 2
Inter-correlations* of Scores on the Raven, PMA and Draw-A-Man Tests

	Raven	V	P	Q	Mo	S
Primary Mental Abilities:						
Verbal Meaning (V)	.30					
Perceptual Speed (P)	.21	.62				
Quantitative (Q)	.35	.67	.62			
Motor (Mo)	.20	.32	.40	.31		
Space (S)	.32	.58	.62	.60	.63	
D-a-M	.21	.52	.43	.52	.39	.52

* $r = .24$ Significant at .01 level.

References

1. Burke, H.R. Raven's Progressive Matrices: A review and critical evaluation. J. Genet. Psychol, 1958,93,199-228.
2. Raven, J.C. Guide to Using Progressive Matrices (1947), New York, Psychological Corporation, 1947.
3. Thurstone, Thelma G., Thurstone, L.L. Examiner Manual for the SRA Primary Mental Abilities (ages 6 to 8) Chicago, Science Research Associates, 1953.

25. LINGUISTIC BACKGROUND AND INTELLIGENCE

To Study the relationship between linguistic background and intelligence, two groups of Panjabi children, one bilingual and the other monolingual, were administered tests of verbal ability and non-verbal intelligence. The bilingual group was found superior on a test of non-verbal intelligence. However, no difference was obtained between the groups with respect to verbal ability in the native language. The results support a transfer-accretion model for the development of intelligence and abilities.

Introduction

While performance of North American native children on spatial and non-verbal tests approximates White norms, that on verbal skills was found greatly inferior. (Havighurst, 1970). Depressed educational achievement and a high dropout rate among American Indians reflect similar findings. (Hawthorn, 1967; Havighurst, 1970). Edington (1970) has suggested that the use of an Indian language by native children may cause difficulties in the acquisition of English, and consequently adversely affect school achievement. However, Lambert and Anisfeld (1969) found positive relationship between bilingualism and intelligence. Again it has been pointed out that the more diversified sociolinguistic background of bilinguals favours the development of a more complex structure of mental abilities for them than for monolinguals. Bilinguals were, besides, found superior on both verbal and non-verbal intelligence tests when socio-economic status was controlled. Ferguson (1954) proposed transfer-accretion model for the development of intelligence, according to which abilities are learned and generalised acquisitions mediated by cultural environment. If such variables as socio-economic status, sex and age are controlled, the more diversified experience of the bilingual might lead to intellectual advantage in non-verbal tests of intelligence. For verbal tests in his own language, a monolingual might perform as well as a true bilingual because the basis for transfer is common.

The present study is aimed at testing the following hypotheses:

1. Bilingual *Ss* score significantly higher than monolingual *Ss* on a non-verbal intelligence test.

2. There is no difference between bilinguals and monolinguals on a Punjabi verbal ability test.
3. For bilinguals, Punjabi verbal ability scores correlate positively with reported use of Panjabi in the home.
4. For bilinguals, there is no relationship between non-verbal intelligence and use of English in the home.

Procedure

Sample: Two groups of boys, aged 9-11 and all attending school, formed the sample. Each group consisted of 50 boys, from Patiala schools, belonging to an average socio-economic stratum. Their intelligence range was 95-110 I.Q. (Lorge Thorndike Non-verbal Form A, level 3). All the available boys were tested irrespective of grade level achieved at school. This involved grades 3 to 5, so that for both the groups less than 10 per cent of eligible *Ss* would have been missed through dropping out of school.

The unilingual group was from an ordinary Government school in which boys of average means are admitted. The principal occupation of the family heads was business in the local market, the monthly income was rupees four to five hundred, the only language used in the home or taught in the school was their native language Punjabi. The families chosen were relatively isolated from superior social influences. They were residing in old residential houses located in thickly populated streets of Patiala town.

A second group of 50 bilingual (English and Punjabi speaking) boys was tested in a comparably small suburb of Patiala. The town is rather less isolated. The principal work available to the families of the boys was clerical, the monthly income was rupees four to five hundred, the languages taught in the school were English and Punjabi. The families were scarcely exposed to superior social influences. They were residing in small one-two-roomed quarters located in the olden streets of Patiala.

Both the samples were thus matched for the critical variable of age, sex and socio-economic status. They were representative of 9-11 years–old boys for the respective communities, and sampling error due to absenteeism or dropping out is regarded as minimal.

Tests: Lorge Thorndike Intelligence Test Non-verbal Form A, level 3 (1954) was used to test intelligence. Socio-economic status, bilingualism, and parents' use of Punjabi in the home were assessed by questionnaires administered to the boys. A measure of verbal ability in Punjabi was provided by the boys' scores in the test of verbal ability administered during their final examinations in the school.

Results

As shown in Table 1, the bilingual group scored significantly higher on the non-verbal intelligence test. There was no significant difference with reference to verbal ability in Punjabi. This verifies hypotheses 1 and 2.

For the bilingual group, a correlation of .69, significant at .01 level of confidence, was obtained between reported parental use of Punjabi in the home and the boys' Punjabi verbal ability scores. This confirms hypothesis 3.

Hypothesis.4 was also confirmed, when a slight positive, though not significant, correlation (.19) was found between reported parental use of Punjabi in the home and intelligence.

Table 1
Means and Stand Deviations: Nonverbal Intelligence and Verbal Ability in Punjabi

	Bilingual (N = 50)		Monolingual N = 50		
	X	*SD*	X	*SD*	*t*
Intelligence...	109.95	6.72	105.02	4.12	4.44*
Verbal ability in Punjabi	66.60	6.20	64.79	5.25	1.47

* Two-tailed test, $p = 01$; df = 98

Discussion

The results obtained support the hypotheses derived from Ferguson's transfer-accretion model for the development of abilities. Bilingualism may be beneficial to the development of non-verbal intelligence, as a result of the more diversified basis for transfer to subsequent ability development that two language systems provide.

The results tend to show that while the use of Punjabi in the home relates to verbal ability level among bilingual Punjabi children, the use of a foreign language by the individual need not adversely affect his acquisition of Punjabi.

It has often been seen that the verbal ability scores of Punjabi children, together with their resultant under-achievement at school, tend to be low; this may be due to the quality of Punjabi used in the home. Hawthorn (1967), in a survey of several Indian communities in Canada, found that the usual everyday conversations among Indian children and adults are deplorably limited. Questions are often answered in monosyllables by children as well as adults. Culture frequently warrants silence from children in the presence of adults. The Punjabi spoken by adults is often inaccurate and inadequate in vocabulary, and reading is virtually unknown to children. It is suggested that these factors, rather than the presence of two languages, adversely affect the verbal performance of Punjabi children.

Again, the equivalent performance of both groups on the verbal ability test suggests that uncontrolled cultural variables, such as degree of contact with superior social influences, may be operating, because in the present study the bilingual group was relatively less isolated from the larger urban community. Nevertheless, any comparative study of bilingualism faces a related problem in so far as groups differentiated in terms of linguistic background inevitably differ with respect to social and cultural factors.

To sum up, it may be concluded that bilingualism has a favourable influence on non-verbal intelligence provided some cultural differences, besides those produced by bilingualism per se, across the two groups studied here are controlled.

References

Edington, E.D. "Disadvantaged Rural Youth", *Review of Educational Research*, 40:69-85,1970.

Ferguson, G.A. "On Learning and Human Ability", *Canadian Journal of Psychology*, 8:95-112,1954.

Havighurst, R.J. "The Education of Indian Children and Youths", *National Study of American Indian Education: Summary Report and Recommendations*, Series 4, No. 6, U.S. Office of Education, Washington, D.C., 1970.

Hawthorn, H.B. (ed), "A Survey of the Contemporary Indians of Canada", Indian Affairs Branch, Ottawa, Canada, 1967.

Lambert, W.E., Anisfeld, E., "A Note on the Relationship of Bilingualism and Intelligence", *Canadian Journal of Behavioural Science,* 1:123-128,1969.

Lambert, W.E. Peal, E., "The Relationship of Bilingualism to Intelligence", *Psychological Monographs*, 27: (Whole No. 546), 1962.

Vernon, P.E., "*Intelligence and Cultural Environment*", Methuen, London, England, 1969.

Lorge, Irvin, and Thorndike, Robert L. "*Level 3, Form A, Non-verbal Battery*". Houghton Mifflin Company Boston, N.Y. 1954.

26. CAN I.Q. PREDICT ACADEMIC SUCCESS

Intelligence Tests scores are often used to predict academic success. This is done by drawing correlations between the I.Q. scores and criteria of academic success such as teachers' ratings, so as to develop equations which will help us predict the pupils' academic achievement. Innumerable coefficients of correlation have been computed for such purposes. These coefficients, even relatively low ones, may serve when we are thinking in terms of groups, but these values, even pretty high ones, may give erroneous predictions when we are considering the individual. The following Scattergram, which represents r = .78, shows relationship between Arithmetic achievement and intelligence that the writer found in his study of a random sample of students of Government Basic School, Patiala, in the spring of 1974, is a case in point:

When coefficients of correlation and equations are used to predict a pupil's academic success, we are working under the assumptions that the nature of the individual's past is constant and will continue into the future, and that academic success depends solely on intelligence as shown through IQ. This "deterministic" approach to the measurement of individual differences appears to be faulty, owing to the clear possibility that the two assumptions underlying this approach may not be proved. A pupils' motivations, interests, and other factors are not

SCATTERGRAM

Lorge-Thorndike Non-Verbal Intelligence Test Level 5 Form A: I.Q.

	80-84	85-89	90-94	95-99	100-104	105-109	110-114	115-119	120-124	125-129	130-134	135-139
125-129										1		
120-124									2			1
115-119						1	2	3	1	2	1	1
110-114							2	3	1	4	1	
105-109						2				2	1	
100-104						2	1	2	1		1	
95-99						2	2	1				
90-94				1			1	1	1		1	
85-89							1	1	1			
80-84				1		1		1				
75-79				1								
70-74		1										

always constant from grade to grade. A simple failure may readily affect the attitude toward schoolwork, a good teacher may suddenly intensify his interest in Arithmetic; but an equation which we use to predict his academic success cannot take these unpredictable factors of life into account. Thus test scores or coefficients of correlation, though of utility in planning programmes of instruction, may not prove much efficacious for predicting academic success.

As not unsoften seen, pupils with the highest IQ do not invariably obtain the highest scores in schoolwork, because many factors, other than intelligence, influence academic success, the importance of these factors varying from pupil to pupil. In fact, the prediction of human behaviour is very difficult because of a great many factors-social, cultural, genetical and psychological–that affect human beings. A pupil's academic success may be affected by what school he happens to join, how often he changes schools, which teachers he is assigned to, whether his parents give importance to his studies, soon and so forth.

Consequently the "deterministic" approach should give place to a realistic approach in which individual differences may be measured on a more feasible assumption that pupil is highly dynamic, his past nature may not continue into the future, and his achievement or academic success may be influenced by many factors, both known and unknown. The statistics of this approach may present many difficulties. Nevertheless, it would be worthwhile to investigate the nature, extent and cause of individual variability on the premise of this more promising premise.

References

1. Clyde H. Coombs, *A Theory of Psychological Scaling*. Engineering Research Institute Bulletin No. 34, Ann. Arbor: Uni. of Mich. Press, 1952.
2. Jerzey Neyman. "Indeterminism in Science and New Demands on Statisticians," *J. of Amer. Statist. Assoc.* LV (December, I960), pp. 625-39.

27. I.Q. AND ACADEMIC ACHIEVEMENT

Many a time the teachers are baffled when bright students fail, or are on the brink of failure, or show a sharp disparity between their I.Q. and academic performance. Whenever their achievement is distinctly poorer than might be expected from their scores on an intelligence test, the students tend to be termed as bright under-achievers, unusual or maladjusted scholars. They are so called because of the well-known assumption that I.Q. as measured by an intelligence test must correspond with success in academic subjects. That this assumption is untenable, and that high I.Q. and as high academic achievement may not go together are the hypothesis of this study.

Procedure

Sixty-two students (31 boys and 31 girls) chosen randomly from 5th and 6th grades (age group 12 to 16) of the Lawrence School, Sanawar formed the sample. The school is a well-known and high-standard public school where children from the above-average social and economic strata are admitted through a comprehensive admission test held at all-India level.

The Lorge-Thorndike Intelligence Test (Level 5 Form A–non-verbal) was used to measure intelligence. This test is made up of figure analogies, figure-classifications and number series requiring 27 minutes working time in all. Thirty minutes before the children started work were used in distributing test-booklets and answer-sheets, filling in the particulars and reading directions. To ensure that the students clearly comprehended what they were required to do, answer-sheets were scored by hand by means of the Rights Key and the raw-scores read against the students' C.A. (Chronological Age) on the Norms-Table to find their I.Q.'s.

Mean percentages of the students' aggregate achievements in the two tests (in all subjects) held during April and May 1964 were taken as their scores in academic achievements.

The students were also ranked on intelligence by their tutor who knows them fairly individually, having had ample opportunities of personal contact through varied curricular and co-curricular programmes.

Coefficients of Correlation between I.Q.'s and Intelligence Ranks, I.Q.'s and Achievement Scores, Intelligence Ranks and Achievement scores were drawn through Rank-Difference Method. S.E.'s (Standard Error) of the 3r's were calculated through the classical formula $\left(SE = \frac{1-r^2}{N}\right)$ and the significance of each 'r' derived through 't' formula and Fisher's table of 't'.

Table 1

		Coefficients of Correlation r	SE	Level of Significance
Between I.Q.'s and Intelligence Ranks	Boys	.40	± .14	.01
	Girls	.50	± .13	.01
Between I.Q's and Academic Achievement	Boys	.12	± .17	.04
	Girls	.45	± .03	.01
Between Intelligence Ranks and Academic Achievement	Boys	.60	± .10	.01
	Girls	.85	± .05	.01

Table 2

(a) Where there is perfect correlation between I.Q. ranks and Intelligence Ranks

	Number
Boys	1
Girls	2

(b) Where there is perfect correlation between I.Q. ranks and Academic Achievement

	Number
Boys	0
Girls	0

Table 3

(a) Where there is a difference of 2 or more between I.Q. ranks and intelligence ranks

	1 Difference of 0 to ± 2 No. of Students	2 Difference of 3 to ± 8 No. of Students	3 Difference of ± 9 to ± 23 No. of Students
Boys	10	11	10
Girls	9	11	11

(b) Where there is a difference of 2 or more between I.Q. ranks and ranks on Academic Achievement.

	1	2	3
Boys	5	9	17
Girls	8	9	14

Table 4

Means and Standard Deviations of Raw Scores in Intelligence Test

Sample	N	Means	Standard Deviations
Boys	31	36.63	10.16
Girls	31	32.97	8.15
Difference	3.66		
Significance of difference–Not significant			

Findings

1. I.Q.'s determined by the intelligence test and the rankings on intelligence made by the teacher show a significant, though not high, correlation. Whereas the I.Q.'s has been derived by converting the raw scores from American norms, this should not on the whole disturb the relative position of an individual's I.Q. The low correlation may be owing to faulty ranking (by the teacher) which is possible as the teacher, while judging his ward's intelligence, is inevitably influenced by the students' academic achievement, pleasant manners, popularity, enviable conduct and the like.
2. Though there is a somewhat significant correlation between I.Q. and academic achievement in the case of girls, such correlation in case of boys is too poor to be significant. This confirms the hypothesis of this study that variation in academic achievement may not be following the same, directional variation in intelligence or that intelligence (as measured by intelligence test) and academic achievement may not go together.
3. The correlation between teachers' rankings on intelligence and academic achievement is good and significant both in case of boys and girls. This, however, should not be taken as favouring the belief that intelligence and academic achievement go together because, as already stated, the teachers' rankings may be too subjective to be considered equivalent to scores of an intelligence test.

4. There is not a single case of 1 to 1 relationship between I.Q. and academic achievement and a good many cases where there is a wide disparity between I.Q. ranks and ranks on academic achievement. In case of I.Q. ranks *versus* intelligence ranks the position is, however, much better. This in fact has led to the findings at 2 and 1 above.
5. Though boys on the average show a greater score than girls on the Lorge-Thorndike Intelligence test, the difference between the means of boys and girls is not significant.
6. Amongst the top students (whose I.Q. is above 109) there are 9 under-achievers among boys and 5 among girls.

Discussion

Poor correlation between I.Q. and academic achievement in most cases may be due to the fact that the mere possession of good intelligence never guarantees good academic achievement. Several factors other than intelligence like will to achieve, study habits, methods of teaching, facilities of work at home, parental guidance, schooling and the like contribute toward academic achievement. Since none of these "other factors" were controlled in this experiment, academic achievement cannot be said to be the logical outcome of intelligence alone. Also, academic achievement itself is never dependent upon intelligence only; the above-mentioned factors may also duly contribute towards it. A high correlation between I.Q. and academic achievement, thus, should in no case be expected.

Secondly, the study reveals that cases of bright under-achievers are not uncommon. That they are under-achievers appears to be wrong notion if those who always expect a substantial correlation between a person's I.Q. and his academic achievement believe that low achievement in case of bright students must be for reasons non-intellectual *i.e.* poor emotional adjustment, poor motivation and the like. Even when poor achievement and emotional stress show some relationship, it cannot be said with certainty, without further evidence, that the former is due to the latter. Some under-achievers may be excitable in their reactions. But this does not prove that their excitability is responsible for poor achievement in subjects. Even "achievement conscious" is open to several interpretations. When his parents do not seem to set high standards before him, it is not because they feel unconcerned about their ward, but because they have become discouraged or think it useless or unkind to be coaxing him all the time or they might be valuing other achievements more than his achievements at school. Thus, non-intellectual factors may not be responsible for under-achieving.

Thirdly, it is doubtful whether he is actually under-achieving. The expectations placed on him may be unrealistic, based on a misconception of the potentialities of a high I.Q. and of the varied abilities measured by the test which yields the so-called I.Q. An I.Q. is usually derived from the composite score on a test that includes many sub-tests such as ability to judge relationships, reasoning, grasp, abstract thinking etc. An individual may earn a high I.Q. without being equally good in his abilities on these sub-tests. Intelligence test scores account for only a limited part of individual differences and hence their inadequacy in portraying all the intellectual qualities. Again, one may be called under-achiever because he is not keen to meet the usual academic requirements but is using his mind in other ways. He is called an under-achiever by his teacher who wants everyone to learn what he teaches. History shows many examples of persons who were not so good at school but became great men by their efforts later. A bright under-achiever may be wiser and more mature than the one who doggedly secures high marks in his school subjects. This, however, may not be always true.

Fourthly, there are more under-achievers among boys than girls. This is in keeping with the usual observation that boys far exceed girls in problem behaviour, reading difficulties, lack of seriousness etc., though this evidence is not conclusive.

As such, it is felt that unless we know something more about a child than what an intelligence test indicates we should not jump to the conclusion that his academic achievement is below par.

28. INTELLIGENCE, CURIOSITY AND ACHIEVEMENT

Abstract

A self-rating inventory designed to identify groups of students differing in curiosity was administered to the male groups differing in intelligence level who had been randomly selected from 350 eighth class male students attending three urbans high schools. The students' aggregate marks in the school examination served as their achievement. The differences in intelligence between the means of high-, medium-, and low-

curiosity students were significant at .01 level or better. The relationships between intelligence and curiosity, intelligence and achievement, achievement and curiosity were significant in the case of all the three groups at .05 level or better.

Introduction

Self-rating instrument, if effective, would be less time-consuming both for the pupils and the teacher because it would be easier to administer and quicker to score. The success of self-rating instruments with children has been attributed by Baker (1) to the fact that the problems of children are so close to their lives that they can hardly help answering what applies to them. Jackson (2) showed that the use of self-inventories was as effective as ratings or interviews.

Maw and Maw (4) demonstrated that self-ratings of curiosity can be used as effectively as combined teacher-peer ratings of curiosity. They constructed a 41-item self-rating instrument, each item of which was meant to measure behaviour logically considered to indicate some aspect of curiosity. Some items were described in positive terms, others in negative terms. The responses were to be given by ticking one of the four words written against each item *i.e.*, never, sometimes, often, always. Thus a response showed the extent to which an item like "I like to explore strange places" pertained to a respondent. The split-half reliability of the test is .91. The test, which was constructed for fifth grade American children, was validated against combined teacher-pupil ratings of curiosity.

This instrument was studied item by item to examine whether any items were such as would call up associations with the culture the test had originated from. None of the items was found to be biased in favour of any culture. Hence the test was employed for the present study.

The study was conducted on 122 eighth class students of three high schools of Patiala. These students were randomly selected from a total of 350 male students on the rolls of the three schools. Most of the students came from middle class urban homes.

The above instrument was administered to the sample and the curiosity scores obtained. To make sure that reading ability would not be an important factor in the test results, the statements were read to the pupils as they followed and checked their forms. Those scoring from 35 to 49 were placed in the low-curiosity group, those from 50 to 74 in the medium curiosity group, and those from 75 to 89 in the high curiosity group.

Since previous studies show that intelligence is moderately correlated with curiosity, each of the three curiosity groups were administered Lorge-Thorndike Intelligence Test Non-verbal Form A level 5(3) to obtain their I.Q's. To determine the relationship of intelligence and curiosity with achievement, the students' aggregate marks in the school examination were collected from the school records. These marks were out of a maximum of 500 (100 for each of the subjects of English, Mathematics, Science, Social Studies and Punjabi – the regional language).

Results

The high-medium, and low-curiosity groups were found to be dissimilar in I.Q. when the differences between means were tested for significance by the CR test. Table-1 shows that the three curiosity groups are significantly different from each other on intelligence. These differences are all in the expected direction.

Table 1
Mean Differences in Lorge-Thorndike Intelligence Quotients for High-, Medium-, and Low-Curiosity Groups

Groups	*N*	*Mean*	*S.D.*	*High/ Medium*	*High/ Low*	*Medium/ Low*	*Significance*
High-curiosity	56	112.86	7.4	9.69			.01
Medium-curiosity	53	100.36	6.6		23.18		.01
Low-curiosity	13	87.33	1.7			13.03	.01

Table 2 is evident of the significant differences in the curiosity level between the three groups initially separated on the basis of their scores on the test. These differences too are as expected.

Table 2
Mean Differences in Curiosity for High-, Medium-, and Low-Curiosity Groups

Groups	*N*	*Mean*	*S.D.*	*High/ Medium*	*High / Low*	*Medium/ Low*	*Significance*
High-curiosity	56	80.04	5.3	9.90	–	–	.01
Medium-curiosity	53	63.68	4.9		8.12		.01
Low-curiosity	13	42.07	2.1			11.01	.01

Table 3 reflects significant relationship between intelligence and curiosity, intelligence and achievement, achievement and curiosity in the case of all the three curiosity groups.

Table 3
Inter-correlations Between Intelligence, Curiosity and Achievement for the Total Group (T), High- (H) Medium- (M), and Low-Curiosity (L) Groups

	Intelligence				Curiosity				Achievement			
	T	H	M	L	T	H	M	L	T	H	M	L
Intelligence					.81	.49	.40	.87				
Curiosity									.85	.83	.71	.87
Achievement	.79	.52	.32*	.50*								

*Significant at .05 level. The rest of the r's are significant at .01 level.

Discussion

That those who have higher intelligence may have more curiosity and those who have lower intelligence may have less curiosity is evident.

Whether intelligence is due to curiosity or curiosity is due to intelligence cannot be asserted. Since, however, intelligence or at least most of it is still believed to be inborn, it may help arouse or even develop curiosity which is of course developed owing to several other factors, both innate and environmental. That intelligence and curiosity are significantly related in the case of each group echoes the same finding.

That each group differs significantly from every other in their curiosity shows that this instrument may be very useful in identifying groups of children differing in curiosity levels.

The significant relationship between intelligence and achievement or between curiosity and achievement is understandable. Intelligence leads to greater learning and so does curiosity and hence the contribution of intelligence or curiosity to achievement, which is the product of learning, though the effect of other factors on achievement may not be ruled out.

Summary and Conclusions

Maw and Maw(4) self-rating instrument for identifying groups of children differing in curiosity, when applied to 122 eighth class children differing in intelligence level, demonstrated that the differences in curiosity and intelligence are in the same direction, that curiosity and intelligence are highly related, that curiosity is related to achievement also, and that the instrument is capable of identifying groups of children differing in curiosity.

References

1. Baker, H. (1945): "Introduction to Exceptional Children." New York: The MacMillan Company, 479-480.
2. Jackson, J. (1946): "The Relative Effectiveness of Paper-Pencil Tests, Interviews, and Ratings as Techniques of Personality Evaluation," *Journal of Social Psychology*, XXIII, 35-54.
3. Lorge, I, and Thorndike, R.L. (1957): "The Lorge-Thorndike Intelligence Tests, Level 5, Form A." Houghton Mifflin Company, Boston.
4. Maw, W.H. and Maw, E.W. (1968): "Self-Appraisal of Curiosity." *The Journal of Educational Research*, Vol. 61, No. 10, July-Aug., 462-465.

29. INTELLIGENCE AND TEACHING SKILL

"John is highly intelligent, but his marks in the teaching skill examination are low"; "Teaching supervisors seem to have a grudge against Savita whose lesson has been assessed as poor, though she is a talented student" –such remarks are the natural outcome of an implicit belief that intelligence and teaching skill go together. Many students and professors believe that the greater the intelligence, the greater is the teaching effectiveness.

It was to study this belief that the present study was undertaken.

That this belief is erroneous and that factors other than intelligence also contribute to teaching effectiveness were the *hypothesis* of the study.

Procedure

The study was conducted on the teacher trainees of the Government Training College, Jullundur. Thirty two students (men and women in equal number) chosen at random from the lot of 200 were given the Lorge Thorndike Intelligence Test, Level 5 (non-verbal). This test is a group of intelligence tests made up of "Figure analogies, Figure classifications and Number series", the three sub-tests requiring 27 minutes' time in all. Forty minutes before the start of the test were used in distributing the test booklets, answer sheets, filling in particulars and explaining the directions. To ensure that the students understood what they were required to do, a few examples were illustrated. Raw scores were later converted into intelligence quotients from the relevant table of norms.

The teaching skill assessment of the students in respect of their most recent discussion lesson was taken up. The I.Q.'s and teaching skill assessments were correlated through the product-moment method. The discussion lesson is just a trial-lesson that the students deliver during the course of their training.

Data:–

A.M. of I.Q. Scores	:	92.70
A.M. of Teaching Skill scores	:	55.00
(Number) N	:	32
S.D. of I.Q. scores	:	12.16
S.D. of Teaching Skill scores	:	03.82
'r' between I.Q. & Teaching Skill	:	00.17
S.E. of 'r'	:	+.07

Interpretation

(i) Poor correlation between I.Q. scores and Teaching Skill scores suggests that factors other than intelligence may contribute towards teaching effectiveness.

(ii) This goes to prove that intelligence and teaching skill may not always closely go together. Factors like methods of teaching, maturity, the teacher's personality, the supervisor's own norms of judgement and allied conditions may also count towards the teaching skill.

(iii) The experiment of course does not lead to the conclusion that intelligence does not contribute towards teaching effectiveness; it just indicates that the factors contemplated above may so influence the teaching skill that a higher intelligence score alone may not always guarantee a correspondingly higher score in teaching effectiveness.

Limitations

Neither the intelligence test not the test of teaching skill was standardised for the population under study. To that extent, the measurements may suffer from poor reliability and validity. The results of this study therefore need to be verified by applying more suitable tests both for intelligence and teaching skill on a fairly large sample of teacher-trainees.

30. A POPULARITY, INTELLIGENCE, ECONOMIC STATUS AND ACADEMIC ACHIEVEMENT

Positive correlations between educational level of parents, socio-metric status, intelligence test scores and school marks were shown in research on American school children (2, 4). This finding stood verified in a study conducted on elementary school children in Brazil (3). A similar study of secondary school children in Brazil (3) showed that social status, intelligence, and academic success are positively intercorrelated, but that social status does not correlate as highly with these variables as it does in the elementary school sample; and that socio-metric leadership ratings and intelligence test scores were negatively correlated, although each of these ratings was positively correlated with school marks.

The present study intended finding out the correlations between intelligence, academic achievement, popularity and economic status (as indicated by parents' income). The hypothesis was that such correlations are positive and significant for Indian school children.

Procedure

The sample consisted of: a group of 110 elementary pupils (belonging to fourth classes of Junior Model School, Government Girls School, and Lyallpur Khalsa School located in Jullundur City) ranging in age from 8 to 12 years, with a mean of 10.2 years and a standard deviation of 1.6, and a group of 100 secondary students (belonging to eleventh classes of Senior Model School, Fentanganj, Girls Higher Secondary School, and Saindass Anglo-Sanskrit School located in Jullundur City) ranging in age from 15 to 18 years, with a mean of 16.7 years and a standard deviation of 1.3.

Popularity was determined by socio-metric technique. Each child was asked to name the three children in the class that he would prefer to work with, the three he would prefer to play with, and the three he would like to eat with. Scores were then computed for the children nominated, by giving them a "3" for each time they were named the first of any of the trials of children listed third. The total score obtained by each child was then divided by the number of children in the class, with a view to comparing the scores from one class with those of other classes. The scores each child received from half the class were correlated with those he received from the other half, in order to determine the reliability of the technique used. This reliability came to .69.

Intelligence was tested by IPAT's (1) Culture Fair Intelligence Tests (Scale 2 for elementary pupils and Scale 3 for "secondary students"). The reliability of these tests was found by correlating scores on form A with scores on form B. The reliabilities thus derived for the three classes of elementary pupils were .72, .69, and .76, while those for the three classes of secondary students were .61, .50, and .71. Reliabilities were calculated separately for the three classes in case of each group to prevent the introduction of surplus variance (in their's) which correlations based on combined groups do introduce.

Data regarding the economic status were obtained from school records, which reported the income of child's parents. These data were converted to scores by giving score values of 1,2,3,4,5 to the income groups of 0-150, 151-300, 301-500, 501-800, 801-1200 (in rupees respectively).

Data on academic achievement were also obtained from school records which reported the students' results in the previous two house tests. The marks in all the subjects were totalled up and the total converted into a percentage score to provide a composite measure of each student's academic achievement.

Findings

The results for the elementary pupils are given in Table 1 and those for the secondary students in Table 2 below:

Table 1
Correlations Between Popularity, Intelligence, Economic Status, and Academic Achievement for 110 Elementary Pupils (Fourth Class)

	Popularity	Intelligence**	Economic Status	Achievement Academic
Popularity	–	.44	.47	.49
Intelligence	–	–	.48	.71
Economic Status	–	–	–	.39

* The correlations are all significant at .01 level.
** Derived from the sum of the scores obtained on both forms of the test.

Table 2
Correlations between Popularity, Intelligence, Economic Status, and Academic Achievement for 100 Secondary Students (Eleventh Class)

	Popularity	Intelligence***	Economic Status	Achievement Academic
Popularity	—	.36*	.28*	.50*
Intelligence	—	–	.19**	.65*
Economic Status	—	–	–	.20**

* Significant at .01 level
** Significant at .05 level
***Derived from the sum of the scores obtained on both the forms of the test.

Positive and significant correlations reported in Tables 1 and 2 confirm the hypothesis. It seems that as far as these children are concerned, popularity, intelligence, economic status and academic performance is positively intercorrelated, just as they (at least three of them) are in the United States and Brazil.

The results for the secondary students, reported in Table 2, show that the correlations of popularity and intelligence with economic status, correlation of popularity with intelligence, and that of economic status with academic achievement, though positive and significant, are not so high as in the case of elementary pupils. This may be due to the fact that the schools included in the secondary school group are highly selective. Even in the highly urbanized city of Jullundur, not more than 15 per cent of children of school age enter secondary school. The Senior Model School (one of the constituents of the sample) also has the reputation of being among the elite of the Government Secondary Schools in the state. Therefore, the lower correlations among these variables, as contrasted with similar correlations in the case of the elementary school, may be explained in part by restriction of range to the upper end of the scale of ability. The extent to which this selection operates socio-economically is shown by the fact that the parents of the secondary school students averaged at least two income groups above those of the elementary school children. Moreover, the lowest level of parents' income in the case of secondary school students was equal to the average for the elementary school parents. But all that has been conjectured here in support of these comparatively low correlations should have rendered the correlations of popularity and intelligence with academic achievement also low. This, however, is not the case and hence the doubt whether the restricted range of the sample has anything to do with the correlations that are low. If high correlations of intelligence and popularity with academic achievement are justified on the plea that high level of intelligence or greater social recognition help in improving academic performance, the fact that the two ways leading to academic success are mutually exclusive, as is reflected by the two high amidst the other low correlations, may not fit in here except for being incidental. Further research alone can throw light on this finding.

The generally positive and significant correlations yielded by this study are too obvious to need any justification, though it may not be fair to attribute them to cause-effect relationships in the absence of requisite evidence to this effect.

Summary

A study of 110 elementary school children and 100 secondary school students in Jullundhur showed that popularity, intelligence, economic status (as indicated by parents' income), and academic achievement are positively correlated, as they are in similar studies in the United States and Brazil. The magnitude of correlation coefficients was, however, not as high in case of the secondary students as in that of the elementary pupils. This may be due to the selective nature of the sample of secondary students, though this cannot be assertively stressed.

References

1. Institute for Personality and Ability Testing, 1602-04, Coronado Drive, Champaign, Illinois, U.S.A.
2. Liddle, G. "Overlap among Desirable and Undesirable Characteristics in Gifted Children." *J. Educ. Psychol*, 1958, 49, 219-223.
3. Lindgren, H.C., and Guedes, Hilda De Almeida. "Social Status, Intelligence and Educational Achievement." Readings in Educational Psychology (Henry Clay Lindgren) John Wiley and Sons, INC, 1968, 88-93.
4. Warner, W.L., Meeker, M., and Ells, K.: "Social Class in America." Chicago: Science Research Associates, 1949.

V. ACHIEVEMENT AND ITS CORRELATES

31. READING ABILITY AND SCHOLASTIC ACHIEVEMENT

Children who are halting and faulty in reading have not, seldom been found to be low in their achievement in various subjects. Reading ability is a very important prerequisite to learning and hence to achievement, more so in the school situation where reading, writing and learning seem to follow, one from the other in same sequence.

The present study was designed to find the relationship of reading ability, evaluated by teacher gradings, to a wide range of learnings in the elementary grades. Pinpointedly, the investigator attempted to know how the marks in reading correlate with marks in seven other subject areas and to find any difference in such correlation for different grade levels. The seven subject areas were Arithmetic, Social Studies, Science, Music, English Composition, Art and Punjabi comprehension, and the grades were 3, 4 and 5. The study was longitudinal in that the same children were screened every year. Since the children at the three grade levels studied were rated by different teachers, the study yields a measure of consistency of the relationship of the reading ability to scholastic achievement.

Method

The subjects were twenty-eight children (boys and girls in equal number) of Junior Model School, Jullundur. They represented a fair sampling of children from the average to above average socio-economic strata. The mean intelligence quotient (culture free Intelligence Test Scale 2 Forms A, B by Cattell R. B. and Cattell A.K.S.) of the subjects was 105, with a range from 95 to

125. The children's average achievement scores in each of the seven subjects were recorded a week before they were promoted to 4th, 5th and 6th grades from their erstwhile 3rd, 4th and 5th grades respectively. This average score was the simple arithmetic mean of their marks in the three tests in each subject that they took in a year-long session at each grade level. Their final reading grades for each grade level (excellent, very good, good, fair and unsatisfactory) recorded at the close of the session were correlated with their average achievement scores in each subject for the corresponding grade level, through the rank order correlation method. Inadequate and slovenly as our school records sometimes are, there were cases for which achievement scores in one or more subjects or reading grades for one or more levels were missing. Such cases were discarded so that the number studied here was reduced to 128 (from 139 originally taken up) whose reading grades as well as achievement scores in each grade level were available.

Results and Discussion

Table 1 presents all the correlations sought to be obtained. All the correlations, except Art 5, and music 3, 4, 5 are at the 1% level of significance. The Art 5 correlation and music 3, 4, 5 correlations fall below the 5% level. The correlations on the whole remain quite consistent for the particular subject area throughout the three grade levels.

The Art correlations show an appreciably high relationship between art and reading in the lower grades (0.89) with a considerably lesser relationship in the middle (0.49) and upper (0.22) grades. Greater utilisation of art in elementary reading activities, *i.e.* use of illustrative drawings in developing sight words, explaining tales read, giving attractive form to concepts etc., may be responsible for the significant correlation at the third grade level. The progressively lower correlations at the 4th and 5th grade levels may be due to a diminished stress in these grades on the integration of art with reading, a lesson which Art teachers might well learn to make their teaching more purposeful and effective. There is no gainsaying the fact that the most school's interestingness of subjects for children sometimes tends to decrease as they proceed from lower to higher grades. Among the reasons leading to this sad state, reduced use or no use of art in reading activity may be one.

Table 1
Rho-Coefficients Between Reading Marks and Marks in Seven Subject Areas for the Third, Fourth and Fifth Grades

Area	Grade Level		
	3	4	5
Arithmetic	0.81	0.75	0.79
English composition	0.92	0.80	0.86
Punjabi comprehension	0.82	0.74	0.75
Science	0.94	0.76	0.81
Social Studies	0.89	0.83	0.73
Art	0.89	0.49	0.22
Music	0.18	0.14	0.15

The low Music correlations at all the three grade levels indicate that the relationship between music and reading is rather poor. Music teachers' obsession that teaching of music unlike other subjects are a teaching of skill rather than of subject matter may be responsible for this relationship. It is this obsession which might have led to lack of integration of music with reading or to lack of ability to supply musical concepts, talents or forms to reading activities as also to everyday life. Music teachers need to emphasise the application-side of music so that children can make reading more palatable and interesting. Teachers find it hard to make an intensive-reading lesson interesting; children fail to get motivated or interested in a reading lesson. Reading lesson tends to be dull and prosaic. Incorporating music with reading, besides other measures, may develop reading ability.

High relationships in case of other subject areas are what may be expected. These subjects essentially warrant reading before one could learn them. In the activities of these subjects reading ability, therefore, plays a vital part. Secondly, verbal ability such as that found in reading does lead to success in scholastic subjects. That is why a good reader shows a more favourable attitude toward schoolwork and does better in all activities including those which are not directly based on reading. The converse is true for the poor reader. Thirdly, better the reading, better is the comprehension of subject and hence a better achievement score. Thus, reading ability and scholastic achievement are found to be considerably related.

Summary

In the study meant to know how reading ability, as evaluated by teacher gradings, correlates with achievement scores in seven subject areas, it has been found that, in five of the seven areas studied, achievement scores are significantly related to reading for grades 3, 4 and 5. In the areas of Art and Music, reading ability probably plays no true role, except in so far as these subjects are doubtlessly related to reading activities. High correlations need not give the impression that there is a causal relationship between reading ability and a subject area. Variables such as motivation, intelligence, personality and interests should also be taken into account while examining the total picture of school achievement.

No significant differences in the correlations from lower to higher grades were found except in Art. The difference in the art correlations may be due to the greater use of art in learning to read at the lower grade levels than that at the higher grade levels.

The correlations, in brief, prove that reading ability has an important and congruous relationship to scholastic achievement in the elementary grades. Further studies of this kind involving factors other than reading ability, which lead to progress in scholastic subjects, would go a long way in making the findings of this study more authentic.

Nevertheless, teachers, more so language teachers, should not be nonchalant toward their very important objective of developing reading ability, because this ability seems to have a decisive edge over other abilities in the matter of improving scholastic achievement. There should be no letup in reading enterprises, because reading ability has assumed ominous significance in the context of the present widened curricula and greater teaching-learning requirements.

References

1. Emmet, Arthur Hinkelman, "Relationship of Reading Ability to Elementary Scholastic Achievement." *Educational Administration and Supervision*. Vol. 42, No. 2 (February, 1956), pp. 65-67.

32. INFLUENCE OF PREPARATION ON ACHIEVEMENT

"Whether preparation is really necessary for showing achievement or improvement in achievement especially at the school or college level" is the problem which has of late been intriguing educators and laymen alike. Teachers who are staunch believers of 'work for worth' have always been harping upon thorough preparation for examinations or achievement test, while those who are thinkers, writers or idealists want the students to depend most on mental gymnastics-through-thinking, reasoning and seeing relations when, posed with a problem. Whether preparation for a test influences their achievement and if so to what extent in the case of B.Ed. students is the question under study here.

The investigator's experience provides ample evidence in favour of the belief that for the purpose of showing good achievement on tests which cover a prescribed syllabus of topics a deliberate preparation in terms of learning the materials contained in the topics is helpful. Preparation enhances achievement is thus the HYPOTHESIS of this study.

Method

The study was conducted on the writer's class of 50 B.Ed. students (23 boys, 27 girls) in the subject of Educational Psychology. The students had been taught the topics of Nature of Educational Psychology. Nervous System, Group Behaviour, Instincts, Emotions, Learning, Memory, Intelligence, Personality, Delinquency, Exceptional children, and Attention. They were given an assignment of two questions on each topic after a topic was completely taught. The assignment meant writing detailed answers to these questions at home.

Thereafter, in one of the teaching periods, the writer called upon the students to choose just one question, on any one of the topics already taught them, and to write an answer to it giving as much details as they possibly could. They were told not to confine themselves to the questions given in the assignments. As the students did not at all know of or even expect this totally surprise test, they initially showed blank faces and a sense of astonishment but became quite receptive and well-adjusted when told that the test was in a spirit of experiment alone and in no case in a bid to judge or report on their performance. They were given 40 minutes for writing their answers, after which the scripts were collected. It was an essay-type test in which all aspects of a question were to be dealt with in a descriptive style in English language. The scripts were marked by the writer out of 10 maximum marks on the same day.

Immediately after the Test, the students were advised to make thorough preparation for the question which they had chosen and attempted in this test. They were told that they had four days to do such preparation after which they would be called upon to write detailed and, this time, well-prepared answer to their question, again in a 40-minutes period. The second test was held at the assigned time and the scripts collected. The students before starting this test confirmed that they were prepared for it. The scripts again were on the same day marked out of ten marks by the writer. While marking the scripts on both occasions, the answers given in the standard textbook prescribed for the syllabus were strictly kept in view. The students were not told at the start of the first test that they would be subjected to the second test, after four days, of the same question.

The data collected were analysed to find out the influence of preparation.

Results

Table 1
Mean Differences Between Girls and Boys in Tests I and II

N	Mean Test I	Mean Test II
Girls 27	3.4	6.1
Boys 23	3.1	1.7
Difference	0.3	4.4

Table 2
Improvement shown in achievement as a result of preparation. 2 per cent girls in after-preparation-test get 50 per cent (of maximum marks) more marks

2% Girls and 4% boys "	40%	"
30% Girls and 22% boys "	30%	"
18% Girls and 16% boys "	20%	"
2% Girls and 2% boys "	10%	"

2% boys show no improvement i.e. their marks in test II are lesser than those in test 1 by 1.

Table 3
Means and Standard Deviations of the Tests I & II

		Means		Standard Deviations	
	N	Test I	Test II	Test I	Test II
For the total Sample	10	3.3	19	1.02	0.29
SE	.14	.12	.12	.03	
Difference	2.6		0.73		
Significance	Highly significant at .01 level and beyond			Highly significant at .01 level and beyond	

Table 4

Co-efficient of Correlation Between Tests I & II

	N	r	Level of significance	
For the total sample	10	.77	.01	Highly significant
For girls	27	.84	.01	"
For boys	23	.61	.04	"
Difference	between r's of girls and boys		0.45	Not significant

Findings

1. A Chi-square test showed a value of 32 indicating no significant difference in the marks obtained by the boys and girls. Consequently, the two sexes were treated as one homogeneous group. Insignificant differences between the boys and girls in their achievements in both the tests, as shown in Table 1, also justify the same contention.
2. Tables 1-2. Girls on the whole show a slightly higher achievement than boys both in the surprise test and the after-preparation test. Maximum marks *i.e.* 6 in test I and 8 in test II are also obtained by one girl and two girls respectively. Again, girls alone show maximum increase of marks as a result of preparation.

   Whereas more girls than boys show improvement of 20 to 30% marks, more boys than girls improve their marks by 40%.

   In matter of minimum improvement, the boys and girls stand equal to each other. Only one boy in the sample failed to improve upon his previous performance.
3. Table 3. Highly significant difference between the S.D.'s of the two achievements shows a great tendency to reach the average score; it also makes one suspect a true difference in variability between before-preparation and after-preparation scores.
4. Table 4. Highly significant correlations for the total sample as well as for boys and girls separately show the close relationship between the students' marks in test I and those in test II, showing thereby that the improvement, presumably as a result of preparation, may be directly and positively related to their achievement before preparation.

Insignificant difference between the r's of boys and girls indicates that in the matter of relationship, between their before- and after-preparation achievements, which is close and positive in this experiment, the boys and girls do not stand much apart.

Discussion

The investigator realises that, since the experiment has been performed on a selected sample, the results may not truly represent the findings which a similar experiment on a large and unselected sample may yield. He visualises many a factor other than preparation which might have influenced the student's second achievement and which were not controlled. Such factors may be the will to do well in the test II (which might not be there while appearing in their surprise test), mental preparation as distinct from study, wrong choice of a question and the like. He also appreciates the pitfalls of the unstandardised essay type tests used in the experiment, though he took care to mark the scripts objectively keeping in view the stand and answer of each.

Without however generalising the results revealed by this study, it may be said that the hypothesis stands verified.

Though there are no sex differences in the matter of enhancement of achievement because of preparation, girls as compared to boys are a little better off. It may be due to greater seriousness and anxiety to do well on the part of girls whose entry to the teaching profession as also to other out-of-home jobs is since very recently becoming more popular, competitive, and go-forward type.

Preparation rather than any other factors (which though not controlled can be said to be equally varying for each student) has, it seems, enhanced achievement, though the degree of enhancement varies from one to five marks in a test carrying a maximum of ten marks. This is what may be expected.

Teachers need to stress on the students' need for preparation before appearing in any test, especially when the test covers a set of certain prescribed topics.

'Surprise' element may have contributed to the greater unevenness of performance in test 1, since the students' initial, original differences (in intelligence and acquired equipment) seem to have played a greater part in the absence of requisite preparation. Much less deviation from the average in test II is evident of a fair evenness of performance brought about presumably by preparation. This finding is authenticated by the fact that whereas 62% of the students failed to reach upto the average in test I, only 26% fall below the average in test II.

'How much a student can prepare so as to show achievement' depends, as would be expected, upon his capacity to learn, to assimilate, to retain and perhaps to recall. Difficulties and limitations imposed by circumstances in the way of his preparation for the test also matter a great deal. In all these factors, there are wide individual differences which are bound to be reflected correspondingly in the after-preparation test. This may explain the positive relationship between the students' scores in test I and those in test II. How much he prepares or learns is very much related to what the student is. What he manifests after preparation is dependent upon what he is equipped with before preparation.

Summary

Fifty B.Ed. teacher trainees (23 boys, 27 girls) were tested in educational psychology before and after preparation for the test. They made a free choice of one question they were to attempt in the surprise test and prepared the same question thoroughly for the after-preparation test. No sex differences were noticed in the scores of the students in either of the two tests. Preparation seems to have led to significant enhancement of achievement in case of both boys and girls. A good and positive relationship between the students' scores on the two tests seems to favour the belief that the enhancement caused by preparation in achievement is related to, if not dependent upon or attributable to the students' initial equipment which in the main is reflected in his performance before preparation.

33. PROBLEMS AND ACHIEVEMENT

In order to verify the hypothesis that adolescent boys and girls have problems that affect their school achievement, 424 ninth and tenth grade students from Government Multipurpose Higher Secondary School and Modern Higher Secondary School of Patiala were given Mooney Problem Checklist in February, 1968, collected in May, 1968 Co-efficients of correlation computed between the seven areas and a composite score of the Mooney and the four subject-test scores and a composite score of the examination yielded inverse relationship between the number of problems on the Mooney and the student achievement test scores of the examination. The relationship was significant at.01 level.

Educators have often hypothesised that adolescents have problems which may adversely affect their scholastic achievement. Sandefur and Bigge (2) found statistical evidence to support this hypothesis in a study they made of an adolescent group in America.

Procedure

In a bid to determine the relationship between the problems of adolescents and their scholastic achievement, 324 ninth and tenth grade students belonging to below average to above average socio-economic strata of the state (the proportion of each stratum in the total population), from the Government Multipurpose Higher Secondary School and Modern Higher Secondary School of Patiala, were administered Mooney Problem Checklist (1) in February, 1968. In early March, 1968, these students appeared in their final promotion examinations in which essay-type tests in various subjects are given. In April, May, 1968 the results of these examinations were collected.

The students, in groups of 36 each at a time, were asked to complete the Mooney Problem Checklist (Junior High School Form) which contains 210 items, 30 in each of these areas: Health and Physical Development (HPD); School (S); Home and Family (HF); Money, Work, and the Future (MWF); Boy and Girl Relations (BG); Relation to people in general (PG); Self-centered concerns (SC). This checklist is designed to reflect the problems which a student experiences and willingly expresses. The number of problems checked in each area forms the problem score of that area; intensities of problems cannot be reflected. The total number of problems checked in all areas forms an individual's composite score.

On the achievement side, the examination yields four subject-test scores besides a composite score, reflecting over-all performance, which is an individual's aggregate of the scores in all the four subjects, *i.e.*, Languages, Social Studies, General Science, and Mathematics.

Coefficients of correlation were then computed between the seven areas and a composite score of the Mooney and the achievement tests. These coefficients are given in Table 1.

Table 1
Co-efficient of Correlation (Inverse) between Problems (on the Mooney Checklist) and Achievement Scores (yielded by the examination)

Problem Areas	Languages	Social Studies	General Science	Mathematics	Composite
HPD	.09	.08	.09	.06	.07
S	.32*	.25*	.29*	.36*	.46*
HF	.28*	.17**	.27*	.30*	.33*
MWF	.12	.11	.10	.09	.12
BG	.02	.06	.07	.04	.08
PG	.08	.08	.11	.06	.05
SC	.07	.05	.12	.03	.12
Composite	.21*	.20*	.16**	.18*	.27*

* Significant at .01 level.
** Significant at .05 level.

Findings

As is evident from Table 1, the correlations between the number of problems reported by the student in the area of health and physical development and achievement (in all subjects and in the composite) were not significant. The number of problems reported by students in the school area correlated significantly (at .01 level) with achievement in the four subject-tests and with the composite score. The coefficients of correlation between the number of problems reported by students in the area of home-and-family and their achievement (in all subjects and in the composite) were also impressive; correlations significant at .01 level were found between home-and-family problems and achievement in languages, general science, Mathematics and the composite achievement score, while correlation significant at .05 level was found between home-and-family problems and achievement in the test of social studies. Relationships significant at .01 level were found between the total number of problems (in all areas) reported by students on the Mooney and achievement scores in all the subjects except general science in which case such relationship was found to be significant at .05 level. The composite achievement score was found to be correlating at .01 level with the composite number of problems reported by the student.

The results of this study, though suggestive, seem to ditto the findings of the investigation made by Sandefur and Jeanette (2).

That problems relating to school adversely affect the student's scholastic achievement warrants that the school must delve into all such factors concerning adolescent's concern with school as tend to deteriorate the adolescent's curricular achievement, with a view to either eradicating these factors or reducing the intensity of their impact.

References

1. Mooney Problem Checklists (New York: Psychological Crop, 1950).
2. Sandefur, J.T. and Jeanette, Bigge. "An Investigation of the Relationship Between Recognized Problems of Adolescents and School Achievement." *Journal of Educational Research, 59*, 10, 1966, 473-74.

34. FAMILY CONFLICTS AND SCHOLASTIC ACHIEVEMENT

Several research in the field of personality suggest a relationship between interparental conflict and academic achievement.

Such studies as have established relationship between family influence and academic achievement reveal that maternal attitude (Drews and Teahan, 1957), home discipline (Kent and Davis, 1957), and parental involvement (Rosen and Andrade, 1959) are significantly related to the child's academic achievement. Studies stressing ego-defensiveness (Haggard, 1957) and test anxiety (Sarason and Davidson, 1960) assert that the ego-threatening aspects of family environments determine child's academic success or failure. Other studies (Baruch, 1937; Manis, 1958; Nye, 1958) indicate a close relationship between inter-parental conflict and disturbance in child behaviour. An identical study (Kramer and Fleming, 1966) suggests that parental differences of opinion may provide a fruitful strategy for exploring differences in child behaviour.

Most of the researches on academic achievement refer to family conflict, but the question of determining the relationship between family conflict and children's IQ or scholastic achievement has often remained unattended. The present study is an attempt to gauge this relationship. As interparental differences of attitudes or reactions are closely related to family conflict, such differences, precisely, were the ones indicated when the two parents expressed opposite, conflicting, contradictory or otherwise different attitudes toward children.

The study was conducted in four steps: constructing a questionnaire to elicit interparental differences of attitude; administering the questionnaire to quantify these differences; dividing the children into three groups, *i.e.* the small, average, and the big, representing in respective order the parents showing low, average and high difference scores on the questionnaire; comparing the group scores on the criteria of IQ, and scholastic achievement (aggregate marks in the last three tests – in English, Mathematics, General Science, Social Studies and first language, each test in these five subjects having been given after a three month interval).

The *hypothesis* tested in the study was that there may be significant differences among children of the three groups in IQ and scholastic achievement (of children whose parents possess less conflicting, opposite or otherwise different attitudes). The phrase "parents possess different attitudes" here means that the attitude of one parent toward children, or towards things concerning children, is different from similar attitude of the other parent, or more precisely that one parent responds to a question-seeking-attitude toward children differently from the other parent.

Method

The sample consisted of 125 pairs of Jullundur suburban parents and their third-, fourth- and fifth- grade children. The total children in the three grades came to be 214; about two-thirds of the children of these groups were represented in the sample.

The parents of these children, in varying numbers, attended PTA's meetings at which the questionnaire was administered. In *four such meetings the work* was completed. Fathers and mothers were seated in separate, though adjoining, rooms when they were asked to answer a questionnaire. They were just told that their responses to the various items in the questionnaire were aimed at knowing their attitudes toward children with a view to making PTA's more effective and school programmes more useful for children. After the questionnaires were completed and collected, a highly illustrative and interesting talk on psychology of children was delivered by a psychology lecturer so that the subjects could get no opportunity to discuss the items of the questionnaire they had just completed. This procedure was followed in each of the four meetings.

Vague and unstructured statements, 30 in number, constituted the questionnaire which was intended to seek natural responses, the inferences from which could not be guessed by the parents. "Parents should indulge in fondling and loving their children openly", "A child should not be coerced to wear clothes he does not relish," "Parents should punish the child when he does any wrong", "A child should not be stopped from doing anything" were some of the questions which were essentially so phrased that parents were provoked to respond differently. They were required to respond by ticking 'yes' or 'no', the two words having been placed opposite to each statement.

The scoring of the questionnaires was done in terms of the number of differences between father and mother in their responses to the items, *i.e.* each item on which father ticked "yes", and the mother "no" or *vice-versa,* was given one score point; the items on which both the parents ticked either "yes" or "no" were ignored; if either parent omitted responding to a particular item, the item was given one score point; and if more than one item was omitted by either parent, that child, and his parents, were not included in the data. The score points were then totalled up and each family given a total difference score. These scores ranged from low to high *i.e.* from 2 to 18 differences. The group of children whose parents scored from 2 to 6 was named as small group; the children whose parents scored from 8 to 11 formed the average group; and the group of children whose parents scored from 13 to 18 was called as big group. To select distinct groups, it was found necessary to omit from consideration those children whose parents gave a difference score of 7 and 12. The groups became unequal in number when the extreme parental-differences groups were selected.

The three groups were then compared on the criteria of IQ and scores through Lorge-Thorndike Intelligence Test-Form A Level 3, and scholastic achievement scores from school records of the children. Means of scores for each group and he scores were computed for statistical purposes; differences between the groups were considered significant when the he reached the .05 or .01 levels.

Results

The differences between children in the small and average, the average and big, and small and big groups were found significant in IQ and scholastic achievement as shown in Table 1. In other words, the IQ and scholastic achievement of children whose parents showed low interparental differences of attitudes were found to be notably different from the IQ and scholastic achievement of children whose parents showed average or high interparental differences of attitudes, and so also was the case with the average *versus* big group. Similarly, significant differences emerged between boys in the small and average, the average and big, and the small and big groups in both IQ and scholastic achievement, as shown in Table 2. Results in case of girls coincide with those in the case of boys and are given in Table 3.

Table 1
Differences Among Children in Small, Average and Big Groups (Representing Increasing Numbers of Interparental Differences/ Conflicts) in IQ and Scholastic Achievement

Scale	Small	Average	Big		t	
	N/39	N/46	N/37	S-A	A-B	S-B
	M	M	M			
IQ	109.10	104.50	99.00	2.24*	2.08*	3.04**
Scholastic achievement	60.13	58.35	52.48	2.06*	2.04*	3.10**

* Significant at .05 level.
** Significant at .01 level.

Table 2
Differences Among Boys in Small, Average and Big Groups (Representing Increasing Numbers of Interparental Differences/ Conflicts) in IQ and Scholastic Achievement

Scale	Small	Average	Big		t	
	N/21	N/21	N/19	S-A	A-B	S-B
	M	M	M			
IQ	108.26	104.00	98.01	2.11*	2.09*	2.95**
Scholastic achievement	56.04	50.10	42.17	2.10*	2.36*	3.06*

* Significant at .05 level.
** Significant at .01 level.

Table 3
Differences Among Girls in Small, Average and Big Groups (Representing Increasing Numbers of Interparental Differences/Conflicts) in IQ and Scholastic Achievement

Scale	Small	Average	Big	t		
	N/25	N/25	N/18	S-A	A-B	S-B
	M	M	M			
IQ	109.95	105.02	100.00	2.12*	2.46*	2.80*
Scholastic achievement	70.82	66.60	62.79	2.14*	2.10*	2.82

* Significant at .05 level.

Discussion

That there are significant differences among children of the three groups in IQ and scholastic achievement tends to indicate that interparental differences/conflicts have some relationship with the children's IQ and scholastic achievement. That such differences exist for the whole sample, as also for boys' and girls' groups treated separately, reflects that interparental differences/conflict bear a relationship with IQ and scholastic achievement of children, irrespective of the children's sex. These findings tend to confirm evidence regarding the differential influence of family conflicts on the functioning of boys and girls. Again, the significant differences mentioned above, being in the same direction and showing as they do significant and consistent decrease in the children's IQ and scholastic achievement with increase in the family's interparental differences/conflicts, tend to establish that an inverse relationship may exist between interparental differences and children's IQ or scholastic achievement. It appears that greater the degree of interparental differences/conflicts, lesser the children's IQ and scholastic achievement. Lesser differences in IQ and scholastic achievement between the small and average groups as compared to those between average and big and to those between small and big are what may be expected.

That the differences, in IQ and scholastic achievement, between the three groups were a function of differences in intelligence of the parents in the respective groups cannot be asserted in the absence of data concerning parents' IQ scores. That such differences were caused by the family's interparental differences is also difficult to state because personal factors like hard work, amount of intellectual exercise, schooling, etc. which may influence children's academic achievement, and environmental factors like disruptive family conditions, parental influence, learner's field etc., which too can so influence, were not controlled in this investigation.

Nevertheless, a close relationship between interparental differences and children's academic achievement is clearly indicated by the consistency and identity of results obtained in the case of the whole group and the two sub-groups. These findings suggest that interpersonal differences or family conflicts to which these differences are inevitably related may well be a productive variable for the study of child behaviour. More research using this variable with criteria associated with emotional conflicts in children, or that using other indices of conflict between parents, may throw more light on the causation of a wide variety of child behaviour. Family conflicts influence a child adversely as revealed by the psychology of growth and development, and hence perhaps the apparent feasibility in the logic thrown up by the results of the present study.

Summary

A study designed to examine the relationship between interparental differences/family conflicts and children's academic achievement revealed significant differences between children in the small, average and big groups (representing low, average and high interparental differences) in IQ and in scholastic achievement. The differences, which were found for both boys and girls, revealed an inverse relationship between interparental differences and children's academic achievement. The study suggests that parental differences (in attitudes toward children) or family conflicts may prove a useful variable for investigating differences in the behaviour of children.

References

1. Baruch, Dorothy W. "A study of reported tension in interpersonal relationships as coexistent with behavioural adjustment in young children". *Journal of Experimental Education*, 1937, G, 187-204.
2. Drews Elizabeth M., and Teahan, John E. "Parental attitudes and academic achievement," *Journal of Clinical Psychology*. 1957,13, 328-331.

3. Haggard, EA. "Socialization, personality, and academic achievement in gifted children". *School Review*, 1957, 15, 388-414.
4. Kent, Norman and Davis, D.R. "Discipline in the home and intellectual development". *British Journal of Medical Psychology*, 1957, 25, 27-33.
5. Kramer, David P. and Fleming, Elyse S. "Interparental differences of opinion and children's academic achievement." *Journal of Educational Research*, 1966,693, 136-138.
6. Manis, M. "Personal adjustment, assumed similarity to parents and inferred parental evaluations of the self". *Journal of Consulting Psychology*, 1958, 22, 481-485.
7. Nye, F. Ivan, *Family relationships and delinquent behaviour*. New York: Wiley and Sons, 1958.
8. Rosen, B.D. and Andrade, R. "The psychological origins of achievement motivation". *Sociometry*, 1959, 22,185-218.
9. Sarason, S.B., Davidson, K.S., Lightfall, F.F., Waiter, R.R., and Reubush, B.K. *Anxiety in elementary school children*. New York: Wiley and Sons, 1960.

35. RELATIONSHIP BETWEEN ACHIEVEMENT SCORES AND SELF-ESTIMATES

Achievement in subjects depends upon the knowledge and information within an individual's conscious mind. It does not tap the unconscious. Thus the individual is well aware of how well he has fared in the subject. Some relationship would be expected between his achievement scores as awarded by the examiner and an independent self-estimate of his performance. To prove this HYPOTHESIS and to determine the magnitude of such relationship the present study was undertaken.

Method

An essay type three hours' question paper containing 15 questions, of Educational Psychology syllabus that they had covered in the classroom, was given to 48 teacher-trainees (23 boys and 25 girls) with a note to attempt any five questions; each question carried 18 marks. Shortly afterwards, the scripts were evaluated by the investigator (their lecturer in Psychology) and the awards (achievement scores) kept away. No marks were put on the scripts. A week later the investigator told the trainees his own answers to each of the 15 questions with instructions that they should evaluate their answers keeping in view the answers which were expected of them. The independent self-estimates of their performances were thus collected. Efforts were made to control other factors which could affect the trainees' self-estimates. To do this the investigator read every word of the answers and awarded marks on the basis of the answers he had in his mind, and the trainees were required to put their own award on an answer immediately after they heard the investigator's corresponding answer. The only thing kept fluid, as far as possible, was the evaluative ability.

Table 1
Means and Standard Deviations of The Sample

Scores	N	Means	Standard Deviations
Achievement Scores	48	40.6	8.9
Self-estimates	48	41.4	7.1

Means and standard deviations of the achievement scores and self-estimates were calculated and the correlation coefficients for the two evaluations computed, using the Pearson product-moment method.

Table 2
Means and Standard Deviations and Mean Differences for Boys and Girls in the Sample

Sample	N	Means		Standard Deviations	
		Achievement scores	Self-estimates	Achievement scores	Self-estimates
Boys	23	36.9	39.6	9.1	7.4
Girls	25	44.5	43.2	8.7	6.8
Difference		–7.6	–3.6	...	...
Significance	...	.001	.001	...	...

Table 3
Correlation Coefficients (r) and Standard Error (SE) (Calculated Through Classical Formula)

	N	*r*	*SE*
Between achievement scores and self-estimates in general	48	.75	± 0.6
Between boys' achievement scores and self-estimates	23	.80	±007
Between girls' achievement scores and self-estimates	25	.62	±.12

Interpretation

1. Of the 48 students 16 were found above average, 13 average, and 19 below average in their achievement.
2. Considering the mean of self-estimates, 16 were found above average, 15 average, and 17 below average.
3. The range of achievement scores is 34, while that of self-estimates is 28, showing that the dispersion of achievement scores is larger than that of self-estimates.
4. The achievement scores deviate more from their mean than the self-estimates do from their mean. The two evaluations are thus patterned differently.
5. On the whole, the trainees over-estimate themselves though the magnitude of this over-estimation is not much.
6. Girls on the average score considerably more than the boys in their achievement, as well as in their self-estimates.
7. Boys on the average over-estimate their performances, while the girls under-estimate their performances a little.
8. Whereas the girls on the average score above the means of the sample both in their achievements and self-estimates, the boys generally score below the said means both in their achievements and self-estimates.
9. Girls' scores both in achievement and self-estimate deviate less from their means than boys' scores do from their means.
10. The correlation coefficient between achievement scores and self-estimates of the trainees is as high as .75 with a standard error of -.06, while the r's between achievement scores and self-estimates of boys and between those of girls are .80 and .62 respectively. Boys have been able to judge their performance better and more accurately than the girls.

Conclusions

There is a significant relationship between achievement scores and self-estimates, this relationship being somewhat greater in the case of boys than in that of girls. This also reflects the fair validity of essay-type examinations, which are often decried, in relation to self-estimates. Students may not be poor judges of their own performance provided they know what is expected of them.

And if they know before the examination what kind of answers are expected of them, they may come up to the instructor's expectations in the matter of their subject-achievement. This fact warrants the need of discussing in the class specific questions on a topic after it has been taught. The lecture method needs to be supplemented by discussion and assignment methods to give students an experience of handling questions and applying the theoretical concepts in everyday use.

36. COMPARATIVE ACHIEVEMENT OF TWO SUBSTANDARD GROUPS OF HIGH SCHOOL STUDENTS

Abstract

Two groups of high school students, admitted to a high school, were those who were below the minimum academic standards. The students in one group were routinely treated in their new class. The second group was given special guidance, additional teaching and more assignments. The two groups were matched for intelligence, and their achievement as measured by grade point average (GPA) was compared over four quarters. The quarters ' as well as cumulative GPA's yielded a significant difference between the two groups. A possible effect of the special treatment is suggested by the study.

The high schools have been constantly increasing their admission requirements owing to the pressure of numbers on their enrolment. The basic minimum academic requirements for admission into a local high school (9th class) since 1965 stood at (a) a second division (50 per cent marks) in their final promotion examination of the previous class (8th) and (b) 45 per cent marks in an admission test comprising Arithmetic and English composition. In 1970 these requirements were relaxed, permitting exceptions based on other evidence indicating the probability of success, for no more than 5 per cent of the entering high school class.

Students admitted under this relaxation had been below the minimum on only one of the two basic academic requirements, *i.e.* their marks in their final promotion examination ranged from 42 to 48 per cent; therefore they need not be conceived of as seriously deficient academically nor considered as the disadvantaged or the culturally deprived. As these students were undoubtedly marginal, they provided the school an opportunity to make efforts for improving their achievement.

Method

In April 1970 a group of 74 students was admitted as exceptions in that they did not meet one of the two basic admission requirements, as described in the preceding paragraph. The group, which was composed of boys only and was in the age-group 13-14, was divided into two equal sub-groups of 37 each for the purpose of giving differential treatment. Both the groups were matched on intelligence (Lorge-Thorndike form A non-verbal level 4). Assuming that the variation of independent influences on the student's achievement is essentially the same in several quarters as within one quarter, the two groups were compared in their achievement (GPA) over four quarters ending their promotion to the next class (10th).

The students in one group (A) were given no special treatment; they were not identified or grouped in any way, and no extra tutoring, counselling or assignment was given. For all practical purposes, they were as any other entering high school students and were permitted to continue as such for the entire period of four quarters. The students in the other group (B) were given one extra period a week in each of their subjects (English, Mathematics, Social Studies, General Science, Hindi/Panjabi). Two specially deputed teachers followed the total progress of each student, encouraging and implementing added counselling when deemed necessary. These students were given one additional assignment a week in each subject, the special teachers checking and correcting the assignments. This was done for all the four quarters.

The two groups were compared on their achievement as measured by their GPA on completion of each quarter's work and on the basis of cumulative record of the four quarters. The special treatment given to the second group was not extended after the four quarters of attendance.

Results

The correlation between intelligence test scores and cumulative GPA for this study sample was found to be .21. This low relationship is not unexpected in so far as the study group was composed of students deficient in one of the basic minimum requirements of admission. The quarter and cumulative averages were obtained from the records of the school and t-tests were computed. The results are presented in Table 1.

Table 1
Groups A and B compared on Mean GPA's

GPA's in	*Group A (Routine treatment)*			*Group B (Special treatment)*			*t*	*Level of Signifi-cance*
	N	*Mean*	*S.D.*	*N*	*Mean*	*S.D.*		
1st quarter	37	1.236	.69	37	1.414	.52	1.28	n.s.
2nd quarter	37	1.269	.58	37	1.512	.46	2.18	.05
3rd quarter	37	1.320	.71	37	1.754	.76	2.86	.01
4th quarter	37	1.282	.59	37	1.862	.71	3.07	.01
Cumulative	37	1.289	.56	37	1.722	.57	2.68	.01

These results indicate that though there was no significant difference in the achievement of the two groups in the first of the four quarters investigated, significant to very significant differences in the achievement of the two groups in the subsequent three quarters, as also in the cumulative, emerged. And these differences are in favour of the "special treatment" group. Therefore, guidance, additional teaching and more assignments does seem to enhance the achievement of this group.

Discussion

As is usual in academic prediction equations, previous performance, in this case the grading received in the 8th class, carries the greatest weight. While the two groups in the present study were matched on intelligence, the group treated routinely had a slightly higher 8th class mean average of 4.139 compared to 3.989 for the group treated specially. The fact that the former group could not maintain this superiority in achievement in any of the four quarters shows that special treatment did the trick and that the initial superiority of the routinely treated group was too small to give this group any advantage to excel the "special treatment" group or at least to counter-balance the special treatment given to the latter.

Though other factors which could differentially affect the achievement of the two groups during the period of the study were not controlled, greater achievement of the "special treatment" group continuously for all the three quarters suggests that guidance, additional teaching and more assignments invested in this group may have a substantial influence.

The factor that seems to be exerting a strong influence on achievement was the number of hours carried. In each quarter "special treatment" group carried a mean of 14.2 hours, while the "routine treatment" group carried a mean of 8.5 hours, a difference of 5.7 hours. Though the other benefits afforded to the former group also continued throughout the period of study, the strong influence of hours carried is implied.

Summary

Two groups of high school students with matched intelligence scores, who failed to meet part of the minimum basic academic requirements, were admitted in a high school in 1970. One group was routinely treated, while the other was given special guidance, additional teaching and more assignments, for the four quarters ending with their promotion to the next class. A comparison of their GPA in each quarter, individual and cumulative, yielded significant differences in level of achievement in favour of the "special treatment" group, suggesting the influence of special guidance, additional teaching and more assignments. It would, however, appear that more studies of this type involving added variables and stricter controls should be made before any generalization can be made.

VI. PERSONALITY AND ADJUSTMENTS

37. PERSONALITY STRUCTURES OF COLLEGE AND SCHOOL STUDENTS

Abstract

Personality differences that exist between school boys, school girls, college boys and college girls were studied by administering Cattell's 16 PF to school and college students (50 males and 50 females of each category). An analysis of variance indicated that the four groups were significantly different on ten of the sixteen personality factors. College students, both boys and girls, were found more emotionally stable, assertive and venturesome than school students, both boys and girls. Both school and college girls were found more tenderminded, shrewd and apprehensive than school boys; and college boys were more emotionally stable, assertive, venturesome, trusting and forthright than both school and college girls.

There is a paucity of research dealing with whether personality differences exist between college and school students. An important issue hindering such research is the choice of instrument. The basic question in this regard is what devices are available for measuring personality, and from these how is one to choose the most appropriate measure? Rating has been used most often for measuring the student personality despite the limitations of the rating method. Perhaps many experimenters feel more confident in using ratings as against personality inventories in their research.

Lough (10) and Blum (1) doing research in this area found that the Minnesota Multiphasic Personality Inventory (MMPI) was not a useful instrument for differentiating between student teachers and students in other curricula. LaBue (8), however, found that the MMPI did differentiate between persistent and non-persistent teachers. Again, Hedlund (7) found that two MMPI scales (pa and L) differentiated between good and poor teachers.

Research utilising Cattell's Sixteen Personality Factor Questionnaire (16 PF) (4,6,9,11) showed contradictory results. Gatzels and Jackson (5) suggest that the 16 PF has two specific advantages which warrant its use in this type of research: (1) it provides scores of factors that are not purely evaluative, and (2) it derives from an extensive programme of long theoretical and empirical work.

DeBlassie (3) determined the extent to which personality differences exist between persistent teachers and prospective teachers, using the 16 PF, and found that only slight differences exist between the two groups.

The purpose of this study was to determine whether personality differences exist between college students having at least three years' college education and school students in the terminal year of the school. The extent to which personality differences exist between these groups was assessed by Cattell's 16 PF.

Procedure

16 PF profiles were obtained for two samples of Ss. One consisted of a random sample of 50 male and 50 female Ss who were in the last year (B.A. Part III) of their graduate course. This was the college group hereafter referred to as college boys, college girls. The second sample, again random, consisted of 50 male and 50 female Ss who were in the terminal year (10th class) of their high school. This was the school group hereafter referred to as school boys, school girls.

Results

Analysis of variance was used to compare the personality structures of the four sub-groups, while t-test was used to test the significance of differences between any two groups on each of the personality factors which showed significant F ratios.

Table 1 shows the sten-score means, standard deviations, and F ratios on the 16 PF scales for each of the male and female subgroups, while Table 2 contains the various t-test combinations for the factors showing significant F ratios. Table 1 indicates that the four subgroups differ significantly on ten of the sixteen factors assessed by the 16 PF. College students differ from school students on the following factors: (1) Less intelligent *versus* more intelligent; (2) Affected by feelings *versus* Emotionally Stable; (3) Humble *versus* Assertive; (4) Shy *versus* Venturesome; (5) Tough-minded *versus* tender-minded; (6) Trusting *versus* Suspicious; (7) Forthright *versus* Shrewd; (8) Placid *versus* Apprehensive; (9) Undisciplined Self-conflict *versus* Controlled; (10) Relaxed *versus* Tense.

More specifically the following conclusions can be drawn from Table 2:

1. School girls are more humble, shy, tender-minded, suspicious, shrewd, apprehensive and tense than school boys. They are, however, less intelligent and emotionally stable than the latter.
2. College boys are more emotionally stable, assertive, venturesome, tender-minded and forthright than school boys.
3. College girls are more emotionally stable, assertive, venturesome, tender-minded, shrewd, apprehensive and controlled than school boys.
4. College boys are more intelligent, emotionally stable, assertive, venturesome, trusting and forthright than school girls.
5. College girls are more intelligent, emotionally stable, assertive, venturesome and controlled than school girls.
6. College girls are more humble, shy, suspicious, shrewd, controlled and tense than college boys. They are, however, less emotionally stable than the latter.

Table 1
Means, SD's and F Ratios in Sten-score Units on the 16 PF Scale, for the Four Subgroups

16 PF	School Boys		School Girls		School Boys		School Girls		Ratios F
	X	SD	X	SD	X	SD	X	SD	
A Reserved *vs.* Outgoing	3.75	1.21	3.63	.94	3.95	1.15	3.50	.94	1.60
B Less Intelligent *vs.* More Intelligent	5.87	1.45	4.98	1.70	6.19	2.14	6.01	2.10	4.11**

C	Affected by Feelings *vs.* Emotionally Stable	3.42	.96	2.15	1.07	4.98	1.10	3.95	.97	66.09**
E	Humble *vs.* Assertive	3.56	1.34	2.41	.98	4.65	1.24	3.97	1.17	26.5**
F	Sober *vs.* Happy-Go-Lucky	2.72	1.18	2.63	.97	2.98	.96	2.81	1.31	.90
G	Expedient *vs.* Conscientious	2.80	.84	2.91	.92	2.72	.97	2.56	.96	1.27
H	Shy *vs.* Venturesome	3.95	.89	3.62	.76	4.97	1.11	4.21	1.12	17.14**
I	Tough-minded *vs.* Tenderminded	2.72	1.62	4.12	.96	3.57	2.10	3.75	2.14	5.60**
L	Trusting *vs.* Suspicious	2.50	1.21	2.95	.82	2.24	.77	2.73	1.12	4.70**
M	Practical *vs.* Imaginative	3.23	1.12	3.01	2.41	2.93	1.41	3.13	2.14	.26
N	Forthright *vs.* Shrewd	2.72	.88	3.89	1.71	2.16	.98	3.98	1.11	27.10**
O	Placid *vs.* Apprehensive	2.13	1.23	3.21	2.13	2.76	2.43	2.98	1.71	2.90*
Q_1	Conservative *vs.* Experimenting	3.21	1.03	3.33	2.03	3.31	1.14	3.52	1.28	.04
Q_2	Group Dependent *vs.* Self-Sufficient	3.91	1.79	4.12	1.92	4.23	1.31	3.80	1.06	.78
Q_3	Undisciplined Self-Conflict *vs.* Controlled	3.42	.97	3.56	.96	3.51	1.21	4.02	1.02	3.30*
Q_4	Relaxed *vs.* Tense	2.42	1.21	3.16	1.19	2.03	.86	3.01	1.37	10.03**

* = .05 Significance Level.
** = .01 Significance Level.

Table 2
Mean Comparisons of the Four Groups on the tenl6 PF Scales with Significant F Ratios

Factor	Means				
	School Boys	School Girls	Diff/M	t	P
B	5.87	4.98	.89	2.81	.01
C	3.42	2.15	1.27	6.24	.01
E	3.56	2.41	1.15	5.00	.01
H	3.95	3.62	.33	6.30	.01
I	2.72	4.12	–1.40	4.69	.01
L	2.50	2.95	–.45	2.12	.05
N	2.72	3.89	–1.17	4.30	.01
O	2.13	3.21	–1.08	3.60	.01
Q_3	3.42	3.56	–.14	.71	NS
Q_4	2.42	3.16	–.74	5.01	.01
	School Boys	College Boys			
B	5.87	6.19	–.32	.87	NS
C	3.42	4.98	–1.56	7.50	.01
E	3.56	4.65	–1.09	13.34	.01
H	3.95	4.97	–1.02	5.05	.01
I	2.72	3.57	–.85	2.24	.05
L	2.50	2.24	.26	1.28	NS
N	2.72	2.16	.56	3.02	.01
O	2.13	2.76	–.63	1.74	NS
Q_3	3.42	3.51	–.09	1.87	NS
Q_4	2.42	2.03	.39	1.39	NS
	School Boys	College Girls			
B	5.87	6.01	–.14	.01	NS
C	3.42	3.95	–.53	26.64	.01
E	3.56	3.97	–.41	5.15	.01
H	3.95	4.21	–.26	4.20	.01
I	2.72	3.75	–1.03	2.68	.01
L	2.50	2.73	–.23	.98	NS
N	2.72	3.98	–1.26	6.30	.01
O	2.13	2.98	–.85	2.02	.05
Q_3	3.42	4.02	–.60	3.01	.01
Q_4	2.42	3.01	–.59	1.89	NS

	School Girls	College Boys			
B	4.98	6.19	–1.21	3.13	.01
C	2.15	4.98	–2.83	12.10	.01
E	2.41	4.65	–2.24	10.02	.01
H	3.62	4.97	–1.35	7.07	.01
I	4.12	3.57	.55	1.68	NS
L	2.95	2.24	.71	4.44	.01
N	3.89	2.16	1.73	6.15	.01
O	3.21	2.76	.45	.92	NS
Q_3	3.56	3.51	.05	.07	NS
Q_4	3.16	2.03	1.13	1.73	NS

	School Girls	College Girls			
B	4.98	6.01	–1.03	2.69	.01
C	2.15	3.95	–1.80	8.83	.01
E	2.41	3.97	–1.56	7.22	.01
H	3.62	4.21	–.59	2.50	.05
I	4.12	3.75	–.37	1.32	NS
L	2.95	2.73	–.22	1.18	NS
N	3.89	3.98	–.09	.10	NS
O	3.21	2.98	.23	.65	NS
Q_3	3.56	4.02	–.46	2.30	.05
Q_4	3.16	3.01	.15	.58	NS
B	6.19	6.01	.18	.42	NS
C	4.98	3.95	1.03	15.70	.01
E	4.65	3.97	.68	2.82	.01
H	4.97	4.21	.76	4.40	.01
I	3.57	3.15	–.18	.04	NS
L	2.24	2.73	-.49	2.54	.05
N	2.16	3.98	–1.82	8.68	.01
O	2.76	2.98	–.22	52	NS
Q_3	3.51	4.01	–.51	2.28	.05
Q_4	2.03	3.01	–.98	4.30	.01

Table 3
Comparisons of the Four Groups on 16 PF Scales, with their Means

	College Boys	College Girls	School Boys	School Girls
B	6.19	6.01	5.87	4.98
C	4.98	3.95	3.42	2.15
E	4.65	3.97	3.56	2.41
H	4.97	4.21	3.95	3.62
	School Girls	College Girls	College Boys	School Boys
I	4.12	3.75	3.57	2.72
			School Boys	College Boys
L	2.95	2.73	2.50	2.24
	College Girls	School Girls	School Boys	College Boys
N	3.98	3.89	2.72	2.16
	School Girls	College Girls	College Boys	School Boys
O	3.21	2.98	2.76	2.13
	College Girls	School Girls	College Boys	School Boys
Q_3	4.02	3.56	3.51	3.42
	School Girls	College Girls	College Boys	School Boys
Q_4	3.16	3.01	2.42	2.03

Table 3 indicates the order (decreasing) in which the four subgroups stand on the ten personality factors in which they differ. The following conclusions emerge from this table:

1. College students more than school students are intelligent, emotionally stable, assertive and venturesome.

   On these four factors, college boys, college girls, school boys and school girls stand in a decreasing order of their scores.

2. Girls, whether school or college, are more tender-minded, suspicious, shrewd, apprehensive, controlled and tense than boys, whether school or college.

   On tender-mindedness and apprehensiveness, school girls, college girls, college boys and school boys stand in a decreasing order of their scores.

On suspiciousness and tension, school girls, college girls, school boys and college boys is the order.

On shrewdness, such order is college girls, school girls, school boys and college boys, while on being controlled it is college girls, school girls, college boys and school boys.

Discussion

It is evident from the results of this study that considerable personality differences exist between college and school students. Place of women in Indian society, their age-old confinement in homes and their proverbial role of home-makers right until recently, their subordinate position *vis-a-vis* men, their conformity and blind allegiance to men and to man-made rules and regulations of conduct, lack of opportunity to forge their way ahead in the Indian world of men-all this coupled with the difficult, stressful and strained life of adolescent girls who in India are still chaperoned when stepping out of home—and the resultant inability to express themselves probably precipitates their already inhibited way of life, and hence the finding that school and college girls more than school and college boys tend to be humble, tender-minded, suspicious, shrewd, apprehensive and tense; and hence also the finding that the school and college girls may be less emotionally stable and seemingly less intelligent than their male counterparts.

Greater freedom, more carefree environment, exceedingly greater opportunities to express and characteristics of approaching adulthood that they are developing, combined with more outgoing and adventurous life, that the college provides, tend to make college boys, and to some extent college girls, more emotionally stable, assertive, venturesome and forthright than school boys and school girls.

Several implications from this study might be considered. The fact that college and school students seem drastically different in terms of personality structure suggests that regardless of the type of education a student receives (school education *vs*. liberal arts), personality structure may influence his success as a student or as an adult late". It may be borne in mind, however, that personality structure is only one, though perhaps the most important one of the criteria that should be used in attempting to define the successful individual. That college education or college life seems to foster certain personality factors, that school life does not, is another finding that this study suggests, though it is not possible to rule out the influence of age, sex, the place of the two sex groups in a culture, and of other factors on the college-going student.

The results of this study need to be cross validated in order that the findings take on sounder meaning. These results, as at present, indicate only possible trends because of the small number of Ss. used. The use of a larger N would correct the limitations and errors caused by a small number of Ss.

If replication and cross-validation of this study on large N's indicates similar results, a study to determine the degree to which other variables, as well as personality structure, might be related for success as an individual would be worthwhile. The use of analysis of variance, as in the present study, is just a step to isolate variables which may influence success in life. But the correlational techniques, both simple and multiple, would help to determine the contribution that a number of variables, considered simultaneously, might make toward the variance in terms of the criterion variable (success as a student or in life).

References

1. Blum, L.P. "A Comparative Study of Students Preparing for Five Selected Professions Including Teaching." The Journal of Experimental Education, 16: 31-65,1947.
2. Callis, R. "Change in Teacher-Pupil Attitudes Related to Training and Experience." Educational and Psychological Measurement. 10: 718-727,1950.
3. DeBlassie, Richard R. "A Comparative Study of the Personality Structures of Persistent and Prospective Teachers." The Journal of Educational Research, Vol. 64, Number 7, March, 1971, pp. 331-333.
4. Erickson, H.E. "A Factorial Study of Teaching Ability." The Journal of Experimental Education, 23:1-39, 1954.
5. Getzels, J.W.: Jackson, P.W, "The Teacher's Personality and Characteristics," in Gage, N.L.(Ed.), Handbook of Research on Teaching, Rand McNally and Co., Chicago, 1963, pp. 506-582.
6. Hadley, S.T. "A Study of the Predictive Values of Several Variables to Student Teaching Success as Measured by Student Teaching Marks" Teachers' College Bulletin of State Teachers' College, Indiana, Pennsylvania, 60:1-10,1954.
7. Hedlund, P.A. "Cooperative Study to Predict Effectiveness in Secondary School Teaching." Third Progress Report, University of State of New York and State Department, Albany, 1953.

8. LaBue, A.C. "Personality Traits and Persistence of Interest in Teaching as a Vocational Choice." Journal of Applied Psychology, 39: 362-365,1955.
9. Lamke, T.A. "Personality and Teaching Success." The Journal of Experimental Education, 20: 217-259,1951.
10. Lough, Orpha, "Women Students in Liberal Arts, Nursing and Teacher Training Curricula and the Minnesota Multiphasic Personality Inventory," Journal of Applied Psychology, 31:437-445,1947.
11. Montross, H.W., "Temperament and Teaching Success," The Journal of Experimental Education, 26: 711-716,1957.

38. A DIAGNOSIS OF ABNORMAL PERSONALITY PATTERNS

Normality being a matter of degree rather than that of kind, people who are seemingly normal almost in every sense of the term may have an abnormal personality pattern or two lurking beneath the adequately adjusted surface of their persona. The abnormal personality patterns are sometimes too deep-seated to cause any alarm or disruption in one's normal functioning. These patterns may, however, exhibit their existence by seriously interfering with one's day-to-day behaviour when (i) there is a particular environmental stress, (ii) puzzling or threatening social factors overwhelm one, (iii) one's self-concept or cultural milieu gets into conflict, or whenever his personal inadequacy faced with an offensive situation lands him in a fix.

Reversely, persons having deviant personality patterns are not, in the usual sense of the word, mentally ill, nor are they in need of psychological treatment. A deviant personality pattern revealed by a test does not indeed mean that the subject is not operating within the normal range, unless other information about the person confirms such findings of the test. It was with such *hypothesis* in mind that the present study was undertaken.

The *purposes* of the study are (i) to assay those traits that are commonly characteristic of disabling psychological abnormality, (ii) to examine the empirical validity of the test, which reveals those traits, through information about the subjects obtained from other sources, and (iii) to find out whether the abnormal personality patterns, in those subjects, interrupt normal functioning.

The *procedure* is: (i) use of the Minnesota Multiphasic Personality Inventory (individual form MMPI) which provides, in a single test, scores on the more important phases of personality.

The test comprises 550 statements covering a wide range of subject matter. The subject sorts all the statements into three categories, *i.e.*, True, False, cannot say. His responses, as shown in these categories, are counted so as to yield scores on four validity scales (?, L, F, K,) and nine clinical scales (Hypochondriasis-HS, Depression-D, Hysteria-Hy, Psychopathic deviate-Pd, Sex Interest-Mf, Paranoia-Pa, Psychasthenia-Pt, Schizophrenia-Sc, Hypomania-Ma). The scoring is done after the three successive steps–sorting out the cards containing significant responses, entering these on the Recording sheet, and applying the scoring key templates to this sheet. The raw scores thus obtained are then transferred to the Profile side of the recording sheet, where the Profile is plotted after adding the appropriate amount of the K factor. This was done for all the 32 individuals covered in the study. The test was applied to a sampling of persons known to have certain abnormal, though undefined, characteristics in their behaviour. The individuals were local post-graduate students. (ii) Comparison of the individual data with the behavioural data collected from persons who know the subjects intimately.

The brief data are tabulated on pages 188 and 189.

Interpretation

(a) A glance at the profiles shows that highest points on certain scales exist on the profiles of individuals Nos. 4 & 22 to No. 32. This is because of the complex mixture of abnormalities in these individuals. Such abnormalities are evidenced by a T score of 80 or above, in all these cases, of one or more scales.

Reports of the tutors who know them very intimately indicate clearly that these persons are more or less severely disturbed –the more elevated the profiles and the higher these scores are, the more disturbed is the person, so that the severeness of disturbances increases as one proceeds from individual No. 22 towards the one at No. 32. The tutors gave only such symptoms, as given below, which were prominent in the persons' behaviour, without giving any clinical name; in some cases they reported almost in an undefined way that the persons sometimes showed queerness, disorder and make believe in their behaviour. The scales given in brackets have been put by the investigator to name the abnormality associated with the symptoms reported by the tutors:

Individual	Corrected RAW SCORE															Abnormal Personality Patterns
Females	?	L	F	K	Hs	D	Hy	Pd	Mf	Pa	Pt	Sc	Ma	Si	Scores	Tendencies towards
1.	17	6	4	17	16	26	20	21	37	10	22	26	19	24	45–63	
2.	13	6	6	19	14	26	18	21	31	8	28	28	19	24	48–63	
3.	25	6	7	19	13	15	17	20	28	14	27	30	23	16	41–68	
4.	11	3	14	14	10	29	9	32	31	13	35	39	21	47	33–82	Psychopathic Deviate, Schizophrenia, limited social interest.
Males																
5.	11	5	5	15	11	16	15	19	25	8	21	22	19	16	41–59	
6.	8	3	3	16	11	20	18	15	26	11	25	26	18	27	41–61	
7.	9	4	7	16	10	18	19	18	19	10	20	28	22	16	41–63	
8.	13	7	3	20	11	18	17	18	20	9	25	27	16	17	42–65	
9.	16	4	3	16	16	22	21	16	27	4	23	23	18	22	38–65	
10.	2	3	7	13	13	23	18	23	30	14	30	30	24	34	41–69	
11.	10	10	1	24	13	20	23	25	25	9	26	26	17	20	45–65	
12.	15	3	15	9	10	25	17	23	23	10	27	31	12	25	38–70	
13.	5	5	13	16	14	22	22	27	29	10	26	31	25	29	54–70	
14.	6	5	5	15	10	20	14	20	31	5	26	25	19	29	41–71	Tendency towards femininity.

15.	4	2	2	19	17	24	25	27	21	7	26	27	24	14	39–71	–do–
16.	41	5	8	20	16	21	21	23	29	8	32	33	18	27	50–71	Schizophrenia.
17.	14	5	6	11	8	25	10	24	28	12	30	35	14	41	38–75	Schizophrenia.
18.	3	9	5	25	11	23	23	27	24	13	30	35	20	2	46–75	Schizophrenia.
19.	14	4	13	14	13	22	18	17	23	13	7	35	20	26	47–75	Schizophrenia.
20.	12	3	10	10	14	19	16	15	31	8	29	36	25	27	41–77	Schizophrenia, tendency towards femininity.
21.	19	3	13	9	7	16	10	26	28	17	28	32	28	29	39–79	Paranoia, Hypomania.
22.	17	8	3	18	12	29	17	21	30	8	24	26	22	15	40–80	Depression.
23.	3	4	10	10	8	21	16	24	20	16	26	38	29	21	48–81	Paranoia, Schizophrenia, Hypomania.
24.	6	3	8	13	13	24	22	23	30	16	32	37	29	32	55–81	–do–
25.	2	5	10	11	13	26	24	26	38	16	32	34	29	22	47–85	Depression, tendency towards femininity, Paranoia, Schizophrenia, Hypomania.
26.	24	5	13	12	16	29	29	35	28	14	32	42	20	32	58–88	Depression, Hysteria, Psychopathic Deviate, Schizophrenia.

27.	25	2	19	8	15	34	19	32	36	10	39	39	19	49	55–92	Depression, Psychopathic Deviate, tendency towards femininity. psychasthenia, Schizophrenia, limited social interest.
28.	2	4	9	11	20	34	25	26	35	15	32	38	25	31	56–92	Hypochondriasis, Depression, tendency towards femininity, schizophrenia.
29.	19	7	15	13	18	30	26	27	29	16	38	46	31	31	56–96	Depression, paranoia, psychasthenia, schizophrenia, Hypomania.
30.	4	2	14	10	18	37	29	36	33	18	35	42	22	34	61–99	Depression, hysteria, tendency toward femininity, paranoia, psychasthenia, schizophrenia.
31.	5	2	16	12	12	26	22	29	30	23	44	54	30	34	52–111	Depression, psychopathic, Deviate, Hypomania, paranoia, schizophrenia, Hypomania.
32.	0	5	23	14	20	25	30	35	42	25	43	56	40	22	47–115	Hypochondriasis, Hysteria, Psychopathic, Deviate, tendency towards femininity, Hypomania, Schizophrenia, Psychasthenia.

(i) Under anxiety regarding physical functions (Hs).

(ii) Diffidence, pessimism, worrying, aloofness, fear of stark realities (D).

(iii) Emotional immaturity, complaining of cramps or of other physiological diseases, fits (Hy).

(iv) Drinking, indifference to social traditions or morality, excitement over a social deeds (Pd).

(v) Undue interest in the members of the opposite sex (Mf).

(vi) Suspicious, being high strung, fear of being persecuted (Pa).

(vii) Unrealistic fears, overdoing, inability to concentrate, too much self-assuring (Pt).

(viii) Unusual thoughts, shifting moods, whimsical behaviour, eccentricity, discordant style (Sc).

(ix) Overactivity and depression alternatively, overambitious, anxious to bring reforms overnight (Ma).

(x) Participating in very few extra-curricular activities, limited social contacts (Si).

(b) The profiles of individual No. 14 to No. 21, though not showing very high points, indicate just one or two abnormalities only, evidenced by a T score varying from 71 to 79 on the scale or scales concerned.

Tutors' reports on these persons are not much alarming. Undue interest in the female (Mf), queer thoughts & behaviour (Sc), doubting things and persons (Pa) and overactivity (Ma), were the only abnormalities sometimes seen in the day-to-day behaviour of these persons who are not markedly disturbed. These persons usually go about their jobs like normals. In certain situations, however, they manifest the abnormality shown against them.

(c) The Neurotic profiles (in which two or more of the scales Hs, D, Hy are dominant) are those of the individuals Nos. 26 and 28.

The Behaviour-problem profiles (in which two or more of the scales Pd, Mf, Ma are dominant) are those of the individuals Nos. 25 and 27.

The Psychotic Profiles (in which the scales Sc, Pa, with D and Ma are dominant) are those of the individuals Nos. 29,30,31,32,23 & 24.

(d) The scores of individuals Nos. 1 to 3 and 5 to 13 lie within the T scores 40 to 70 (considered to be an average score). These individuals lie more on the side of normality than that of abnormality. The tutors' experiences with these individuals confirm this finding.

(e) The individual No. 4 has been reported by the tutor to be friendless, aloofish (Si), having disordered thinking (Sc), and indifferent to social conventions (Pd). This confirms her elevated scores on the three scales.

(f) Validity of Scores:

(i) In some cases though the? score is quite high, the percentage of? items belonging to each scale is almost negligible. In most cases, however, the? score is not appreciable. The number of items, therefore, on which the subject "cannot say" or is doubtful is not significant in any case.

(ii) The L scores vary from 2 to 7 in 29 out of 32 cases; this is not significant. In all these cases, therefore, there has been no appreciable attempt on the part of the subjects to place themselves in the most acceptable light socially. The investigator's experience with the subjects confirms this finding because he found that all these subjects, being unduly keen to know something about their personalities, went out of their way to cooperate and give genuine responses to the best of their understanding and abilities. The L Scores 8,9 and 10 of the remaining subjects. No. 22,18 and 11 respectively do not invalidate other scores of these subjects which have withstood the test of empirical validity as said in paras a, b above. These at worst reflect defensiveness on the part of these subjects.

(iii) The F scores vary from 1 to 16 in the case of 30 subjects; the scores of these subjects are, therefore, not likely to be invalid for such causes as subjects' carelessness or inability to comprehend the items, or scoring or recording errors. In most of these cases, the scores obviously are quite rational and relatively pertinent.

The F scores 19 and 23 of the remaining subjects' No. 27 and 32 respectively may be attributable to the subjects' attitude of self-criticism at the deliberate or unconscious level, their carelessness or most probably their language difficulty, but there is reason to believe tutors' reports confirming the finding as in (a) & (b) above

– that even in these two cases the high F scores have not materially affected the profiles, more so when several of the clinical scales show T scores around 50 to 60.

(iv) The K scores vary from 8 to 20 in the case of 30 subjects; this is neither too high nor too low. It may not, therefore, be wise to interpret any form of defensiveness or attitude of self-criticism or wish to appear in an unfavourable light on the part of these individuals. Besides, having used the K score as a correction factor for several other scores which in turn stand validated through other criteria, it may mean anything in terms of the test-taking attitude, short of falsification of other scores.

The K scores 24 and 25 of the remaining subjects Nos. 11 and 18 respectively are rather high. But these being the case of low F and high K, K scores do not tend to be indicators of any form of defensiveness, nor a worthwhile distorting factor.

From the above discussion, it may be safe to assume that the responses of the subjects, on the whole, have yielded a valid set of scores. It can be said with a fair degree of confidence that the M.M.P.I. used on this sample has yielded fairly valid scores in spite of the subjects' comparatively inadequate educational experience, their language difficulties and their different cultural milieu.

Limitations

(i) The inventory has been used on some individual cases only. The application of its group form may reveal more information regarding the possibility of its universal application and uniform interpretation.

(ii) Nothing has been done, in this experiment, to calculate test-retest-correlation in order to know the reliability coefficient or to validate the scores with another standardised test having similar scales in order to know the validity coefficient.

(iii) It would be worthwhile to calculate inter-correlational 'r's between the scores on different scales in order to see such abnormality patterns which tend to go together.

(iv) A statistical treatment of the data derived from the use of the inventory on a large and stratified sample may yield more information.

39. PERSONALITY DIFFERENCES AMONG MOST POPULAR AND LEAST POPULAR GRADUATES

Abstract

Graduates, 300 students, who earlier joined post-graduate classes in arts, were administered a 5-choice sociometric scale designed to identify most popular and least popular students. This variable, popularity status, was then analysed in relation to the personality characteristics measured by the California Test of Personality. Scores made by the most popular students on each trait of the personality test differed significantly from those made by the least popular group. The popularity status of the students was found relatively constant.

To associate with others in one way or another is an ever-present need of human existence. In fact we are always dependent upon such association for our comfort, joy and security. That certain patterns of interaction in social relationships are all pervasive warrants that factors related to social acceptability be identified. Why are some individuals highly accepted by their peers while others are cold-shouldered or even actively rejected by them? What personality patterns characterise the socially accepted and the socially rejected individuals? Answering these questions may reveal the patterns of interaction that permeates social relations. Further, a study of the personality factors related to social acceptability and unacceptability can suggest measures for improving the status of those individuals who are not so popular. The present study is an attempt to accomplish this by analyzing the relationships between popularity status and personality characteristics.

Design and Methodology

Male students (N = 300) studying in the first year of post-graduate classes in arts of Punjabi University formed the sample of the study. They were matched for age and intelligence. Ten classroom groups, two each in the subjects of Political Science, History, Hindi, Punjabi and English, were used in the study. All of them were arts graduates.

A sociometric scale was constructed with the aim of measuring the sociometric acceptability of the Ss in their respective peer groups. It was a 5-choice scale, each category of which was assigned a numerical weight. The scores of each student on this scale were computed.

Students in each group who obtained the twenty highest scores on the scale were identified. These together constituted the most popular group, while those having the twenty lowest scores formed the least popular group of students. In this way, 100 most popular and 100 least popular students were identified.

The California Test of Personality was employed to measure the chosen personality traits. This test was administered to the two groups *i.e.*, two hundred students, and scores were computed for each of the personality traits. The traits included were self-reliance, personal work, personal freedom, withdrawal, belongingness, nervousness, social standards, social skills, anti-social tendencies, school relations, community relations and family relations. The first six constitute the Personal Adjustment Category of the test, while the latter six represent the Social Adjustment Category. An analysis of variance, multiple classification, was computed to determine the differences in the personality traits of the most popular and the least popular groups.

The same sociometric scale was administered to each of the initial 300 students once again, after about two months from the date of first administration. Correlations were drawn between the scores obtained by Ss identified as most popular or least popular on the first administration and the scores the same Ss made on the second administration. This was done to know whether the popularity status of students undergoes a change or remains constant.

Results

Table 1 presents an analysis of the differences in scores made by each popularity group on each of the traits measured.

Table 1

Personality Differences on Each Trait as Revealed through Analysis of Variance

Popularity groups .. P.G.
Subject groups .. S.G.

Personality trait	Source of variation	df	F
Self-reliance	Between P.G.	1	112.75
	Between S.G.	4	2.08
	Interaction	4	6.93

Personal worth	Between P.G.	1	95.22
	Between S.G.	4	1.93
	Interaction	4	0.69
Personal freedom	Between P.G.	1	70.46
	Between S.G.	4	2.72
	Interaction	4	0.78
Belongingness	Between P.G.	1	62.92
	Between S.G.	4	2.04
	Interaction	4	5.81
Withdrawal tendencies	Between P.G.	1	41.75
	Between S.G.	4	13.89
	Interaction	4	2.06
Nervousness	Between P.G.	1	36.94
	Between S.G.	4	3.01
	Interaction	4	7.12
Social standards	Between P.G.	1	21.70
	Between S.G.	4	0.85
	Interaction	4	0.92
Social skills	Between P.G.	1	161.42
	Between S.G.	4	2.92
	Interaction	4	3.05
Anti-social tendencies	Between P.G.	1	69.75
	Between S.G.	4	1.02
	Interaction	4	1.89
Family relations	Between P.G.	1	231.32
	Between S.G.	4	32.72
	Interaction	4	42.11
School relations	Between P.G.	1	101.66
	Between S.G.	4	0.39
	Interaction	4	22.31
Community relations	Between P.G.	1	40.61
	Between S.G.	4	1.78
	Interaction	4	18.26

Table 2
Personality Differences on Personal Adjustment and Social Adjustment as Revealed Through Analysis of Variance

Category	Source of variation	df	F
Personal adjustment	Between P.G.	1	272.61
	Between S.G.	4	1.59
	Interaction	4	7.50
Social adjustment	Between P.G.	1	231.42
	Between S.G.	4	3.82
	Interaction	4	2.14

Table 2 gives the analysis of variance computed to reveal difference in mean total scores for each of the two broad categories of adjustment measured by the test. The said differences are between the two popularity groups.

Significant differences between the most popular and least popular groups, at the .05 and the .01 levels, were found on each component of the personality test. When the scores made by each subject group were analysed, a significant difference was found on two components of the test *i.e.,* family relations and withdrawal tendencies. When the factor of interaction between subject group and popularity group was probed, the analysis revealed a significant difference on six components of the test, *i.e.,* self-reliance, belongingness, nervousness, family relations, school relations and community relations. Again, significant differences (.01 level) exist between the two popularity groups on total personality and total social adjustment scores.

The coefficient of correlation between the two administrations of the test in the case of the most popular and least popular groups came to .89.

Discussion

These findings unequivocally suggest that most popular and least popular graduates differ significantly on a number of important personality traits. No generalisation is, however, possible in this case, as in the case of any finding of a relationship between measures of personality characteristics. Only further research will show whether individuals attain high social status because they possess certain personality traits or whether they develop these traits as a consequence of having attained high social status.

The popularity status of students tends to remain relatively constant through time, though this fact has been determined over a short time span.

40. ADJUSTMENT AND SELF-ACCEPTANCE

Several recent studies show that adjustment as such is fairly related to self-acceptance. A broad conclusion of most of these studies is that those who are more well-adjusted have greater self-acceptance than those who are less well-adjusted. Taylor and Combs (6), for example, demonstrated that better adjusted children, as determined by the California Test of Personality were able to accept more damaging statements about themselves than were less adjusted children. Their argument is that "a maladjusted person is one who is heavily threatened and too rigid in his defences against threat to accept mildly threatening truths about himself". Rogers (4) defines the well-adjusted individual as one able to accept all perceptions, including those about self, into his personality organisation. He states that the relationship between self-acceptance and adjustment seems to increase as adjustment improves. Combs (1) and Snygg and Combs (5) point out that "a phenomenal self is adequate in the degrees to which it is capable of accepting into its organisation any and all aspects of reality". It is to demonstrate similar relationship between self-acceptance and adjustment that this study has been undertaken.

Hypothesis

The well-adjusted person would accept more unflattering (or even threatening) facts about himself than would the less well-adjusted person.

Procedure

Two hundred high school students (male and female in equal numbers) of approximately similar socio-economic condition, educational level and age from four schools of the urban area of Jullundur were administered the tests in May-June 1966. Bell Adjustment Inventory was used as a measure of adjustment. Though this inventory is not an ideal instrument for distinguishing between the more well-adjusted and the less well-adjusted, it did well for the purpose of classifying the population into the upper and lower 50 per cent in terms of adjustment score obtained on the inventory. Thus two groups of students, one group better adjusted than the other on the basis of an external criterion, were found.

To measure the extent to which these students would accept damaging statements about themselves, a list of statements which appeared to be equally applicable to or even true of all boys and girls, though self-disparaging if admitted, was drawn. Four teachers were asked to suggest new statements and to criticise those on the list drawn by the investigator. The following fifteen statements emerged as a consensus:

1. At times I abuse my parents.
2. Sometimes I copy from the notes of my classmates.
3. When I know I shall not be caught, I steal or tell lies.
4. At times I disobey my teachers.
5. At times I indulge in false excuses to get out of things I dislike.
6. At times I say indecent words or things.
7. Sometimes I am fussy over trifles.
8. Sometimes I shirk work that I am supposed to do.
9. At times I have been mischievous with my classmates.
10. At times I am uncharitable to those who love me.
11. Sometimes I am unsportsmanlike in my behaviour.
12. At times I brag about my qualities before others.
13. At times I do not keep tidy.
14. At times I am unkind to the young's of little birds, and animals.

This list was cyclostyled and presented to all the children of the two groups about a month after they were administered the Bell Adjustment Inventory. What they were told was: "Here is a list of things students of your age sometimes do. I would like to know which of these is true of you. Check the statements which hold good for you, fold the list and return it. You may or may not put your name on it; no one else will come to know of your answers which are strictly confidential."

The students took about ten to fifteen minutes in returning the lists duly filled in.

Results of the Experiment

The results were analysed and the summary of results is shown in the Table 1 below:

Table 1
Mean Adjustment score, mean number of Disparaging statements checked and critical ratios of the differences for males and females

	Mean Adjustment Score	Mean No. of Disparaging Statements Checked	Mean S.D.	SE/ Mean	CR
			Males		
Lower 50%	27.6	4.7	2.3	.32	6.03
Upper 50%	61.4	8.8	3.8	.53	
			Females		
Lower 50%	34.3	5.6	2.8	.40	4.00
Upper 50%	68.7	8.0	3.2	.45	

The hypothesis, that those having greater adjustment score have checked more self-disparaging items than those having lesser adjustment score, stands amply proved. This is true of both males and females. Evidently, relationship between the ability to accept disparaging statements about self and adjustment is positive and it withstands the shocks of demonstratedly carried out experiments.

The group result as shown in the table was also observed in quite a few of the individual cases. The male student, who obtained the highest adjustment score in the group, checked all except two of the items on the list as true of himself. The opposite tendency was observed in the cases of those having low to very low adjustment scores. The female student who checked just three items was the one whose adjustment score is lowest among the females.

Limitations

A statement may look disparaging to one and not at all or not so disparaging to another depending upon how one interprets it for himself. Tests based on marking or accepting such statements may, therefore, suffer from a serious flaw that the individuals' response may be determined in part or in whole by their subjective interpretation of a statement rather than by what the test-maker means by that statement. This may be the chief limitation in the case of the list of statements and the Bell Adjustment Inventory used in this experiment, as also in the case of several personality tests used by psychologists in various studies. It would be, therefore, worthwhile to test the hypothesis of this study through measures of adjustment and instruments for measuring self-acceptance other than those used in the present study.

Summary

An attempt to demonstrate a relationship between ability to accept disparaging statements about self and adjustment was made by asking high school students, classified into more well-adjusted and less well-adjusted group, through Bell Adjustment Inventory to check on a list of fifteen apparently disparaging statements those true of themselves. The more well-adjusted students checked significantly more statements than did the less well-adjusted students. The male students in general appear to be less well-adjusted and consequently capable of less self-acceptance than female students.

References

1. Combs, A.W. 1949. A phenomenological approach to adjustment Theory, *J. Abnorm. Soc-Psy-School*. 44: 29-55.
2. Downie, N.M., *Fundamentals of Measurement:* New York: Oxford Univ. Press.
3. Garret, H. *Elementary Statistics*. New York: Longman's Green, 1956.
4. Rogers, C.R. 1947. The organisation of personality. *Amer. Psychologist*. 2: 358-68.
5. Snygg, D.C., Combs, A.W. *Individual Behaviour. A new frame of reference for Psychology*. New York: Harper, 1949.
6. Taylor, Charles and Combs, Arthur W. "Self-Acceptance and Adjustment" in *Contribution to Modern Psychology*. 1958. Oxford Univ. Press. New York.

41. EFFECTIVENESS OF MOTIVES

Several factors or situations serve as motivating stimuli to work and effort on the part of people. Competition and co-operation are a few of such stimuli or motives. Maller (2) studied the effect of competitive and co-operative motives upon the work efficiency of American school children and found that though both the competitive and co-operative conditions provided effective motivation, competition proved to be more effective than co-operation as a motive. Two other experiments performed in America, one with pre-school and high-school children (7) and other with college students (6), have yielded almost similar results.

Mead (3) studied whether the competition motive is stronger in several primitive tribes in North America, Africa, and Pacific. He found that the relative capacity of competitive and co-operative motives to influence the behaviour of an individual depends upon the nature of the cultural influences to which he has been subjected. May and Doob (5), commenting on Maller's and others' experiments on the subject, point out that such experiments show only the relative strength of certain motives in specific cultural circumstances, not the absolute strength of these motives in all cultures.

Present Experiment

The present study attempts to measure the relative effectiveness of two motives–competition and co-operation–for the work of graduate students undergoing teacher training in the Government Training College for Teachers, Jullundur, and M.G.N. Training College for Teachers, Jullundur. The subjects, 384 in number, ranged in age from 18 to 22 years. The males and females were in equal number. The students who had graduated from different degree colleges and had just started their year-long training in the two training colleges were representative of three different socio-economic levels *i.e.* middle-class-characteristic of small communities, poor-characteristic of crowded localities of unskilled labourers, and well-to-do characteristic of professional and business classes.

To determine the effectiveness of the two motives, competition and co-operation, the experiment was planned so as to compare the work of the subjects under three different conditions of motivation: a competitive condition, a co-operative condition, and a neutral condition.

For the purpose of this experiment, the competitive condition is that which stimulates the individual to strive against other individuals in his group for a goal object of which he hopes to be the sole, or a principal possessor. The co-operative condition is that which stimulates an individual to strive with the members of his group for a goal object of which is to be shared equally among all of them, while a neutral condition is a controlled condition devoid of any motivation (1).

Method and Procedure

The subjects were required to complete as many problems of simple addition as possible within twenty minutes' time. Each problem consisted of the addition of two two-place numbers like 15 and 32, or 46 and 17. The problems were presented to the subjects on 2 typed sheets, 50 problems to a sheet. All the subjects completed these problems under three conditions. The subjects were classified into 8 groups of equal number. The group designated as A, B, C, D, E, F, G, H, were made by picking out, through stratified sampling, individuals from both males and females so that the number of subjects of each sex was same in every group. The three conditions were induced by variation in the instructions.

In unmotivated condition the students were given the instructions: "This is just for practice. Begin adding when I say 'start' and go on doing so until I say 'stop'. Don't write your name on the sheets." In competitive condition the instructions given were: "Let us find out your speed of work in addition. Let us see who is the fastest, the next fastest, third fastest, and so on to the slowest in your group. Those who do fast work will be rewarded. Each one of you has a good chance to win. Start adding when I say 'start' and go on doing so until I say 'stop'. The greater the number of problems you solve, the greater is your chance of scoring over others in the group. Write your name on top of the sheets." In co-operative condition the instructions given were: "We would find out which group is fastest, second fastest, third and so on. The groups doing fast work will be rewarded according to their position. Your group has a good chance to win. Your group will score over other groups if the number of problems all of you solve for your group is maximum. Don't write your own name on sheets but do write the name of your group."

Entire work was completed in one session, divided into 11 periods of 4 minutes each. Each of the periods involved 2 minutes' work on each of the two separate sheets of addition-problems.

The subjects worked for one period under the control condition, and for five periods (a total of 20 minutes) under each of the two motivating conditions. After the subjects worked under the control condition which was always provided in the first period, they worked under the competitive condition for one period, then under the co-operative condition for one period, again for one period under the competitive condition, followed by one period under co-operative condition, and so on in alternate succession until they completed working for five periods under each of the two motivating conditions. The number of problems done per minute by each subject constituted the subject's score, under the control and under each of the two motivating conditions.

Results

The results of the experiment are placed in the Table below:

Table

The average number of problems done per minute, under the unmotivated condition and under each of the two motivating conditions, by the students

Group	Condition		
	Unmotivated	Competitive	Co-operative
A	28.4	32.3	33.4
B	32.2	33.0	38.5
C	24.7	27.9	30.5
D	27.3	30.5	31.6
E	26.2	28.5	33.0
F	31.3	33.7	34.8
G	29.2	33.2	37.0
H	30.3	34.2	38.1
Average of all groups	28.7	31.7	34.7

As is evident from the Table, the competitive as well as the co-operative conditions effectively motivated the subjects, because in both the cases the number of problems solved significantly exceeded the number solved under the unmotivated condition; and competition was found to be a more effective motive than co-operation of the work-for-your-group kind. Since all the eight groups were alike in regard to their composition *vis-a-vis* socio-economic status and cultural background of the subjects, the study could not say whether the differences in the effectiveness of the three conditions are true of all persons and in all cultures. These differences, however, are statistically reliable. Again, individual differences within each group were noticed; for instance, one-sixth of the total number of subjects actually worked faster when the motive was co-operation than they did when the motive was competition. Practice seems to have increased the difference in the effectiveness of the two motives; for example, the average score for the first competitive period was 32.7 and the score for the first co-operative period was 31.9, thus showing a difference of only 0.8 problems between the scores obtained under the two conditions. The scores for the final competitive and the final co-operative periods were 34.4 and 29.4 respectively. Thus, the difference between the scores obtained under the two conditions rose to 5.0 problems, though the score under the competitive condition showed a gain of 1.7 problems and the score under the co-operative condition showed a loss of 2.5 problems.

Discussion

The findings of this study support Maller's view. Competition is more effective a motive for work and effort than co-operation and that the differences in effectiveness of the two motives tend to increase with practice.

It is, however, difficult to generalise that competition always surpasses co-operation in its motivating effectiveness, unless competition and co-operation with the members of one's own group (characteristic of this study) be regarded as considerably representative of all the competitive as also of all the co-operative situations in which the graduate students often find themselves. The types of competition may vary from one situation to another, the benefits accruing from the two motives may be differently perceived, the value-dimensions and personality-types of individuals may be divergent – these and some other factors may be lie, unless the influence of the two motives is exhaustively studied under all possible conditions, that competition motivates more than co-operation. The value of competition as a motive or its status relative to that of co-operation is difficult to measure by the use of just one kind of competitive situation. Similarly it is difficult to assess the value of co-operation or its status relative to that of competition. Varieties of co-operative situations as also of competitive situations should be involved in experiments of the type performed in this study before concluding whether co-operation is a more effective motive or competition.

Moreover, differences in the motivating effectiveness of competition and co-operation may be owing to differences in culture which, there are reasons to believe, emphasise, breed, encourage or inspire one motive more than another.

Instincts like those of self-assertion and acquisition may seem to justify that competition is deep-seated in human nature; and instincts like those of gregariousness and sex may claim that co-operation is equally inherent. Even if this plea is granted, cultures, socio-economic factors and social set-up are likely to influence the instinctively fixed co-operative or competitive behaviour to the extent of making the two motives equally powerful or making either of them a more powerful motive than the other.

One social order may foster co-operative behaviour. Another may develop the creed of competition and individual rivalry. 'Which of these better serves human life and human ideals' is a question which begs an answer from philosophers, sociologists and educators alike. And whatever the answer, it would warrant that education should, besides other things, aim at setting up a social order which strives to devote itself to the desired behaviour, co-operative or competitive as the case may be.

If, however, Maller's (2) and other findings are explained by the argument that American children are brought up in the culture which lays great emphasis on personal ambition, rivalry and individual success, and the nature of which is basically competitive, how is the similar finding of this study regarding Indian students to be explained? The "culture" argument valid in the case of American children is certainly not valid in the case of Indian sample, because Indian culture is substantially different from American culture, especially with regard to its emphasis on "competition" value and the behaviour leading to and from it. Consequently, the experimenter is tempted to believe that the 'competition' motive, because of its very nature, may be more powerful than the 'co-operation' motive which, perhaps again because of its very nature, may be relatively less potent. Is man, irrespective of caste, creed, sex, culture or nationality, motivated more by a competitive rather than a co-operative situation? Is it in his very blood or nature to do more work under the competitive condition than the co-operative condition? The answers to these questions may be attempted by future researchers.

Summary

The study devised to study the relative effectiveness of competition and co-operation as motives to work was done by subjecting a representative group of 384 graduates (males and females in equal number), undergoing teacher training in two Training Colleges of Jullundur, to an experiment planned to compare their work under three different conditions of motivation *i.e.* competitive, co-operative and neutral. The subjects were required to solve as many problems of simple addition as possible within a stipulated period, under all the three conditions separately. Whereas both competition and co-operation proved to be effective motives to the work, competition surpassed co-operation as well as "no motivation" as a motive to work. Practice effect tended to increase the difference in the effectiveness of the two motives. That both Americans and Indians are found to be more motivated by 'competition' than by 'co-operation' seems to suggest that not culture but the very nature of competition and that of co-operation is such that competition is a more powerful motive than co-operation.

References

1. Graffs, Leland W., Schneirla, Theodore C., Robinson, Elsa E., Gilbert, Ralph W., *Recent Experiments in Psychology*, New York: McGraw-Hill, 1950, pp. 40-62.
2. Maller, J.B., "Co-operation and Competition, an Experimental Study of Motivation." *Teachers College Contributions to Education*, 1929, No. 384.
3. Margaret Mead., *Co-operation and Competition among Primitive Peoples*. New York: McGraw-Hill, 1937.
4. May, M.A., and L.A. Doob, "Competition and Co-operation." *Social Science Research Council*, 1937, Bulletin 25.
5. Sims, V.M., "The Relative Influence of Two Types of Motivation on Improvement." *Journal of Educational Psychology*, 1928, Vol. 19, pp. 480-484.
6. Sorokin, P.A., M. Tanquist, M. Patten, and C.C. Zimmerman, "An Experimental Study of Efficiency of Work Under Various Specified Conditions." *American Journal of Sociology*, 1930, Vol. 35, pp. 765-782.

VII. ATTITUDES AND INTERESTS

42. STUDENT ATTITUDES TOWARDS COLLEGE *Vis-a-Vis* UNIVERSITY

It has been generally observed that the majority of students doing post-graduate degree course at colleges are those who had preferred to go to a university and who, though rejected in university admissions, were so strongly motivated towards a post-graduate degree course that they eventually seized upon the chance to pursue such a course, albeit at a college. In this study the attitudes of such students to their college and the course were investigated, the hypothesis being that students who went to colleges in the belief that colleges were the second-best alternative to university could compare the college unfavourably with university (or what they thought a university would be like) and would therefore, at least initially, show a largely negative attitude towards the college.

The data were collected from three sources. Firstly, a questionnaire was filled by 120 post-graduate students (in the subjects of Economics, Political Science, English and History) admitted in an arts college. The questionnaires were given to them after they had completed one month of their courses. Secondly, 20 of these students were selected for personal interview at the end of their first year at a college, when their attitudes were studied in depth. Finally, a stratified random sample of students who had just completed the first year of their college course was contacted, by means of selecting all relevant students from a small sample of arts colleges, chosen so as to be representative in terms of geographical region, size and type of the post-graduate course offered. These students (90) were also asked to fill the questionnaire.

The students who were in their first term at a college were asked first what advantages and disadvantages, if any, they felt a college had over a university, from the point of view of a student taking a post-graduate course. Just over a quarter (26 per cent) thought there were no advantages, compared with only 8 per cent who thought there were no disadvantages in a college compared with a university. A wide variety of factors were mentioned by those who saw either advantages or disadvantages in a college. Factors stated most frequently are shown in Tables 1 and 2.

Table 1
Advantages of a College Compared with a University (Factors stated most frequently)

	Percentage*
Class being smaller, students get more individual attention	35
Teachers are more friendly and approachable	21
There is more freedom and less restrictions	10
Students are encouraged and helped in learning	9
Teachers provide ample material in the subject	8

* The total from which these percentages were calculated is the total number of students who mentioned any advantages.

Table 2
Disadvantages of a College Compared with a University (Factors stated most frequently)

	Percentage*
Lack of adequate library facilities	29
Social and cultural life (that the university offers) is lacking	20
University degree carries higher status	15
Inadequate hostel accommodation	12
Staff not as qualified as in university	10

* The total from which these percentages were calculated is the total number of students who mentioned any disadvantages.

Twenty* of these students interviewed at the end of their first year revealed facts that highlighted their attitudes towards

---

* The sample consisted of 12 men and 8 women; 7 were aged nineteen, 10 aged twenty and 3 over twenty. Eight were doing Science courses, five Social Science courses and 7 other Arts courses. All had originally stated that they would have preferred to get into university.

college *vis-a-vis* university. As may be expected, there was a correlation between how well the student was doing in his course and how well he liked the college. Only one out of the 20, having failed in her examination, said that she had enjoyed her first year. Two who had passed their examinations had, however, decided to leave college. Most of the students hesitated to express their opinion of the colleges as a whole, saying that they could only judge the merits of the college they were attending, though many of them thought that in general all colleges were, in terms of superiority, status and advantages, next only to the university. Four out of the 20 had, however, so changed their opinions that they were now glad that they had gone to a college rather than a university. Three of these students highly eulogized the colleges they were attending, saying that their colleges enjoyed good reputation, that lectures were of high level, lecturers were friendly and sympathetic, and that they could get adequate material in their subjects. Post-graduates, being in smaller numbers, as they were, enjoyed more freedom and privileges. The remaining three students who were happy at their college also praised the good teaching, the approachability of the staff and the congenial social climate. The main dislikes of these students were the roll call at lectures, lack of cultural amenities, dull buildings, and lack of friends from the other sex.

Eight of the 20 students showed largely unfavourable attitudes. They complained mostly about the teaching and about the social life and curricular facilities. They thought the lecturer's knowledge was outdated and the lectures boring. They bemoaned the lack of tutorials, lack of inspiring climate and the fact that there would be a non-university (done at a college) degree. Their general feeling was that a post-graduate degree in a college (outside the university) was of a lower status, and that they in the college had to work harder owing to lack of academic and library facilities that their counterparts in the university enjoyed. They disdained the fact that there was no liaison between their lecturers and the examiners (as was the case in the case of the post-graduates' courses at the university), and that, therefore, their lecturers could give them no guidance on the questions likely to be asked in the examination.

When asked the question "Do you think the colleges, or the universities, or both should expand to admit increasing number of students who wish to do a degree these days," about a quarter of them thought that both should expand, a little more than a quarter that the colleges should expand, and a half thought the universities should take in more students. Those favouring college expansion were of the view that in college individual attention was paid and that it catered for the slower worker who was not up to university standard. Those favouring university expansion felt that colleges should concentrate on graduate courses only and that at college a post-graduate student feels second-class.

Of those favouring university expansion only three were doing arts or social science courses; conversely, the majority of those who think colleges or both colleges and universities should expand were doing science courses.

Thus, on the whole, the majority of these students (especially those during arts or social science courses) retain a largely unfavourable attitude towards doing a post-graduate degree at a college. Some students who do not show such attitude favour college for the individual attention, friendly staff and aid to the slower worker which the college provides.

Sixty-five per cent of the students doing arts or science courses, who were questioned after one year at a college, had applied for university compared with just under a half (38 per cent) of those doing science courses. All students were asked whether or not they now felt that they would have preferred to go to university or to a college; 63 per cent of those doing arts or social sciences would have preferred to go to a university compared with 42 per cent of those doing sciences. They were also asked if their preference had changed since being at a college. The answers (in total only) are given in Table 3.

Table 3
Whether students would prefer to have gone to a University or College

Now preference	*Percentage*	*Earlier Preference*	*Percentage*
University	59	University	70
College	23	College	15
No preference	16	No preference	13
No answer	2	No answer	2
Total	100		100

A change of opinion, though slight, has taken place, though it has been in favour of college rather than *vice versa*. This ties in with the fact that whereas just over half the students found their college much as they expected, 25 per cent had found it better than expected compared with 18 per cent who had found it worse than expected.

The students in this sample were asked, as in the case of the first sample, the advantages and disadvantages of a college compared with a university. Similar proportions thought there were either no advantages (25 per cent) or no disadvantages (9 per cent). Some advantages had assumed greater importance and others had declined. Fewer students now thought the college provided more individual attention (though this was still one of the most frequently stated advantages) and more students stressed the fact that they were provided with ample material in the subject. Lesser students found the staff more informal and friendly. The most frequently stated advantages are shown in Table 4.

Table 4
Advantages of a College Compared with a University
(Factors Stated Most Frequently)

	Percentage*
More individual attention because of smaller classes	16
Provided ample material in the subject	11
More informal and friendly staff	11
Students encouraged and helped	11
More freedom and less curbs	10
Better teaching	9
Lesser non-academic activities	9

* The total from which these percentages are calculated is the total number of students who saw any advantages.

As expected, the number of disadvantages mentioned increased. The most important disadvantages seen by the students were almost similar to those that were found by the sample questioned at the beginning of their first year. The only noticeable difference was that "less qualified staff' swept to the top of the list, being mentioned by nearly 35 per cent of those who stated any disadvantages. (See Table 5).

Table 5
Disadvantages of a College Compared with a University
(Factors stated most frequently)

	Percentage*
Less qualified staff	35
Inadequate library facilities	24
Lack of social and cultural life	16
Less prestigious degree	10
Inadequate hostel accommodation	8
Lack of facilities	7

* The total from which these percentages are calculated is the total number of students who saw a disadvantage.

Conclusion

From an exploratory study of this nature only tentative conclusions can be drawn. Perhaps more information is required about individual colleges and their post-graduate courses, in order to discover to what extent students' attitudes, correlate with such factors as the degree of professor-student contact, the extent to which individual attention is paid, the degree of freedom provided to students and the like. Broadly, however, it is evident that where the college is seen to perform a function distinct from the university, the attitudes of students tend to be more favourable. The college is least favoured where the comparisons with universities are most obvious – for example, in the cultural and social life, the academic atmosphere, and the library facilities.

Perhaps university is a sanctum sanctorum of the elite, intellectual if not economic or intellectual and economic together, who bask in the sunshine of dialectics and intellectual gymnastics spiced with a socio-cultural panorama in the leisurely and generously free environs that are not destined for the less sophisticated and the less endowed, who must wriggle through the drab and dreary path of non-intellectual, competitive exercises dulled by a conspicuous void of things cultural in the temporal and deliberately restrained climate of the college.

43. STUDENT ATTITUDES AND SCHOLASTIC PERFORMANCE

Abstract

An educational problem that occasions deep concern among teacher educators is whether students' attitudes toward school are related, as they should be, to their academic performance. In a critical and experimental study aimed at examining this relationship, 320 ninth class students (162 boys, 158 girls) were subjected to two questionnaires that assessed attitudes toward their schools. IQ's achievement test scores (examination marks), and course grades were collected. Each teacher judged each of his students' overall satisfaction with school. The results show that the correlations between students' attitude (or satisfaction) scores and scholastic scores were negligible, that there were no sex differences, that the teachers' judgements were better than chance but that they related more closely to the students' academic record than to the latter's expressed attitudes, and that the students are satisfied most with the schoolwork and activities, but least with their teachers. Lack of relationship between satisfaction and success in school raises many eyebrows among teacher educators.

Attitudes reflect satisfaction or dissatisfaction. Satisfaction and success go together. Successful people appear satisfied, and unsuccessful people dissatisfied, when asked about the conditions surrounding their achievements. In school, students who are doing well might express contentment when asked to describe their school experience, and those who are doing poorly might express discontentment. In other words, scholastic performance and attitude toward school are, at least logically, related to each other. Surprisingly, however, educational research has not yet verified this contention. Indeed, several researchers (Diedrich, 1966; Jackson and Getzels, 1959; Malpass, 1953; Tenenbaum, 1944; Tschechtelin, Hipskind, and Remmers, 1940) have shown that scholastic success and attitudes toward school are typically unrelated to each other. If further research also demonstrates that success (as shown by high academic achievement) and satisfaction in school (as shown by attitudes toward school) are not closely related, it should provoke anxious thinking among teacher educators and researchers alike.

Is scholastic performance linked to attitudes (which may vary from satisfaction to dissatisfaction) toward school? Are teachers sensitive to differences in their students' attitudes toward school? Do teachers expect that good performance and satisfaction in the case of their students are related? The present study is designed to answer these questions.

Method and Procedure

A total of 320 ninth class students of five schools in a predominantly Punjabi, working-class suburb of Patiala (10 classes located in 5 schools; N = 162 boys, 158 girls) served as the subjects (Ss). They were randomly chosen from a total of 660 students (340 boys and 320 girls).

The pupils' mean IQ, as measured by the Lorge-Thorndike Intelligence Test Non-Verbal, form A, Level 5 (1957) was 101, with a standard deviation of 8.4. The 10 ninth class teachers (6 men, 4 women) also participated in the study by judging how satisfied each student was with his experiences in school.

At the close of the school term, the investigator administered two attitude questionnaires to the students during regular class periods. To ensure frank and truthful answers, Ss were assured that their responses would not be shown to their teachers or to anyone else connected with their schools. The two questionnaires were:

1. The Student Attitude Scale (KSAS). This was an attitude scale developed some years ago (Kakkar, 1966) and designed to elicit responses concerning general satisfaction or dissatisfaction with four aspects of school life: The school as such, teachers, schoolwork and future expectations from school. The test-retest reliability of the scale was 0.69. It contained 40 descriptive statements, each followed by five possible responses: fully agree, agree, undecided, disagree, and fully disagree. These responses reflected very favourable, favourable, neutral, unfavourable, and very unfavourable attitude respectively. A student's response to each item was scored 4,3,2,1, or 0 depending on the degree to which his reply reflected a positive attitude toward his school. Thus, the possible range of scores was from 0 to 160. A score value was multiplied by the number of times a statement was mentioned in a grouping such as "agree" or "disagree," *i.e.* multiplying 30 by 3 if a statement has been mentioned by 30 students in the "agree" column. The multiplicands in all the five columns were then totalled to determine the score value of each statement.

The mean scores for the sample of ninth class pupils were 106.9 for boys and 117.3 for girls. Standard deviations were 16.5 and 11.8 for boys and girls respectively. Test-retest reliability was .82. The following are sample items:

9. My school is an attractive place for me.
17. My teachers take personal interest in me.
30. The work done in my school gives me inspiration.
38. School provides us training for social life.

2. The Michigan Student Questionnaire (shortened version), developed (Flanders, 1965) to assess students' attitudes towards their present teachers and schoolwork. It contained 37 statements, each followed by four possible replies: strongly disagree, disagree, agree, and strongly agree, a student's response to each item being scored 4,3,2, or 1 respectively, showing the degree of positive attitude toward his school and his teacher. Thus the possible range of scores was from 37 to 148. The mean scores for the sample of ninth class pupils were 103.4 for boys and 112.8 for girls. Standard deviations were 15.6 and 11.9 for boys and girls respectively. Test reliability for the total sample, based on a variation of the Kuder-Richardson formula appropriate for weighted scores (Ferguson, 1951), was .74. The following are sample items:

12. What we learn in this class makes one want to learn new things.

16. This teacher certainly knows how to teach.

23. I really like this class.

The correlation between responses to the Student Attitude Scale (KSAS) and the Michigan Student Questionnaire was .89. Thus the relationship between the two questionnaires is high enough to justify the use of both in a study of students' attitudes.

Teachers' judgements of student attitudes towards school were gathered personally from the 10 ninth class teachers who were requested to assemble for a two-hour session on a holiday. The teachers, firstly, were shown sample items from the Student Attitude Scale (KSAS) and were asked to predict how their students might respond to the statements in the scale; this was done to train the teachers in understanding how a student's response reflected satisfaction or dissatisfaction with his school experience. Then each teacher was given a list of his students and instructed to divide the group into three sub-groups by classifying his students into three levels of satisfaction: "most satisfied," "satisfied," and "least satisfied." He was then led to separate from within the two extreme groups a smaller number of students (one-fourth of each group) who seemed to be "very satisfied" and "very dissatisfied." Thus, each student's attitudes were classified by his teacher into one of the five categories *i.e.* "most satisfied," "very satisfied," "average," "very dissatisfied," "most dissatisfied." In each classroom the approximate fractions of students in the five categories were: 1/12,1/4,1/3,1/4, 1/12. To treat the ratings quantitatively, the values 15,12,10,8 and 5 were assigned to the five groupings, the highest value representing the attitudes of students whom the teachers had classified as "most satisfied."

Scholastic performance consisted of two measures, *i.e.* (i) achievement scores in English, Mathematics, Social Studies and Science in the final (external) examination, (ii) grades as given by the S's teacher in the above four subjects.

In order to determine the attitudinal statements favoured most and those favoured least, the statements in the Student Attitude Scale (KSAS) were ranked in a descending order of their favourableness on the basis of the score value of each statement.

Results

The findings with respect to the relationship between attitudes toward school and measures of scholastic performance are shown in Table 1.

Table 1
Correlations Between Student Attitudes and Scholastic Performance

Scholastic Performance	Student Attitudes			
	Student Attitude Scale (KSAS)		Michigan Student Questionnaire	
	Boys	Girls	Boys	Girls
Examination Scores				
English	.14	.13	.09	.08
Mathematics	.19*	.18*	.12	.15
Social Studies	.16	.11	.07	.09
Science	.18*	.19*	.13	.14
Teacher Grades				

English	.13	.12	.06	.08
Mathematics	.16	.18*	.09	.11
Social Studies	.09	.10	.10	.06
Science	.11	.13	.09	.09

* p < .05.
N = 162 boys, 158 girls.

Some features of this table are notable. Firstly, all the correlation coefficients are small, though some of them are significant. Secondly, the magnitude of correlation coefficient (r's) with the examination scores is the same as that with teachers' grades. Thirdly, the coefficients by and large are higher in the case of the Student Attitude Scale (KSAS) than in that of the Michigan Student Questionnaire, though the differences are not significant. Fourthly, although most of the coefficients are higher when examination scores are a measure of scholastic performance than when teacher grades serve as that measure, the differences are trivial. Fifthly, there are no significant sex differences.

Thus, these data tend to strengthen the results of other investigators who found no significant relationship between attitudes toward school and scholastic achievement. Success-satisfaction relationship in the context of school persists in being elusive.

Table 2 contains: (i) correlations between the teachers' judgements of students' satisfaction and the scores derived from the students' responses to the two questionnaires, (ii) correlations between the teachers' judgements and the two measures of students' scholastic performance, and (iii) correlations between the teachers' judgements and the students' IQ.

Table 2
Correlations Between Teachers' Judgements and Measures of Student Attitudes, Scholastic Performance, and Intelligence

Students	Student Attitudes		Scholastic Performance				IQ
	Student Attitude Scale (KSAS)	Michigan Student Questionnaire	English	Mathematics	Social Studies	Science	
Boys	.35	.29	.56	.58	.51	53	.52
Girls	.31	.28	.45	.46	.41	.59	.47

N = 162 boys, 158 girls.
p < .01 in case of all the r's.

The findings reveal that students' satisfaction with school is fairly visible to teachers and that it can be judged by the teachers with greater-than-chance accuracy. They also show that teachers tend to expect achievement and satisfaction to be more closely related than the two, in fact, are. Evidently, the correlations in Table 2 reveal that when teachers resort to judge how a student will respond to an attitude questionnaire, they emerge nearer to describing how well the student is in his academic achievement than to how he feels about his experience in school.

Thus, these data tend to indicate that teachers are fairly sensitive to differences in their students' attitudes toward school, and that teachers expect that good performance and satisfaction are related.

Of the 10 statements favoured most, as many as 6 show attitude toward schoolwork, 2 toward future expectations from school, 1 toward school as such, and 1 toward schoolteachers. The students seem to be satisfied most with the work and activities in the school. Of the 10 statements favoured least, as many as 4 show attitude toward teachers, 3 toward future expectations from school, 2 toward school as such, and 1 toward schoolwork. The students seem to be least satisfied with their teachers and very pessimistic about what the school can do for their future.

Discussion

The relationship between scholastic performance and attitude toward school, or that between success and satisfaction in school, though theoretically and even logically inevitable and close, is unexpectedly absent or negligible. There might be several factors responsible for this provocative finding, provocative because if success or achievement in school does not determine attitude or satisfaction, teacher educators must pause to find: "what else will" and "how else to create satisfaction," or "what conditions in or out of school contribute toward satisfaction or dissatisfaction with school", or "is scholastic success a goal worth aiming at when it cannot yield satisfaction with school."

First, and most probable, the range and intensity of student attitudes are not as great as responses to the questionnaire indicate and, hence, are not too potent to affect behaviour. Students may not be hating or loving school but, instead, be feeling rather neutral about their school experience. Second, teachers may be behaving in ways that effectively undermine the natural connection that exists between attitudes and achievement. In most classrooms, students have to willy nilly master the minimal curricular objectives whether they like it or not. Assignments are clearly defined, deadlines are set, and frequent checks are made by teachers to verify whether the work is being done as required. Third, over-ambitious parents, in a bid to make their child pile up achievements or successes, irrespective of his capacities or interests, may behave in a manner that weakens whatever link between attitudes and achievement still survives. Fourth, several classroom conditions such as domineering teacher, lack of psychological safety, absence of psychological freedom, requirement of being obedient, compliant or conformist and the like.

That the teachers, parents and the classroom climate may offset or counteract the natural consequences of differences in students' attitudes, or that these formidable elements in the students' lives perhaps snap the legitimate connection between success and satisfaction, may pique teacher educators and stimulate them to reform the situation.

References

1. Died rich, R. "Teacher perceptions as related to teacher-student similarity and student satisfaction with school." Unpublished Doctoral Dissertation, University of Chicago, 1966.
2. Flanders, N.A. "Teacher influence, pupil attitudes, and achievement." Cooperative Research Monograph, No. 12 (OE-25040), Washington, D.C.: United States Government Printing Office, 1965.
3. Jackson, P.W. and Getzels, J.W. "Psychological Health and Classroom Functioning: A Study of dissatisfaction with school among adolescents," *Journal of Educational Psychology*, 1959, 50, 295-300.
4. Kakkar, S.B. "Student Attitude Scale (KSAS)," State College of Education, Patiala, 1966.
5. Lorge, Irving, and Thorndike, Robert L. "The Lorge-Thorndike Intelligence Tests." Houghton Mifflin Company, Boston, 1957.
6. Malpass, L.F. "Some relationships between students' perceptions of school and their achievement." *Journal of Educational Psychology*, 1953, 44, 475-482.

44. SOCIAL ACCEPTANCE AS RELATED TO SCHOOL TENURE

Jack Frymier, assisted by Dr. Bernard Corman and Dr. Arthur Combs (1), found that incoming members may be rejected by an established group simply because they are not a part of the group for any period of time. It may be interesting to determine whether or not acceptance or rejection is related in any way to school tenure (length of time the students attend the school together).

The present study was intended to determine if there was any difference between the extent to which members of these groups were (a) accepted or rejected, (b) singled out as being members of a dissident group hankering for power, and (c) singled out as isolates.

Method

The school in which this investigation was conducted had an enrolment of approximately 1,200 students from class I through XI. In class I through VIII there were two sections of 40 students each, but from IX through XI there were four sections of that size for each class level. As the number of students was doubled at the IX class level, each up-coming VIII class section was split into two groups of 20 students each, and an additional 20 students from other local schools were added to these groups to make four sections of 40 each.

For the purpose of this study the students who had been admitted in this school at the VIII or IX class level were designated as "juniors", while those who had been there in this school since their early elementary classes were designated as "seniors".

A sociometric questionnaire having the following questions was administered to six of the twelve sections in classes IX through XI. In all 223 students were involved, 102 "seniors" and 121 "juniors":

(1) Name the two students you would prefer to sit with in your class.

(2) Name any students you would prefer not to sit with in your class.

(3) Name the two students you would like to work with in your class.

(4) Name any students you would prefer not to work with in your class.

(5) Do you think there is a dissident group in your class, whose members are always hankering for power? If so, name them here.

(6) Name any students you feel are neglected or ignored by others.

The students were instructed that they must, in any case, answer questions 1 and 3, and that they may answer questions 2,4,5 and 6 only when they felt that way about some particular classmate.

When a student was named in response to question 1 or 3, he was assumed to be enjoying social acceptance to a degree. When he was named in response to question 2 or 4, he was considered to be subjected to rejection to a degree. Again, those named in response to question 5 were assumed to be enjoying extreme acceptance in the situation and the ones mentioned against question 6 were recognised for their extreme rejection. Thus it was assumed that questions 1 to 4 reflected peer acceptance or rejection, while questions 5 and 6 indicated students' recognition of these factors within their class groups.

Scoring

A student whose name was mentioned in response to question 1 or 3 was given one plus score for each mention (plus taken as acceptance). A student whose name was mentioned against question 2 or 4 was awarded one-minus score for each mention (minus taken as rejection). The scores of those four questions were added together for each student and the mean score and standard deviation for the "seniors" group and "juniors" group calculated. Whether this acceptance or rejection was by a "senior" or by a "junior" was also recorded.

The number of times a student's name was mentioned in response to question 5 was noted and the mean scores and standard deviation for the "seniors" and "juniors" groups calculated. This was also done for question 6 regarding the neglected. Thus the scores for questions 5 and 6 were all positive numbers, while the scores for questions 1 to 4 were both positive and negative numbers.

Results

The results of these computations are tabulated below:

Table 1
Acceptance and Rejection of "Seniors" and "Juniors"
(Derived from Responses to Questions 1 to 4)

Group		Mean Score	Standard Deviation
Seniors	....	+2.32	3.92
juniors	....	–0.12	5.40

N.B. -- Acceptance is indicated by plus score and rejection by minus score.

Further analysis of the data showed that "seniors" accepted other persons within the "senior" group (mean = +1.64), but rejected "juniors" (mean = –.92). Conversely, "juniors" accepted "seniors" (mean = +.78) and other "juniors" (mean = +.37). This tends to reveal that those students (seniors) who had attended school together for a longer period of time were accepted to a greater degree than were those (juniors) who had been together in the school for a smaller duration. Besides, rejection came mostly from the "senior" group rather than from both groups impartially.

Table 2
Degree to which Students were Singled out as being Members of a Dissident Group Hankering for Power (Derived from Responses to Question 5)

Group		Mean Score	Standard Score
Seniors	....	+3.55	3.61
Juniors	....	+1.03	1.60

Members of the senior's group were pointed out as being members of power-hungry subgroup (mean = 3.55) more frequently than were the "juniors" (mean = 1.03). Such a distinct and significant difference seems to have been caused by the fact that there was perhaps something fundamentally different in the way these students were functioning within their own sections.

Table 3
Degree to which Students Figured as Isolates
(Derived from Responses to Question 6)

Group		Mean Score	Standard Deviation
Seniors	....	0.86	2.41
Juniors	....	2.73	4.30

"Juniors" were singled out as isolates (mean = 2.73) far more frequently than were members of the "seniors" group (mean= .86).

Further analysis of the data showed that, of the ten students enjoying highest social acceptance, six were "seniors" and four were "juniors", whereas, of the ten students subjected to severest rejection, two were "seniors" and eight were "juniors".

Eight of the ten students, most frequently singled out as being members of a power-hungry group, were from the "senior" group and two were "juniors".

Lastly, of the ten students mentioned most often as isolates, one was a "senior" and nine were "juniors".

Discussion

That "juniors" were rejected far more than "seniors" echoes the finding arrived at by Jack Frymier (1). That it takes time to win social acceptance and that an established group shows considerable reticence in welcoming new members to its fold are perhaps fair conclusions emanating from this study. Those who accept may need time and opportunity to understand, judge and later be convinced of the merit of an incoming member, and they may tend to avoid the risk involved in accepting the later straightaway and hence perhaps the said conclusions.

Another phenomenon suggested by the study is that when a considerable number of persons enter an established group simultaneously, certain forces may be generated within the situation which leads to the original members uniting into a stronger and more solid unit, accepting their own members, but barring out new incoming members without sufficient consideration. This acceptance and rejection seem to stay and also seems to be invariably noticed by the members of both groups. Natural tendency of a group to become highly integrated and cohesive when faced with the threat of infiltration from outside may be the basis of this phenomenon.

Members of the older group forming dissident subgroups for seeking power over others may be the sequel to the unwelcome entry of new-comers and a reaction to the real or imagined fear that the juniors might interfere with or even share the powers and privileges of the seniors. Similar reasons appear to account for the finding that juniors, by and large, were isolated.

References

1. Jack Frymier— Acceptance and Rejection as related to length of school attendance *Journal of Educational Research,* Vol. 53, No. 3, Nov. 1959, pp.112-114.

45. SOCIAL ACCEPTANCE AND SCHOOL SUCCESS

Socio-metrically, popular children are well-adjusted, dependable and friendly. Besides, they tend to succeed in schoolwork. Sociometry provides a means of studying social acceptability which the present study attempts to assess.

Moreno's Sociometric test consists in an individual choosing his friends from his immediate group of which he is a member. The individual in this test is asked to reveal the members of the group with whom he would prefer to associate in one or more given situations. Greater understanding of pupils' needs and a basis to form more effective class groups are the chief advantages that the teacher can well utilise as a result of a sociometric test. The adolescent is gradually being weaned from parents and family control in favour of the social milieu made up by his classmates; consequently acceptance by the group is highly significant for him. He can do little to affect his own score in the sociometric test and hence the accuracy of such a test.

Purpose

(i) To organise and quantify children's social acceptance score-amongst the members of their own class with a view to understanding the status and changes in their friendship patterns, so that the teacher could use this understanding to organise more effective class-groups in various situations and to provide for the isolates some specific social experiences within their own sphere of competence.

(ii) To ascertain whether more popular children succeed more in schoolwork.

Hypothesis

Children look for friendly relations with others of their own group, this being their essential developmental need. They may need the same or different friends in different situations. Those who succeed in their schoolwork form good social relationships with their peers.

Method

Thirty-seven children (17 boys and 20 girls) of 4th standard, age group 10, of Junior Model School, Jullundur were asked to make their first, second and third choices on these three items:

(i) Your very best friends in the class.
(ii) Those with whom in the class you would like to sit on the same desk.
(iii) Those whom in the class you would prefer as companions in a work project.

They were assured that no one would come to know of their choices which were required to help the school in making more congenial groups for different purposes.

Sincere answers obtained from all the children in the class were charted. The choices were graphically represented on sociometric tables. In determining social acceptance score the first choices were multiplied by three, second choices by two, and third choices by one. The children who were from an average to above average socio-economic strata of urban part of Jullundur had attended their previous standards in the same school.

The validity and significance of the social acceptance scores were checked and interpreted in the light of similar information obtained from the class teacher. Validity coefficient, through Rank-Difference method, was calculated between the teacher's rankings of pupils' social acceptance and social acceptance scores derived from the sociometric test.

The assumption that children who succeed in their schoolwork also succeed in establishing social relationships was tested by computing Rank-Difference Coefficients between the sociometric scores and school success as derived from their aggregate achievement scores in three previous tests. Rank-Difference Correlation was also computed between teachers' rankings of pupils' social acceptance and the pupils' success in schoolwork.

Data

Tabular analysis of the three choices: Tables (1a) to (1f) represent 1st, 2nd, 3rd choice of boys and girls on the three items. The alphabets A to T represent the pupils tested. The social acceptance score is derived as mentioned in the method above. Items 1, 2, 3 are the questions on which the pupils were asked to make their choices. Tables 2, 3, 4, 5 quantify the children's social acceptance scores and their relationships with school success and with teacher's ranking of the children's popularity.

Findings

Table 1a – Boys M, G, and O–the stars-are most popular. M enjoys maximum social acceptance. In popularity they are in this order:

M-G-O-BE-CI-NP-A-L-DHQ-FJK (No dash between the letters showing that persons are equal on social acceptance score)

F, J and K aspire to friendship relations with other boys. but since no other children choose them as best friends, they are regarded as isolates in friendship patterns. D, H and Q are least popular as they were chosen by no more than one boy each. The mutual friends are: A & C, B & E, B & I, E & I, A & M, G & H, G & M, D & P, G & P, L & O, N & O. B, E and I form a clique.

Table 1b – In their preference for the classmates with whom they would like to sit on the same desk, the boys again choose most M, O, and G; M excels all others in popularity. In social acceptance score on this item, they are in the order: M-O-G-E-B-CINP-L-A-H-KQ-DFJ. D, F & J aspire to sit on the same desk with others; but since none prefers to sit with them, they are found as isolates. No more than one boy likes to sit with K & Q. Those who mutually like to sit with each other are B & E, G & H, B & I, E & I, A & M, G & M, K & M, L & O, L & N, E & O, N & O, G & P; H & P. B, E, I, & G, H, P are two cliques.

Table 1c – In the boys' preferences for companions in a work project, G, M & O are accepted most. G excels all others in popularity here. In social acceptance score on this item, they stand in the order: G - MO - B - E - P - CN - AI - LQ - DH - FJK. F, J & K want others to be their companions in a work project; but since none chooses them as companions, they stand isolated. D & H are chosen by no more than one boy Those who mutually choose each other as a companion are A & C, B & E, A & M, G & M, O & N, O & E, D & P, G & P, M & P. Amongst the boys G, M & O are highest on social acceptance score and F, J, K are isolates, while D, H are least popular.

Table 1d – Girls G & N - the stars - are most popular; G enjoys maximum social acceptance. F and H aspire to friendship relations with other girls; but since no other girls choose them as best friends, they are found as isolates in friendship patterns. D, I, K,

L, S and T are least popular-though in equal degrees-as they were chosen by no more than three girls each. In popularity the girls stand in this order: G - N - B- R- AM- C - JO - EPQ - DIKLST - FH. The mutual friends are B & D, A & M, G & I, D & N, G & N, M & N, A & O, C & O, G & O, I & Q, E & R, P & R, J & T.

Table 1e – In choosing classmates to sit with on the same desk, N is chosen most of all followed by G and B. In social acceptance score on this item they stand in this order: N-G-B-M-R-A - CD - O - H - EIJKT - LPQ - FS. F and S wish to sit with others, but since none wishes to sit with them, they are found as isolates. L, P, Q, F and S are least preferred as no more than 2 or 3 girls want to sit with them. Those who mutually choose each other to sit with on the same desk are B & D, B & G, B & N, A & M, A & O, C & O, D & N, E & R, G & N, H & K, I & Q, L & M. B, G, Nn, D form a clique.

Table 1f – In choosing classmates for companions in a work project, G and N are chosen most of all, though in equal degree. In social acceptance score on this item, they stand in this order: GN-BM-P-A-IR-D-O-CJ-EHLQI-S-FK. F & K want others to be their companions in a work project, but since none chooses them as companions, they stand isolated. F, K, S, E, H, L, Q, T are least popular as they are chosen by nil to two classmates only. Those who mutually choose each other here are A & M, A & O, B & D, B & N, C & O, G & I, G & N, G & S, Q & I, J & T, L & M, P & R, Q & R.

Among the girls G & N are highest on social acceptance score, and F, H, S, K are isolates while L, P, Q, E, H, S and T are least popular.

Table 2 – On aggregating the social acceptance score, boys stand in this order of popularity: M-G-O-E-B-C-IP-N-A-L - HQ- D - K - FJ, which confirms the finding under Table lc.

Table 3 – In case of boys, r's between Sociometric Acceptance (SA), Teachers' Ranking of social acceptance (TA) and School success (SS) are:

	TA	SS
SA	.69	.73
TA	x	.85

Teachers' ranking of the boys' social acceptance and sociometric acceptance of boys show fair correlation. Teachers' ranking of the boys' social acceptance shows greater correlation with the boys' school success than the boys' sociometric acceptance. Greater social acceptance generally leads to more school success. Teachers seem to judge the boys' social acceptance more accurately than the sociometric test.

Table 4 – On aggregating the social acceptance scores, girls stand in this order of popularity: N - G - B - M - AR - CIP - DO - J - E - QT- L - HK - S - F, which confirms the finding under Table 1f.

Table 5 – In case of girls, r's between Sociometric Acceptance (SA), Teachers' Ranking of Social Acceptance (TA), and School Success (SS) are:

	TA	SS
SA	.71	.50
TA	x	.64

Teachers' ranking of the girls' social acceptance and sociometric acceptance of girls shows greater correlation than the similar correlation in case of boys. Social acceptance found by sociometric test shows lesser correlation than that ranked by teachers with school success. That greater social acceptance generally leads to more school success, and those teachers judge the boys' social acceptance more accurately than the sociometric test are true both in the case of boys and girls.

Conclusions regarding the sample under study

1. Most of the children, both boys and girls, aspire for social acceptance or friendly relations amidst their immediate group.
2. The degree of social acceptance or popularity varies from one individual to another.
3. A few stars on top of social acceptance score and a few isolates at the bottom border round the majority of moderate social mixers.
4. Mutual friends and small cliques are a characteristic feature of children's group.
5. Those chosen as friends on the 1st item tend to be chosen to sit with on the same desk or to be companions in a work project. This is more truer about the stars than about others. Isolates are not chosen on any one of the three items generally. Thus the children tend to choose the same friends in different situations.
6. No boy has named any girl on any of the three items; the reverse is also true. This is evident of the boy-boy and girl-girl friendships which alone are characteristic of our social life.

7. There are no sex differences in matters of aspiring for social acceptance or friendly relatives, and of choosing the same friends to sit with or to make companions in work-projects.
8. In general, children, both boys and girls, who succeed in their schoolwork tend to establish good social relationships and greater social acceptance than those who enjoy less school success.
9. Socio-metrically popular children tend to be characterised as fairly popular by their teachers as well.

Recommendations

The validity and significance of sociometric popularity having been checked and interpreted in the light of information obtained from teacher's observation, the teacher of the children in this study was advised (i) to provide, for the isolates and the least popular, specific kinds of social experience, more interaction-opportunities for developing friendly peer relations, guidance to increase their social attractiveness by improving their skills and social standards as well as building up their confidence in friendship rules, (ii) to consider the desirability of cliques in his classroom, (iii) in the matter of looking at isolates and cleavages to consider all such factors as religious and cultural backgrounds, intelligence, personal development and appearance, length of time in the group, and socio-economic status.

References

1. Guilford, J.P.: "Psychometric Methods", New York: McGraw—Hill, 1954.
2. Groulund, N.E.: "Sociometry in the Classroom", N.Y. Harper, 1959.
3. Arden N. Frandsen: "Educational Psychology", McGraw-Hill, 1961, pp. 493-495.
4. N.M. Downie. "Fundamentals of measurement". Oxford Univ. Press, N.Y. 1961, pp. 293-297.
5. Noll, V.H., and Noll, R.R.: "Readings in Educational Psychology", Macmillan Coy. N.Y. 1962, pp. 381-388.
6. Junn C. Nunnally, Jr.: Tests and Measurement". McGraw-Hill, 1959, pp. 391-393.

Table 1 a
Item 1

Chooser	A	B	C	D	E	F	G	H	I	J	K	L	M	N	O	P	Q
A			1				3						2				
B					2				1						3		
C	2						3								1		
D			2										1			3	
E		2							1			3					
F		1							2						3		
G								3					2			1	
H							1						2			3	
I	3	1			2												
J			3				2						1				
K							2						1				3
L		3												2	1		
M	3		2				1										
N		3			1										2		
O					3							2		1			
P				3			1						2				
Q					2								3		1		
Social Acceptance Score	4	10	8	1	10	0	15	1	8	0	0	3	18	5	13	5	1

Table 1 b
Item 2

Chooser	A	B	C	D	E	F	G	H	I	J	K	L	M	N	O	P	Q
A			2				3						1				
B					2				1						3		
C							2						1		3		
D				2									1			3	
E		3							2						1		
F		2			3										1		
G								3					2			1	
H							1						2			3	
I		1			2								3				
J			3				2						1				
K							2						1				3
L		3												2	1		
M	2						1				3						

	A	B	C	D	E	F	G	H	I	J	K	L	M	N	O	P	Q
N					2							3			1		
O					3							2		1			
P							1	3									
Q		3			2										1		
Social Acceptance Score	2	8	5	0	10	0	16	2	5	0	1	3	22	5	17	5	1

Table 1 c
Item 3

Chooser	A	B	C	D	E	F	G	H	I	J	K	L	M	N	O	P	Q
A			1				3						2				
B					2			1							3		
C	3													2	1		
D			2										1			3	
E		1						3							2		
F		1										2		3			
G								3					2			1	
H							1						3			2	
I	3	1			2												
J			2				1						3				
K							2						1				3
L		2												3	1		
M	3						1									2	
N					1										2		3
O					2			3						1			
P				3			1						2				
Q		3			2										1		
Social Acceptance Score	3	12	7	1	11	0	15	6	0	0	0	2	14	7	14	8	2

Table 1d
Item 1

Chooser	A	B	C	D	E	F	G	H	I	J	K	L	M	N	O	P	Q	R	S	T
A			2										1		3					
B				3			2							1						
C		3												2	1					
D		1					3							2						
E			3				2											1		

F					2											3		1		
G									1					3			2			
H											1	3							2	
I							1							3			2			
J		2												3						1
K		3					1							2						
L	2												1	3						
M	1											2		3						
N				2			1						3							
O	3	2	1																	
P										2			3					1		
Q							2		1					3						
R					2											1				3
S		3					1							2						
T	2									1					3					
Social Acceptance Score	8	10	6	3	4	0	19	0	6	5	3	3	8	17	5	4	4	9	3	3

Table 1e
Item 2

Chooser	A	B	C	D	E	F	G	H	I	J	K	L	M	N	O	P	Q	R	S	T
A			2										1		3					
B				3			2							1						
C		3												2	1					
D		2											3	1						
E		2											3					1		
F					3													2		
G		2											3	1						
H				3							1			2						
I							1							3			2			
J			3	2			1													
K								3						2					1	
L	3												1	2						
M	1										2			3						
N		1		3			2													
O	3	2	1																	
P		2		3										1						
Q							2		1									3		
R					3									1		2				

S					3		1											2		
T	2									1					3					
Social Acceptance Score	7	14	6	6	3	0	15	4	3	3	3	2	9	25	5	2	2	8	0	3

Table 1 f
Item 3

Chooser	A	B	C	D	E	F	G	H	I	J	K	L	M	N	O	P	Q	R	S	T
A							1						2		3					
B				2									1	3						
C							2								1	3				
D		1					3							2						
E				3									1	2						
F								3								1		2		
G									2					1					3	
H		1							3							2				
I							1							3			2			
J	1			3																2
K							1	3						2						
L	2						3						1							
M	2										3			1						
N		1					2						3							
O	3	2	1																	
P				3										2				1		
Q							2		1									3		
R					2							3				1				
S							1						2	3						
T				3						1				2						
Social Acceptance Score	8	11	3	6	2	0	20	2	6	3	0	2	14	19	4	9	2	6	1	2

Table 2
Social Acceptance Score–Boys

Boys	Item No.			Total Score	Rank
	1	2	3		
A	4	2	5	11	10
B	10	8	12	30	5
C	8	5	7	20	6

D	1	0	1	2	14
E	10	10	11	31	4
F	0	0	0	0	16.5
G	15	16	15	46	2
H	1	2	1	4	12.5
I	8	5	5	18	7.5
J	0	0	0	0	16.5
K	0	1	0	1	15
L	3	3	2	8	11
M	18	22	14	54	1
N	5	5	7	17	9
O	13	17	14	44	3
P	5	5	8	18	7.5
Q	1	1	2	4	12.5

Table 3
Social Acceptance and School Success–Boys

Boys	Rank on Sociometric Acceptance	Teacher's Ranking of Social Acceptance	Rank on School success
A	10	11	9
B	5	6	6
C	6	4	3
D	14	10	10
E	4	3	4
F	16.5	15	12
G	2	2	2
H	12.5	8	8
I	7.5	13	16
J	16.5	14	15
K	15	17	13
L	11	7	14
M	1	1	1
N	9	16	17
O	3	12	7
P	7.5	5	5
Q	12.5	9	11

'r' between Sociometric Acceptance and Teacher's Ranking = +.69
'r' between Sociometric Acceptance and School Success = +.75
'r' between Teacher's Ranking and School Success = +.85

Table 4
Social Acceptance Scores–Girls

Girls	Item No. 1	2	3	Total Score	Rank
A	8	7	8	23	5.5
B	10	14	14	38	3
C	6	6	3	15	7.0
D	3	6	5	14	10.5
E	4	3	2	9	13
F	0	0	0	0	20
G	19	15	20	54	2
H	0	4	2	6	17.5
G	19	15	20	54	2
I	6	3	6	15	7.0
J	5	3	3	11	12
K	3	3	0	6	17.5
L	3	2	2	7	16
M	8	9	14	31	4
N	17	25	20	62	1
O	5	5	4	14	10.5
P	4	2	9	15	7.0
Q	4	2	2	8	14.5
R	9	8	6	23	5.5
S	3	0	1	4	19
T	3	3	2	8	14.5

Table 5
Social Acceptance and School Success–Girls

Girls	Rank on Sociometric Acceptance	Teacher's Ranking of Social Acceptance	Rank on School Success
A	5.5	6	2
B	3	1	3
C	7	7	5
D	10.5	14	12
E	13	12	18

F	20	13	8
B	3	1	3
G	2	3	14
I	7	5	11
H	10.5	20	10
J	12	15	15
K	17.5	8	17
L	16	9	7
M	4	4	1
N	1	2	4
O	10.5	11	9
P	7	10	6
Q	14.5	19	20
R	5.5	16	16
S	19	18	19
T	14.5	17	13

'r' between Sociometric Acceptance and Teacher's Ranking = +.71
'r' between Sociometric Acceptance and School Success = +.50
'r' between Teacher's Ranking and School Success = +.64

46. STUDENTS' ATTITUDES TOWARDS SCHOOL LIFE

From the time a child enters school to a few years later he seems to be interested in his school life, probably because school provides him a new place to satisfy his needs. He starts feeling that, besides home, school is a place where things are interesting, attractive and worthwhile. But there occurs a change in his attitudes to the things in school as he advances from 7th and 8th classes towards high school classes. To gauge the types of such changes the present survey was undertaken.

Method

356 students (both boys and girls) in classes III to VI and 290 students (both boys and girls) in classes VII to X of 4 local schools (2 boys schools and 2 girls schools), chosen randomly, were asked to write on a slip what they liked most and what they disliked most in their school. They were asked to say so only about the things, activities or people in school.

The slips were collected in a few minutes and the likes and dislikes classified in a few broad categories. The results are shown in a table on next page (p. 237).

Findings

1. A glance over the table indicates that as children move up through the classes, many of them BECOME less keen about things in schools (subjects, books, talks, teachers), and relatively more interested in recess periods, sports, holidays, students (all of which are things outside the classroom).
2. Though there is an obvious decline in their interest in academic work as the students advance in grades, a considerable number of them retain interest in it *i.e.* whereas 78.5 per cent of the students in classes III–VI mentioned academic subjects or things belonging to academic programme as what they liked most, at the VII–X class level 53.5 per cent mentioned items in this category.
3. The high school children, more often than the younger children, expressed dislike of teachers, the academic programme, discipline, rules and orders.
4. There is no appreciable difference in their attitude towards art activities as the students advance in grades.
5. Both likes and dislikes towards students show increase as the youngsters advance in years.

Discussion

Decline of interest in school, when the students are on the road to adolescence, may be due to such reasons as–adolescence adds to their interests which the school cannot readily fulfil, most adolescent are more critical and less suggestible than they were when they were younger, high school requires of them more academic work and study than the earlier classes, onset of maturity reminds them of downright realities (of which they were not so pointedly aware before) such as being poor and backward in the subject and in academic skills, poor study habits and the like.

Maturity and increasing need to be self-dependent may make adolescents dislike teachers and rules. Strong likes and dislikes towards students are an indication of the adolescents' bid to sustain definite social relations and group loyalties.

The school programme must be comprehensive and attractive so as to satisfy a variety of needs and interests that the adolescents have. Teachers, besides being mature, sympathetic and friendly in their out-look and behaviour must not signify authority and fear.

Table showing percentage of students' extreme likes and dislikes (classified in some categories) in schools

Things in schools	Like most	Dislike most	Like most	Dislike most
Class	III to VI	III to VI	VII to X	VII to X
Age	7-11	7-11	12-16	12-16
No of Students	356	356	290	290
Academic subjects, classroom, wall magazine, library books, talks etc.	78.5	41.6	53.9	46.3
Art, drawing, painting, pictures, dramatics etc.	11.00	5.8	10.5	4.2
Sports, games, play, recess, holidays etc.	5.5	5.9	28.8	3.2
Teachers, discipline, rules, orders etc.	3.5	0.4	0.8	9.0
Students	1.5	4.0	3.8	7.5
Other people and other things	0	0.3	0.8	1.0

N.B. Things irrelevant and those mentioned by too few were discarded.

References

1. Coleman, J.S., 1959. "Academic Achievement and the Structure of Competition." H.E.R.
2. Allen, E.A., I960. "Attitudes of Children and Adolescents in School". Education Research.
3. Jersild, A.T., I960. "Child Psychology". Prentice-Hall.
4. Symonds, P.M. 1942. "Adolescent Fantasy". N.Y.C.U.P.

47. RECREATIONAL INTERESTS OF HIGH AND LOW IQ STUDENTS

Summary

Recreational interests of 62 high and 50 low IQ boys, and 53 high and 60 low IQ girls in the 9th, 10th and 11th classes of higher secondary schools were studied by a checklist of 30 items. IQ 110 and above formed the criterion of high IQ, while IQ 85 and below formed that of low IQ. Preferences of the upper 50 per cent and lowest 50 per cent of the high IQ and the low IQ groups respectively were compared. School activities were more common in high IQ students, both boys and girls. Individual, out-of-doors, and aggressive activities were more popular in low IQ boys. Low IQ girls, like their male counterparts, indulged more in aggressive activities. High IQ girls were conspicuous for their preference of social recreation such as walking together, talking together, eating together, sitting together in restaurants or parties and talking, and even studying together.

Related Research

Smith (6), Lehman and Witty (4), Leach (3), Reeves and Slater (5), Bell (1), Gross (2) and others have surveyed the recreational interests of school children of different IQ ranges. Their general finding is that children of different IQ levels take part in different types of activities. Some of their specific findings are: (i) High IQ students have more mature and wider interests and hobbies than their low IQ counterparts; they also are drawn more towards the school activities. (ii) Dramatics, writing, group discussion, listening to talks, and book reviews attract high IQ students, while social activities are preferred more by low IQ students. (iii) Manual activities, more active and exacting games, and vigorous interests are less preferred by high IQ students.

Method

Government Senior Model Higher Secondary School for Boys and Govt. Girls Higher Secondary School of Jullundur, considered as being fairly typical of schools in the urban sectors of the Punjab State, were chosen for the study. The total population in the two schools was 1,928, and the average IQ of the students was 100.

Of the 563 students in Higher Secondary classes (9th, 10th and 11th), 80 per cent were administered the Lorge-Thorndike Intelligence Test Level 4 Form A Non-verbal. The students of IQ's 110 or above and 90 or below were set apart for the purpose of studying the significant differences in recreational interests between high and low IQ students. Such students comprised approximately the upper 50 per cent (of high IQ group) and the lowest 50 per cent (of low IQ group) of the students who were tested for intelligence. Their actual numbers were 62 high and 50 low IQ boys, and 53 high and 60 low IQ girls.

A checklist consisting of 32 items of recreational interest or activities most popular with the students of these two schools was prepared. These items were: playing Badminton, Basketball, Football, Hockey or Volleyball; going together for walks, shopping or excursions; riding bicycles; eating together in restaurants or sitting together in groups and talking; listening to records or radio, dancing; going to cinemas, playing pranks or playing cards; attending school athletics or other school programmes; participating in school dramatics, discussion groups, talks and red-cross activities; wrestling, boxing or racing; studying together; having parties, sewing, gardening or preparing dishes; swimming, hiking; studying alone, thinking or brooding or going out alone. A column for "any other activities" not covered in the checklist was provided.

The checklist was administered to the students classified according to their IQ levels and the frequency of responses for each item on the checklist determined. The chi-square test of significance was utilised to know whether differences in frequency of response to each item were statistically significant.

Findings

The differences at the five per cent level of confidence, between high IQ and low students in relation to the recreational interests they like were:

All the lowest IQ boys in 9th, 10th and 11th classes participated significantly more frequently in playing football, volleyball, hiking, fighting and riding bicycle, while their more intellectually sophisticated peers played significantly more badminton, attended and participated in more school activities, both curricular and cocurricular.

Class-wise analysis of boys showed that 9th class students of low IQ went for fishing and boating or on other out-of-door errands to a greater degree, while in 10th and 11th classes the same ability group showed greater participation in going to cinemas and eating together in restaurants as well as going for fishing and boating. The 10th and 11th class boys of the high IQ group went for swimming or hiking significantly more often than their low IQ peers. Thus most of the significant differences showed significantly greater participation by the lowest IQ boys.

Lowest IQ girls of all the three classes took part significantly more in playing hockey or football with their classmates, while high IQ girls of these very classes showed significantly greater preferences for playing badminton, going for swimming and excursions, sitting in restaurants and talking, enjoying parties, going to cinemas, attending to and participating in school athletics, dramatics or other school programmes, and studying together.

Class-wise analysis of girls showed that 9th class students of high IQ participated significantly more often with their classmates in going for swimming, eating together in restaurants, going to school athletics and other school programmes. The low IQ girls of the same class had greater interest in playing basketball, going for fishing, and meeting other people. In 10th and 11th classes, the high IQ girls took significantly greater interest in going on excursions or picnics, enjoying parties, and going for school athletics. The highest IQ girls in these classes checked significantly more often activities such as playing cards, listening to radio, reading together and going in for discussion. Thus most of the significant differences of girls at the three classes went in favour of those who had higher IQ's.

Discussion

Boys of low intelligence more often go in for the more individual, out-of-door recreational interests, with few or no other persons as companions. Low IQ girls, like low IQ boys, tend to also take part more often in aggressive types of activities. Probably, lonely or individual activities alone satisfy the needs of low IQ students. Social interests can be pursued with at least a fair amount of intelligence which those having low IQ lack. Generally, unskilled and unselected recreational interests is perhaps what may be expected to be popular with the dull students, as social, skilled and selected interests draw their origin as well as vitality from brightness or greater intelligence potential.

Going in for school activities is significantly more popular with boys and girls of high intelligence, showing that such activities may fulfil the needs of the more intelligent to a greater degree than those of the less intelligent. Scholastic work requires at least a normal amount of intelligence and hence this finding.

Girls of high intelligence are significantly more interested in recreation involving a social set-up such as is there in parties, eating together in restaurants and talking together. This is what may be expected because greater intelligence makes the mare go in socials.

Students of very high intelligence tend to be mature, judicious, and highly selective in the matter of choosing recreational activities. This is probably because maturity and discrimination in social as well as individual functioning stem from the basic intellect inherent in an individual.

The findings of this study, though not very much different from those of similar studies undertaken elsewhere, are highly suggestive.

References

1. Bell, Howard M. "Youth Tell their Story" (Washington, D.C.. American Council on Education, 1938).
2. Gross, Frank P. "*Activities of Bright Versus those of Dull Students*". Journal of Educational Research, Vol. 60, No. 6, Feb., 1967, pp. 283-85.
3. Leach, Kent W. "*Intelligence Levels and Corresponding Interest Area Choices of Ninth Grade Pupils in Thirteen Michigan Schools*". Journal of Expert. Edu. XXII (June, 1954), pp. 369-383.
4. Lehman, H.C., and Witty, P.A. "*Play Activities and School Progress*". Journal of Educational Psychology, XVIII (1927), pp. 318-26.
5. Reeves, J.W., and Slater, Patric. "*Age and Intelligence in Relation to Leisure Pursuits*". Occup. Psy. XXI (1947), pp. 111-124.
6. Smith, H.P. "*A Study in the Selective Character of American Secondary Education: Participation in School Activities as Conditioned by Socio-economic and Other Factors*". Journal of Edu. Psychology, XXXVI (1945), pp. 229-46.

48. AN EXPERIMENTAL STUDY OF NATIONALITY PREFERENCE

To determine empirically whether the methods of Rank Order and paired comparisons yield results which are essentially similar, and in a bid to determine preference for nationality of individuals who in this variously shrunken world are in contact, physical, psychological or other, with people of different nationalities, 70 individuals, male and female in equal number, chosen at random from a group of 300 graduate teachers (the sample was representative in that the proportion, in it, of teachers of different socio-economic levels coincide with such proportion in the state's total population of graduate teachers) of Punjab were given slips of paper on which were listed seven different nationalities: English, American, Japanese, Russian, Chinese, German and French. The group collected at one time was instructed as below, using the method of Rank Order:

"Imagine that teachers of the seven nationalities listed arrive here and that you are required to have as a family guest a teacher of one of these nationalities. Look at the list carefully, then assign number 1 to the nationality of the teacher you would most prefer to have; number 2 to the nationality preferred second, and so on, until the least preferred nationality is assigned number 7. Take as long as you like to make the rankings. If you happen to be "undecided' on any two nationalities, choose one or the other instead of ranking them the same. All the seven nationalities must be assigned a rank and no two ranks should be the same".

In the slips distributed, the nationalities were written in many different orders so that no bias should attach to the serial listing of a given nationality when all subjects were considered.

From the ranks given to different nationalities, the order of preference for each nationality was determined by giving the rank values of 7,6,5,4,3,2 and 1 to the first, second, third, fourth, fifth, sixth and seventh preference respectively, multiplying the number of each preference of a nationality with the corresponding value, adding all the seven multiples below each nationality, and then ranking each nationality, on the basis of its total value score, as shown in Table 1. The table also shows per cent positions and scores derived by transmutation of rankings (2). This was done on the assumption that "nationality preference" follows the normal probability curve in the general population. This assumption was justified because differences at extremes of the trait are relatively much greater than differences around the mean, as it should be. The mean ranks assigned to each nationality were determined from the data. Distributions of the rankings for nationalities rated near the bottom or top were skewed, as would be expected. The mean ranks and the standard deviations of the distributions are shown in Table 2.

Table 1
Showing the Total Value Scores, Ranks, per cent Position and Normal Curve Scores of Different Nationalities

Nationality	Total Value Scores	Rank	Per cent Position	Normal Curve Score
American	413	1	7.14	78
Russian	352	2	21.43	66
English	321	3	35.71	57
Japanese	279	4	50.00	50

German	272	5	64.30	43
French	241	6	78.57	34
Chinese	104	7	92.86	22

Table 2
Showing nationality preferences derived by method of rank order

Nationality	Mean Rank	Standard Deviation
American	2.10	1.26
Russian	2.97	1.59
English	3.41	1.74
Japanese	4.01	1.73
German	4.11	1.83
French	4.56	1.38
Chinese	6.51	1.26

To make ranked data comparable, rank orders were converted into per cent ranks in which higher values represent the more desirable standing as shown in Table 3(1).

Table 3
Showing per cent ranks of nationalities as derived by rank order method

Nationality	Rank as in Table 1,2	Per cent Rank
American	1	93
Russian	2	79
English	3	64
Japanese	4	50
German	5	36
French	6	30
Chinese	7	7

The second stage of the experiment involved the method of paired comparisons, in which S is forced to make independent judgement of each stimulus with every other stimulus. The group was instructed as below:

"Now you will be given a slip of paper on which are written two nationalities, with a note that of the two you should tick the one you would prefer, for the purpose of having as a family guest a teacher of one of these two nationalities. You should indicate a preference for one or the other nationality, instead of indicating "no choice" when you happen to be uncertain. After you have done this on one slip, you would be given several other slips one by one for similar action".

The second slip was distributed after collecting the first slip from all the subjects, the third after collecting the second, the fourth after the third and so on, for a total of 21 paired comparisons to be made in respect of the seven stimuli involved in this experiment.

From the number of cases one nationality was preferred to the other, as ticked in all the slips, the total frequency of preference for each nationality was determined and the mean frequency of preference for each computed, as given in Table 4. The percentage of total preferences obtained for each nationality, and the percentage of preferences one nationality obtained over the others are shown in Table 5. The percentage of preferences all the nationalities were found to enjoy over a particular nationality are given in Table 6, and the nationalities which were preferred more than other nationalities along with the preferences the former got as against the latter, in Table 7.

Table 4

Showing frequency of preference, mean preference and rank order derived from the method of paired comparisons

Nationality	Total frequency of preference	Mean frequency of preference	Standard deviation	Rank order
American	315	3.24	1.71	1
Russian	266	3.04	1.67	2
English	241	2.94	1.65	3
Japanese	234	2.93	1.97	4
German	218	2.83	1.66	5
French	169	2.67	1.64	6
Chinese	27	2.55	1.57	7

Table 5

Showing percentage of total preferences and percentage of preferences for each nationality as against the other nationalities (method of paired comparisons)

Prefer	TO							
	American	Russian	English	Japanese	German	French	Chinese	Total
1				2				3
American	..	61	73	63	73	83	97	75
Russian	39	..	51	61	61	71	96	63
English	27	49	..	57	56	59	97	57

Japanese	37	39	43	..	60	61	94	56
German	27	39	44	40	..	71	90	52
French	17	29	41	39	29	..	87	40
Chinese	3	4	3	6	10	13	..	6

N.B–Figures under col. 2 denote percentages of the cases in which one nationality (col.1) is preferred to every other. Total (col. 3) shows percentage of total preferences each nationality obtained.

Table 6

Showing percentage of preferences all the nationalities enjoy over a particular nationality (method of paired comparisons)

Nationality Preferred to	Nationality Preferred							
	American	Russian	English	Japanese	German	French	Chinese	Total
1				2				3
Chinese	97	96	97	94	90	87	..	94
French	83	71	59	61	71	..	13	60
German	73	61	56	60	..	29	10	48
Japanese	63	61	57	..	40	39	6	44
English	73	51	..	43	44	41	3	43
Russian	61	..	49	39	39	29	4	37
American	...	39	27	37	27	17	3	25

N.B.–Figures under col. 2 denote percentages of the cases in which nationalities in col. 2 are preferred to the nationality mentioned against them in col 1. Total (col. 3) shows the percentage of total preferences against the nationality in col. 1.

Table 7

Showing nationalities which were preferred more than certain other nationalities and the number of preferences former obtained as against the latter (method of paired comparisons)

	American	Russian	English	Japanese	German	French	Chinese
			Nationalities preferred more than Col. X				
No. of such Nationalities	Nill	1	2	3	4	5	6
Names of such Nationalities	–	American	American Russian	American Russian English	American Russian English Japanese	American Russian English Japanese German	American Russian English Japanese German French

No. of preferences obtained by nationalities in Col. X when compared to nationalities preferred more	–	27 as against American	53 19 as against American 34 as against Russian	83 26 as against American 27 as against Russian 30 as against English	105 19 as against American 27 as against Russian 31 as against English 28 as against Japanese	108 12 as against American 20 as against Russian 29 as against English 27 as against Japanese 20 as against German	27 2 as against American 3 as against Russian 2 as against English 4 as against German 9 as against French
Average No. of preferences each nationality in col. X got when compared to nationalities preferred more	0	27	26.50	27.67	26.25	21.60	4.50

	Nationalities preferred more than Col. X						
	American	Russian	English	Japanese	German	French	Chinese
No. of Nationalities not preferred more than itself (col. X)	All the other 6	5	4	3	2	1	None
Names of nationalities not preferred more than itself (Col. X)	Russian English Japanese German French Chinese	English Japanese German French Chinese	Japanese German French Chinese	German French Chinese	French Chinese	Chinese	

Results

Total value scores and normal curve scores (Table 1), besides determining ranks 1, 2, 3, 4, 5, 6, 7 for American, Russian, English, Japanese, German, French, Chinese nationalities respectively reveal that:

1. American nationality is preferred: 4 times as much as Chinese, about twice as much as French, about one-and-a-half times as much as German, Japanese and English, and about one-and-a-quarter times as much as Russian nationality.
2. Russian and English nationalities are preferred: 3 times as much as Chinese, about one-and-a-half times as much as French, and one-and-a-quarter times as much as German and Japanese nationalities.
3. Russian nationality is preferred a little more than English.
4. Japanese, German and French nationalities are preferred about two-and-a-half-times as much as Chinese.
5. Japanese and German nationalities are equally preferred, though they are preferred a little more than the French.

Mean ranks and their magnitudes (Table 2) affirm the ranks as well as the differences in nationality preference concluded from Table 1.

Table 3, which affirms the above results, tells further that American nationality is more preferred (theoretically) than 93%, of the group, Russian than 79%, English than 64%, Japanese than 50%, German than 36%, French than 30%, and Chinese more preferred than 7% of the group of nationalities taken in this study. The term 'theoretically' here refers to the fact that the nationality's own rank is partly assigned to the higher group and partly to the lower. Whereas only 7% of the group are preferred more than American nationality, as many as 93% of them are preferred more than the Chinese. Whereas Japanese nationality is in the middle of the preference scale, each of the nationalities-American, Russian, English, Japanese and German–is equidistant from its successor (as in the descending order of per cent ranks given here) on the preference scale. Very little distance between French and German nationalities and a big gap between French and Chinese in the matter of the magnitude of preference, as already evident from Tables 1,2, are shown by Table 3 also.

From Table 4, it is immediately apparent that the method of paired comparisons gives almost the same results as those obtained by the methods of rank order. This was also shown by Kate's study (3). In one sense, the two methods may be identical. When S ranks, he should, evidently, compare each stimulus with every other stimulus if his ranking is to be careful and objective. If he does so, he would be using the method of paired comparisons. The chief advantage of the method of paired comparisons over that of rank order lies in the fact that by paired comparison S is bound to make independent judgement of each stimulus with every other stimulus. In the case of rank order S may not make such a thorough analysis.

A more detailed account of nationality preferences emerges from Tables 5 and 6.

Whereas 75 per cent (maximum) of the total preferences cast by the Ss are bagged by American nationality, when this nationality is paired with every other in turn, only 40 per cent of the total preferences come in the lot of French nationality, when placed in similar situation. Six per cent, least of all, is the share of Chinese nationality when paired with every other. Russian nationality stands 12 per cent lower than American and 6 per cent higher than English, while Japanese and German nationalities lie in close proximity to English when subjected to similar comparisons.

Preference for each nationality as against the other nationalities is depicted below. The nationality on the left is preferred to each of the nationalities given against it on the right. The parenthetical figure is the percentage of cases in which the former is preferred as against the latter:

American	Chinese (97),	French (83),	German and English	(73),
	Japanese (63),	Russian (61),		
Russian	Chinese (96),	French (71),	German and Japanese	(61),
	English (51),	American (39),		
English	Chinese (97),	French (59),	German (56),	Japanese (57),
	Russian (49),	American (27),		
Japanese	Chinese (94),	French (61),	German (60),	English (43),
	Russian (39),	American (37),		
German	Chinese (90),	French (71),	Japanese (40),	English (44),
	Russian (39),	American (27),		
French	Chinese (87),	German (29),	Japanese (39),	English (41),
	Russian (29),	American (17),		
Chinese	French (13),	German (10),	Japanese (6),	English (3)
	Russian (4)	American (3)		

Conversely, a picture of the preferences enjoyed by several nationalities over a particular nationality is drawn below. The nationalities on the left (in each horizontal line) enjoy preference over the nationality given against them on the right. The parenthetical figure is the percentage of cases in which each of the former is preferred to the latter. The figure bracketed with total is the percentage of total preferences against the nationality on the right.

American (97), Russian (96), English (97), Japanese (94), Chinese
German (90), French (87), Total (94)

American (83), Russian (71), English (59), Japanese (61), French
German (71), Chinese (13), Total (60)

American (73), Russian (61), English (56), Japanese (60), German
French (29), Chinese (10), Total (48)

American (63), Russian (61), English (57), German (40), Japanese
French (39), Chinese (6), Total (44)

American (73), Russian (51), Japanese (43), German (44), English
French (41), Chinese (3), Total (43)

American (61), English (49), Japanese (39), German (39), Russian
French (29), Chinese (4), Total (37)

Russian (39), English (27), Japanese (37), German (27), American
French (17), Chinese (3), Total (25).

In preference to each of the American, Russian, English and German nationalities as many as four (excluding French and Chinese) of the six nationalities are preferred in most cases.* In preference to Japanese, only three of the six nationalities excluding German, French and Chinese are preferred in most cases.* In preference to French as many as five (excluding Chinese) out of the six nationalities, while in preference to Chinese four excluding German and French out of the six nationalities are preferred in most cases.* Again, when paired to other nationalities, five (excluding French and Chinese) of the seven nationalities were preferred in most cases.*

Of the nationalities preferred in paired comparisons, American, Russian, English and German are preferred to Chinese and French in most cases,* while Japanese are preferred to Chinese, French and German in most cases;* French are preferred to Chinese only, and Chinese to French and German in most cases.* Again, when paired to other nationalities only two (Chinese and French) of the seven nationalities are voted against in most cases.

Whereas no nationality has been preferred more than American, one nationality (American) has been preferred more than Russian, two (American, Russian) more than English, three (American, Russian, English) more than Japanese, four (American,

* "Most cases" here refer to the percentage which exceeds the average-percentage derived from the percentages in vertical columns of Table 5, 6.

Russian, English, Japanese) more than German, five (all except Chinese) more than French, and six (all the others) more than Chinese (Table 7).

Japanese got the highest number of average preferences when paired in turn to the three nationalities preferred more than itself. Russian, English, German and French come next in descending order, when these nationalities are paired in turn to the respective nationalities preferred more than themselves. All these five nationalities, except the French, lie in close proximity to each other in the matter of average number of preferences they got when compared, in pairs, to the nationalities preferred more than themselves. The lowest average of this nature is obtained by Chinese nationality.

Conclusions

The nationalities in descending order of the magnitude of preference are American, Russian, English, Japanese, German, French and Chinese. American nationality is preferred most and Chinese least of all. Whereas American nationality is preferred more than 3 times as much as French, and about twice or more than twice as much as German and Japanese, it is preferred several times as much as Chinese, and it is preferred as much more than Russian as Russian more than English.

The method of paired comparisons gives almost the same results as those obtained by the method of rank order.

American nationality is preferred most to Chinese and least to Russian, while Chinese is preferred least to American and most to French. Russian nationality is preferred most to Chinese and least to American, while Chinese is preferred almost least to Russian. English nationality is preferred most to Chinese and least to American, while Chinese is preferred least to English. Japanese nationality is preferred most to Chinese and least to American, while Chinese is preferred half as much to English as to French. German nationality is preferred most to Chinese and least to American, while Chinese is preferred to German nearly as much as it is preferred to French. French nationality is preferred most to Chinese and *vice versa*. It, like Chinese, is preferred least to American.

Whereas no nationality is preferred more than American, one nationality is preferred more than Russian, two more than

English, three more than Japanese, four more than German, five more than French, and six more than Chinese.

These results however, need to be further validated, through replication of the study on larger and differential samples, before they can be generalised.

References

1. DuBois, Philip H. "An Introduction to Psychological Statistics", Harper and Row, New York, 1965, pp. 75-76.
2. Garrett, Henry E. "Statistics in Psychology and Education", Allied Pacific Pvt. Ltd., 1962, pp. 328-29.
3. Havner, Kate. "An Empirical Study of Three Psycho-Physical Methods", J. Gen. Psychol., 1930, 4, pp. 191-212.

49. TEACHING ABOUT RELIGION IN SCHOOLS

Information and knowledge of religion may help in inculcating higher values, teaching about religion may elevate the morale of the taught through precepts, scriptural injunctions would raise their moral and social standards and such like beliefs led the investigator to Seek educators' views on the subject.

Procedure

As many as 72 Headmasters/Headmistresses/other administrators connected with High or Higher Secondary Schools formed the sample. The method used was more or less a standardized interview in which the opinion of each individual in the sample was sought on a single question: "Should the high Schools teach about religion the way they teach other curriculum"? The study was spread over a number of months as the investigator sought the opinion of one individual at a time as and when he got an opportunity of meeting him or her. Their views in original having been recorded, an attempt was made to analyse the same into 'pro' and 'anti' categories. Some of the interesting arguments supporting their views were also revealed. No suggestion or opinion favouring or controverting their expressed opinion was given with a view to obtaining their initial unbiased views only. Other factors like the religion or faiths of the individual, the type of school he/she was connected with, his/her age etc. were not controlled, but all the educators who gave their opinion had at least fifteen years' experience in teaching or administration or both.

Results

1. 68 per cent favour teaching about religions in the high/higher secondary school curriculums.

An old headmaster having 25 years school experience came out: "Content of many religions especially their basic premises, beliefs and goals would promote national integration and international understanding". An educator grown pretty grey under the heavy though enriching load of responsibilities that her 20 years' stay in the school entailed commented: "Teaching about religions would work wonders if the content of such teaching is carefully planned and imparted by teachers who could easily keep up an unprejudiced, objective view-point". An administrator betraying an inspiring glow on his face, which clearly depicted the inevitable signs of aging in school itself, remarked: "We could produce peace-loving, democratic individuals through teaching about religions, the foundations of religions having been laid on the gospels of truth and love of mankind." "Each high-school student should be taught about religions if we want our nation to imbibe high moral values", remarked a grey-haired headmistress who has dedicated all that is hers in the service of education? "God help our country when our children are denied any instruction about religions", commented an administrator who had spent a valuable part of his life in education. "Religion is about the only source our children can draw inspiration from", said a retired educator whose only vocation was education.

Some of these views seem to be adequately weighty, while others may be argued against on the plea that schools can, and perhaps most of them are, teaching moral and spiritual values without teaching about religion. Nevertheless, it is hard to form any opinion in favour of 'teaching about religion' without taking into account the opposite views which follow presently.

2. 28 per cent are against teaching about religions. Most of them anticipate trouble if such teaching is done, while others think that all that religion implies can be taught without importing religion in the classroom.

A brilliant headmaster blurted out: "We may run the risk of producing bigots if we teach about religion". "For God sake do not infuse religious teaching, if you want our children to prosper in this wide world and if you feel communal troubles be avoided," chuckled a rosy-cheeked headmaster who had seen a lot of life in school. "School should not take over the work that legitimately belongs to religious institutions", replied an aging headmistress who is in education for two decades. An educator who is devoted to education since the prime of his life opined: "Why can't home do most of religious teaching? We are already over-burdened". "Let not our children become too much religion-conscious in this international world", declared an enthusiast who keeps education so near and dear to his heart. A veteran educator believes, "Within the limited time the schools can teach, they are already bound to teach certain moral and spiritual values, but they cannot and should not assume the major responsibility in this behalf."

Such are some of the views at the other extreme which betoken the belief that teaching about religion should not form part of the curriculum in high school. All the same it is difficult to endorse this view before looking at the views, which tend to strike a balance, as hereunder. Though very few respondents offered these, it is worth our while to consider them.

3. Some are of the view that "Comparative religions" be taught at the Higher Secondary level where the subject may be chosen as an elective". "Let the children out of their school time participate in religious instruction managed for them in local religious institutions", stated a middle-aged educator. "The facts of religions may be placed before our High School students without any comment, in favour or against. Let them judge for themselves," offered a hoary headmistress. "Let our history courses offer enough teaching about religion without instituting religion (as such) as one of the subjects in curriculum," mentioned an administrator who worked in many schools.

4. Some of the more interesting responses are: "Knowledge of right and wrong may not always lead to right conduct. Let us develop in students an urge to do what is right". "Teachers through their own examples indirectly teach values to students". "Schools are doing their bit to teach morals, what more do you want?" "Supervised games teach good sportsmanship, democratic classrooms present ideals of citizenship; religion would do no better." The coming generation must be spiritually strong to withstand the onslaught of conflicting ideologies and hence the need for religious teaching." "We should not shrink from discussing questions of moral significance with pupils when the situation so demands." "You cannot teach about religion effectively in schools."

The purpose of this study is not to offer any comments on the facts revealed, but to leave the question open for the experts to discuss and arrive at their own conclusions. It is fallacious to decide about this vital issue without taking into consideration the cultural background, the strength of religions, and the genius of our own country.

VIII. MEASUREMENT AND EVALUATION

50. MY CONCEPT OF A GOOD EVALUATION PROGRAMME IN A SECONDARY SCHOOL

Education aims at full development of the student-development in all aspects of his personality. Evaluation, curricula, teaching technique, books are at best only the tools or means to achieve this aim. It is imperative that these means are best developed and made use of for the sake of education. Whether the curriculum is suitable or the teaching technique is useful or the books serve the purpose is known to the educator through evaluation. In other words, that education is doing well, or if not, where it requires modification, is evident to us through evaluation and hence the vital role of evaluation, which should therefore be seen in the total context of the educational process and not as an end in itself. When we say that education means the fullest development of the child's personality, evaluation of one kind or another must check up whether the development is taking or has taken place. If evaluation is to play such an important and great part in the field of education, it must not be made so lightly as at present. It must be flawless from every point of view, so that it is efficient. If evaluating technique tests all that education caters to, it has served its purpose. If it does not, do away with such techniques and introduce others which serve education. Any evaluating programme must lead to test the outcomes of education. We do not want evaluation for its own sake.

Secondary education being the backbone of the child's future–academic or vocational–is scheduled to involve certain essential developmental tasks. An efficient and comprehensive evaluation programme alone, which involves the testing of aspects (of growth) other than academic achievement and which includes the use of techniques other than written examinations, can tell us whether a secondary school is performing all such tasks, and if so, to what extent. It is in this indispensable sense that the concept of a good evaluation programme needs to be discussed here.

Assumptions and Purposes

Evaluation is based upon some basic assumptions which need to be kept in view. Firstly, education aims at bringing about changes in human behaviour. Evaluation seeks to find out the extent to which each of these changes has taken place. Secondly, human behaviour is too multiphased to be explained by a single score and a result of the evaluations is only a part of the whole; thirdly, tests alone are too inadequate to evaluate an individual. Any reliable and valid information that helps a teacher in better understanding a pupil and leads to assisting the pupil in his development is useful. Fourthly, the nature of evaluative techniques used affects the pupils' learning and the teachers' teaching; pupils will study subject matter alone if they are evaluated on subject-matter-content; and the teachers too would stress upon it at the expense of everything else that they are meant to impart.

These assumptions imply that evaluation should be comprehensive enough to encompass all the varied aspects of pupil's growth and development, that data from all sources including tests should be put together to give a whole picture of the individual, that diverse evaluative measures be used to appraise and understand different phases of an individual's achievement and that the type of evaluation influences both learning and teaching. The chief purpose of educational evaluation is to promote and improve learning. It is to achieve this purpose that evaluation attempts:

(i) To yield information for promoting pupils, reporting to parents and grading,
(ii) To select the pupils and to motivate them,
(iii) To evaluate the effectiveness of certain teaching methods and that of the entire educational programme with a view to improving them, and
(iv) To give data for educational and vocational guidance.

Evaluation, like any other system, should subscribe to a democratic pattern of living to which we are pledged. Democracy recognizes the worth and dignity of every individual, evaluation must also do like-wise. But we injure their sense of worth and well-being when we give low grades to children having low mental abilities, comparing them with their classmates who have high mental ages. Such children, if moved to classroom situations, where they find activities more commensurate with their abilities, would enjoy success and satisfaction which a democratic philosophy promises. All individuals need to experience success in order to live a normal living. If they do not have such experience in one way they attempt to have it in another, even undesirable way.

The problem child or a delinquent is often a poor student who, being unable to achieve success, resorts to stealing or doing other mischiefs in order to appear as somebody to be reckoned with or as someone who is important. Of the ten delinquents of fifth grade whom the writer studied through case history method as many as eight (who were truants, boasters, liars,....or bullies) were poor scholars. Some of our evaluating activities may be directly responsible for putting some children on such dubious paths.

To solve this problem, the teacher needs to be aware of individual differences and to be more flexible and willing to do something about such differences. The classroom group is too heterogeneous to be free from wide variations in individual achievement. All the same, unless pupils have experience of success, they do not have enough motivation to learn. This motivation is not forthcoming if the child with a low grade is posed with the problem of competing with a classmate having a fairly high grade. On the other hand, if his progress is compared against his own ability, while he is improving, he will be motivated to continue his efforts so as to achieve success. Grading or evaluation done on the latter basis would be certainly more useful. Progress evaluated on the basis of a pupil's own ability to learn not only stimulates below average students to improve, but motivates the bright students as well who otherwise do no more than just adequate to excel the average students even without making much effort. Teachers through such evaluation will be respecting pupils' personalities and contributing towards the development of each pupil within the limits of his abilities. Placing reasonable targets of achievement before the child may be another way of motivating him to improve.

Psychology Behind Evaluation

To be most effective, educational evaluation should make use of the best available techniques and well known psychological principles.

First principle is that for evaluation of achievement to be successful the students should be ready for it. Just as we can teach a child to read or to walk only when he has reached a certain stage of mental and physical development, we can evaluate a student more profitably when he has the readiness to undergo testing. A student is ready when he appreciates and accepts the values and purposes involved. When the student knows that basically all evaluation is to help him, it is easier to make him receptive towards testing.

Related to the principle of readiness is the second principle that, for evaluation to be purposive and reliable, motivation is necessary. A pupil's progress on a test is directly related to his motivation. When motivated, his performance is much better than when motivation is lacking. The mere awareness of the fact that they have something to gain as a result of good performance makes students motivated enough to put in their best–to do which they would necessarily learn more effectively.

Twenty students of ninth class were given by the writer a test in general English without any previous notice. They showed an average achievement score of 20.5. After a week they were given the same test, this time after motivating them on the plea that those showing good performances would be chosen for some work projects. Their average score rose up to 27.8. Though other factors were not controlled, motivation obviously led to improved learning. Even such factors as fatigue, pain and sickness do not slow down the performance of students who are highly motivated.

Thirdly, evaluation to be significant and acceptable to the students must result in pleasure, success, rewards. When high marks or grades follow the evaluation, students welcome testing and regard it as important and useful; but how do these tests bring success or pleasure is the question that demands an urgent answer.

If the tests demand rote memory for good marks, the students will become good crammers. If they require student to apply learnt principles in everyday life or to solve problems, the students will study with the aim of becoming best equipped to do well on the test items. Similarly the teachers will also use one or the other method of teaching depending upon the requirements of evaluation. It is in this sense that the type of evaluating technique used determines or influences the students' method of learning and the teachers' technique of teaching. What do we want the students to become, what changes shall we bring in the students after a year's teaching of the subject or in other words what objectives of teaching a particular subject do we want to achieve, are the questions which determine what kind of evaluation technique we should have, besides of course determining such things as the teachers' method of teaching, learning experiences, students' method of study, the curriculum, the books. Evaluation must therefore be based on the objectives of teaching a subject at a particular stage. Achievement tests constructed on this basis can lead to pupil's satisfaction, pleasure and success. This constitutes the fourth psychological principle of evaluation.

The writer, in an attempt to construct an achievement test (in B.T. educational psychology) based on certain objectives of teaching the subject, found that the objective-based evaluation was fairly reliable and valid. A gist of the research study follows.

Sixty-one questions which comprised 26 'true-false' items, three 'matching' items and 32 'best answer' items were devised after consulting the subject syllabus. The objectives were (i) to enable teachers to devise, to use and to test new principles of learning educational techniques; (ii) to acquaint them with the chief contributions of great educationists and psychologists in the field of educational psychology; (iii) to assist school children in developing right values and in resolving their social and emotional problems; and (iv) to assist children in becoming worthy citizens.

The try-out of the test under construction was carried out on 128 teachers undergoing training at the Government Training College, Jullundur during 1958-59. The sample included equal number of men and women trainees. The questions contained 74 items in all. Each correct answer carried one mark, while every incorrect or omitted answer carried no mark. The maximum score was 74.

Item Difficulty

An analysis of the data revealed that 56 per cent of the items had difficulty indices between .25 and .75; 40 per cent had indices larger than .75 and 40 per cent smaller than .25. Items of moderate difficulty constituted 29 percent of the entire lot.

Item Validity

The validity index (discriminating power) of each of the 74 items was calculated by Biserial Correlation. Fifty-four per cent of the items had validity indices of .20 or above; 24 per cent of the items had zero validity; a few had negative indices also. It is apparent that in the final selection of the items those with validity indices below .20 will have to be excluded.

In the exact distribution, 53 trainees scored above the mean (26.98). Twenty-six made the average score (26-27) while 49 trainees scored below the average. The standard deviation of the scores worked out at 5.02.

The Reliability of the Trial Test

The reliability of the test was determined by the Split-Half Method and the correlation co-efficient (r) calculated by the Pearson Product Moment method. The correlation between the two halves came to be .65. The reliability co-efficient as worked out by the Spearman-Brown Prophecy formula came to .79.

Validity of the Test

A study was made of the correspondence between the scores of trainees on the try-out and their scores in the final essay-type examination. The correlation co-efficient came to be .60. This is a reasonably high figure. It can be expected that after the test has been finalized by eliminating the unreliable and the less discriminating items, the predictive value of the test will increase further.

Teachers can think of the objectives of teaching their own subject, define them into the behaviour changes expected in the child who is lucky enough to achieve the objective and frame the test items both essay and objective-type meant to seek the same answer. They may consult the present higher secondary syllabus to borrow the content of the test items. The actual techniques of constructing test items based on this approach, though well known, cannot be discussed here for lack of space.

Again, evaluation is more fruitful in terms of human learning if students are constantly intimated or told in a meaningful way as to how well they are faring.

When answer scripts are duly marked and returned promptly, the students show greater interest in learning and testing than when the same are returned after a long time or are not returned. Experiments conducted by the writer in this behalf have demonstrated the good effect of immediate knowledge of results on learning.

Lastly, evaluation results in greater learning when students through day-to-day teaching are made aware of what is expected of them in answer to certain questions on a topic. This may warrant discussion, project or other methods besides the usual lecture method to which a teacher is tempted to resort.

The writer, after having evaluated the scripts and having noted the marks on a separate sheet, asked the B.T. students to evaluate their own answer books in educational psychology. They were to give marks to each essay-type answer after the writer read out the correct answer expected from them. As high as .75 co-efficient of correlation, which was found between the students' self-evaluation and their achievement scores (as given by the writer), clearly shows that if the students know how they are expected to deal with a question they would certainly do better.

Incidentally, evaluation, in this experiment of self-evaluation, again warrants the need of reforming teaching techniques.

What to Evaluate

Our evaluative activities are in the field of achievement which comprises the outcomes of educational instruction. The school testing programme mostly deals with the achievement of children in mathematics, science, language, social studies and the like, which shows that their evaluation is limited to certain abilities and skills. Obviously, this is not enough to obtain an evaluation of the objectives which the school is meant to achieve. Intelligence, aptitudes, personality, interest, and attitude are other fields in which we should evaluate.

Evaluation in the Final Analysis

Evaluation in the final analysis must help education. It should diagnose weaknesses of educational processes and hint at removing these weaknesses, it should motivate the students as well as teachers, it should lead to better teaching and better learning, and it should aim at realizing the objectives of education.

51. EVALUATING AN ORIENTATION COURSE

Orientation courses by and large help in finding or correcting one's mental relations and principles. The beneficiaries are induced to apply their mind in or to be receptive toward the training, instruction or apprenticement to which they have cast their lot at a given time. The course may be likened to an introduction, a preface on an elementary treatise preceding the act of ushering in new entrants, novices or probationers in a formal course of studies or profession.

Of all the departments, Education Department is obliged, perhaps quite legitimately owing to the multitudinous requirements of education, to run orientation courses for all and sundry. It has often been observed that these courses tend to soften the new entrants' struggle in education, help their adaptation to a new environment and bring harmony between them and their new love. This happy spectacle has often been manifesting especially if the orientation course was well-planned, well-organised and efficiently run. Conversely, when orientation courses are haphazardly run, poorly planned and tactlessly executed, they have been found to be no more than mere exercises in futility.

Whether an orientation course has been of some utility, or whether it has achieved the purposes it aimed at or whether it seems to be based on its objectives, and if so to what extent, are questions which can be answered only after some sort of post-orientation-evaluation is done. In fact it is highly necessary to evaluate an orientation course not only to estimate whether it has been useful and successful, but also to improve upon it with a view to making it more effective. Evaluation helps in avoiding the pitfalls which tended to make the course slip-shod and insipid and in repeating, even intensifying, the features which led to definite advance on the part of those attending the course.

With this aim in mind, the writer attempted, on the last day of the course, to evaluate newly recruited college lecturers' orientation course lasting three weeks held in June-July, 1967 in the State College of Education, Patiala.

This course has been introduced by the Panjab Education Department for the last four years with a view to orientating the college lecturers, who are fresh entrants to the profession and who are blissfully innocent of any training whatsoever towards teaching, and giving them training which aims at making them more effective and efficient. Unlike school teachers, lecturers are not exposed to any pre-service training and are put in the saddle by being appointed directly, after obtaining their academic degrees. That, therefore, they need some training, for the nature of a lecturer's job is essentially the same as that of a teacher's except that the former's wards are comparatively grown-up and have somewhat different needs, led the Department to believe that an orientation course would stand the lecturers in good stead in the matter of understanding education, its purposes, its psychology and the ways it should be imparted. As such, the orientation course comprises of talks, discussions and seminars on major topics of Foundations and Principles of Education, Psychology of Education and Methods of Education. The idea is to introduce the theory and practice of education in a well-coordinated and well-correlated way so as to inspire the lecturers for and instill in them the grand aim and meaning of education, as also the ways human minds absorb education, with a view to helping them understand various problems of education and the ways and means of solving such problems. In short, the course is meant to make them experts for the jobs entrusted to them.

Method

A small questionnaire, containing only 14 questions preceded by a paragraph giving its purpose and instructions to give free, frank and pointed answers, was administered to all the forty–four lecturers (males and females in equal numbers) undergoing the course. No identifying data were collected–they were asked to omit even their names–so that they had the fearlessness and outspokenness as also the freedom from responsibility and from the horror of being held to ransom, all of which are the proud privileges of being anonymous.

Working under the belief that those orientated are the best judges of how the course went with them and to what extent they had benefited from it toward the purpose they were called for, the evaluation was confined in this study to seeking the lecturers' bold replies to the questions contained in the questionnaire.

Since the purpose was to evaluate this course, not courses of this nature as such, questions were chiefly meant to seek opinions on each step or part of the programme of this course, besides asking for concrete suggestions to make future courses more palatable and effective.

The programme consisted of three lecture periods (one for each of the three subjects of 'Principles of Education', 'Psychology of Education' and 'Methods of Education') followed by a discussion period in which general problems of education, experiences of teachers and ways of improving educational set-up were mutually discussed by the lecturers and the resource personnel. In each of the three periods, a resource person talked for 40 minutes on a topic after which 20 minutes' discussion, questioning and answering took place. The discussion period was of one hour's duration. The resource personnel were lecturers, senior lecturers, readers, and Principal of this College besides a few experienced principals and educationists from outside. In the afternoons, the lecturers were expected to browse over relevant educational material in the college library, and to review a book each of their choice. At the end, the lecturers were asked to answer three questions out of nine (essay-type) set on various topics covered in the course.

Findings and Discussion

(a) All the respondents like to teach, 94 per cent of them like their present jobs of lecturers and as many as 97 per cent like to stick to the teaching profession.

It is a happy augury that a predominantly large majority of the lecturers orientated in this course is a contented lot of teachers who are satisfied with what they are and who would like to serve the profession.

(b) 60 per cent of the lecturers think that it is a good idea to give new lecturers an orientation course, while 31 per cent, who do not think so, regard the course as useless, unnecessary or waste of time. Informal discussion on the utility of the course led to reduce the latter percentage to 11.

This speaks highly of the orientation course under evaluation. Most of the lecturers seem to be favourably inclined to the idea chiefly because of the considerable impact the course left on them.

(c) 66 per cent of the sample agree that this course should (as it is) comprise of Principles, Psychology and Methods of Education in a broad way, while 34 per cent do not agree.

But, when asked if they could suggest other subjects that the course should comprise of, besides or in place of the above three subjects, only 29 per cent of the whole lot say that they can suggest other subjects. Of these only 4 per cent came out with the suggestions that subjects like Political Science, Ethics, Teacher-Student Problems, and general national problems be also included. 31 per cent say that they are unable to suggest anything, while as many as 40 per cent regard silence on this question as a better part of valour.

Taking the latter figures into account, it is apparent that the small minority of individuals who claim to disagree with the contents of the course do so without being able to justify their disagreement. They fail to suggest alternative subjects.

It may be safely concluded that most of the lecturers are satisfied with the contents of the course and that these contents attempt to achieve the aims of the course. Out-of-class meets revealed that the lecturers in general found the talks on these subjects interesting, worthwhile and conducive to learning. Many educational problems, of which they were only vaguely conscious and which often stared them in the face before coming for this course, became problems which they felt deeply interested in and which they thrashed out excitedly in a bid to identify and solve. This may be a very desirable outcome of the deliberations of this course.

(d) Two-thirds of the group think that the duration (3 weeks) of the course is enough. Of the remaining one-third who say it is not enough, only a few (6 per cent of the total) suggest that it should be from 6 weeks to 6 months.

When asked whether the duration should be more, 34 per cent reply in the affirmative and 66 per cent give negative answers, showing that the lecturers have been fairly consistent in their reactions.

Most of them do not believe that the orientation course should be longer than what it is. Probably they think that the object of the course has been achieved in the period for which they have attended the course.

However, their feeling that a longer course will slice off a bigger chunk of their well-earned summer vacation might have led them to believe what they do. That they do not want a longer course may therefore be owing to the fact that the course interferes with and takes away a good part of their vacation. If the course were held in the working days, instead of in the vacation as at present, a much more favourable reaction to the question "should the duration be more" might have been forthcoming.

(e) As many as 80 per cent of the group feel that three lecture periods per day (one for each of the three subjects as at present) will suffice. Of the remaining 20 per cent who say that this will not suffice, only a negligible few suggest that the number of lecture periods should range from 4 to 6. That they want no more than 3 periods is reiterated when only 20 per cent say 'yes' and 80 per cent say 'no' to the question whether there should be more lecture periods per day.

A large majority of the lecturers think that one period daily for each of the three subjects is enough to meet the requirements of their course. In fact that is what may be expected because more than one period for each subject every day, especially in the case of the subjects which are quite novel to the individuals, may tax the patience of any audience, no matter how interesting the fare provided.

The possibility that they are all the time conscious of being deprived of a part of their long holiday is also not ruled out. Three periods, they might be thinking, leave a good part of their day intact and more periods would leave very little of it, and hence a three-period day saves their vacation to some extent. This is what may be guessed only, as they have not said it in so many words.

The lecturers' responses regarding the duration of the course as also the number of daily periods should not be understood as contrary to their otherwise favourable reactions, as already discussed, towards teaching, the profession and the orientation course.

(f) 74 per cent of the respondents like to have a 40-minute lecture followed by a 20 minute discussion in each period, as against 26 per cent who would like to have more discussion than lectures. That discussion is more palatable and interesting than lecture, especially for the grown-up post-graduate intellectuals as the present audience is, further confirmed when as many as 46 per cent of the lecturers answered in the affirmative (as against 54 per cent who said 'no'), when asked whether it should be a "free-for all" discussion in every period. This is what may be expected.

A large majority of them however want discussion following the talk. This shows their desire to learn new concepts and ideas and their curiosity to clarify their thinking soon after, through questioning and discussion. The writer observed this state of affairs almost daily, after the group settled down following a few days' furor and excitement that are the inevitable concomitants of a beginning course. Even incessant questioning and a keen desire to express and discuss their own views were invariably observed, which portends well for the course under evaluation.

(g) That the lecturers are equally divided between 'Ayes' and 'Nos' on 'whether there should be a discussion period in addition to the lecture periods should cause no surprise, because those for 'Ayes' are repeating no more than their desire for discussion, more discussion as revealed earlier, and those for 'Nos' regard discussion period as redundant when each of the three lecture periods involves ample discussion. Most of those who favour more discussion and less lecture in each period or a free-for-all in every lecture period, as shown in the previous paragraph, seem to cast their votes to the 'Nos' here. Their tendency to have lesser periods on the days which form substantial part of their vacation, as shown in (d) and (e) above and as honestly expressed by them in calmer moments during informal confabulations, may not be ruled out. Nevertheless, this should not make one suspects their desire to attend the orientation course.

(h) Lecturers show their intellectual fervour and evidence of being erudite and interested in matters educational, as also a desire to profit from this course, when as many as 80 per cent of them say that they would like to go and browse over relevant educational material in the college library, in the afternoons. This betokens well of the course.

(i) Proverbial aversion and repugnance toward examination, as may be expected because nobody wants to be examined or judged, is evident as only 31 per cent say yes, as against 69 per cent who say no, when asked whether they would like to take a small test at the end. In fact, human nature abhors examination and hence this finding. Examination is an anachronism which is hard to do away with owing to its distinct merit that it, as nothing else can, saves education from slump.

(j) 70 per cent or more of the respondents think that this short course may help them in: making their teaching more effective, understanding the basis of education, dealing with students, making students' learning more effective, making students more responsive, and handling educational and social problems.

Most of the lecturers appear to be considerably responsive and benefiting from the course in the sense that they consider themselves to be more competent, after the course, in handling the teaching-learning situations and educational problems. The course, it seems, left an imprint on their minds, as depicted and even verbally disclosed in off-handed intervals. Change of attitude towards teaching, and willingness to understand and solve educational problems were also discerned at times in many of the lecturers.

(k) When asked to give concrete suggestions to make this course more effective, many different and varying suggestions were thrown up. Very few of the lecturers agreed on any one of the suggestions, barring only a few.

Highest percentage (46) is of those who want the Department to pay travelling allowance to and from home, and daily allowance to cover their boarding expenses.

Forty per cent of the lecturers like to have talks from and enjoy discussion with great educationists, well-known and highly qualified people of wide experience and highly learned authorities. Since all of them are masters of their subjects and have an intellectual bent of mind, they are keen to have an exchange of thought with persons who matter, besides those in this college who lecture on technical subjects. To have the honour of listening to and discussing with great personages, well-known people of prestige and power and supreme public figures puffs up our ego and lends us a sense of pride and privilege, and hence perhaps this suggestion.

Twenty-three per cent want the course to be held at a hill-station. Grueling heat of the plains and their grievance that they would have spent their vacation at a hill-station, if they were not called for this course, may have led to this concerted demand.

Next percentage (14) is of the lecturers who do not want the discussion period. This has been discussed at (2) above. Same is the percentage of those who suggest that the course should be more practical and less theoretical. Too much of theorizing is likely to become dull and hence this suggestion.

The respondents who suggest that the course should be held before appointment and those who want that educational trips and excursions should be interposed in between are 11 per cent each.

If to attend this course is a necessary condition for confirmation, as stated by the Department in a recent circular, there is a lot of sense in the suggestion that the course should be held before appointment, and immediately after selection by the Public Service Commission.

Educational trips to vitalize the theory extended by the talks may do some good.

Other suggestions which were made by 7 or lesser per cent of the lecturers are more library facilities, conducting the orientation course subject-wise on Summer Institute pattern, making it more broad-based and less technical, reducing the number of periods, replacing this course by a seminar of lecturers after every three years, confining the course to a discussion on teacher-student problems, making the course free of cost (expenses on travel and food must be fully borne by the state), stopping it forthwith, making it a correspondence course, giving lecturers more opportunity to address and discuss. Some of these suggestions may be of value in making the course more effective, but most of them are not consistent with the aims of the orientation course.

In the achievement test, at the end 2 of the lecturers scored 60%, 7 scored between 50 to 59%, 21 between 40 to 49%, and 14 between 33 to 39%. Their performance on the whole, though satisfactory, leaves much to be desired. This may be partly due to their resentment for the examination.

Conclusions

Orientation course for new lecturers is a useful feature which may be retained. The course may consist of the Philosophical,

Sociological and Psychological Basis of Education, Methods of Education and Guidance (in short all that forms the basic content of teacher training), since the idea is to give college teachers elementary teacher training which, unlike school teachers, they are not required to get before appointment. Teacher-student problems, moral and general issues as well as those that concern college education may be highlighted and thoroughly discussed within the ambit of the subjects mentioned above. Theory should be given vitality by infusing in it practical implications and by discussing how theoretical precepts can be given practical implementation and concrete shape.

Three-weeks' or a months' duration is enough, but the lecturers if possible may be compensated for this drain on their summer vacation by crediting an equivalent number of days in their leave account. The number of periods and their division into lecture and discussion sub-periods may be kept as it is. There is a need to give greater opportunity to the lecturers to express themselves. Let them pose problems, initiate dialogues, suggest remedies from all of which the resource personnel may discover cues to start their planned talks.

Material and books relevant to the talks they listen to may be kept available in the college library. There should be no formal examination at the end; but they may be given assignments for the important topics covered in the course so as to keep their interest and curiosity alive.

Actual expenses on travelling and food should be paid, as otherwise the orientation course may cost them considerably.

Lectures by the resource personnel should include talks by the elite in the field of education. Making some hill-station the venue would be an added attraction and a consummation so devoutly wished.

Despite all the fanfare with which an orientation course or for that matter any course starts, dullness and gross indifference are bound to set in if we fail to handle the situation with great circumspection and to solve the day-to-day matters deftly. Education presents an adventure, a thrill, a challenge, even provocation which we should enjoy and squarely meet rather than get ruffled at. While we are imparting education, we are likely to meet a barrage of questions, even of fire, from those to whom we sell our wares. We may get scratched or even injured at the hands of those who, though sitting at our feet, attempt to embarrass us with their hair-splitting pointers. We may be grilled on matters to which we are unable to do full justice. Our tactless treatment of a topic or situation may throw up excitement and agitation. All this need not sweep us off our feet, nor cause us excruciating headaches too painful to recover from. Keeping ourselves at the altar of reason without getting bogged down in emotional upsets or entanglements, preparing ourselves to face the onslaughts of our critics with the force of argument and knowledge as also of intellect, throwing our erstwhile vanity and pride to the winds at least for a while, we should valiantly, and yet with all humility, face the situations and try to mollify the excited listeners with satisfying answers and pain-relievers galore, so as to stall further embarrassment to us.

Mercifully for us, many of our educands are too indifferent to challenge us and our knowledge. This should not land us in the reverie that we are highly successful genii who are turning our wards into gold. Probably the sermons we give, the education we claim to bestow or the instruction we, day in and day out, inflict, may be too insipid to make them a glow or excited enough to be sceptical of us and our oratory. There is a great possibility that we are caught napping and found below par m what we are upto. For want of adroitness or owing to personal inadequacy and insufficient readiness, we sometimes are tempted to make uncharitable references. We should make it a point to resist such temptations, as this may spark off a major row, even pandemonium, making our audience hurl invectives or make menacing gesticulations on us. To meet all the justified criticism, however, we should be on our guard and keep a strategy of ever-readiness, in refreshing contrast to the smug satisfaction that our wards are too docile to raise their heads or our teaching too fool-proof to permit censure.

We should not, like the unwary, be lured into the dark by-lanes of slumber and charm of a false sense of prestige and complacency. Let us do some rethinking on educational problems which are nearer the hearts of those who are ensnared in these problems.

52. MEASUREMENT OF TEACHING SKILL

Skills are much more tangible and more readily observable than knowledges or concepts. Teaching-skill is no exception. An insightful and expert observer can form a fairly accurate guess of teaching-skill when a teacher is at work. If the observer is adequately experienced in the technique of supervising and evaluating teaching performance of teacher-trainees, his expertise and consequently his evaluation of the teaching skill would become all the more reliable and objective.

2. The investigator took up this study to verify the Hypothesis that the training college lecturers, who train teachers in the theory, methodology and practice of teaching, have a sufficient teaching experience (say five years or more), and have supervised and evaluated the teacher-trainees' teaching performance for about the same period are fairly accurate and dependable in evaluating teaching-skill.
3. The Purpose of the study is envisaged to be the revelation of a suitable criterion or method to (i) measure teaching-skill of teacher-trainees, (ii) discriminate between good and bad teachers, and to (iii) make a judicious selection of teachers.
4. The Sample of the study is 158 teacher-trainees (both boys and girls in equal No.) of Government Training College for Teachers, Jullundur (1960-1961 session). The evaluators are the lecturers possessing requisites mentioned in para 2 above.
5. The Procedure has been to observe a 40 minutes' lesson of a trainee and to evaluate it. The trainee, having been informed of the date and time of his lesson a week in advance, is fully prepared for the task. His second lesson is similarly evaluated after an interval of two months or about by an observer different from the one who observed his first lesson. This is done for each of the 158 trainees.
6. Each trainee takes up two teaching subjects, so that one of his lessons is in one subject and the other in the other subject. While evaluating the lesson it is the methodology and the teaching-skill that are predominantly emphasized, so that it is assumed that the trainee's teaching-skill is the commonest factor in his lesson or that his performance is saturated with a conglomeration of qualities conducive to dexterity in teaching. The limitations of such assumption are, however, appreciated by the investigator.

What the observer sees in order to evaluate a lesson or what factors according to him are involved in teaching-skill is left to an individual observer, who perhaps looks to the lesson as a whole—its methodology, its effectiveness, interestingness, its capacity to invoke pupil's participation and all that goes to make his lesson worthwhile. Placed as they are and given the efficacy, as indicated in para 2 above, the observers are expected to be able to judge a lesson from its gestalt impression. Care has however, been taken to keep the conditions, regarding each of the observer, constant.

ANALYSIS OF DATA

1. *Averages:*	Mean of achievement in lesson I	...	51.6
	Mean of achievement in lesson II	...	52 6
2. *Correlation Coefficients:*	Achievements of 158 students 'r' between achievements of lessons I and II		

3. *'r' between Different Lessons*

	English	Hindi	Hist.	Punjabi	Sc.	Mth.	Snsk.	Geog.	Mc.	Drg.
English	–	.56	.79	.77	.93	.68	.84	1	1	–
Hindi	–	–	.84	–	–	.1	–	–	.83	–
History	–	–	–	.77	1	1	1	1	–	–
Punjabi	–	–	–	–	–	–	–	1	1	–
Science	–	–	–	–	–	.75	–	–	–	–

Abbr. Mth = Mathematics
Snsk = Sanskrit
Hist = History
Geog = Geography
Mc = Music
Drg = Drawing

Findings

1. Correlation between the two evaluations (2 above) shows that the two observers of each lesson are fairly near each other in their judgement. Their evaluation of teaching-skill may thus be said to be fairly accurate and dependable.
2. Correlations between the two evaluations (2 above) shows that the students' performance in teaching is fairly consistent.
3. Correlations at 3 shown in the above table cannot be regarded as significant as the number of trainees having the combinations of subjects which have shown these high correlations is less than 10 in each case.

4. Correlations between History and Punjabi, Science and Mathematics, History and Hindi, English and Science, English and History, English and Mathematics, all showing reliable evaluation and consistent achievement, may also be due to the fact that a common medium of instruction (Punjabi in first 2, Hindi in the next, English in the last 3) might have contributed towards consistent achievement.

All the correlations, especially those between English and Sanskrit, English and Hindi, English and Punjabi, Hindi and Music, which do not have much in common, show at best that the most predominating common factor between the correlating lessons is the teaching-skill shown by the trainees.

Limitations

1. The method of evaluating teaching-skill, though well-tried, is not standardised.
2. The study yields results which need further verification through similar and improved techniques.

53. EXAMINATIONS: AN OPINION STUDY

Educationists, public men and students have been decrying examinations for a long time past. Arguments of all kinds from "it is frightful" to "it serves no purpose" have been advanced against examinations. Student community, naturally, finds enough meat in all such arguments and tends to favour the slogan: "abolish examinations". Man by nature does not like to be examined. The very suggestion "I would be judged", whatever be the mode of judgement, sweeps us off our feet.

Essentially, examination is only a means to promote the ends of education. Questions like "why should this means be employed"? "why not do away with this means"? "in what way does examination serve the ends of education"? etc. made the writer seek, in this study, opinions on examinations. The study makes no assumptions; nor does it advance any hypothesis.

Sample and Method

B.T. students of Government Training College, Jullundur (Session 1965-1966) formed the sample. 184 students (male and female in equal numbers) were asked (i) to answer the question "Should examinations be held? in "yes" or "no". They were further asked (ii) to justify their answers in detail, writing in favour of examinations, if they answered "yes" and writing against it, if they answered "no".

The sample was a well-shuffled group of individuals coming from lower middle to upper middle socio-economic strata of the urban area of Jullundur City, and it could be considered as being fairly representative of a large and unselected, though comparable, population.

No suggestions were given. The students were permitted to write anything in response to the second question [(ii) above]. There was no time limit, though all of them returned their sheets within about forty minutes.

The 'yes' and 'no' answers were separated and arguments given by those who said 'yes' and those who said 'no' were separately listed and analysed.

Findings

Number of those who said 'yes': 97 (51.8%)
Number of those who said 'no': 87 (46.4%)

More than one reason, for both 'yes' and 'no' was given by each student. The number of reasons given varied from 2 to 8. Similar reasons were given by most, so that each reason found mention many times.

Discussion

The reason most frequently mentioned in favour of examinations was that they assess our abilities and achievement. Some of the reasons standing next in order of frequency of mention are: "It evaluates our performance"; "It points out our weaknesses which we can then improve"; "Lest teachers and students should become lazy"; "Otherwise knowledge will remain below par"; "Fear of examination stimulates hard work, self study"; "This is the only check up on teachers"; "This gives the evidence and reward of work done"; "Otherwise students won't study"; "It helps permanent learning"; "Lest those who don't work should also pass"; "Otherwise teaching and learning becomes dull routine"; "Success in it gives self-confidence"; "It prepares for a vocation, life, realities ahead"; "It makes us attain knowledge systematically"; "It develops a sense of competition;" "It gives student a purpose to work for, makes him active".

Thus examination is favoured on the pleas that it evaluates, it stimulates proper learning and proper teaching, it prepares the individual for life ahead and it makes education fruitful.

The least number of responses in favour of examinations come from those who are conscious of the 'fear' aspect of examinations and who would like that examinations be shorn of this unpleasant accompaniment. This aspect finds maximum mention in the responses of those who give an emphatic 'no' to the question, "should examinations be held?", as a justification for their opposition to examinations.

Some other reasons (in the 'no' category) standing next in the order of frequency of mention are: "It does not assess ability"; "It is merely copying of whatever is there in books"; "It keeps knowledge shallow"; "In it, success is a matter of chance only"; "Only crammers get good marks"; "It makes bookworms"; "It does not lead to development of intelligence"; "It amounts to getting a degree by fair means or foul."

Thus examination is disfavoured most on the pleas that it causes fear, it does not assess anything, it does not lead to real learning or effective teaching, and it kills initiative. Least mention has been made of the reason that "examination leads to use of foul means for passing".

Whereas a large majority of the respondents favour examination on the plea that examination evaluates learning, an equally large majority disfavour it on the opposite plea that it does not evaluate learning. That examination, if rightly and objectively planned and suitably conducted, makes reliable and valid evaluation has withstood the shocks of several researches. The opposite plea has perhaps been nursed by those who have had the bitter experience of having been subjected to defective examination and/or those whose lot in examinations has often been failure.

Whereas those favouring examination claim that examination leads to proper learning and teaching, those disfavouring examination say that it does not. The latter opinion is perhaps due to the impression, that examination tests memory alone and not knowledge or growth, that our present day examination invariably gives. There is no denying the fact that if examination tests memory, it is only memory which the student will train and the teacher will help train. It is in this sense that the type of examination questions in the question paper influences the students' method of learning and teachers' method of teaching. Memory training to the neglect of other aspects of growth and development is encouraged by the evaluative instruments which do not correspond to or stem from the objectives of teaching a subject. The tests, which really test whether and to what extent the objectives of teaching a subject (which in turn are aimed at achieving the child's growth) have been achieved, make for proper learning which follows proper teaching.

In fact, most of what makes examination detestable is attributable to the prevailing type of examination and the way it is held. Many reasons given by those who disfavour examination owe their origin to these factors.

'That it makes education fruitful', as claimed by the protagonists of examination, is perhaps the most important argument in favour of examination. Examination, like books, curriculum, teaching techniques, and teachers, is a tool to be employed in the service or interest of education. It is not an end in itself. At best it is a means to an end which is education. It, however, is a tool which is more important than the other above-mentioned tools because it, through its results, can determine and choose the other tools. It should, therefore, be a very sharp and efficient tool so that it not only diagnoses what is wrong with education as a whole, or with any of the other tools employed in the service of education, but it also leads to suggesting the remedies. Thus examination can help achieving all that education aims to achieve.

Fear element in any examination will perhaps remain, as the very nature of examination is such that humans abhor it. We do not want to be judged. Any attempt to judge us therefore lands us in a state of trembling. All the same, examination is what we cannot do without. No system of education can flourish or can attain its aims without the active support of examination. Those who opt for abolishing examination have not been able to suggest any other method or alternative which could perform the same functions or cater to the same needs as the examination performs or caters to. There is however an urgent need to so reform examination that it causes no more than the minimum fear which is inevitable simply because it happens to be examination.

Table 1
Favourable Arguments

S. No.	Reasons given by those who say 'yes'	Per cent frequency of mention rounded off to the nearest unit
1.	It judges our abilities, knowledge, achievements	76
2.	It evaluates our performance	71
3.	It points out our weaknesses which we can then remove	68
4.	Otherwise knowledge will remain below par	67
5.	Fear of examination stimulates hard work, self-study	67
6.	Lest teachers and students should become lazy	67
7.	This is the only check upon teachers and students	65
8.	This gives the evidence and reward of work done	65
9.	Otherwise students won't study	65
10.	It helps permanent learning, ensures learning	65
11.	Lest those who don't work should also passes	63
12.	Otherwise teaching and learning become dull routines	63
13.	Otherwise there is a waste of funds on education	63
14.	It enables teachers to test and improve their methods	63
15.	Success in it gives self-confidence	61
16.	It prepares for a vocation, life, realities ahead	62
17.	It makes us attain knowledge systematically	60
18.	It develops a sense of competition	60
19.	It gives student a purpose to work, makes him active	57
20.	Without it evaluation may involve corrupt practices	55

21.	It removes frustrations of failure and leads to success and adjustment	52
22.	It develops habits of organising material, of discriminating between fact and fiction	50
23.	It develops thinking and reasoning	43
24.	It helps in selection for services etc.	40
25.	It differentiates between good and poor achievers	34
26.	Education can't prosper without it	33
27.	It tells parents whether or not their money on their children is well-spent	32
28.	It strengthens teacher-pupil relationship	32
29.	It is very good, but it should be such that it causes no fear, dread or nervousness	26

Table 2
Unfavourable arguments

S. No.	Reasons given by those who say 'no'	Per cent frequency of mention rounded off to the nearest unit
1.	It makes me afraid, unhappy, ill, nervous	66
2.	It does not assess ability or personality	64
3.	It is merely copying of whatever is there in books	62
4.	It keeps our knowledge shallow, as reading for examination is scanty or limited, ignoring basic knowledge	59
5.	It is a chance; if questions are those, we have prepared, we succeed; otherwise we fail	57
6.	Because only crammers get good marks	55
7.	It does not take stock of a student's all round or yearly progress	54
8.	It amounts to getting a degree by fair means or foul	52
9.	It makes book-worms	52
10.	It does not lead to development of intelligence	52
11.	It does not lead to permanent learning	44

12.	It does not develop thinking and imagination	
13.	Teachers lose initiative and originality while teaching from an examination point of view	
14.	It fails to develop comprehension and understanding	33
15.	Very little preparation makes you pass an examination	33
16.	It leads to bad methods of teaching	32
17.	It represses independence and critical thinking	26
18.	It results in scare, suicides, mental cases, inferiority, depression, etc.	25
19.	It demands mechanical details	25
20.	It leads to foul means of passing *i.e.* copying, bribing, etc.	25

54. MASS FAILURES AT HIGHER SECONDARY LEVEL

It was with feelings of both optimism and pessimism mixed together that the conversion of the high school into the higher secondary school was effected in Punjab ten years ago*, the new campaign was launched with the lofty purpose of bringing our schools in line with the modern multipurpose schools meant to pace up with the needs and requirements of the present industrialised world. The change was a suspect, to start with, in so far as its superiority to the ten-year-school was concerned. Perhaps it was not welcomed with open arms or accepted unequivocally as a reform; and perhaps this negative attitude has been a stumbling block until today in making the higher secondary system a success. This kind of attitude has been so intense that a rethinking, on whether the change should continue or be annulled, has also been there. Schools desiring to revert to the old system, which in fact had become their too intimate a life-partner to dispense with, however great the allurement against it, have in certain cases already regressed to their earlier stage without any qualms of conscience.

An event, however, of notable importance occurred as soon as the new system approached its weaning stage after about a few

* Though this too has since given place to 10 + 2 system.

years of life. Cries of mass failures at the higher secondary level echoed in the State's educational world. Almost all the higher secondary schools were so affected. The writer was provoked to make a study of the causes leading to this problem.

The inability of schools and even educands to adjust to the sudden change from high school to higher secondary school, inadequate preparation for the change on the part of both the schools and the educands, and the schools' failure to meet the requirements of the new system were assumed to be a few, among the various reasons, responsible for mass failures.

Method and Procedure

The study, which was confined to the higher secondary schools of Jullundur District, entailed a close examination of the higher secondary results of the three years (1961,1962,1963) following the introduction of the new system, commencing from the student getting into 9th class in the year 1958. Besides examining the results of both core and elective groups, a look into the causes of failures subject-wise (as indicated by the Headmasters/ Headmistresses) and a study of such factors, as the teacher-pupil ratio, the qualifications of teachers, the matric pass percentage of five years ending with 1958, the number of students and staff in 1958 (before the introduction of the new system) and that in 1963, was made with a view to arriving at important causes leading to mass failures.

A detailed proforma to collect the particulars mentioned above was sent to as many as 34 schools (75% of the ones switched over to the new system). However, though unfortunately, only 19 schools returned the proformas and that too after about four months' effort which involved issuing several reminders, making repeated telephonic calls and sending expediters to the District Education Officers.

Besides, relevant records on mass failures maintained by the Circle Education Officer were examined and three interviews with the District Education Officer sought with a view to reviewing the data supplied by the heads of the schools. Ten heads of the schools (out of the present sample) were interviewed when matters pertaining to the general fall in the result percentage were freely and informally discussed.

The results were compared with the University pass percentage and with their own pass percentage of five years preceding the year of switch-over to the new system. Of the causes leading to failures at the higher secondary level only such causes were retained as the findings of this study as were duly corroborated by the District Education Officer under whose control the schools were.

The higher secondary system involves two university examinations, *i.e.*, one at the end of the 10th class and the other at the end of 11th class, which are called the core and elective results respectively. The core consists of six subject's compulsory for all the students, while an elective group (there are seven elective groups in all) consists of four subjects to be chosen out of six or more. While analysing the results in this study, only the aggregate results of both the core and elective groups were considered.

Findings

1. The schools' high matric results (70 to 95 per cent) consistently for five years preceding the introduction of the higher secondary scheme and the low higher secondary results (ranging from 70 to 32 per cent) consistently for three years succeeding the introduction of the new scheme show sharp decline in results following the change-over. The University's over-all results show an exactly similar decline, which indicates that the schools under study have fared as well or as ill as all the schools of the State put together and that factors concerning the introduction of the new scheme alone may have led to this deterioration.

   The said deterioration in the results was further probed into. The causes of fall in result percentages commonly put forth in the proforma by the heads of the schools and those revealed in the talks with the District Education Officer and with the ten headmasters who were interviewed were as follows:

   (a) Hasty and thoughtless implementation of the new scheme, especially in the matter of making prior provision of suitably qualified staff and necessary equipment for teaching the theory and practice of various elective groups.

   (b) Poor stuff (students), particularly with regard to achievement levels in English, mathematics and science, as those failing in these subjects in the middle standard examination were promoted.

(c) Faulty split-up of the curriculum, *i.e.*, the core is emphasized for the first two years and the elective group taught in the last one year only. Consequently, the electives get neglected, even though the courses in the electives are heavy and fairly advanced.
(d) Indiscriminate admissions in the 9th Class.
(e) Wrong selection of the elective groups, there being no scientific guidance.
(f) Overcrowding in the Higher Secondary classes.
(g) Frequent transfers of experienced teachers.
(h) Lack of proper weeding out up to and at the delta stage, resulting in the promotion of students who are weak in one or more subjects.
(i) Frequent cases of long maternity leave by women teachers, especially in girls' schools.
(j) Faulty allotment of teaching subjects, *i.e.* the qualification or suitability of a teacher for a particular subject is not kept in view while allotting him a time-table.
(k) Increased work-load of teachers.
(l) Ignorance of teaching methods for the higher secondary subjects, as the existing teachers are attuned to the training meant for teaching at the high school level.
(m) Lack of contact between parents and teachers; this contact is essential for making a consistent and collective approach towards the improvement of educational standards.
(n) Increasing use of guides, emphasis on rote memory, lack of supervised study, decreasing attention to written work.
(o) Lack of laboratory equipment for science subjects.
(p) Frequent deputation of teachers to attend seminars and workshops.
(q) Enhanced school timings which leave no time for self-study and lesson-preparation.
(r) Faulty implementation of the internal assessment scheme, especially in the sense that it does not serve its purpose of guidance and motivation.
(s) Faulty system of external examination in that the question papers are set by persons who may not be actually teaching higher secondary classes.

2. The results of all the core subjects, both of the schools under study and of the University as a whole, have likewise shown a decline (from 94.4 to 78.0 per cent) for all the four years commencing from 1960, indicating that factors associated with the introduction of the higher secondary system may have contributed to this fall in results. In fact, an all-round deterioration in the results of almost all the subjects of the two groups (Humanities and Science), which alone most of the schools offer, has been observed.

   The causes of this fall, as commonly revealed in the proformas and the interviews with the District Education Officer and the headmasters, were found to be the sudden stoppage of the objective-type tests current prior to 1962, poor stuff especially in mathematics and English and overcrowding in classrooms.
3. Comparing the results of the core subjects and elective groups of the three years following the introduction of the higher secondary system, it was found that the result percentages of core subjects each year were higher than those of the elective groups. The cause revealed by the headmasters and the District Education Officer was that the students prepared for the core for two years (9th and 10th classes) and for the elective group for one year (11th class) only, while the courses for the elective groups were fairly heavy and of a high standard. Nevertheless, the over-all picture in the core was not found as dismal as in electives.
4. The differences among boys' and girls' schools in matters of (i) the results in the core or electives, (ii) the continuing decline in these results, and (iii) the degree of such decline, were found insignificant.
5. Besides the falls in result percentages caused in most schools by factors associated with the introduction of the higher secondary system, the result percentages touched a new low in some of the schools under study owing to factors peculiar to those schools alone. Whereas in 1961, 70 per cent of the schools showed a below-university result in electives and 50 per cent of them showed a below-university result in the core, in 1962 and 1963, the percentages of such schools as had shown below-university results were 67 (electives), 53 (core); and 63 (electives), 43 (core) in 1962,1963 respectively.

That the core had an edge over the electives in the matter of results is thus evident. The causes revealed were a paucity of qualified staff to teach the electives, inadequate equipment for teaching science and technical groups, wrong selection of elective groups, poor standards of teaching the newly introduced subjects, students' poor level of achievement in English, science and mathematics, and failure to attend to individual difficulties in overcrowded classrooms.

6. Whereas the result percentages of most of the elective groups in 90 per cent of the schools under study, were found in close proximity to each other, those of the science group were found invariably lower than those of the humanities group. The causes of this disparity were found out to be inadequate preparation for teaching, insufficient laboratory equipment, and less qualified staff for teaching the subjects in the science group.
7. In rural schools, besides the causes for mass failures which were common to most schools, the wastage of time caused in coming to and going from the school adversely affected the studies.
8. In 10 per cent of the schools which abounded in students from backward classes, consistently poor standards of achievement in English and science subjects led to high figures in failures.
9. Consistently poor results in English, one of the subjects in all the elective groups, were revealed. This may be due to the short weighting this subject is subjected to ever since our new policy on language teaching in schools.
10. Poor results in Fine Arts and Home Science groups in the schools which offered these groups were stated to be due to paucity of qualified staff and necessary equipment.
11. The teacher-pupil ratio did not seem to go with the result percentage, as quite a few schools having a higher teacher-pupil ratio tended to be lower in their pass percentages. Whereas the staff in each school was considerably raised on a high school's conversion into higher secondary school, no improvement in results was noticed. Instead, a steady and in some cases sharp deterioration in the results followed.
12. The number of students on roll was not found to be in any way related to the pass percentage.

13. Qualifications of teachers did not seem to matter in the matter of making the results good or poor, as schools with more highly qualified staff were not, in quite a few cases, found to be showing better results than those with less highly qualified teachers.

    Though most of the assumptions stated at the time of taking up this study stand verified from the findings, it may not be fair to conclude that the higher secondary system cannot withstand the hazards standing in its way. Perhaps any new system is bound to meet hurdles the way this system is meeting. Mass failures may serve as a pointer to its shortcomings, the way it is being run and thence to efforts for improving it and over-coming the impediments which seem to be hindering its growth.

55. EFFECTS OF DIFFERENT TEACHING METHODS ON LEARNING

That different teaching methods produce little or no difference in learning has been the consistent conclusion of several researches (1,2, 3,6,7). Another set of researches (4,5) prove that the effect of class size on learning may be little or none at all.

One obvious implication is that the teaching methods employed by the researchers are not distinct or unique enough to produce significant differences in the amount of acquired learning. Another is that the class sizes kept are not too different in magnitude to produce notable differences in the amount of learning or perhaps an exactly similar teaching method such as a limited lecture material is blurted out before a class irrespective of its size.

This study aimed at examining alternative hypotheses, *i.e.*, different teaching methods produce differential amounts of learning; effects of class size on learning occur.

The present study was so designed as to evaluate (i) the effect of discussion method as also that of lecture method on learning, (ii) whether a small class or a large class of students does better when taught by the same teaching method.

To evaluate a particular teaching method effectively, testing of the students was done immediately after the method had been employed thereby avoiding contamination by the additional variable of outside study. This procedure would be a more direct test of the effects of the teaching situation *per se* and would therefore be more likely to reveal its effects.

Quizzes for which the students had not prepared were used to know whether students in a small class would do better than students in a large class.

Method and Procedure

Of the 200 students enrolled in the author's Educational Psychology class, 40 were chosen randomly for the experiment. These 40 students were divided into two groups of 20 each. Each student in one group was very closely equated with a student in the other group on the basis of the three hourly house examination they had last taken in the course that year.

The two groups were summoned to the class on the same day, *i.e.*, one at 8 a.m. and the other at 9.30 a.m. They were earlier told that they would be taught one of the topics of Educational Psychology out of the 10 topics still to be taught. One group was taught the topic of 'Mental Hygiene and Education' through lecture method from 8 a.m. to 9.30 a.m., while the other was imparted the same lesson by discussion method from 9.30 a.m. to 11.00 a.m. Since none of the students knew the topic to be taught, they had neither prepared the said topic nor were expecting it to be taught. There was no communication between the two groups as there was no time interval between the end of the lecture period and the commencement of the discussion period. During the last 20 minutes of the lecture period and again during the last 20 minutes of the discussion period, the students in each class were given a quiz which specifically covered the material that was presented in the lecture and the discussion periods. The students had typically received a few weeks' notice for examination before this time, but were clearly not expecting and had not prepared for this quiz. In order to avoid biasing the lecture or discussion in favour of the quiz material, the quiz was constructed by a junior member of the author's[1] department and was not seen by the author until after it was administered. The quiz was multiple choice, containing 15 questions. The two groups of 20 students each were compared in their performance on the quiz.

The second part of the experiment was to know the effect of class size on learning. By a flip of a coin, of the two groups of 20

1. Author is the writer of this paper, who taught the groups and performed this experiment.

each made earlier, one group was selected for the small class and the other group was merged in one of the two large classes of 80 each. Thus, the Ss for the experiment consisted of two equated groups of 20 students each, one group in a small class of 20 students and the other group in one of the large classes.

The small class met at 8 a.m. and the large class met at 9.30 a.m. It was arranged that the small class meet earlier in the day than the large class so that in the event the students communicated information to each other about the topic taught or about the examination, the bias introduced would operate against the likely hypothesis (if at all this were the hypothesis) that students in a small class would do better than students in a large class in quizzes for which they had not prepared. Questioning of the students after examination revealed that the amount of communication was just about nil. Prior to teaching they were just told that they would be taught one of the 9 topics still to be taught. Since none of the students knew the topic to be taught, they had neither prepared the topic nor were expecting it to be taught.

Both the classes were taught the topic of 'Personality Assessment' by lecture method and the author repeated exactly the same material to the two classes. During the last 20 minutes of the lecture period, the students in each class were given a quiz that specifically covered the material presented in the lecture. The students were vaguely aware that the examination would be held sometime but were not at all aware that it would be held immediately after teaching nor were they prepared for the quiz. As in the case of the first phase of the experiment, this quiz too was constructed by a junior member of the author's department and was not seen by the author until after it was administered. It, as before, was multiple choice containing 15 questions. The two groups were compared in their performance on the quiz.

Results

The quizzes of 20 students in the lecture class and those of the 20 students in the discussion class were scored by assigning one point for each correct answer. For each student, quiz score was thus obtained. Whereas the mean of the group taught by discussion method was 11.28, that of the group taught by lecture method was 7.15, showing the difference, in favour of discussion method, significant at .01 level.

Again, the quizzes of the small class and its matched counterpart in the large class were scored by assigning one point for each correct answer. For each student, a quiz score was thus obtained. Whereas the mean of the small class was 9.36, that of its matched group in the large class was 6.29, showing the difference, in favour of the small class, significant at .01 level. An alternative method of analysing the results was to correlate the quiz scores of the small class students with those of their matched counterpart in the large class. The Pearson Product-moment coefficient came to 0.29, showing that the correlation between the scores of the small class and its matched counterpart in the large class is too low to be taken note of.

Discussion

The results confirm the hypotheses that different teaching methods produce differential amounts of learning, that discussion method may be superior to lecture method of teaching, and that small class may benefit more than a large class when taught by the same teaching method. These hypotheses may be particularly true when learning is evaluated in quizzes which specifically cover classroom material and for which the students had not prepared. One cannot be certain, of course, about the role attributed to extra study.

Another specific conclusion which can be drawn from the data is that in order to test the effect of a particular classroom technique, evaluation should be done immediately after the technique is employed. Waiting until the final examination, or any other announced examination, confounds the problem by permitting many other variables to creep in, one of the most obvious of which is extra study. This is what seems to have happened in the case of studies, quoted in the first para of this paper, which go against the hypothesis that different teaching techniques produce different amounts of learning. In fact there are genuine difficulties of controlling some of the extraneous variables in the case of experiments on teaching methods. Many of the experiments on teaching methods might have led to significant differences if the evaluation procedure avoided contamination by such factors as extra study.

Why does discussion method lead to greater learning than lecture method? The answer lies in the fact that discussion method arouses such concomitants as interaction among the students and the teacher, thinking on the part of the students as well as the teacher, clarification of concepts, relationship between various contents of the lesson, feedback, motivation and the like, all of which facilitate and enhance learning and most of which are not catalyzed by lecture method which is more or less a one-way affair consummated by a verbalist teacher. That discussion method, because of its very nature, operates more profitably in a small class (as in this experiment) than in a large class might have aided in confirming this hypothesis.

The fact that, in previous studies, the variable of class size has so repeatedly been found to produce no significant effect on the amount learned, and has yet yielded significant differences in the present experiment, implies that a restudy of other teaching variables using different measuring techniques might be more fruitful than it has previously been.

The data indicate that students in the small class learned significantly more in class than the students in a large class. The difference of about 3.06 points on a test which had a mean score of about 9.36 was fairly large, considering the relatively small variance of the difference scores and the fact that the small *versus* large class variable was limited to only one lecture per quiz. Furthermore, there was no attempt to utilize the unique advantage of a small class by permitting more questions or discussions.

What was the specific variable operating in the large and small classes which produced the difference? As Buxton (2) has opined, class size, like time, is not a variable by itself, rather it is an abstraction in which other variables tend to operate. In evaluating the course at the end of the year, almost all the students in the small class spontaneously commented that they found it easier to pay attention in the small class and that they had become more interested. Casual observations by the author corroborated this. The students in the small class seemed to be much more alert in their listening as well as notetaking behaviour. Rarely, if ever, were they observed in behaviours which are not uncommon in very large classes, such as talking to each other, pinching others, staring out of windows, reading, mimicking, etc. Undoubtedly, the very proximity of the lecturer in the small class acts as an inhibitory influence on these behaviours.

Perhaps the variable of class size had nothing to do with the obtained differences. It is possible that something like a "Hawthorne effect" was operating in which the students in the small class felt more significant, and more highly motivated because a special class had been instituted for them. This possibility, and similar ones, such as unintentional lecturer bias, or that students perhaps learn more at 8 a.m. than at 9.30 a.m. or 11.00 a.m., do not reduce the significance of the major finding, namely that differences as a result of teaching technique manipulations were found on quizzes but may not be found on a prepared – for final examination for which adequate time interval permits extra study.

That discussion method, as compared to lecture method, produces greater learning in a small class and that lecture method, again, produces greater learning in a small class than in a large class, reflect that class size, not so much the teaching method, may be the *raison d'etre* of the major finding.

Summary and Conclusions

Twenty students in a class taught by lecture method were compared on examination performance with a matched group of students taught by discussion method. The hypothesis that discussion method of teaching leads to greater learning than lecture method was confirmed. Again, the hypothesis, that the small class would do better on quizzes which specifically covered the classroom material and for which the students had not prepared, was verified when 20 students in a small class were compared on examination performance with a matched group of students who were in a large class. The implications of this methodological procedure were discussed in relation to other research on the effectiveness of different teaching methods.

References

1. Birney, R. and McKeachie, W. "The teaching of psychology: A survey of research since 1942." Psychol. Bull., 1955, 52, 51-68.
2. Buxton, C.E. "College teaching, a psychologist's view." New York: Harcourt Brace. 1956.
3. Good, C.V. "Colleges and Universities — VIII. Methods of Teaching." Encyc. educ. Res., 1950, 42, 273-278.
4. Kidd, J.W. "The question of class size." J. Higher Educ., 1952, 23, 440-444.

5. Nachman, Martin; and Opochinsky, Seymore. "The effects of different teaching methods: A methodological study." J. of Educ. Psych., 1958, 49, 5, 245-248.
6. Otto, H.J., and Von Borgersrode, F. "Class Size." Encyc. Educ. Res., 1950, 42, 212-215.
7. Wolfle, D.L. "The first course in psychology." Psychol. Bull., 1942, 39,685-712.

56. MEASURING TEACHER TRAINEES' TEACHING SKILL

Skills, being tangible, concrete, and definite, are said to be easily perceptible and measurable. However, this is less true of the teaching skill which, as distinct from other skills, involves in its measurement such attitudes of the teacher as predict how well he will get along with pupils in inter-personal relationships and how well gratified he will be with teaching as his vocation. Besides, good teaching essentially depends upon how good, harmonious, and satisfying is the two-way relationship between teacher and pupil. Such vital requirements of teaching render somewhat difficult the investigator's measurement of teaching skill. How far our measurement of teaching skill of teacher-trainees is consistent and reliable and how far a trainee's teaching skill in one subject is related to his skill in another are the two main purposes of this study.

The specific hypothesis to be tested is that our technique of measurement of trainee's teaching skill is reasonably accurate and reliable and that there is a good relationship between a candidate's teaching skill in one subject and that in another.

Method

Subjects. The subjects were 182 teacher-trainees of Government Training College for Teachers, Jullundur (Punjab State, India), 1961-62 session. The two sexes were about equally represented.

The evaluators were lecturers (instructors) of the College faculty, each possessing a minimum experience of five years in teaching theory and methodology of teaching and in guiding and evaluating trainees' teaching practice.

Procedure. A trainee was observed during two different 40 minute periods while teaching classes of a secondary school. He was informed of the date of each observation a week in advance so as to permit him to prepare detailed lesson notes and be ready for the task. The second observation was made two months after the first, by a different observer, and while trainee taught a different subject from the first. Evaluation was on a point basis, marks being allotted up to a maximum of 100. This procedure is called "internal assessment".

In addition, trainee's marks on the two lessons were combined and this total then correlated with his score in teaching skill in the University passing-out test. This test is another classroom teaching evaluation, employing the same criteria of evaluation as the internal assessment, but two examiners are employed and both are from outside the College.

Effort was made to ensure that all the observers evaluated the lessons on a common basis or that their criteria for giving credits were kept constant. This was done by asking the observers to keep in view such items as knowledge of subject-matter, ability to organise it, clarity of presentation, ability to create interest and use aids effectively, sympathetic attitude toward pupils and general effectiveness. Though it is disputable to assume that these qualities alone constitute teaching skill, it was thought proper to tabulate them for observers so as to make evaluation uniform and consistent.

Results

The product-moment correlation between the two internal assessments was .69 (standard error .04).

Specific correlations between internal assessments relative to subjects taught by trainees were as follows:

Subject taught	*r*	*N*	*S.E.*
Hindi and History	.67	18	.11
Panjabi and History	.56	49	.16
English and Mathematics	.74	17	.10
Mathematics and Science	.59	40	.10
History and English	.75	58	.05

Correlation between combined internal assessment scores and University passing-out scores was .68 (S.E. .04)

Discussion

The correlation between internal assessments is a measure of the reliability of the method and its magnitude here indicates that our internal assessment of teaching skill is quite reliable and dependable.

The array of similar correlations between subjects taught suggests that the assessments are little colored by the subject being taught, or, seen in terms of the trainees, indicate that trainees teach similar and dissimilar subjects about equally well. In other words, their skills tend to be stable and consistent.

Finally, the extent of the correlation between internal assessment and University (external) assessment indicates a notable agreement between the two, again supporting the reliability of the technique, and speaks favourably of our ability to assess trainees' teaching skill.

57. STANDARD OF ENGLISH IN SECONDARY SCHOOLS

The Investigation

The off-repeated charge that the standard of English is constantly falling in the schools in our country appears to be fairly true when one studies the appalling shape of the language used and accepted in schools. Assuming, and perhaps legitimately, that whether the people speak and hear good English would in the ultimate analysis be determined by schools, the charge is well founded. Schools can guarantee good English of the future scholars the way they ensure certain quantitative standards of curriculum.

The writer gets an opportunity to visit the local high schools every year in order to supervise the practical work of the B.T. students under training. This visit is spread over a period of six weeks. During the time the B.T. students are free from the lectures and teaching work allotted to them, they are required to correct the exercise books of their pupils, so that the room where they and their supervisor sit is stacked with rows of exercise books arranged on open shelves. The writer, during his such visits in the last three years examined from these stacks a sampling of the high school students' exercise books in English composition, carefully noted down the common errors in usage, and later classified these errors in several categories. As many as 300 exercise books picked out randomly in both boys' and girls' schools (having a well-shuffled and almost equal stock of children from all kinds of socio-economic strata of society) were gone through. A common error was considered as such when it was committed by at least twenty students. The categories or broad areas of errors noticed in the students' written work are given below in order of their frequency and occurrence:

Common Errors of Pupils

1. Incorrect use of tenses especially of irregular verbs like see, give, stick, buy.
2. Incorrect uses of the numbers and tenses of the verbs is, are, was, were.
3. Pronouns *i.e.* use of I, me, he, him, she, her, they.
4. Spellings: words, pronounced somewhat or slightly different from the way they were written, were usually mis-spelt.
5. Agreement of nouns, in number, with the verbs and their tenses.
6. Faulty punctuation.
7. Use of possessive pronouns: my, mine, his, her, ours.
8. Structure of interrogatory sentences, mistakes like "what you will do" instead of "what will you do". "Why he comes" instead of "why does he come"?
9. Incorrect use of prepositions and conjunctions (in, at, on, with).
10. Wrong use of the definite articles 'a', 'an'.
11. Defective knowledge of the use of capital letters.
12. Use of personal pronouns in compound structures such as 'Mohan and I (as subject), 'Mohan and me' (as object), 'to Mohan and me' (as object of preposition).
13. Use of 'who' and 'whom' while referring to persons *i.e.* "who did he go there with" instead of "with whom did he go there"?
14. Interchangeable use of 'its and 'it's'.
16. Using double negative as 'I don't have no books' etc.
17. Incorrect use of idioms.
18. Interchangeable use of "shall" and "will".
19. Poor structure of complex sentences: "She is one of those students who is......".

Possible Causes of Errors

The question "what are these errors due to" was then probed into through (i) intimate contacts with teachers of English, (ii) visits to schools and classes, (iii) study of school time-tables and (iv) conversations with students. The following causatives of the problem were discovered:

(a) A poor command of the language of teachers teaching English.
(b) Shortage of qualified teachers, resulting in English being taught by those less qualified or unqualified to teach the subject.
(c) Classes too large to permit individual attention.
(d) Very little attention paid to the exercises in English composition.
(e) Avoiding word-to-word correction of exercise-books.
(f) Failure to encourage well-spoken English.
(g) Teachers' and parents' failure to encourage the habit of reading good English literature in the pupils.
(h) Teachers' failure to recognise the importance of the teaching of English.
(i) Failure to diagnose the causes of bad English.
(j) Faulty methods of teaching English.

A glance at the list of errors might at first sight alarm the teacher, but he should take it for granted that it is not a problem which cannot be solved. If the teacher just makes up his mind not to allow the errors to go undetected in the students' spoken as well as written English, he has won half the battle. It has often been seen that teachers tolerate most of these errors and let these go unnoticed; hence the above suggestion. The usual practice is that the teachers grade the students' performance in written English as A, B, C etc. without giving much constructive help in the form of correcting an error, pointing it out, drawing pupil's attention to it, or taking the trouble of giving drill and practice in the corrected form.

Suggestions for Improvement

A look at the causes of the errors may induce the teacher teaching English to believe that he is helpless in the matter, but he very much needs to know that quite a few of the causes are such as he alone can alleviate.

The following suggestions are offered to schools with a view to making their teaching in English more effective and successful:

1. Encourage the habit of reading in the pupils. Higher classes may read material that has excellent literary qualities.
2. Provide ample opportunities for speaking both on the individual and group levels.
3. Encourage the writing of exercises from simple descriptive compositions to original and creative ones.
4. Teach specific skills like spelling, letter-writing.
5. Encourage the translation of expressions and structures in the mother tongue into English and *vice versa*.
6. Encourage the use of dictionary.
7. Encourage the pupils to listen into radio programmes in English.
8. Encourage critical and purposeful reading and discussion of standard books in English literature.
9. Provide challenging experiences which require the use of language.
10. Give guidance in the selection and use of appropriate and effective words and phrases as well as in the increase of vocabulary.
11. Emphasise on organization and precision of written materials.
12. Ensure that the pupils know the parts of speech: noun, pronoun, verb, adjective, adverb, preposition, the voices and tenses of the verb. Teach them to recognise the main parts of a simple sentence (subject, verb, objects, and complement) and the main parts of a complex sentence (the main clause and its supporting subordinates).
13. Pay individual attention depending upon child's needs and potentialities.

Teachers Teaching English

The home as well as the school lay the foundations on which rests child's future learning. Once the child learns the essential skills of language, his success, which largely depends upon efficient reading, writing and speaking, in all schoolwork is very much facilitated. Besides, his competence in language helps him to develop social understanding and aesthetic sense, and to explore more about himself and the world around him. His ability to use the language effectively will give him a certain amount of poise and self-confidence.

Good teachers of English, or for that matter of any subject, may not be the natural products of a teacher training programme. Teaching skill, in spite of keen perception and insight, like any other skill, is imbibed from deliberate observation and efforts to follow and seek assistance of a good teacher. Practical experience under expert guidance is most beneficial. A very regular and vigorous ing-service programme of training teachers would perhaps solve the problem of producing good teachers of English.

A conscientious teacher may be correcting spelling, punctuation or other mistakes in the pupils' exercises and yet he may not be fostering good English. Students be taught a great deal of grammar and yet be incapable of writing good English. They will not develop good English without practising the knowledge of grammar in every-day use. Similarly a piece of composition may have no grammatical errors and yet may not be a good English exercise because it is slipshod, haphazard, and colourless, it contains nothing of real import and is ambiguous. Good English implies clear thinking, proper organization of thought content, and selection of choicest words that convey the thoughts directly and effectively. Language, like social customs, is a human behaviour which changes with time. Norms of human behaviour change from one period to another; so do the norms of language. There is such a thing as the acceptable standard of human behaviour in a certain period. Parallel to this standard and exactly in conformity with it is the norm of a language which alone can be called good English. So it may be noted that good is a relative term here and not a measure of any absolute standard. More correctly, good English may just be a standard of the kind scholars of English, who possess normal intelligence and aptitude for the language, can accept and utilize.

The teacher teaching English in the high school has a two-fold function. He has to teach English as a language and as literature. The former is aimed at the use of the language in day-to-day life, and the latter attempts to develop aesthetic sense and literary expression. If the teacher teaches English through objectives and methods determined by the needs of his pupils and the nature of the language, and if literature is taught with reference to the same needs and in terms of the distinct qualities of literary art, the two aspects (*i.e.* linguistic and literary) supplement and complement each other.

It might be argued that faced as we are with the question of national language in India, it is futile to think of or try for good English; but the fact remains that English is still retained as an essential subject at both the high school and University levels. In spite of the rising tide of nationalistic sentiment in our fast-developing country, the role of English as a necessary second language at the levels of Government, trade, educational and inter-state communication is considered vital and immense. Besides, there has been a phenomenal expansion of secondary education preparatory to University disciplines in humanities, science, Arts, medicine as well as technical training. In the secondary schools imparting such education, English enjoys a pivotal position both as a discipline of value in itself and as a necessary medium of study in other fields. As such it is vitally necessary to keep up the standard of English. Let us, therefore, attempt to make our teaching of English efficient enough to make it possible for students to be good in English.

References

1. Benjamin S. Bloom, "Evaluation in Secondary Schools", pp. 201-230. A.I.C.S., Near Delhi.
2. Trevers, Robert M.W. "Introduction to Educational Research".
3. Cronbach, lee, J., "Essential of Psychological Testing", pp. 368-386.
4. Mario Pei, The story of language. "The New American Library", 1960.
5. L. Clark Keating, "Language for the Gifted", N.A.G.C. Ohio.

IX. VALUES, THEIR ORIGIN AND DEVELOPMENT

58. VALUE SCORES OF TEACHER TRAINEES AND COLLEGE TEACHERS

Andrews (4), using the "Study of Values" (1) on 564 teachers and principals, found significant differences for teachers of eight different subject areas and for principals on four of the scales, namely theoretical, economic, aesthetic and political. He found that teachers of social studies tended to score high on the aesthetic and political scales. Anderson (2), using the same test, on 19 secondary and 19 college history teachers, found college teachers scoring significantly higher on the aesthetic scale, lower on the economic scale. Bledsoe (5), administering the "Watson-Glaser Critical Thinking Appraisal" and the "Study of Values" on educational administrators, elementary and secondary teachers both male and female, found significant difference between scores of men and women on the aesthetic scale, significant difference between scores of administrators and secondary teachers on the economic scale, and between elementary and secondary teachers on the aesthetic and religious scales, and a significantly positive correlation between age and scores on the aesthetic scale. Gowen (7), using the "Study of Values" on education majors, concluded that gifted students tended to score significantly higher on the theoretical and political but lower on the economic and religious scales than did the general students. Kelley (11), administering the same test along with other tests on 300 engaged couples in 1935-38 and again after 20 years, found that scores on the economic, social and political scales remained about the same, that scores of men on the theoretical and aesthetic scales came down significantly and the scores of both men and women on the religious scale rose up significantly after the lapse of time. Sternberg (12), applying the same test along with the Kuder Preference Record and MMPI on students from nine subject areas, discovered sharpest differences in these tests between majors in music and English when compared with those in science, and found significant correlation between the aesthetic scale and tendencies toward maladjustment on the MMPI.

The present study, like the studies reviewed above, uses the well-tried "Study of Values", with a view to comparing the value scores of 25 teachers trainees and 25 college teachers matched for sex (males only), subject (Master's degree in Political Science whether getting teacher training or teaching in liberal arts colleges), age (24-29 years), academic ability (second division in M.A., *i.e.* 50 to 59 per cent marks), and socio-economic status (as revealed in interviews). The teacher trainees were selected from the batch of 340 B.Ed. students undergoing training for becoming secondary school teachers in State College of Education, Patiala (Session 1967-68), and the College teachers from liberal Arts Colleges of Patiala. The trainees at the time of testing had almost completed their training. These trainees had not taught at all, while the college teachers had taught in college for 2 to 5 years.

Findings

A summary of the scores on the study of values is given below in Table 1.

A glance at the table shows that on three of the six scales, namely theoretical, political and religious, there are almost no divergences between mean scores for the two groups; while on the remaining three scale, namely, economic, aesthetic and social, such divergences are there, though these are not wide enough. This is what may be expected, when the differences between the two groups of teachers were reduced to a minimum with regard to such considerations as sex, subject, age, academic ability and socio-economic status.

Table 1
Summary of Scores on the Study of Values

Group	Theoretical	Economic	Aesthetic	Social	Political	Religious
25 Teacher Trainees –						
Mean	36.39	34.53	32.40	35.25	36.72	31.34
S.D.	4.52	5.69	8.52	6.30	4.85	8.02
25 College Teachers –						
Mean	38.07	31.27	39.42	39.96	36.29	32.69
S.D.	4.02	5.20	5.02	8.92	5.27	9.00

This similarity in the means of the would-be high school and college teachers may also be owing to the facts that the persons in the two groups belong to the same culture [assuming that it is culture which tends to build up one's values (6,8,9)], that high school teachers in the present times are really more like college teachers than was the case in the past, that, being young as the high school teachers in this study are, they have more recently been in contact with college teachers and perhaps have assimilated their values.

Differences, in the means of the two groups, though slight in the case of most values, may be because different peer relations and expectations may cause some differences to appear, and because time (after graduation) spent in slightly different tasks may influence the scores after some years.

Significantly (.01 level) higher mean of college teachers on the aesthetic scale may be explained by the fact that the study and understanding of higher literature warranted by the requirement of enhancing knowledge and teaching the grown-ups, and development of artistic interests, which the arrangement of and participation in dramatics and other allied activities tend to promote (both of which promote aesthetic value), are abundantly available to college teachers and scarcely to the trainees who have yet to commence their teaching career.

Significantly (.05 level) higher mean of teacher trainees on the economic scale may be owing to the financial stringencies (caused by acute unemployment) they are often in and consequently a strong economic motive behind their present venture – both of which are not so strong in the case of the present day college teachers who are very well paid.

Significant differences in aesthetic and economic scales were revealed in Anderson's study (3) also in the same direction in which such differences have been shown by this study. Higher and significant (.05 level) mean of college teachers on the social scale may be due to interest in people aroused by the same influences which lead to liberalization of one's opinion about teacher-pupil relations. The social value items of the values' test are concerned with human relations which are the subject of much of the work in a liberal Arts Colleges. Teacher trainees, contrarywise, are not so much exposed to the said influences and hence perhaps their lesser score on the social scale.

Viewing the magnitude of mean scores, the means which are rather low when compared with the general norms for men are those of theoretical (both groups), economic (both groups), aesthetic (teacher trainees), political (both groups) and religious (both groups) scales, while the means of aesthetic (college teachers) and social (both groups) scales are not significantly different from the general norms for men. The S.D.'s obtained indicate that the scores on the religious and social scales (both groups) and on aesthetic scale (teacher trainees) are consistently more varied than on other scales.

A comparison (Table 2) of the value scores of the sample in this study and of a comparable sample of American subjects (young high school teachers and young college teachers, aged below 35) tested in an identical study (2) may be of some interest here.

Except on economic and social scales, American subjects (both school and college teachers) have consistently scored significantly (.01 level) higher than their Indian counterparts. There are several possible reasons for this phenomenon: (i) On the theoretical scale empirical and rational approach embodied in American culture and education may have given American subjects an edge over their Indian counterparts in whose culture and education emphasis on the said approach is comparatively less; (ii) Comparatively greater provision of artistic interests and training in American education might be developing Americans' aesthetic value more than Indians'; (iii) Much greater awakening, pragmatic philosophy and a sense of self-enhancement in American subject may be the cause of their higher scores on the political scale as compared to the corresponding scores of their Indian counterparts whose idealistic philosophy and altruistic culture seem to have cramped political value; (iv) Emphasis, in American education, on synthetic approach to the diagnosis and

Table 2

A Comparison of Indian and Americas Sebjects on "Study of Values"

Group	N	Means						S.D.'s					
		T	E	A	S	P	R	T	E	A	S	P	R
Indian School teachers	25	36.39	34.53	32.40	35.25	36.72	31.34	4.52	5.69	8.52	6.30	4.85	8.02
American School teachers	19	45.09	34.62	41.55	38.45	43.37	37.72	7.68	8.19	13.86	4.11	4.27	10.26
Significance of Mean Difference	...	.01	n.s.	.01	n.s	.01	.01	...	...	...	...	...	...
Indian College teachers	25	38.07	31.27	39.42	39.96	36.29	32.69	4.02	5.20	5.02	8.92	5.27	9.00
American College teachers	19	43.17	27.09	47.18	39.18	42.18	40.27	6.99	7.92	7.64	8.02	5.49	12.38
Significance of Mean Difference	...	.01	n.s.	.01	n.s.	.01	.01	...	...	...	...	...	...

solution of problems and on the concept of unity may account for the American subjects' relatively higher score on religious scale.

On economic and social scales the subjects of the two countries are alike, probably because the tendencies to be practical and businesslike which promote economic value may be the natural consequence of American philosophy and the newly-acquired characteristics of young Indians tested in the present study, while altruistic tendencies conducive to social value may be imbedded in both Indian and American cultures. Unless, however, further evidence from future researches is forthcoming, these arguments in support of the differences and similarities between the value scores of Indian and American samples may not be too strongly emphasized.

Summary

The "Study of Values" administered to 25 teacher trainees and 25 College teachers, matched for sex, subject, age, academic ability and socio-economic status, revealed among the two groups significant differences on economic, aesthetic, and social scales and almost no differences on theoretical, political and religious scales. A comparison with comparable American population revealed significant differences in favour of American groups in all scales except economic and social.

References

1. Allport, G.W., Vernon, P.E. and Lindzey, G., "Study of Values". (3rd ed.) Boston: Houghton Mifflin, I960.
2. Anderson, Alvin, L., "A Comparison of Study of Values Scores for Selected Secondary and College Teachers". The Journal of Educational Research, Vol. 60, No. 2, Oct. 1966, pp. 86-89.
3. Anderson, Alvin, L., "Personal and Situational Factors Affecting the Choice Between College and Secondary Teaching". Unpublished Ph.D. Dissertation, University of Oregon, 1964.
4. Andrews, John, H.M., "Administrative Significance of Psychological Differences Between Secondary Teachers of Different Subject Matter Fields". Alberta Journal of Educational Research, III (December, 1957), pp. 199-228.
5. Bledsoe, Joseph, C., "A Comparative Study of Values and Critical Thinking Skills of a Group of Educational Workers". Journal of Education Psychology, XLVI (November, 1955), pp. 409-17.
6. Gordon, Leonard, V. and Kakkar, S.B., "A Cross-Cultural Study of Indian and American Interpersonal Values". The Journal of Social Psychology, 1966,69, pp. 339-340.
7. Gowan, J.C., "Achievement and Personality Test Scores of Gifted College Students". Journal of Educational Research, VII, pp. 105-9.

8. Kakkar, S.B. and Leonard V. Gordon, "The Interpersonal Values of Indian Teacher Trainees". The Journal of Social Psychology, U.S.A. 1966,69, pp. 341-342.
9. Kakkar, S.B., "A Cross-Cultural Study of Values". The Research Bulletin (Arts), Panjab University, No. LV(1), 1967, pp. 1-17.
10. Kelley, E. Lowell., "Consistency of the Adult Personality". American Psychologist, X (November, 1955), pp. 659-81.
11. Sternberg, Carl., "The Relation of Interests, Values and Personality to the Major Field of Study in College". Unpublished Ph.D. Dissertation, New York: University, 1953.

59. IMPACT OF TRAINING ON VALUES

Does training influence values? Literature on values does not provide a categorical answer to this important question. Most of the researches on teachers and their preparation have not made any objective assessment of the effects of teacher training on students (2,5,6,7). A recent study (8) concluded that the personality patterns of male students differed from those of the female students both at the beginning and end of the teacher training course, that the changes occurring in each group, as observed after teacher training, were too few to be taken note of, and that the values of the males changed more than those of the females. The study also hinted at the possibility that the training may have influenced the social and economic values of the males, not females.

This research is an attempt to assess and evaluate some of the changes occurring in the values of a group of graduate teacher trainees during the course of training.

Method and Procedure

The Allport-Vernon Lindzey Study of Values (British Version) (1,9) was employed to assess and evaluate the values. This test, which is standardised, reliable and valid, has been amply used in the work reviewed by Duffy and Dukes (3, 4). It tests empirically Spranger's theory (10) that people can be classified according to their attitudes or values. It is specifically designed to measure the relative importance of these six basic values: Theoretical (having dominant interest in the discovery of truth, and being empirical, critical, rational, intellectual in approach); Economic (having interest in what is useful, being practical and a good businessman); Political (being interested in personal power, not necessarily limited to the field of politics); Social (having love of people, being, sympathetic, kind and altruistic); Aesthetic (having artistic interests, valuing form and harmony); Religious (being mystical, seeking to comprehend the cosmos as a whole).

The test was administered in August 1967 immediately before the training course started and again, to the same group, in March, 1968 at the time the training came to an end, and the scores registered on the two occasions were compared to evaluate the change caused during the training. The findings were compared to the findings yielded by a comparable study made for British teacher trainees.

The students taking the Education degree course (B.Ed.) in the State College of Education, Patiala, in the session 1967-68 participated in the study. Of the 268 students on roll, those who had graduated in April, 1967 examination, were in the age range of 19 to 24 years and have had no teaching experience formed the subjects. Such subjects numbered 150 (100 men and 50 women). Thus, education, age and teaching experience which can, among other factors (that were not controlled), influence students' values were controlled, so that the subjects under the experiment formed a fairly homogeneous group whose values were placed under the influence of, at least ostensibly, a single variable called teacher training course. The sample was fairly representative of similar population all over the state of Punjab. The subjects came from below-average to above-average socio-economic and educational strata of the state.

Results

Having obtained the scores for all the six values, means and standard deviations of the scores were calculated, separately for the men and the women in the group, and the differences between the means for the two sexes tested for significance using t-test. The results of the calculations for values measured before training and those measured after training are given in Table 1 and Table 2 respectively.

Table 1
Means, Standard Deviations and Significance of Difference between the Means of Men and Women for Values Measured before Training

Value	Group	N	Mean	S.D.	Difference of means	Significance level
Theoretical	Men	100	32.01	4.26	3.01	t = 4.56 >.01
	Women	50	29.00	354	-	
Economic	Men	100	28.30	4.24	-	t = 6.16 >.01
	Women	50	32.80	4.54	4.50	

Political	Men	100	25.56	5.92	4.56	t = 4.85 >.01
	Women	50	21.00	4.67	-	
Social	Men	100	40.70	4.81	4.40	t = 5.56 > .01
	Women	50	36.30	4.40	-	
Aesthetic	Men	100	21.43	6.09	-	t = 3.46 > .01
	Women	50	25.33	3.70	3.83	
Religious	Men	100	32.00	7.32	-	t = 2.76 >.01
	Women	50	35.87	9.86	3.87	

Table 2

Means, Standard Deviations and Significance of Difference Between the Means of Men and Women for Values Measured After Training

Value	Group	N	Mean	S.D.	Difference of means	Significance level
Theoretical	Men	100	32.28	3.66	2.79	t = 4.50 > .01
	Women	50	29.49	4.54	-	
Economic	Men	100	26.00	4.67	-	t = 5.29 > .01
	Women	50	30.45	5.60	4.45	
Political	Men	100	25.22	4.80	4.42	t = 5.45 > .01
	Women	50	20.80	5.30	-	
Social	Men	100	43.00	6.30	3.60	t = 3.78 > .01
	Women	50	39.40	3.80	-	
Aesthetic	Men	100	21.50	5.40	-	t = 4.67 > .01
	Women	50	25.33	3.70	3.83	
Religious	Men	100	32.00	6.51	-	t = 2.81 > .01
	Women	50	34.53	8.00	2.53	

Significant differences between the scores of the men and women students, on both occasions, when they were tested, warranted treating them as separate groups.

Table 1. Before training, fairly significant to highly significant differences were found between the various value scores of men and women students. The range-line of this increasing significance paralleled the line of values in this order: religious, aesthetic, theoretical, political, social, economic. The men's scores exceeded the women's significantly on social, political and theoretical values, the significance of such excess being on the decrease in the same order; while the scores of the women exceeded those of the men significantly on economic, aesthetic and religious values, the significance of such excess being on the decrease in the same order.

Whereas the highest degree of significance was in favour of women excelling men in economic value, the lowest too was in favour of women surpassing their male counterparts in religious value.

The highest degree of significance in favour of the men, next only to that in favour of the women, was in respect of social values.

Whereas the order of values for men, according to the magnitude of the value scores, from highest to lowest, was social, theoretical, religious, economic, political and aesthetic, that for the women was social, religious, economic, theoretical, aesthetic and political.

Table 2. After training, the differences between the scores of men and women students ranged from fairly significant to highly significant, the value order of this increase in significance being political, economic, aesthetic, theoretical, social, religious. The men's scores significantly exceeded the women's and the women's scores exceeded the men's on the values on which they had so exceeded each other in their scores on the tests administered before training, except that the significance of such excess before training was more in the score of social than in that of political value, while the significance of such excess after training was more in the score of political than in that of social value.

Whereas the highest degree of significance was in favour of men excelling women in political value, the lowest went to women surpassing men in religious value. The highest degree of significance in favour of women, next only to that in favour of men, was in respect of economic value.

The order of values both for men and women, according to the magnitude of the value scores, remained the same as it was before training.

The differences between the scores before training and those after training, of both men and women, when examined, were found to be too small to be significant at even 5 per cent level, for all values except social and economic. The mean score on social values of both men and women had increased significantly, while their mean score on economic values had decreased significantly.

Table 3. The highest degree of such significance of difference was in favour of women excelling men in social values. Also men's gain in social values matched their loss in economic values.

Conclusions

(i) The values of the men students, as revealed by this study, differed from those of the women students, both before and after the teacher training course.

Table 3
Change in Means and S.D.'s and Significance of the Change—Before to After Training N=100 Men and 50 Women

Value	Before after training	Mean		S.D.		Difference of 'before'		Significance of difference after' means	
		Men	Women	Men	Women	Men	Women	Men	Women
Theoretical	Before	32.01	29.00	4.26	3.54	-	-	n.s.	n.s.
	After	32.28	29.49	3.66	4.54	00.27	00.49	.05	.05
Economic	Before	28.30	32.80	4.24	4.54	2.30	2.35	sign.	sign.
	After	26.00	30.45	4.67	5.60	-	-	at .01	at .05
Political	Before	25.56	21.00	5.92	4.67	00.34	00.20	n.s.	n.s.
	After	25.22	20.80	4.80	5.30	-	-	at .05	at .05
Social	Before	40.70	36.30	4.81	4.40	-	-	sign.	sign.
	After	43.00	39.40	6.30	3.80	2.30	3.10	at .01	at .01
Aesthetic	Before	21.43	25.03	6.09	6.20	-	-	n.s.	n.s.
	After	21.50	25.33	5.40	3.70	00.07	00.30	at .05	at .05
Religious	Before	32.00	35.87	7.32	9.86	-	1.34	n.s.	n.s.
	After	32.00	34.53	6.51	8.00	-	-	at .05	at .05

(ii) Changes occurring in each group during the period of training were only minimal.
(iii) The only significant changes observed were in social and economic values of both men and women students.
(iv) The changes mentioned in (iii) above were in terms of promoting social value and devaluing economic value.
(v) Women, more than men, improve on social value and deteriorated on economic value.
(vi) Women's improvement on social value was found to be somewhat higher than their deprovement on economic value.
(vii) Men's improvement on social value was found to be as much as their deprovement on economic value.

That the changes observed in both open and women students were caused by the training they underwent between the two testings is not indisputable, but that nothing which the student teachers under study experienced during the same period had significantly changed their values, at least as many as four on the test used, may be safely said. The training course may have influenced the social and economic values of both men and women, but the other four values seem to have stayed put. Nevertheless, this research tends to give out that the teacher training may influence at least some aspects of students' personality or values to at least some extent. If it is assumed that the significant changes in most values and the significant ones in a few may have been caused by external factors (not controlled in this experiment), other than the teacher training course, exclusively or in combination with the training course, the pattern of changes as also its magnitude in case of each value would have been different from the one we now have. Since original pattern of scores on each value has survived the training course, it may be safely said that external factors have not influenced the students' values even if training too has not contributed much to change in values. This may suggest that inherent factors like the students' ability to absorb the influences conducive to the enhancement of one or more values might have resulted in the changes observed in this study.

Even inherent factors make themselves felt only when they are roused to action by environmental stimuli which in the present study were chiefly the teacher training course and allied factors.

Discussion

Though the results yielded by this research fail to permit any categorical statements about the influence of teacher training on the 150 students involved, yet they are suggestive of reflection and further research.

Only small changes in the patterns of scores on the values' test indicate, if not affirm, that by the time they reach a post-graduate stage students have entered adulthood, with their personality patterns already established. The tenets of personality or the value systems evaluated by the values' test seem to be relatively stable, in that they underwent almost no change during the period of teacher training. Alternatively, it may be said that the qualities assessed by the values' test may not be susceptible to training.

A period of only 6½ months between the two testings is perhaps too small to be adequate for effecting any substantial changes in the value systems or personality patterns almost permanently laid down during the plastic years of earlier stages of growth. It is possible that the student teachers for elementary education, who start their training when younger (after matriculation) and undergo a much longer training course (two years), may manifest marked changes in their values. Their personality patterns are likely to be less developed at the start of the training course than those of the graduate students, and the greater duration of their course may let certain inevitable influences of teacher education affect them indelibly. If the changes, if any, in the personality patterns of these students during the teacher training course are compared with those shown by a group of the same age and similar socio-economic status, following a degree course in liberal arts, the differences between the results of the two groups may reveal differences between the impact-potential of a teacher training course and that of a liberal arts course. If, however, the two groups show no difference in the changes their respective courses bring in them, the changes could be attributed to maturation rather than training of some kind.

The only significant changes found, in this study, were in the social and economic values of the students.

The maximum increase observed was in the social value scores of students, both men and women. These scores symbolise interest in people for their own sake, and may have been affected by the same influences which lead to the liberalisation of men's opinions about pupil-teacher relations. The social value items of the values' test are concerned with human relations which are the subject of much of the work in a teacher-training course. Hence, perhaps, the greatest increase in the social value scores. Of the two sexes, women showed greater increase in social value than men. Men's scores were already very high before training and thus there was lesser opportunity for change in them than in the scores of women, whose scores were originally much lower. The amount of possible change in score may be limited by the nature of the test in that the values' test is too brief and short to offer adequate scope for changes to show up that a longer test generally affords.

Men and women students, almost equally, registered a decrease in economic value. The teacher training course does not lay much stress purely on what is useful or on being a practical businessman. If anything, the emphasis of the course can be said to be deviated towards social value. As an increase in one's score in one value can be achieved only at the cost of the score in another (there being an aggregate of 180 points to be distributed among the six values on the values' test used here), it is not surprising that it was the students' economic scores which diminished when their social scores increased. Their scores on other values remained unaltered.

That only social and economic values underwent a change suggests that not all aspects of the students' values, or for that matter students' personalities, are susceptible to training. That even these two values did not register equal amounts of change tends to prove that the students' values are not equally susceptible to training. That in one (social) of the so-changing values women recorded a greater magnitude of change than men, as also the fact that the magnitude of change in all the values though insignificant is different, one from another, clearly suggest that the effects of the teacher training course may not be quite the same for men and women students. These three, however, are the hypotheses that could be tested with other groups of population, in the co-educational as well as single-sexed colleges of education where the pattern of change in values consequent on training is likely to be different.

It is evident that some of the students' personal qualities or values are likely to be fairly stable by the time they seek admission in the teacher-training college. These qualities should be given the greatest preference while making selection, since there is almost no scope of their being changed considerably during the course. If these are the qualities which can make a good teacher, the presence or absence of them should, among other factors, be a decisive condition for trainees' selection or rejection respectively. There are other qualities or values which are amenable to change by training. If these are the qualities needed for making a good teacher, besides or in place of the qualities of the greatest preference, these should be given the next preference, at least at the outset. In other words teacher trainees should be selected on the basis of the qualities that cannot be changed, and then the training course should attempt to train such other qualities as can be changed.

Political, theoretical, religious and aesthetic values, as defined by the values' test used here, were little influenced by experiences faced during a teacher training course. If, therefore, these qualities are considered desirable in a teacher, such students should be selected who are possessed of these values at the very beginning of a training course.

Many other qualities could also be considered on these lines, but this research produces evidence yielded by only one test. Further researches using tests for other qualities and experimental techniques involving proper control of other factors that can affect values might prove productive and useful.

Which qualities or values are changeable and to what extent, which ones are those that cannot be changed, are such qualities the same or different with students of different sexes and greatly differing ages, are the questions which could be answered by future researches. But unless such answers are obtained, it seems difficult to evaluate the impact the teacher training can exclusively make on students' values.

Indian and British Teachers

Comparison of the outcomes of this research with those of Evan's study reveals (8):

(a) the changes in values occurring during the period of training are equally minimal both in the case of the British and Indian teacher trainees (comparable groups of both men and women);

(b) insignificant changes in the four values of the British men are matched by insignificant changes in the four values of their Indian counterparts. These four values are theoretical, political, aesthetic and religious.

(c) significant (.05) rise in social value of the British men is matched by significant rise (.01) in social value of Indian men;
(d) significant (.05) diminution in economic value of the British men is matched by significant (0.1) diminution in economic value of Indian men;
(e) insignificant changes in all the six value of the British women are matched by insignificant changes in four of the six values of Indian women (The two unmatched are economic and social);
(f) insignificant diminution in economic value of the British women is matched by significant (0.05) diminution in economic value of Indian women;
(g) insignificant rise in social value of the British women is matched by significant (.01) rise in social value of Indian women.

Whereas the findings at (a) to (e) tend to indicate that British teacher trainees are hardly different from their Indian counterparts in most of the values examined in this research, those at (a) and (g) point out that the two populations tend to differ, though not much, in the change they seem to undergo in just two values, during the teacher training period.

If it is assumed that the teacher training course causes change in values, the findings at (a) to (e) may be understood to mean that the teacher training in Britain and that in India are congruent and equally effective in all respects, provided the two populations are exactly alike and comparable, as assumed in this comparative analysis. Since causal relationship between teacher training and value-change has not yet been demonstrated, it would not be fair to conclude that the teacher training in the two countries is equally effective in terms of value orientation. The differences in the nature and extent of the teacher training courses in the two countries are also too marked and too well-known to favour such conclusion. If it is hypothesised that the individuals at the teacher training stage are too mature and grown-up to absorb any change in their values, the above mentioned findings may be understood to denote similarities in the cultural and social upbringing of individuals in the two countries, provided that we assume that the teacher training courses of the two countries are alike and comparable. Perhaps there is some force or dimension, common to the cultures or value-domains of the two countries, which so makes the teacher training instruction so far as its ability to cause value change is concerned.

On the other hand, from the findings at (a) and (g) it may be observed that social and economic values of women may undergo greater change, though the direction of this change is the same, at the hands of the teacher training course in India than that in Britain, other things being equal. But since casual relationship between teacher-training and value-change should be ruled out in the absence of any demonstrable findings to this effect, and since there is reason to believe that the teacher training course in India is not particularly conducive to produce changes in social and economic values of women, the above observation seems far-fetched. If it is surmised that the Indian women teacher trainees, more than their British counterparts, absorb change in their social and economic values, other things being equal, one may observe that the former are more flexible than the latter in regard to these two values or that these values are more firmly set in the latter than in the former. Perhaps there is some force in the Indian culture, absent in the British culture, which motivates Indian women teacher trainees, more than their British counterparts, to absorb change in their social and economic values. It would, however, be unscientific to put much credence in these observations in the absence of any valid evidence.

A comparison of value scores of the British and the Indian subjects before and after training may be of some interest here. Since value differences between men and women teacher trainees before training are in the same direction—as the one in which they are found after training, both in Indian and British subjects, it is evident that there are commonalities and stability (may be owing to cultural similarities) in the value patterns–in so far as men excel women in some values and women excel men in others–of the two countries. Perhaps there is something common to the cultures of the two countries, which keeps up the differences between men and women in regard to their values, in spite of the things like the influence of teacher training to which the trainees are exposed.

Except in political and aesthetic values in which men and women of the two countries are alike in the matter of one sex differing from the other, the direction of value differences between the Indian men and women is opposite to that between British men and women. This is true in the case of value scores both before and after training. Indian and British cultures seem to develop the political and aesthetic values of their men and women in the direction similar to each other. The two cultures seem to resemble each other in some ways.

Whereas Indian men excel women in theoretical and social values, British women excel men in these values. Again, Indian women excel men in economic and religious values; but British men excel women in these values. The intra-national sex differences both in Indian and British teacher trainees may be attributed, in part at least, to their respective cultures, while the international sex differences may be owing to cultural differences between the two countries.

Indo-British Values Across 'Culture' Paradigm: Men teacher trainees in India (both before and after training–see Tables 4 and 5) score higher than their British counterparts in theoretical and social values, and lower in economic and aesthetic values. In political and religious values the two groups are more or less alike.

India's ancient philosophy which emphasises search for truth and altruistic interests seems to account for their (Indian men's) being higher in theoretical and social values, and the same tenets of this philosophy by depreciating the trait of being practical and utility conscious explain being relatively lower in economic values as against the Western philosophy, which is down-to-earth, pragmatic, materialistic, and which hence may tend to make the British somewhat lower in theoretical and social values and higher in economic values.

Being lower in aesthetic values may be owing to little emphasis on artistic and creative interests in India's traditional scholastic programmes as also to her colourless, formless and dull cultural activities which abound in the lives of little children, as against British schools' deliberate and planned programmes of training children's aesthetic sensibilities.

Both British and Indian cultures seem to have their roots in their respective religions which in fact govern the very way of life of their people. Hence the proximity between the Indians and the British in religious value.

The nature and extent of interest in personal power and grounding in political life, which stem from political history and ancient culture, may be almost evenly proportioned in the two nations partly because both of them had an equally checkered political career and partly because India was influenced for over a century by the political hegemony of the British and was later obliged, though not unwillingly, to adopt the English political hierarchy; hence the negligible difference in the political value scores of the two peoples.

Women teacher trainees in India (both before and after training–See Tables 4,5) score higher than their British counterparts in economic and religious values and lower in theoretical, social and aesthetic values. In political value the two groups do not differ from each other.

Indian women more than men, and British men more than women, score higher in economic value, probably because of Indian women's relatively more recent entry in the world of business and vocations and their consequent bid to outdo their male counterparts in being independent and economically self-sufficient, as compared to British women who are neither new entrants in the vocational world nor are they backward in such competition with men. Thus, in economic value Indian women (of the country's newly-emerging social order and the fast evolving culture which in collusion with the industrial and materialistic culture of the West stresses economic values) seem to excel not only their male counterparts in India but also their male counterparts in Britain (who are already scoring higher than the female in their own country) and

Table 4
A Comparison of India (Punjab) and British Teacher Trainees on the Values' Test after Training

	N	MEANS						S.D.'s					
		T	E	P	S	A	R	T	E	P	S	A	R
MALE													
Indian	100	32.01	28.30	25.56	40.70	21.43	32.00	4.26	4.24	5.92	4.81	6.09	7.32
British	32	28.00	30.91	26.66	38.72	23.47	32.25	5.29	6.84	7.63	6.41	7.39	15.81
Difference		4.01	–2.61	–1.10	1.98	–2.04	–0.25						
Significance		.01	.01	n.s.	.05	.05	n.s.						
FEMALE													
Indian	50	29.00	32.80	21.00	36.30	25.03	35.87	3.54	4.54	4.67	4.40	6.20	9.86
British	46	31.24	27.37	21.22	43.96	27.07	29.15	6.26	6.51	5.78	5.92	7.25	13.21
Difference		–2.24	5.43	–0.22	–7.66	–2.04	6.72						
Significance		.01	.01	n.s.	.01	.05	.01						

	N	MEANS						S.D.'s					
		T	E	P	S	A	R	T	E	P	S	A	R
MALE													
Indian	100	32.28	26.00	25.22	43.00	21.50	32.00	3.66	4.67	4.80	6.30	5.40	6.51
British	32	28.59	29.03	26.44	41.25	22.03	32.66	4.68	7.20	6.20	4.90	7.49	15.00
Difference		3.69	–3.03	–1.22	1.75	–0.75	–0.66						
Significance		-.01	.01	n.s.	.05	n.s.	n.s.						
FEMALE													
Indian	50	29.49	30.45	20.80	39.40	25.33	34.53	4.54	5.60	5.30	3.80	3.70	8.00
British	46	31.61	25.76	21.63	44.59	27.50	28.91	6.31	7.49	6.50	5.30	6.76	13.38
Difference		–2.12	4.69	–0.83	–5.19	–2.17	5.62						
Significance		.05	.01	n.s.	.01	.05	.01						

hence their female counterparts in Britain too. All this is an endeavour and with a vengeance to forge ahead, as it seems at least, in almost utter disregard of their age-old (though now-less-stressed and much-less-practised) idealistic and spiritualistic philosophy, as distinct from the West's pragmatic or materialistic outlook (which in a preceding paragraph has been attributed to British men's edge over Indian men in economic value).

Whereas males in India, belonging to the patriarchal society as they do or at least as they did until very recent times, have been exposed to the Western ways of thought and action through education and industry for centuries of foreign rule and have consequently tended to deviate a little from the mystical, religious preachings of the nation's idealistic philosophy, women were not so exposed and were all along, till independence twenty years ago, destined to play the ancient role of home-makers in the hitherto 'world of men' as it existed. This explains Indian women's higher score in religious value. Consequently Indian women found no opportunity to deviate from the erstwhile religious culture, as compared to their British counterparts who under the 'outward' Western philosophy were not so placed and were "marching ahead" all abreast with their male counterparts. Hence, probably, Indian women's edge over the British women in religious value.

That Indian women are scoring below their British counterparts in aesthetic values may be owing to the reasons for which Indian men score below British men in this value, as explained in a preceding paragraph, because training in aesthetics given to women in India or elsewhere perhaps may in no way be different from that given to men in India or elsewhere. Women's higher scores than men in this value, whether in India or Britain, are likely to be owing to women's proverbial, even natural, endowment of relatively higher aesthetic value, as illustrated by Spranger (10) in the study of sex differences on the Allport-Verman-Lindzey study of values.

Indian women's long-protracted backwardness in the matters of forging ahead in fields like education, vocation, business and all else (which in India until very recent history could be justly called masculine fields), that made them somewhat dependent on menfolk, who truly dominated the show, and that may have consequently led to develop in them 'inwardness' and traits of being uncritical, submissive, somewhat self-centred or at least home-centred, seems to have kept them not only below Indian men in their own country in theoretical and social values, but below the British women too who, contrariwise, under the influence of their practical and 'outward' philosophy, are excelling their male counterparts in these values. The paradigm of ideal woman unfailingly and unexceptionably loyal-to-husband, meticulously chaste, most obedient and faithful to the older folk and possessed of all virtues to a fault (preached, for good reasons indeed and for living an ideal and enviable life by the ever-lasting Indian philosophy) may also have contributed toward this deficiency of Indian women.

The reasons Indian and British men may have for being alike in political value seem to hold good for Indian and British women too for being alike in this value.

It would be fair indeed to recognize that the findings of this research may not be generalized except for (i) the specific conditions from which the facts of the present study are derived, (ii) the limited though representative number of the teacher trainees' sample employed, and the (iii) test used. It is necessary to replicate the study (i) on larger and more representative samples from different populations, (ii) with other reliable and valid instruments, (iii) by proper evaluation of dimensional extremities and (iv) under different conditions, before a scientific generalization can be made.

Summary

The influence of teacher training on students' values was estimated, through the use of the 'study of values' test (1) on 150 graduate teacher trainees (100 men and 50 women), controlled for age, education and teaching experience. The test was administered at the commencement, and again at the end of the teacher training course and the test scores on the two occasions compared to evaluate the changes possibly caused by the training course. Minimal changes, except in social and economic values, were found and significant sex differences revealed in all the six values, both before and after the course.

Comparison with Evans' (8) results in a similar study showed identity between the two findings in that: changes in theoretical, political, aesthetic and religious values of males were insignificant, rise in social value and fall in economic value of males were significant.

The comparison showed differences between the two in that: the Indian women showed changes in economic and social values but no change in the remaining four values, while the British women showed no change in any value.

Differences between the value scores (both before and after training) of Indian and British teacher trainees may be attributable to the cultural differences between the two countries.

The general pattern of value scores (men excelling women in some values and reverse in some others) survived the impact of teacher training both in the case of Indian and British teacher trainees, indicating that the training may not affect all aspects of students' personalities (which are by now well stabilized) or at least the aspects examined in this study. Slight changes observed after training in the Indian sample cannot be attributed to the teacher training course alone, especially when the trainees are exposed to the whole wide world and when several other factors, perhaps more potent than the factor of teacher training, which can influence their values, have not been controlled.

References

1. Allport, G.W. Vernon, P.E., and Undzey, G. "Study of Values (3rd Edi), Boston: Houghton Mifflin, I960.
2. Allen, E.A. (1962) "Professional Training of Teachers: A Review of Research." Educ. Res., V. 3, 200-15.
3. Duffy, E. (1940), "A Critical Review of Investigations Employing the All-port-Vernon 'Study of Values' and other Tests of Evaluative Attitude," Psych. Bull. 37, 597-612.
4. Dukes, W.F. (1955), "Psychological Studies of Values," Psy. Bull., 52, 24-50.
5. Evans, K.M. (1959), "Research on Teaching Ability," Edu. Res., 1, 3, 22-36.
6. Evans, K.M. (1959a), "The Teacher-Pupil Relationship," Educ. Res., II, 1, 3-8.
7. Evans, K.M. (1961), An Annotated Bibliography of British Research on Teaching and Teaching Ability," Educ. Res., IV, I, 67-80.
8. Evans, K.M. (1967), 'Teacher Training Courses and Students' Personal Qualities", Educ. Res., X, 1, 72-77.
9. Richardson, S. (1965), "The Study of Values," London: N.F.E.R.
10. Spranger, E. (1928), "Types of Men." Halle: Niemeyer.

60. THE INTERPERSONAL VALUES OF INDIAN TEACHER TRAINEES*

The present study was performed to determine whether a relationship exists between values of Indian teacher trainees, as measured by the Survey of Interpersonal Values (SIV),[1] and their rated effectiveness as teachers; and to compare the values of this group with those of teacher trainees in two other cultures.

At the beginning of the fall semester at the Government Training College for Teachers, 50 male and 50 female teacher trainees were administered the SIV. Toward the end of the senior year, the teaching ability of each subject was evaluated by two different examiners on the basis of two classroom performances. Product-moment correlation coefficients were obtained, separately by sex, between scores on the SIV and the summed ratings of teaching effectiveness. Seven of the 12 coefficients were statistically significant at or beyond the .05 level of confidence. Teachers of either sex rated as being the more effective of the sample tended to be relatively low on Support and high on Benevolence. In addition, for females, favourable ratings were significantly associated with being low on Conformity and high on Independence, and for males, with being high on Leadership.

SIV data were obtained for an augmented senior sample of 73 males and 123 females at the same institution. When means were compared with those of American teacher trainee samples of 25 males and 28 females, it was found that the Indian subjects of both sexes scored significantly lower on Support and Recognition and significantly higher on Conformity and Benevolence than the American trainees. Also, Indian males scored lower in Independence than did their American counterparts; differences for the females approached significance. Means of the Indian female group were compared with those of a sample of 45 female Japanese trainees(1). All mean differences were in the same direction as those found between the female Indian and American groups, with differences for Support, Conformity, Independence, and Benevolence being statistically significant. Differences between Indian and American samples are in directions congruent with differences between characteristics and beliefs of

* Dr. Leonard V. Gordon, New York (U.SA.) was co-researcher and co-author.

the two cultures. The greater similarity between the Japanese and American subjects as compared with the Indian and American subjects may reflect, in part, post-war American influence.

References

1. Gordon, L.V., Survey of Interpersonal Values, Chicago: Science Research Associates, 1960.

61. A CROSS-CULTURAL STUDY OF TEACHERS' VALUES*

While the measurement of the value structure of the teacher trainee has received attention in America, there is a notable lack of research in this area in India. Since the values that an individual holds may affect his relationships with other people as well as his occupational success, the investigation of this particular aspect of personality in the prospective teacher would appear to be most important.

The present study was performed to determine whether a relationship exists between certain interpersonal values of Indian teacher trainees and their rated effectiveness as teachers. This group was also to be compared with teacher trainees in two other cultures on the same values in order to determine the extent to which measures of these values reflect certain known characteristics of the Indian culture.[1]

Procedure and Results

The Survey of Interpersonal Values (SIV) (4) was judged to be relevant for the purpose of the present study by the senior author (Kakkar, S.B.) and his staff. The content was appropriate for educated, English-speaking subjects and the values themselves appeared to have saliency within the Indian culture. Also, previous research with this instrument in America had indicated that the patterning of interpersonal values of teacher trainees was significantly related to evaluations of their performance in the practice teaching situation(6).

The six values measured by the SIV are defined as follows: Support (S)–being treated with understanding, receiving encouragement from other people, being treated with kindness and consideration; Conformity (C)–doing what is socially correct,

* Dr. Leonard V. Gordon, New York (U.S.A.) was co-researcher and co-author.

1. This was done; the studies appear later in this chapter.

following regulations closely, doing what is accepted and proper, being a conformist; Recognition (R)–being looked up to and admired, being considered important, attracting favourable notice, achieving recognition; Independence (I)–having the right to do whatever one wants to do, being free to make one's own decision, being able to do things in one's own way; Benevolence (B)–doing things for other people, sharing with others, helping the unfortunate, being generous; and Leadership (L)–being in charge of other people, having authority over others, being in a position of leadership or power.

As a preliminary step, it was considered important to obtain an estimate of the reliability of the SIV for an Indian sample and to obtain some information regarding the inter-relationships of the dimensions as measured. To this end, the SIV was administered twice to a sample of 22 male and 73 female teacher trainees, with a 17-day interval between testings.

Product-moment correlations between scores in the two administrations (Table 1) indicate that all of the scales have adequate stability for research use with this population in the Indian culture. The pattern of intercorrelations among the scales (Table 1) is very similar to that reported for American and Japanese samples (4,7), with twelve and thirteen respectively of the fifteen correlations being identical in sign, and the respective average deviations being .18 and .14. These findings suggest that the factor structure of the six values in the Indian culture is similar to that found in the Japanese and American cultures, and that these dimensions are reasonably independent of one another.[2]

Table 1
Test-retest reliabilities (Diagonals) and product moment correlations among SIV scales for the Indian Sample (N=95)

	S	C	R	I	B	L
S	(.60)	–.27	.31	–.11	–.29	–.36
C		(.71)	–.30	–.24	.14	–.22
R			(.63)	–.49	–.35	.12
I				(.76)	.14	–.26
B					(.73)	–.49
L						(.66)

2. Satisfactory reliability for the Japanese form of the SIV and a factor structure similar to that of the original have been reported by Kikuchi and Gordon (7).

At the beginning of the fall semester at the Government Training College for Teachers, 50 male and 50 female teacher trainees were randomly selected from the 205 students in the senior class to serve as subjects in the main study and were administered the SIV according to standard procedures. Toward the end of the senior year, the teaching ability of each subject was evaluated on the basis of two lessons taught within an interval of a fortnight. Each of the lessons was rated by two different examiners, each of whom had at least five years of instructional experience in the theory and practice of teaching and in supervising teacher trainees. Each subject's performance was assessed on the basis of a standard set of criteria, which included method of presentation, subject-matter covered, interest elicited, and use of audio-visual aids.

Table 2

Correlations of the SIV scales with the teaching effectiveness criterion

	N	S	C	R	I	B	L
Males	50	–.31*	–.24	–.14	.26	.29*	.32*
Females	50	–.39**	–.30*	–.23	.34*	.33*	.10

* Significant at the .05 level of confidence.

** Significant at the .01 level of confidence.

Product-moment correlation coefficients were obtained separately for male and female subjects between scores on the SIV and the summed ratings of teaching effectiveness (Table 2). It will be noted that seven of the 12 coefficients are statistically significant at or beyond the .05 level of confidence. Teachers of either sex rated as being the more effective were likely to score lower on Support and higher on Benevolence. In addition, favourable ratings are significantly associated with being low on Conformity and high on Independence for females and high on leadership for males.

For purposes of making cross-cultural comparisons, data from the initial testing of the reliability sample and from the validation sample were combined, and means and standard deviations were computed separately for each sex. Means were then compared with those reported for samples of American and Japanese teacher

3. The Japanese teacher trainees were from a state-supported Teachers' College in Japan, while the American samples were equally divided between two private colleges, on the East and West coasts.

trainees (5). The latter samples were of about the same age as the Indian subjects and comparable in socio-economic status.[3]

Compared with the American sample (Table 3), the Indian trainees of both sexes score significantly lower on Support and Recognition and significantly higher on Conformity and Benevolence. Also, Indian males score significantly lower in Independence than do their American counterparts. Sex differences between Indian male and female teacher

Table 3
A Comparison of Indian and American Teacher Trainees on Scales of the SIV

	Means							Standard Deviations					
	N	S	C	R	I	B	L	S	C	R	I	B	L
MALE													
Indian	72	11.1	19.0	9.4	13.2	19.6	17.4	3.4	5.2	3.9	5.7	5.3	5.1
American	25	14.8	13.4	11.2	16.9	16.9	16.8	4.3	7.7	4.1	5.9	6.1	6.8
Difference		–3.7	5.6	–1.8	–3.7	2.7	6						
Significance		.01	.01	.05	.01	.01	ns						
FEMALE													
Indian	123	11.1	22.7	7.0	14.0	22.2	12.9	3.4	4.2	3.4	4.7	3.9	3.5
American	28	15.0	16.6	11.2	16.1	20.0	11.1	5.0	6.0	4.7	7.3	5.1	5.1
Difference		–3.9	6.1	–4.2	–2.1	2.2	1.8						
Significance		.01	.01	.01	ns	.05	ns						

Table 4
A Comparison of Female Indian and Japanese Teacher Trainees on Scales of the SIV

	Means							Standard Deviations					
	N	S	C	R	I	B	L	S	C	R	I	B	L
Indian	72	11.1	22.7	7.0	14.0	22.2	12.9	3.4	4.2	3.4	4.7	3.9	3.5
Japanese	45	14.5	19.7	7.6	16.0	19.8	12.7	3.9	3.0	2.9	4.3	4.2	3.8
Difference		–3.4	3.0	–.6	–2.0	2.4	.2						
Significance		.01	.01	ns	.05	.01	ns						

trainees are quite similar to those obtained for the American sample, with females scoring significantly (.05 level or beyond) higher in Conformity and Benevolence and lower in Leadership. Unlike the Americans, Indian males score higher than their female counterparts in Recognition.

The means of the female Indian and Japanese teacher trainees are presented in Table 4. All mean differences are in the same direction as those found between the female Indian and American teacher trainees, with those for Support, Conformity, Independence and Benevolence being statistically significant.

Discussion

The present findings indicate that certain values originally identified by factor analytic methods in the American culture can be reliably measured for educated, English-speaking subjects in the Indian culture. Also, some of these values are significantly related to rated teaching effectiveness. It is interesting to note that while Conformity appears to be very highly valued in the Indian as compared to the American group, individuals who deviate in the direction of non-conformity tend to be rated as being the more effective. Fleishman and Peters (2) similarly found that, within an industrial bureaucracy, where Conformity is generally considered to be a virtue, the Conformity scale of the SIV had a significant negative validity against rated effectiveness for a supervisory sample.

Indian teacher trainees differ from their American counterparts on the SIV in directions congruent with certain characteristics of Indian culture and beliefs. Indian subjects tend to score lower than their American counterparts on Support, Recognition and Independence and higher on conformity and Benevolence. The Indian virtues of self-realization and spiritual peace reflect the psychological self-sufficiency represented by low scores on the Support and Recognition scales. Seeking recognition is also opposed to humility, which is strongly emphasized in the Indian culture. Dutifulness and obedience are likewise stressed, as is the following of rules of right conduct (*dharma*) which is an essential prerequisite to deliverance (*moksha*), and benevolence is considered to be an enviable virtue.

These findings are similar to those reported by Fuster (3) in comparing Indian and American college students on the Edwards Personal Preference Schedule (EPPS). Significant differences were found for some of the scales which measure constructs similar to those in the SIV.[4] Furster found Indian students of both sexes to be higher on Nurturance (Benevolence) and lower on Dominance (Leadership) than the Americans, and Indian females to be lower on Exhibition (Recognition) and Indian males to be lower on Autonomy (Independence) than their American counterparts.

3. The median intercorrelation between corresponding SIV and EPPS sales is about .49.

Differences in values between female Indian and Japanese teacher trainees are in the same direction as those found between Indian and American subjects, but tend to be smaller in magnitude (the respective absolute average differences being 1.9 and 3.4). The greater similarity between the Japanese and American subjects may reflect in part the post-war American influence in Japan. This interpretation is supported by Berrien's Findings (1, p. 19) that in comparison with rural Japanese high school students, urban students tended to differ in the direction of the American norm on a modified version of the EPPS.

Extensions of the present research now underway include a determination of whether the obtained cross-cultural differences occur for other corresponding American and English-speaking Indian populations, as well as a parallel investigation using a Hindi translation of the SIV.

References

1. Berrien, F.K. *Values of Japanese and American Students*. ONR technical report, Rutgers University, New Brunswick, N.J., January, 1964.
2. Fleishman, E.A. and Peters, D.R. *Interpersonal values, leadership attitudes and managerial "success". Personnel Psychol., 1962,15,127-143.*
3. Fuster, J.M. *Study of Edwards Personality Preference Schedule on Indian College Students. J. Soc. Psychol.,* 1962, 57, 309-314.
4. Gordon, L.V., *Survey of Interpersonal Values.* Chicago: Science Research Associates, I960.
5. Gordon, L.V. Research Briefs: *Survey of Interpersonal Values.* Chicago: Science Research Associates, 1963.
6. Hildebrand, Susan. *The similarity of values and their relation to the ratings of student teachers by their master teachers.* Unpublished Honours thesis, Occidental College, Los Angeles, California, 1962.
7. Kikuchi, A. and Gordon, L.V. *Evaluation and cross-cultural application of a Japanese form of the Survey of Interpersonal Values. J. Soc. Psychol.*, 1966.

62. TEACHER ATTITUDE CHANGE AND VALUE STRUCTURE

Abstract

The Study aimed at finding the relationship of certain interpersonal values (Support, Conformity, Recognition,

Independence, Benevolence, Leadership) to change in attitude (as measured by Minnesota Teacher Attitude Inventory-MTAI) of prospective teachers revealed that the group which showed a more positive attitude scored significantly higher on Benevolence and Conformity and obtained significantly higher course achievement scores. These findings suggested that factors other than attitude change might also be reflected on the MTAI which usually is considered as a valid measure of just attitude change caused by teacher education.

Researchers, in a bid to determine whether attitude change in the sense of developing positive attitudes toward teacher-pupil relationship occurs after teacher training, found that subjects did tend to change in the positive direction on the MTAI (1,10,11). Besides, that certain teacher trainees tend to change in the negative direction on the MTAI subsequently came to light (2). In another investigation, more relevant to the present study, it was found that the group showing positive change scored significantly higher on a deference scale and received significantly higher grades than did the group showing negative change (12).

To investigate the relationship between certain interpersonal values (Support, Conformity, Recognition, Independence. Benevolence, Leadership) and change in attitude resulting from teacher training, the present study was undertaken.

Since teacher training course is chiefly designed to develop positive attitudes toward teacher-pupil relationship which the MTAI is supposed to measure with some degree of accuracy, MTAI was chosen as the most suitable instrument to measure the change in attitude following teacher training. And since MTAI is said to be a valid measure of teacher attitude change and not any other factors, it was hypothesized that there are no value differences between the teacher trainees who change positively and those who change negatively on the MTAI following teacher training, especially because a trainee's value structure at this stage is too established to suffer a change. The two groups of teacher trainees were compared on support, conformity, recognition, independence, benevolence, leadership, and course achievement.

Method

The sample consisted of two groups of 50 students each, one having those students who showed maximum positive change on the MTAI and the other who showed maximum negative change. These students were chosen from a total of 278 teacher trainees who were on roll in the State College of Education, Patiala (INDIA) in the 1967-68 session.

The whole lot of trainees were administered the MTAI in the first week of their admission to the training course and again at the end of the course. The magnitude of the attitude change they showed after training formed the basis of their classification in the two groups. During the first quarter of their training period, the Survey of Interpersonal Values–SIV (7, 8)–was administered which yielded scores on the six values mentioned before. The trainees were also given their letter grades in achievement tests held four times during the session. Each time their achievement was tested in five essential papers, *i.e.* Philosophy, Psychology, Methods of Teaching and School Organization, Indian Education, Guidance and Evaluation. On the basis of a student's aggregate achievement, his grade-point average was calculated which was named course achievement.

Table 1, which gives the pre-post data for the two groups, shows that both groups were almost similar on the Pre-MTAI testing, but significantly different on the post-test.

Table 1
Comparison of Group 1 (Showing Positive Change) and Group 2 (Showing Negative Change) Pre-Post MTAI Testing

	Pre-test Mean	Post-test Mean	Range of Difference Scores
Group 1	17.74	30.29	6 to 51
Group 2	18.26	–4.03	–6 to –51

Table 2, which gives comparisons between the two groups on the variables studied in the analyses, shows that the group showing positive change scored significantly higher on measures of benevolence and conformity, and obtained significantly higher grades than did the group showing negative change. 't' test was employed to determine the significance of difference between the means. The variables of support, recognition, leadership and independence did not significantly set the two groups apart.

Table 2
Comparisons of Group 1 (Showing Positive Change) and Group 2 (Showing Negative Change) on Value Scores and Grade-point Average

Variable	Mean of Group 1	Mean of Group 2	t
Support	11.42	13.47	1.49
Conformity	18.71	14.82	2.72*
Recognition	9.62	10.49	1.21
Independence	15.23	17.75	1.68
Benevolence	20.22	15.96	2.98*
Leadership	17.91	16.27	1.04
Course Achievement	4.01	2.67	3.12*

* Significant at .05 level.

Results and Discussion

The finding that the subjects who showed a positive change in teacher attitudes were characteristically more conformist and benevolent suggested a trait or traits that might have contributed toward determining the direction of attitude change.

The need to conform to the thoughts and attitudes of others, especially to those of teachers, might have gone some way toward fostering the positive change in teacher-pupil attitudes. The positive direction of the change might also have been, at least partly, determined by a democratic atmosphere obtaining in the institution where the course was taught. This finding coincided with the finding, that those who change positively in teacher attitudes were more deferent (12), and with the general finding that individuals tend to change attitudes in the direction of authority figures etc. (9).

If the subjects showing positive teacher attitude change be taken as relatively superior in teaching effectiveness, as they may legitimately be, the present finding concurred with another finding that the teacher trainees possessing greater teaching effectiveness show relatively greater conformity (6,7). Again, that teacher trainees are very high on conformity and not-so-high on other value scales is congruent with the similar findings of other studies as well (5,6,8). The high conformity scores might also have been caused, at least to some extent, by the characteristics of dutifulness and obedience enshrined in Indian culture.

The need to be benevolent towards others, especially towards children, might be an important determiner of direction of attitude change, and this need might have accounted for at least some part of the positive change in teacher-pupil attitudes. The direction of this change might have been determined by the Indian philosophy (with which the course was taught) of doing good to others and being kind and generous (dharma) which is an essential prerequisite to deliverance (moksha). Benevolence in Indian culture is considered as an enviable virtue and hence perhaps the positive change in attitudes toward teacher-pupil relationships.

If the positive change group is considered as the one who is relatively superior in teaching effectiveness as it may genuinely be, the finding that it showed comparatively greater benevolence agreed with the finding that benevolence and teaching effectiveness are significantly correlated (6,7). Again, the high benevolence scores yielded by this study were identical to such scores in other studies (5,6,8).

The other significant finding that the subjects who showed positive change on the MTAI obtained higher course achievement scores corroborated similar result in another study (12). The higher achievement might have stimulated the attitude change in the direction or the philosophy with which the course was taught, of it might have led to maturational development which in turn would result in developing positive attitude change.

The results of this study suggest that other factors, and not attitude change alone, might also be reflected in change on the MTAI, normally attributed to the impact of teacher training. Many factors related to the learning experiences the teacher training often provides tend to mix up with the teacher attitude change that the MTAI is supposed to measure. Individual personality traits, values or personal attitudes, may, besides teacher training, contribute toward producing the attitude change. As such scores on the MTAI may not constitute a valid measure of the attitude change caused by teacher training, further researches of identical nature may establish that, for evaluating the effectiveness of teacher training in terms of its capacity to change attitudes, MTAI may not be solely relied upon.

References

1. Cook, W.W., Kearny N.C., Rocchio, P.D., and Thompson, A. "Significant Factors in Teachers' Classroom Attitudes," Journal of Teacher Education, 1956, 274-279.

2. Eason, M.E., "The Minnesota Teacher Attitude Inventory in Evaluating the Teaching of Educational Psychology," Journal of Educational Psychology, 1956, 47, 271-275.
3. Gordon, L.V., "Survey of Interpersonal Values." Chicago: Science Research Associates, 1960.
4. Gordon, L.V., "Survey of Interpersonal Values," Chicago: Science Research Associates, 1963.
5. Gordon, L.V., and Kakkar, S.B. "A Cross-Cultural Study of Indian and American Interpersonal Values," The Journal of Social Psychology, U.S.A., 1966,69, 339- 40.
6. Kakkar, S.B. "A Cross-Cultural Study of Values," The Research Bulletin (Arts), Punjab University, Vol. LV(1), 1967, 6, 13.
7. Kakkar, S.B. and Gordon, L.V., "The Interpersonal Values of Indian Teacher Trainees." The Journal of Social Psychology, U.S.A., 1966, 69, 341-42.
8. Kakkar, S.B. and Gordon, L.V. "A Cross-Cultural Study of Teachers' Values.," Education and Psychology Review, 1967,172-177.
9. Newcomb, T.M. "Social Psychology," New York: Henry Holt and Co., 1958.
10. Rogers, V.R., and Smith, J.A., "Professional Attitudes of Students in an Intensive Teacher Training Programme." Elementary School Journal, 1956, 57,100-101.
11. Shaw, J., Klausmeier, H.S., Luckes, A.H., and Reid, H.T. "Changes Occurring in Teacher-Pupil Attitudes During a Two-Week Guidance Workshop." Journal of Applied Psychology, 1952, 36, 304-306.
12. Teigland, John, L. "The Relationship Between Measured Teacher Attitude Change and Certain Personality Characteristics." The Journal of Educational Research, Vol. 69, No. 2, October, 1966, 84-85.

63. A CROSS-CULTURAL STUDY OF INDIAN AND AMERICAN INTERPERSONAL VALUES*

Kakkar and Gordon,[1] in comparing a sample of Indian teacher trainees from the Government Training College for Teachers with a counterpart American sample on the Survey of Interpersonal Values (SIV),[2] found significant mean differences between male

---

* Dr. Leonkrd V. Gorden, New York (U.S.A.) was co-researcher and co-author.

1. Kakkar, S.B., and Gordon, L.V. The Interpersonal values of Indian teacher trainees, *J. Soc. Psychol.*, 1966,69, 341-342.

2. Gordon, L.V. Survey of Interpersonal Values. Chicago: Science Research Associates, 1960.

and female groups for five of the six value scales. These differences reflected known value differences between the two cultures. The present study was performed to test the generality of the previous findings for counterpart male and female college and high school samples in the two countries.

The SIV was administered to 36 male and 27 female liberal arts students, and 42 male and 61 female senior high school students from the same general area. The samples were selected so as to approximate the American reference groups in relative socioeconomic status and educational level. The American comparison group consisted of the normative American samples of 1075 male and 746 female college students and 782 male and 666 female high school students.

When means of Indian and American samples were compared, it was found that the direction of the differences mirrored *exactly* those previously obtained between Indian and American teacher trainees. All four Indian groups scored lower than their American counterparts on Support and Recognition and higher than their American counterparts on Conformity and Benevolence. All differences, except that for the high school males on Recognition, were statistically significant beyond the .05 level. In addition, as was the case with the teacher trainees, all four Indian groups scored lower than corresponding Americans on Independence–differences for the two male groups only being significant. No consistent directional differences were found for the Leadership scale.

In general, results of the present study are both internally consistent and correspond very closely to those previously reported for the same values on a different type of sample. The conclusion that obtained differences reflect differences between the interpersonal values of the typical American youth and his educated Indian counterpart, at least from this particular geographical area, appears to be strongly supported. An extension of this research using samples of another part of India is currently underway.

64. A CROSS CULTURAL STUDY OF RESPONSE SETS

Comparing the response sets of American and Japanese students on semantic differential scales through the use of Rorschach inkblots as stimuli, Zax and Takahashi (17) found that the Japanese made proportionately fewer extreme and more neutral responses than did the Americans. Gordon and Kikuchi (6,7), using School Environment Preference Schedule–SEPS (4), concluded that the Japanese made as many or as strong extreme responses as Americans, though they did make more neutral responses than Americans. The former researches attributed the differences in "response styles" to differences in child-rearing practices in the two cultures. The latter ones suggested that cross cultural differences in response sets led to make Japanese neutral responses more than Americans.

The present study attempts to determine whether an extremeness response occurs in the Indian culture-an assumption that Zax and Takahashi made in respect of Japanese culture. Besides it involves a comparison of the response sets of Japanese, American and Indian students. The stimulus material used is meant to impart a uniform rather than a varying meaning to the respondents so as to facilitate interpretation of results. Again, the technique of analysis permits measurement of the extremeness response set without any effect on it of the frequency with which the subjects choose the negative or positive alternatives. Thus cross-cultural response-set comparisons are not left free to be confused or interfered with by cross-cultural differences in responses to content as they incidentally were in the study conducted by Zax and Takahashi (18).

Method and Procedure

The School Environment Preference Schedule or SEPS (4), the research instrument used by Gordon and Kikuchi (7), measures the degree to which the student adopts those attitudes, values, and behaviours that are fostered in traditional school environments. Each of the 24 items in the SEPS is responded to on a five-point scale: "Strongly agree" (SA), "Agree" (A), "Undecided" (U), "Disagree" (D), and "Strongly disagree" (SD). Agreement with any item means acceptance of the bureaucratic norm. Item reversal to control for acquiescence is not attempted because acquiescence itself seems to be characteristic of bureaucratic orientation. The SEPS was administered to random samples of 10th and 11th grade students comparable in socio-economic and educational status

1. The author is grateful to Prof. Leonard V. Gordon, Albany, N.Y. for permitting this action.

to their counterparts in Japan and America who earlier were administered this instrument for an identical research conducted by Gordon and Kikuchi (7).

The analytic method employed in earlier American studies (2, 3, 17) was followed in order to compare extremeness response sets. Relevant data contained in Gordon's study (7) on the response sets of counterpart American and Japanese students were drawn upon to compare the response sets in the three cultures.[1] In the analytic method, these four scores are obtained and correlated: (1) Conventional (C), based on score weights 5, 4, 3, 2,1 assigned to the five response alternatives. (2) Proportion agree (P), or the number of "Strongly agree" and "Agree" responses made. This score is suggested by Cronbach (1) as an operational substitute for the C score since it eliminates extremeness response set variance. (3) Strength of agreement (X), obtained by weighting responses of "Strongly agree" by 2 and "Agree" by 1 and computing the arithmetic mean. (4) Strength of disagreement (Y), obtained by weighting responses of "Strongly disagree" by 2 and "Disagree" by 1 and computing the arithmetic mean. The X and Y scores give an indication of the strength of the extremeness response set at each end of the continuum, largely independent of the number of such responses.

The extremeness response set analysis was performed for the 10th and 11th grade samples, separately by sex and culture. Product-moment correlations–among the four types of scores – were separately calculated for the samples of 150 male and 150 female Indian students and compared with such correlations in respect of Japanese and American students.

There being no significant grade differences on any of the 5 response alternatives, the males of 10th grade and similarly those of 11th grade score treated as one group. This very treatment was given to females for similar reasons. Sex differences were also found not significant, but the sex groups were retained and treated separately because the Japanese and American data for identical sex groups as also identical grade groups were available for comparison purposes.

1. The author is grateful to Prof. Leonard V. Gordon, Albany, N.Y. for permitting this action.

Results

Negative correlations between X and Y scores serve as evidence for the existence of an extremeness response set, because extreme responses to content in one direction would be logically expected to be inversely related to the equally extreme responses to comparable content in the opposite direction. Relationships for all the four samples (males and females of 10th, 11th grades taken separately, Table 1) and for the two samples (males and females of the 10th and 11th grade combined in a group, Table 2) are negative. The magnitude of the correlations for the Indian students (.58, .66) is dissimilar to that obtained for the corresponding American (.41, .35) and Japanese (.42, .39) samples (Table 3) as also to that reported by other investigators (Hamilton 1968). Whereas American and Japanese students are similar to each other in their extremeness responses set, they may be considerably less rigid, less conservative or more liberal than their Indian counterpart in this response set.

Gordon and Kikuchi had noted very high correlations between C and P scores in previous American studies and had therefore substituted response-set-free P score for the C score (1970 c). High correlations between these scores are observed for the Indian (Tables 1, 2), Japanese and American (Table 3) samples. The magnitude of such correlations is also similar.

The very high correlations of the C and P scores with the X scores and the similarly high correlations of the C and P scores with the Y scores (Tables 1,2), found in Indian students, are significant at one per cent level in all the instances. They reflect that the Indian students have as much discriminating power of negative response alternatives as that of positive alternatives. In this respect they are different from their American and Japanese counterparts who show greater discriminating power of negative response alternative as compared with that of positive alternatives (Table 3).

Percentage of "undecided" responses in the three cultures were compared to determine differential tendency, if any, to mark such responses. Per cent responses for each of the five alternatives are presented by sex and cultures in Table 5, while such responses in respect of Indian students are presented by sex and grade in Table 4. It may be noted that for each sex Japanese students marked about twice as many "undecided" responses as did the Americans and about four to five times as did the Indians (the differences being significant beyond one per cent level, Table 6). Whereas no differential tendency to mark the extreme alternatives ("Strongly Agree" and "Strongly Disagree") was noted in the American and Japanese students, marked and significant differences in such tendency were found between Indians and Americans, Indians and Japanese, the differences being highly favourable to Indians in case of the positive extreme and to Japanese or Americans in case of the negative extreme. Balancing the greater tendency of the Japanese to use the middle category is the greater inclination of the Americans and the still greater inclination of the Indians to make the "Agree" responses and the greater tendency of the Americans to make the "Disagree" responses. As many as nine of the twelve differences are statistically significant. Parenthetically, none of the differences between sexes, within cultures, is significant (P .05).

Table 1
Correlations among SEPS Scores for Indian Male and Female Students of Grades X, XI

N is 50 males and 50 females in grade X and 100 males and 100 females in grade XI

Grade		P		X		Y	
		Male	Female	Male	Female	Male	Female
C	X	.91	.83	.90	.90	–.84	–.68
	XI	.92	.88	.91	.88	–.87	–.81
P	X			.74	.52	–.77	–.66
	XI			.74	.82	–.87	–.73
X	X					–.67	–.69
	XI					–.50	–.63

All the r's are significant at .01 level.

Table 2
Correlations among SEPS Scores for Indian Male and Female High School Students

N is 150 males and 150 Females

	P		X		Y	
	Male	Female	Male	Female	Male	Female
C	.92	.87	.91	.88	–.86	–.76
P			.74	.65	–.84	–.71
X					–.58	–.66

Table 3
Correlations among SEPS Scores for Indian, Japanese and American Male and Female High School Students

		P		X		Y	
		Male	Female	Male	Female	Male	Female
C	Indian	.92**	.87**	.91**	.88**	–.86**	–.76**
	Japanese	.77**	.88**	–.08	–.09	–.52**	–.68**
	American	.83**	.82**	–.08	–.28*	–.60*	–.64**
P	Indian			.74**	.65**	–.84**	–.71**
	Japanese			.06	–.05	–.24*	–.52**
	American			.00	–.23*	–.38**	–.23*
X	Indian					–.58**	–.66**
	Japanese					.42**	.39**
	American					.41**	.35**

* Significant at .05 level.
** Significant at .01 level.
C—Conventional
P—Proportion Agree
X—Extremeness Agree
Y—Extremeness Disagree

Table 4
Per cent Responses to Each Alternative (on SEPS) Made by Indian Students of

Grade	Sex		N	SA	A	U	D	SD
			Per cents of response alternating					
X	Girls	...	50	27.12	35.49	8.90	20.55	7.73
	Boys	...	50	26.29	34.28	6.32	21.80	11.15
XI	Girls	...	100	29.70	32.92	7.53	19.80	9.90
	Boys	...	100	29.91	35.36	5.20	18.34	10.56

The per cent differences between the boys of grades X, XI and those between the girls of grades X, XI are not significant in respect of all response alternatives. Sex differences at each grade are also not significant.

Table 5

A Comparison of per cent responses to each alternative made by Indian, Japanese and American Students, Separately by Sex

	Response alternatives					
	N	SA	A	U	D	SD
MALE						
Indian*	150	28.70	35.00	5.57	19.50	10.76
Japanese	285	8.00	16.01	26.07	29.07	19.06
American	192	7.02	23.06	15.04	36.08	17.00
FEMALE						
Indian**	150	28.84	33.78	7.99	20.51	9.18
Japanese	92	6.02	17.09	29.01	32.02	14.02
American	206	5.06	22.02	14.04	37.04	20.02

* Boys of grades X (50), XI (100) together.

** Girls of grades X (50), XI (100) together.

Table 6

Significance of difference between the per cent responses to each alternative made by Indian, Japanese and American Students

Difference between*	Response alternatives					Sex
	SA	A	u	D	SD	
Japanese/ American	...	.05	...	...	...	Male
American/ Japanese	...	...	.01	...	...	Both Male & Female
Japanese/ Indian	.01	.01	...	...	...	Both Male & Female
Indian/ Japanese	...	...	.01	.01	.05	Both Male & Female
American/ Indian	.01	.01	...	...	...	Both Male & Female
Indian/ American	...	...	.01	.01	.01	Both Male & Female

* The nationality after the diagonal is one in whose favour the significant difference lies. In case of Indian students Male includes 50 boys of grade X, and 100 of grade XI, and female includes 50 girls of X and 100 of grade XI.

Discussion

The results indicate that the extremeness response sets are clearly identifiable in the Indian, American and Japanese cultures, though much more so in Indian as compared to the other two cultures. The extremeness response set of Indians is higher than that of Japanese or Americans in its strength or contribution to scale variance. The Japanese and Americans do not differ from each other in the strength of such sets. Whereas none of the cross-cultural differences between corresponding correlation coefficients for either sex, when comparing Americans and Japanese, is significant at five per cent level, most of the cross-cultural differences between corresponding correlation coefficients for either sex, when comparing Indians with Americans and Japanese, are significant at one per cent level.

Again, the tendency to use the extreme alternatives, "Strongly Agree" or "Strongly Disagree", when agreeing or disagreeing, though equally strong in American and Japanese cultures for the present stimulus material, has been found to be highly stronger when using "Strongly Agree" and significantly weaker when using "Strongly Disagree" in Indian culture. These results are evident of the significantly greater bureaucratic orientation of Indian students when compared to their American and Japanese counterparts, as also revealed in a previous study (10).

Whereas substantial differences between the X and Y scores in their relationship to the total scores may be noted in the American and Japanese students (7), such differences do not seem to exist in the case of Indian students who seem to be equally discriminative of both positive and negative alternatives. Their agreeing responses stand positively related and their disagreeing responses stand negatively related to their total responses. This again affirms the previous finding (10) that in bureaucratic orientation Indians far excel their American and Japanese counterparts. Nevertheless it is evident that the X and Y scores may represent functionally different, rather functionally opposite response sets (as indicated by + r's of X and – r's of Y) in India as they do in America and Japan. This tends to prove the American finding (2) that differential weighting of the two response sets can enhance the validity of Likert scales in India as well as it does in America and Japan.

Indian students are significantly less prone than American students to use the "undecided" category when responding. Since American students in turn are less prone than Japanese students to use the said category, as noted by Zax and Takahashi (18), and Gordon and Kikuchi (7), Indian students seem to be least "undecided" among the three nationalities. This finding stands corroborated by relevant scores on the Decisiveness scale of the Survey of Personal Values (SPV) (3), a forced-choice test that is free of this response set. Indian high school students on the average scored significantly higher than Americans who scored significantly higher than Japanese on the said scale of the SPV. As Decisiveness measures the value placed on making quick decisions or taking a definite stand on issues, on this basis Indian students would be expected to select fewer "Undecided" response alternatives than the American and Japanese.

To sum up, Indian high school students, both male and female, are significantly higher than their American and Japanese counterparts on positive response sets including the positive extreme, and significantly lower than counterpart American and Japanese on the "undecided" and negative response sets including the negative extreme. This may be attributed to Indians' excessive bureaucratic orientation (as compared to Americans' and Japanese') that was revealed in an earlier study on SEPS (10). That Indians are greater conformists than Americans and Japanese, as demonstrated in previous studies (8, 12, 13, 14), and in Kakkar and Gordon (1966 a), Gordon and Kakkar (1966) lends additional strength to the possibility that they may be more prone to bureaucratic orientation.

Since the "undecided" responses are bound to decrease in the face of an overwhelming number of agreeing responses, it may not be appropriate to conclude, unless there is other evidence, that Indians are more decisive than Americans or Japanese.

On the other hand, the American and Japanese high school students are reported to be like each other in all their response sets except that of the "undecided" in which the Japanese are significantly higher. Gordon and Kikuchi (7) have said that this is due to the fact, revealed by item analysis data in both cultures, that the "undecided" and "Disagree" responses are very similar to one another in their relationship both to the total SEPS score and to external criteria and that the Japanese therefore may have caused a rise in their "undecided" responses because for them the "undecided" response may simply represent a disinclination to indicate disagreement. The question which, however, still remains unanswered is "Is there something in Japanese culture which makes him act, like a diplomat, as he does in this instance?"

In positive response sets, both average and extreme, Indians excel Americans and Japanese. In the "Undecided" response set, Japanese excel the other two nationalities. In negative responses, Americans score over others in disagreeing while Japanese excel Americans and Indians in strongly disagreeing (Table 7).

Results of this study have important implications in attitude research where Likert format is employed. Significant differences obtained between cultures could well emerge solely from response set differences, or non-significant findings could be due to disregarded response set differences. Thus, the investigator has to be cautious against drawing inferences regarding cultural differences in the absence of response set information. Cross-cultural differences in response sets of Indians and Americans, as also of Indians and Japanese, may be reflected by this study. Whether such differences are due to differences in bureaucratic orientation of the cultural groups concerned or due to the format used in the study, or due to both, and if due to both, what is the extent of each of these two factors, are however, the issues which further research would sort out.

Table 7
Nationalities in Decreasing Order of Per cent Responses to Each Alternative

SA	A	U	D	SD
Indian	Indian	Japanese	American	Japanese
Japanese	American	American	Japanese	American
American	Japanese	Indian	Indian	Indian

References

1. Cronbach, L.J.— "Further Evidence in Response Sets and Test Design." *Educational and Psychological Measurement*, 1950, 10, 3-31.
2. Gordon, L.V.— "Validity of Scoring Methods for Bipolar Scales". *Educational and Psychological Measurement*, 1967 (a), 27, 1099-1106.
3. Gordon, L.V.—*Survey of Personal Values*. Chicago: Science Research Associates, 1967(b).

4. Gordon, L.V.— *School Environment Preference Schedule*. Albany: Author, 1968 (a).
5. Gordon, L.V.—"Are There Two Extremeness Response Sets?" *Educational and Psychological Measurement*, Vol. 1, No. 1, 1971.
6. Gordon, L.V. and Kikuchi, A.—"The Measurement of Bureaucratic Orientation in Japan." *International Review of Applied Psychology* 1970,19, 133-138.
7. Gordon, L.V. and Kikuchi, A.—"Response Sets of Japanese and American Students." *Journal of Social Psychology*, 1970 (c) 82,143-148.
8. Gordon, L.V. and Kakkar, S.B.–" A Cross-cultural Study of Indian and American Interpersonal Values" *Journal of Social Psychology*, 1966, 69, 339-340.
9. Hamilton, D.L.– "Personality Attributes Associated with Extreme Response Style". *Psychological Bulletin*, 1968,69,192-203.
10. Kakkar, S.B.–"Bureaucratic Orientation of Indian Students". *Punjab University Research Bull*. (Arts), Vol. II, No. 2, Aug. 1971,83-97.
11. Kakkar, S.B. and Gordon, L.V.—"A Cross-cultural Study of Teachers' Values". *Education and Psychology Review*, 1966(a), 6,1972-177.
12. Kakkar, S.B. and Gordon, L.V.– "The Interpersonal Values of Indian Teacher Trainees. "*Journal of Social Psychology*, 1966,69, 341-342.
13. Kakkar, S.B.—"A Cross-Cultural Study of Values". *The Research Bulletin (Arts)*, Punjab University, LV, (1), 1967.
14. Kikuchi, A. and Gordon, L.V.—"Bureaucratic Orientation of the Japanese Adolescent." *Japanese Annals of Social Psychology*, 1970 (a) 11, 217-229.
15. Kikuchi, A. and Gordon, L.V.—"Japanese and American Personal Values: Some Cross-cultural Findings". *International journal of Psychology*, 1970 (b), 5,183- 187.
16. Korn, H.A. and Giddan, N.S. "Scoring Methods and Construct Validity of the Dogmatism Scale." *Educational and Psychological Measurement*, 1964, 24, 867-874.
17. Zax, M. and Takahashi, S.–"Response Styles Among Japanese and American Children." *Japanese Psychological Research*, 1967 (a), 9, 58-61.
18. Zax, And Takahashi, S.—"Cultural Influences on Response Style: Comparisons of Japanese and American College Students." *Journal of Social Psychology, 1967 (b)*, 71, 3-10.

65. BUREAUCRATIC ORIENTATION OF INDIAN STUDENTS

Bureaucratisation of the individual in the present day society has been studied by several researchers. Weber (1946), the father of bureaucratic theory, observed that the individual was becoming a cog in the machinery of modern bureaucracy. Blau and Scott (1962) considered this development to be the greatest menace to liberty. Huxley (1946), Orwell (1949) and others projected in fictional literature accounts of the individual's abject surrender to the powers that be. From (1941) observed that such an eventuality might not be unwelcome to most of the victims.

Interest in the nature and development of the bureaucratic personality, in the influence of bureaucracy on an individual's personality and in the traits of individuals who are attracted to or tempted to a bureaucratic environment has been abundant, but research on all these problems has been limited Research on such problems has, however, been undertaken by Gordon (1969) who postulated a personality construct "bureaucratic orientation" (Gordon 1968 a) and who using his instrument, the "Work Environment Preference Schedule" or WEPS (Gordon 1968 b), obtained highly significant results in studies involving individuals who openly resist or reject bureaucratic pressures or highly bureaucratic work environments. The WEPS discriminated between militant teachers and those who refused to strike (Khalique 1970), between army career and non-career motivated United States Military Academic graduates (Bridges 1967), and between Air Force ROTC students who drop out and those who remain (Bronzo 1966). It was also found to be related to a variety of personality characteristics in directions congruent both with bureaucratic theory and prior research findings.

From the WEPS which was based on the scheme of Max Weber (1946) which was meant for adults and older students, Gordon derived directly his instrument, the "School Environment Preference Schedule" or SEPS (1968 c) which measures bureaucratic orientation of the younger student in school setting. SEPS measures the same construct as that measured by the WEPS. It is almost exactly parallel to WEPS, except that its items refer to the school rather than work environments. The use of the SEPS on Indian students and the presentation of data bearing on its validity are the subjects of this study.

Materials, Sample Population and Procedure

Bureaucratic orientation, which means a commitment to the set of attitudes, values and behaviours that are characteristically fostered and rewarded in highly bureaucratized work environments, was assessed through SEPS (1968 c). It is a 24-item form developed to cover a set of these four categories: self-subordination (a desire to comply with the wishes of and to please one's teacher); Uncriticalness (an uncritical acceptance of the opinions of teachers); Rules Conformity (a desire for the security that following rules and regulations affords); Traditionalism (a need to identify with one's school and to conform to the peer-group norm). It is based on a scheme parallel to that of WEPS, but it describes individual rather than organizational characteristics.

The items refer to the school environment and are so worded that agreement would reflect acceptance of the traditional school norm. The five response categories used are: "Strongly Agree", "Agree", "Undecided", "Disagree", and "Strongly Disagree". In the SEPS, as in all Likert Scales, the tendency of the individual to mark the extreme response alternative whether agreeing or disagreeing is prominently revealed. Gordon (1967 a), (1970 a) had found differential weights which nullified this response set at the agreement but not the disagreement end of the continuum so as to enhance the validity of the WEPS, the parent instrument of the SEPS. He later found that the same scoring scheme (two for "Strongly Agree", and "Agree", one for "Undecided" and "Disagree" and zero for "Strongly Disagree") was effective with the SEPS as well (Gordon and Kikuchi 1970). Hence its use in the present study. The test-retest reliability of the SEPS on eighth grade and eleventh grade students is known to be .75 and .62 respectively (1970 b).

Since the SEPS and WEPS measure a comparable construct at the upper grade levels of school, they are likely to be highly related to one another and to bear similar relationships to construct relevant external measures. The data accruing from the present study are pertinent in this behalf.

The SEPS was administered to several samples, selected by simple random assignment, of students in the seventh through the eleventh grades. The WEPS was administered at the eleventh grade level to those students who had taken the SEPS, as also to 100 college students (Liberal Arts), male and female in equal numbers. The number of cases at the seventh through tenth grades was 50 of each sex. At the eleventh grade 100 students of each sex were tested (with the SEPS and WEPS). Correlations with scholastic achievement were drawn at each grade level. The subjects chosen were of a fairly high socio-economic status so that comparison with comparable Japanese and American data, which incidentally were available, could be readily made. They were chosen randomly from Auckland House, Simla (Girls), Bishop Cotton School, Simla (boys), Modern School, Patiala (co-educational), and Senior Model School, Patiala (co-educational)–the schools which are meant for the elite.

The SEPS was also administered to 150 elementary teacher trainees (who had passed their high school), while WEPS was also administered to 100 secondary teacher trainees (who were graduates) of the State College of Education, Patiala. The sex-wise distribution of the numbers chosen randomly from the 300 trainees in the former case and 300 trainees in the latter case was 50 boys, 100 girls (age range 14-18 years) and 50 boys, 50 girls (age range 20 to 28) respectively.

The WEPS was also administered to secondary teacher trainees of the State College of Education, Patiala, with a view to correlating bureaucratic orientation with interest in the teaching profession. This was done for a sample of 67 males and 62 females chosen randomly from 250 persons of each sex. The instrument used to measure interest in the teaching profession was KTAT (Kakkar 1968).

Again the SEPS and WEPS were administered to several samples of school and college students and correlations drawn between bureaucratic orientation and other measures such as personality, attitudes and values.

Results

The SEPS and WEPS were administered to several samples consisting of 100 male and 100 female eleventh grade school students. Separate category scores as well as total scores were computed for both instruments to permit detailed comparisons. It may be noted (Table 1) that the intercorrelations between category scores are highly uniform. When the respective category reliabilities are considered, a single factor appears to account for almost all of the reliable variance in both WEPS and SEPS. The correlation between the total scores on the two instruments comes to .89 when corrected for attenuation due to unreliability. These results suggest that both SEPS and WEPS measure a highly comparable construct and parenthetically support the use of a single total score for each. The means of eleventh grade students, both males and females, on the SEPS and WEPS and the sex-wise correlations between the students' scores on the two schedules (Table 3a), while suggesting the same finding, show further relevance to the validity of the SEPS.

The results of a similar study on a comparable American sample (1970 b) being congruent to the aforesaid results suggest the same hypothesis.

Correlations between the SEPS and WEPS used on 7th and 8th grade students yielded a median value (uncorrected) of .51, reflecting lesser relevance and lower reliability of the WEPS at lower high school grades.

Correlations of the SEPS with scholastic achievement measures, for samples from Auckland House Shimla may be seen in Table 2. All relationships are either negative or highly insignificant, suggesting that in pupil-centered schools such as this the more bureaucratically oriented student tends to be less bright and may do more poorly academically. The less bright student may compensate by a greater adherence to what he considers to be institutionally acceptable behaviour or that the student who depends on his superiors to make decisions for him may be less able to meet situations in which he must function intellectually on an individual basis.

Significant negative relationship of SEPS with intelligence and achievement was also noted in a study in Japan (Kikuchi and Gordon, 1970).

A glance at such results in an American study (1970 b) indicates that (i) in seventh and eighth grades both Indian and American children are alike in that their bureaucratic orientation is inversely related to their scholastic achievement, (ii) in ninth, tenth and eleventh grades the two are not so alike in that the bureaucratic orientation of Indian students, as compared to that of their American counterparts, is less inversely related to scholastic achievement.

Means and standard deviations of all male and female students in the seventh through eleventh grades of the schools are presented in Table 3. In these particular schools, the nature of the school input had been found considerably consistent and stable over the previous five years' period and attrition was very low. A monotonic decrease in means is evident for samples of both sexes beginning at the seventh grade, which reflects a consistent decrease in "bureaucratic orientation" with advancing grade level. Significant mean differences between students in the junior and senior grade students are also evident. Female means in the case of all samples in this study are higher probably because Indian females are higher on conformity than their male counterparts (Kakkar 1967).

These findings regarding Indian students (Table 3) echo those regarding American students as found in a study of the students in the seventh through twelfth grades of a University school in New York (Gordon 1968 c). Indian and American samples are almost alike in the magnitude of sex differences in the same grades and mean differences in different grades. Differences between SEPS and WEPS scores of high school students of India and America are also alike.

A similar decrease in means for the SEPS was found in a study conducted in six junior and three senior high schools in Fukushima and Tokyo, Japan (Kikuchi 1970). For both sexes, and both types of schools mean of the upper class students were found lower than those for the lower class students. For both sexes, large and significant mean differences on the SEPS were found between students in the junior and senior high schools.

The decrease in "bureaucratic orientation" that occurs in the three cultures tends to reflect an increasing need for self-dependence on the part of the youngsters as they grow up, as also a decreasing conformity to environmental constraints within the school itself with increasing grade level. A Japanese study (Kikuchi and Gordon 1969), which concluded that the more bureaucratically oriented the student the more positive his attitude towards school, tends to confirm the same finding when with every increase in grade level students were found to be decreasingly positive in their attitudes towards school.

That Indian high school students have substantially high conformist values than their American counterparts was established in cross-cultural research (Kakkar and Gordon 1966, and Kakkar 1966). These same differences are found on the SEPS (Table 4) between students of comparable socio-economic status in India and United States. Differences in "bureaucratic orientation" of a like magnitude were also found on the WEPS between college samples in these two cultures (Table 5).

SEPS Means of Indian College students (Table 5) tend to substantiate the earlier finding (Table 3) that bureaucratic orientation diminishes with growth. Considering the teacher trainees in the hierarchy "elementary Teachers–Secondary teachers" and so on, analogous to the hierarchy "primary grade students–secondary grade students–college students", the means in Table 3b, 3c also mirror the same finding.

That the SEPS means of Indian teacher trainees, who are higher in growth than school students, exceed those of the 11th grade students who on SEPS stand lowest in their own hierarchy (Table 3), should cause no surprise, because the teacher trainees were found, as revealed in the interviews held subsequently, to have shown their choices on the schedule according to how they as teachers would expect their wards to accept the values and procedures that characterize highly structured or bureaucratized school environments and according to what the most acceptable behaviour in a well-disciplined and authoritative institution ought to be. Teachers as a group, even otherwise, may be excelling other groups in the degree of bureaucratic orientation as and because they do in that of its close correlate conformity (Kakkar and Gordon 1966).

Merton (1940, 1949), Weber (1946) and others theorized that work environments represented by the bureaucratic organisational model would attract individuals with certain specified personality characteristics. In a bid to verify this theory, as also to assess the validity of the SEPS, and to find its constructural similarity to the WEPS, Correlations of the SEPS with a number of personality variables were determined based on the 11th grade student samples.

Correlations between the WEPS and the values measured by the "Survey of Interpersonal Values" or SIV (Gordon 1960) and the "Survey of Personal Values" or SPV (Gordon 1967) had been obtained earlier for two high school samples (11th grade, 50 male and 50 female) and two college samples (50 males and 50 females adult students of Liberal Arts). Highly consistent, significant correlations had been found for all the four samples with four of the value scales, in a positive direction with Conformity and Orderliness and in a negative direction with Independence and Variety (Table 6). Similar relationships may be noted between the SEPS and these same scales for the same high school samples (Table 7). That all values which have significant correlations with the SEPS have been found to be significantly correlated, and in the same direction, with the WEPS (Tables 6, 7) further supports the conclusion that the WEPS and SEPS measure a common construct.

Like adults, students who score high on bureaucratic orientation are inclined to place a high value on conformist behaviour and on being systematic and orderly, and a low value on having personal independence of action and on engaging in new and varied activities. These results, consistently obtained at both the adult and student levels, are in complete agreement with previous findings regarding need satisfaction in bureaucratic environment and with inferences derivable from bureaucratic theory. Parenthetically this particular value syndrome also has been found to be characteristic of tradition-oriented, ritualistic, socially rigid and highly formalised oriental cultures like India's (Gordon 1963,1967b, 1967d). These results are also identical with the results of similar analysis, of data on comparable American samples, made as a part of the construct validation of the WEPS' (Gordon 1968 a, 1970 b) relationships with a variety of personality measures.

Again, significant relationship had been earlier found between the WEPS and five other value dimensions for at least two of the four samples tested, positively with Recognition and Goal Orientation and negatively with Leadership, Achievement and Decisiveness (Table 6). Similarly, significant relationships in a corresponding direction occur for one of the two high school groups between the SEPS and these same scales (Table 7). Except for lack of positive relationship between WEPS (or SEPS) and Practical Mindedness and for lack of negative relationship between WEPS (or SEPS) and Benevolence, the Indian and American samples (Gordon 1970) seem to be alike in the matter of relationship between bureaucratic orientation and certain values or personality dimensions.

Hence the bureaucratic adult's tendency to place a higher value on being treated as important and on having clearly defined work objective, and to place a lower value on having authority over others, on the urge to achieve and on taking quick decisions appears in embryonic form in his younger counterpart. On the whole, these characteristics fit the infamous stereotype of the older bureaucrat, and reflect some of the dysfunctional aspects of bureaucratic behaviour described by Merton (1940).

Significantly positive relationships between (i) WEPS and conformity (on all the four samples–Table 6), (ii) SEPS and conformity (on both school samples–Table 7), (iii) WEPS and Orderliness (on all the four samples–Table 7), and (iv) SEPS and Orderliness (on both school samples–Table 7) support similar relationships between WEPS (and also SEPS) and acquiescence (Couch and Keniston–1960), (Gordon 1970 c, 1970 b).

Significantly negative relationships between (i) WEPS and Variety (on all the four samples–Table 6), and (ii) SEPS and Variety (on both school samples–Table 7) support positive relationships between WEPS (and also SEPS) and dogmatism (Rokeach's Dogmatism Scale 1960), (Gordon 1970 c, 1970 b). Significantly positive relationships between (i) WEPS and Recognition (on 3 of the 4 samples–Table 6), (ii) SEPS and Recognition (on 1 of the 2 school samples–Table 7), (iii) WEPS and Goal Orientation (on 2 of the 4 samples–Table 6), and (iv) SEPS and Goal Orientation (on 1 of the 2 school samples–Table 7) strengthen similar relationships between WEPS and (also SEPS) and authoritarianism (Adorno 1950 – California F-scale), (Gordon 1970c, 1970b). Thus the data on both Indian and American school and college students give vitality to the theoretical assumption that bureaucratic orientation would be positively associated with authoritarianism, dogmatism, and acquiescence, characteristics which are prevalent in bureaucratic environments.

Product-moment correlations between the SEPS and scale of Allport-Vernon-Lindzey Study of Values, based on a sample of liberal Arts female students (N = 50), is presented in Table 8. High SEPS scores are associated positively and negatively, respectively, with the Economic and Aesthetic values, reflecting an interest in what is useful and in the practical affairs of the business world, but little interest in the variety of experience or the artistic aspect of life. Similar relationships found between the WEPS and the study of Values test, though on a Peace Corps sample (Gordon 1968 b), tend to confirm the validity of the SEPS as well as its comparability to the WEPS.

Rank Difference Correlations of the WEPS with interest in teaching profession as measured through K.T.A.T. (Kakkar 1968) are presented in Table 9. Low and insignificant, though positive, relationships show that the analogue "the more bureaucratically oriented the student teacher the more interested in the teaching profession is he likely to be" may not be true. Those who are less interested in the teaching profession may compensate by showing a greater loyalty to the institution or its bosses.

Summary of Results

The SEPS and WEPS seem to be constructively comparable as shown by their close inter-relationships and by the identity of their correlations with external measures. Hence "Bureaucratic orientation", as originally defined at the adult level, may as well be measured in the younger student, with the school setting as the environmental frame of reference.

Decrease in SEPS means with increasing grade level, which has been found for school students in America, India and Japan, reflects changes in organizational expectations and individual needs in that the student, when advancing towards maturity, subjects himself decreasingly to environmental restraints and assumes increasingly independence on his part. Thus, "bureaucratic orientation" decreases with increasing maturity. That these changes do occur in the growing youngsters is what may be expected also.

SEPS shows negative relationships with both intelligence (Kikuchi and Gordon 1970) and school performance and an insignificantly low though positive relationship with interest in teaching profession.

Students with higher bureaucratic orientation are expected to possess more favourable attitudes toward an authoritarian or traditionalistic school environment. This hypothesis was tested by having the 10th and 11th grade students, who were involved in the earlier validation study, to show their attitude toward an authoritarian school environment on a five-point rating scale, favourable-unfavourable. The scale was scored so that high scores would typify a favourable attitude. Correlations between the

SEPS and the attitude ratings for the two grade levels came to .62 and .54 (significant at .01 level) respectively. Thus SEPS shows a positive correlation with favourableness toward an authoritarian school climate.

In case of Indian and American students of school and college, bureaucratic orientation is related positively and significantly to conformity, orderliness, negatively to independence and variety, in case of some groups positively again to recognition and goal orientation and negatively to leadership, achievement and decisiveness, positively also to authoritarianism, dogmatism, acquiescence, and economic value and negatively to aesthetic value.

Indian students at all levels *i.e.,* school, college, teacher training, appear to be more bureaucratically oriented than their American counterparts. Teacher trainees in India, however, are found to be more bureaucratically oriented than other groups probably because they are greater conformists themselves and would expect their wards to be so.

Bureaucratic orientation which, as revealed in studies made in America,* India and Japan, appears to be an important personality construct that seems to owe its determination, modification and re-orientation, in terms of increase or decrease, to the climate in which a person is brought up, educated and made to work. Whether this climate is highly structured, authoritative and awe-inspiring or highly permissive, flexible and democratic may make all the difference in how this construct takes shape. Among the various factors, which make or condition the climate, culture, attitudes, and personality of the individual or group constituting the environment may be more important.

References

Adorno, T.W., Frenkel-Brunswik, Else, Levinson, D.J. and Sanford, R.N. *The Authoritarian Personality*. New York: Harper, 1950.

Blau, P.M., and Scott, W.R. *Formal Organisations*. San Francisco: Chandler, 1962.

Bridges, C. *Prediction of Attrition at the U.S. Military Academy*. West Point: Research Division, U.S. Military Academy, 1967.

Bronzo, A.F., Jr. "Discriminant Analysis of Attrition of AFROTC Cadets." Master's Thesis, Boston College, 1966.

* The author is highly grateful to Dr. Leonard V. Gordon, State University of New York at Albani for the data on American and Japanese students.

Couch A.S., and Keniston, K. "Yeasayers and Naysayers: Agreeing Response Set as a Personality Variable." *Journal of Abnormal and Social Psychology*, LX (I960), 151-174

Fromm, E. *Escape from Freedom*. New York: Farrar and Rinehart, 1941.

Gordon, L.V., *Survey of Interpersonal Values*. Chicago: Science Research Associates, 1960.

Gordon, L.V. *Survey of Interpersonal Values*. Research Briefs. Chicago: Science Research Associates, 1963.

Gordon, L.V. and Kakkar, S.B. "A Cross-Cultural Study of Indian and American Interpersonal Values", *Journal of Social Psychology*, 1966,69, 339-340.

Gordon, L.V. "Validity of Scoring Methods for Bipolar Scales." *Educational and Psychological Measurement*, XXVII (1967), 1099-1106 (a).

Gordon, L.V. *Survey of Personal Values*. Chicago: Science Research Associates, 1967 (b).

Gordon, L.V. "Q-typing of Oriental and American Youth", *Journal of Social Psychology*, 71,1967,185-195(d).

Gordon, L.V. *Correlates of Bureaucratic Orientation*. In proceedings of XVI International Congress of Applied Psychology. Amsterdam: 1968. Swets & Zeitlinger: pp. 291-297 (a).

Gordon, L.V. *Work Environment Preference Schedule*— WEPS. Albany: Author, 1968 (b).

Gordon, L.V. *School Environment Preference Schedule*—SEPS. Albany: Author, 1968(c).

Gordon, L.V. "Are There Two Extremeness Response Sets?" 1970 (a).

Gordon, Leonard V. "The Measurement of Bureaucratic Orientation." *Personnel Psychology*, 1970, 23. (b).

Gordon, L.V., and Kikuchi, A "Response Sets of Japanese and American Students." *Journal of Social Psychology* 1970.

Gordon, Leonard V. "Weber in the Classroom", *Journal of Social Psychology*, 1970 (c).

Huxley, A.L. *Brave New World*. New York: Harper, 1946.

Kakkar, S.B., and Gordon, L.V. "A Cross-Cultural Study of Teachers' Values." *Education and Psychology Review*. 1966, 6,172-177.

Kakkar, S.B., and Gordon, L.V. "The Interpersonal Values of Indian Teacher Trainees. "*Journal of Social Psychology*, 1966, 69, 341-342.

Kakkar, S.B. "A Cross-Cultural Study of Values", *The Research Bull* (Arts), Panjab University, LV, (1), 1967.

Kakkar, S.B. "Teacher-Trainees' Interest in the Teaching Profession." No. 52, S.I.E., Chandigarh, 1968.

Khalique, N. "A Study of Bureaucratic Orientation of Strikers and Non-strikers." Patna University, 1970.

Kikuchi, A, and Gordon, L.V. "Bureaucratic Orientation of the Japanese Adolescent."

Kikuchi, A., and Gordon, L.V. "Bureaucratic Orientation and Attitudes Towards the School Environment", 1969.

Merton, R.K. "Bureaucratic Structure and Personality." *Social Forces*, XVIII (1940), 560-568.

Merton, R.K. "Social Theory and Social Structures". Glencoe: Free Press, 1949. Orwell, G. *Nineteen Eighty-four*. New York: Harcourt Brace, 1949.

Rokeach, M. *The Open and Closed Mind*. New York: Basic Books, I960.

Weber, M. *Essays in Sociology* (Translated by H.H. Gerth and C. Wright Mills). New York: Oxford University Press, 1946.

Table 1
Intercorrelations among SEPS and WEPS "Category Scores" and Total Scores SEPS

	S	U	R	T	Total
Self-Subordination (S)	*.65*	.62	.60	.64	.72
WEPS Impersonalisation (I)	.56	.60	.50	.58	.62
Rule Conformity (R)	.62	.62	*.68*	.56	.71
Traditionalism (T)	.56	.52	.62	*.63*	.67
Total	.68	.62	.66	.70	.73

Note– Common categories are Italicised. "U" represents "Uncriticalness".

Table 2
Correlations of the SEPS with Scholastic Achievement*

Grade	N	R
7	19	–.42
8	28	–.23
9	22	.05
10	22	.24
11	19	.26

* Percentage of total marks in the final promotion examination served as the achievement measure.

Table 3
Means and standard deviations (SEPS) of students in five Grades

	Male			Female		
Grade	N	Mean	SD	N	Mean	SD
7	50	41.30	4.38	50	41.54	3.42
8	50	39.82	5.14	50	40.86	3.74
9	50	38.00	4.86	50	39.70	3.80
10	50	35.90	4.83	50	37.22	5.12
11	100	35.57	6.44	100	36.68	5.48

Table 3a
Means and standard deviations of students on SEPS and WEPS and Correlation between the total scores on SEPS and EPS

	Grade	N	Sex	Mean	SD	Correlation: SEPS	WEPS
SEPS	11	100	Male	35.57	6.44	In Male scores	79*
			Female	36.68	5.48	In Female scores	.66*
WEPS	11	100	Male	36.92	4.84		
			Female	36.78	5.62		

*Significant at .01 level.

Table 3b
Means and standard deviations of elementary teacher trainees on SEPS (who had passed their High School and were undergoing Two Years' Teacher Training)

Sex	N	Mean	SD
Male	50	43.37	5.7
Female	100	44.06	5.2

Table 3c
Means and standard deviations of Secondary teacher trainees on WEPS (who were graduates undergoing One Year Teacher Training)

Sex	N	Mean	SD
Male	50	39.22	4.3
Female	50	39.69	3.9

Table 4
Comparative data on the SEPS for samples of American and Indian High School Juniors and Seniors

	Male			Female		
	N	Mean	SD	N	Mean	SD
Indian	40	39.0	5.0	110	39.8	4.5
American	64	22.0	6.5	59	20.6	7.9
Difference		17.0*			19.2*	

* Significant of .01 level.

Table 5
Comparative data on the WEPS for samples of American and Indian college students

	Male			Female		
	N	Mean	SD	N	Mean	SD
Indian	50	33.90	5.9	50	34.29	4.2
American	81	27.50	6.4	108	27.20	6.1
Difference		6.40*			7.09*	

* Significant at .001 level.

Table 6
Correlation Between the WEPS and Value Scales

	School Males 1 (N=50)	School Females 2 (N=50)	College Males 3 (N=50)	College Females 4 (N=50)
Personal Values (SIV)				
Support	.11	.08	.15	.12
Conformity	.63*	.69*	.60*	57*
Recognition	.19	.27**	.29**	.28**
Independence	–.52*	–.41*	–.63*	–.58*
Benevolence	.11	.13	.18	.21
Leadership	–.16	–.27**	–.14	–.28**
Personal Values (SPV)				
Practical Mindedness	.10	–.02	.18	.10
Achievement	–.29**	.10	–.32**	–.22
Variety	–.46*	–.50*	–.54*	–.56*
Decisiveness	–.27**	–.10	–.28**	–.14
Orderliness	.65*	.70*	.63*	.68*
Goal Orientation	.18	.28**	.21	.27**

* Significant at .01 level.
** Significant at .05 level.

Table 7
Correlations between the SEPS and Value Scales

	School Males	School Females
Interpersonal Values (SIV)		
Support	.12	.10
Conformity	.65*	.73*

Recognition	.20	.28**
Independence	–.54*	–.44*
Benevolence	.12	.15
Leadership	–.18	–.28**
Personal Values (SPV)		
Practical Mindedness	.12	–.04
Achievement	–.28**	.12
Variety	–.47*	–.49*
Decisiveness	–.28**	–.13
Orderliness	.63*	.69*
Goal Orientation	.16	.27**

* Significant at .01 level.
** Significant at .05 level

Table 8
Product-Moment Correlations Between the SEPS and the Study of Values

Values	r
Theoretical	–.03
Economic	.42*
Aesthetic	–.39*
Social	.02
Political	.12
Religious	–.15

* Significant at .01 level.

Table 9
Correlations of the WEPS with interest in the Teaching Profession"

Group	Sex	N	r
B.Ed.	Male	67	.11*
(Secondary teacher trainees)	Female	62	.04*

* Not significant.

66. CORRELATES OF BUREAUCRATIC ORIENTATION

Porter (1966) suggested that industrial psychologists need to study individual differences in the context of organizational theory. Gordon (1968 a) postulated a personality construct, bureaucratic orientation, based on the bureaucratic model. He developed a measure of this construct, using the original scheme of Max Weber (1946) which describes the common denominator characteristics of bureaucratic organisations. The measure named the Work

Environment Preference Schedule (WEPS) has a coefficient of reliability of .90 and test-retest reliability of .65, besides validity r's ranging from .20 to .67 with measures of characteristics typifying acceptance of the bureaucratic norm (1968a, 1971a, 1971b).

Merton (1940), Weber (1946) and others thought that work environments represented by the bureaucratic organizational model would appeal to individuals having certain personality characteristics. As such significant relationships between WEPS and tests of such characteristics would be expected. Correlations between the WEPS and primary personality factors as measured by Sixteen Personality factors Questionnaire Form A (Cattell 1964) may provide one such set of relationships. Presentation of data, based on an Indian sample, and bearing on the validity of the WEPS with certain specified personality factors is the purpose of this study. The 16 PF form used here is the Hindi version of Cattell's original test, as standardized by Kapur (undated) for comparable Indian samples, having split-half reliability coefficients of .49 to .83 and validity coefficients similar to those derived by Cattell.

Method

Forty-eight in-service teachers (35 male and 13 female) posted in the Government elementary schools situated in the rural areas of Punjab State formed the sample. Being in the same salary-scale and belonging to the same social set-up, they stood controlled for socio-economic level. Their educational level was two-years' teacher training following eleven years' school. Age-range and teaching-experience-range were 23-35 and 6-18 respectively. As sex differences in WEPS scores were insignificant, males and females were considered as a single group.

In order to spot out the personality factors which separate high bureaucratically oriented from low-bureaucratically oriented, the group was divided into two sub-groups *i.e.* Low WEPS (who scored 34-40) and high WEPS (who scored 41-47). The difference in the means of the two groups was highly significant at .01 level (Table 1).

Table 1

Means of WEPS Scores of Low WEPS and High WEPS Groups

Group	N	Mean	SD
Low WEPS	19	38.79	1.72
High WEPS	29	43.14	3.32
Significance of Difference .01 level			

Results and Discussion

When the personality behaviour of low WEPS group was compared with that of high WEPS group, significant differences (using analysis of variance) between the two samples, were observed on two factors *i.e.*, C and E (Table 2). On all other factors the differences between the two groups were insignificant.

When the data were examined within the framework of the bipolar descriptions of source traits, both the groups (high WEPS and low WEPS) exhibited very similar patterns of personality behaviour. Manifesting consistent features of cyclothymia, the subjects showing high bureaucratic orientation were warm, sociable and outgoing. They did not differ from those showing low bureaucratic orientation in seeking out people but did demonstrate a lack of emotional maturity. They showed less effective role interaction and democratic procedure than their low WEPS colleagues. They tended to be somewhat submissive and dependent as compared to the latter. This is what may be expected.

Difference in bureaucratic orientation was not found congruent to differences in such personality factors as sociability, intelligence, surgency, superego strength, adventurous nature, being sensitive, paranoid tendency, introversion-extraversion, shrewdness, self-confidence, radicalism- conservatism, self-sufficiency-dependency, sentiment formation and ergic tension.

Table 2
Mean Sten Scores of Low WEPS Group (N=19) and High WEPS Group (N=29)

Factor	Description	Low WEPS group	High WEPS group	F
A	Cyclothyme-Schizothyme	5.94	5.62	.55
B	Intelligent-Dull	8.42	8.10	.44
C	High-ego strength-Low-ego strength	4.73	3.75	7.80**
E	Dominant-Submissive	6.36	5.37	4.23*
F	Enthusiastic-Depressed	6.42	6.44	.12
G	High-superego strength-Low superego strength	6.42	6.25	.37
H	Adventurous-Shy, timid	5.05	5.03	.04

I	Tender-minded-Tough minded	5.63	5.93	.47
L	Paranoid-Adaptable	5.78	6.13	.76
M	Imaginative-Practical	4.42	4.68	.24
N	Shrewd-Artless	5.63	5.34	.90
O	Guilt Prone-Confident	5.21	5.86	1.50
Q_1	Radical-Conservative	6.47	5.89	1.80
Q_2	Self-sufficient-Group dependent	4.57	4.51	.04
Q_3	Controlled-Low self-concept	5.57	5.47	.08
Q_4	Ergic Tension-Relaxed	5.57	5.55	.03

*P <.05. **P<.01

Thus only two separate and distinct patterns of personality behaviour for the high and low groups (on bureaucratic orientation) were revealed. Measured by the 16 PF, two factors (C and E) separated the high group from the low group.

Consistently significant relationships were found between the WEPS and six of the personality factors, in a positive direction with L and O, in a negative direction with A, E, M, and Q_2 (Table 3). Thus, individuals who score high on bureaucratic orientation are inclined to be suspecting, jealous, and timid, insecure. At the same time, they tend to be aloof, stiff, submissive, practical, conventional, and dependent. These results are in complete accord with prior findings regarding need satisfaction in bureaucratic environments and with inferences derivable from bureaucratic theory. Some of these personality factors resemble the opprobrious stereotype of the bureaucratic, and are reminiscent of some of the dysfunctional characteristics of bureaucracy described by Merton (1940).

Table 3
Correlation Between Personality Factors and WEPS

Serial No.	Traits		r
A	Warm	Aloof	
	Social	Stiff	–.33*
B	Bright	Dull	
	Persevering	Quitting	–.006
C	Mature	Immature	
	Calm	Unstable	–.13

E	Dominant	Submissive	
	Aggressive	Mild	–.29*
F	Enthusiastic	Sober	
	Happy-go-Lucky	Serious	–.107
G	Conscientious	Casual	
	Persistent	Undependable	–.13
H	Adventurous	Shy	
	Thick-skinned	Timid	.10
I	Sensitive	Tough	
	Effeminate	Realistic	.05
L	Suspecting	Accepting	
	Jealous	Adaptable	.29*
M	Introverted	Practical	
	Absent-minded	Realistic	–.58**
N	Sophisticated	Simple	
	Polished	Unpretentious	–.03
O	Timid	Confident	
	Insecure	Self-Secure	.69**
Q_1	Radical	Conservative	
	Critical	Tradition loving	–.09
Q_2	Self-sufficient	Group dependent	
	Resourceful	Conventional	–.99**
Q_3	Controlled	Uncontrolled	
	Exacting will power	Lax	.05
Q_4	Tense	Phlegmatic	
	Excitable	Composed	–.15

* Significant at .05 level.
** Significant at .01 level.

Since the WEPS is intended to measure bureaucratic orientaion, it would be expected to correlate positively with measures of actual or expressed willingness to remain in a highly bureaucratised work environment, such as military service.

Data bearing on this hypothesis and also on the validity of the WEPS resulted from another study. College boys undergoing military-type training along with studies under National Cadet Corps programme formed the subjects of this study. Most of the students who join this officer training programme choose to go in as Commissioned Officers in the military service. The investigator administered WEPS to 150 cadets of the National Cadet Corps (N.C.C.) at a local liberal arts college. The cadets were students of the second year of the three-year-degree (graduation) course. By the start of the second year, 40 per cent of the original group had withdrawn from the programme. As may be noted in Table 4, those who remained had a significantly higher WEPS score than those who had withdrawn. The difference is represented by a biserial correlation coefficient of .51.

Again, the WEPS was administered to 394 senior cadets of the National Cadet Corps at the same college two weeks prior to their final graduation examination. Each cadet was asked to indicate on a graphic scale the likelihood of his joining the army after his N.C.C. training. As may be noted in Table 5, a monotonic relationship was found between WEPS scores and the cadets' stated intention. The concurrent validity of the WEPS against this career motivation criterion is represented by a product moment correlation of .46 which is highly significant (.01 level). A monotonic increase in standard deviations reflects a greater homogeneity in bureaucratic orientation among the more highly career motivated.

Table 4
Predictive Validity of the WEPS for NCC Sample Against a Retention Criterion

Group	N	Mean	SD
Remaining	90	40.91	6.7
Withdrawn	60	33.86	5.4
Difference		7.05*	r=.51*

* Significant at .01 level.

The findings of these two studies echo those yielded by the studies of Anthony Bronzo and Claude Bridges referred to by Gordon (1968).

Table 5
Concurrent Validity of the WEPS for NCC Sample Against a Career Intention Criterion

Career Intention	N	Mean	SD
Sure to join	101	41.21	3.6
Likely to join	142	37.39	5.4
Not sure	99	34.41	6.2
Not likely to join	52	28.79	9.5
Total	394	35.62	6.9

Table 6
Means and Standard Deviations for the WEPS

Group	N	Mean	S	Sex
High School Seniors	100	36.92	4.84	Male
	100	36.78	5.62	Female
College students	50	33.90	5.9	Male
Secondary School	50	34.29	4.2	Female
Teacher Trainees	50	39.22	4.3	Male
Elementary School	50	39.69	3.9	Female
Teachers	35	41.22	2.70	Male
	13	41.77	3.18	Female
	48	41.39	2.70	Combined Group

Table 6 presents WEPS means for male and female samples. Very high means are those of elementary school teachers *i.e.* the individuals who had essentially resigned themselves to a highly structured and bureaucratized environment. A minimum of 6 years and a maximum of 18 years was the length of their stay in schools. Secondary school teacher trainees, most of whom would go in for a teaching career in secondary schools (organizations that fit the bureaucratic model warranting conformist, systematic and orderly behaviour on the part of its members), have also fairly high means for obvious reasons. High School seniors come next in the magnitude of their means, while the lowest means are those of college students who, having left the environmental constraints within the school setting, have full responsibility for structuring their own work environment and for making their own decisions.

Highly consistent, significant relationships (based on Indian samples) of WEPS with several value scales, and weak relationship of WEPS with interest in teaching, and scholastic achievement and comparisons of such relationships with identical relationships based on comparable American samples, as revealed in Kakkar's study (1970), provide another set of correlates of bureaucratic orientation. Again, relationships of WEPS with need-achievement, intelligence, academic achievement and interest in teaching find place in another study by Kakkar (1971). In most of the correlations between the WEPS and measures of constructs associated with authoritarianism, dogmatism, acquiescence and external locus of control detailed in these studies, significant relationships in the predicted direction have been noted. Such are the relationships which essentially bear out the validity of the WEPS, a reliable measure of individual differences which Gordon* (1968a) derived from the bureaucratic organizational model and which may serve as a very effective instrument to measure a personality construct- "bureaucratic orientation".

References

Cattell, R.B. (1964). *Handbook for the Sixteen Personality Factor Questionnaire.* The Institute for Personality and Ability Testing, Champaign, Illinois.

Gordon, L.V. (1968 a). *Manual: Work Environment Preference Schedule* (WEPS) Albany.

Gordon, L.V. (1968 b). "Correlates of Bureaucratic Orientation — Proceedings of XVI International Congress of Applied Psychology" Amsterdam: Swets and Zeitlinger, 291-297.

Gordon, L.V. (1971 a). Weber in the Classroom *Journal of Educational Psychology*, (1st issue).

Gordon, L.V. (1971 b). Manual: *Work Environment Preference Schedule* (WEPS). Albany.

Kakkar, S.B. Bureaucratic Orientation of Indian Students, 1970, Punjab University Research Bulletin (Arts).

Kakkar, S.B. Some Correlates of N-Achievement, 1971, Indian Journal of Educational Research.

Kapoor, V.K., and Jalota, S. The Sixteen Personality Questionnaire (Hindi Version — Forms A and B), Undated.

Merton, R.K. Bureaucratic Structure and Personality. *Social Forces*, 1940,18, 560-568.

Porter, L.W. (1966). Personnel Management, in P. Farnsworth, Annual Review of Psychology, Palo Alto, 395-422.

Weber, M. (1946). Essays in Sociology, (Translated by H.H. Gerth and C. Wright Mills), Oxford University Press, New York.

---

* The author is grateful to Dr. Leonard V. Gordon, State University of New York, Albany who supplied the manuals and his findings of WEPS.

X. TEACHERS, THEIR CHARACTERISTICS AND PROBLEMS

67. A STUDY OF TEACHERS' WORRIES

Teaching is an attractive job for such reasons as 'it is a very good opportunity to be creative,' 'it is satisfying as teachers develop children into good citizens', 'environment of work is most congenial', 'teachers' associates in the profession belong to an above-average level of culture,' 'variety in teacher's job is so much that it makes work interesting,' 'it provides many opportunities for growth' and the like. Conversely, teaching job has several disadvantages which cause persistent worries. These worries tend to arouse conflicts and may lead to nervous disorganisation. Nervousness, tension, irritation and consequently a disabling maladjustment often arise from the teacher's professional as well as personal life. It was with this HYPOTHESIS that the present study to gauge teachers' worries was undertaken.

Method

246 teachers (180 males and 66 females) of Jullundur High Schools were asked to list just three factors which caused them persistent or frequent worries. No factors were suggested to them, so as to avoid leading responses. The particulars they were asked to write on their lists were "whether married or single", "whether living with wife/husband and if not why".

700 items were mentioned in all by 246 teachers. These factors were classified into 10 broad categories and the percentages of teachers responding for each category were calculated. Some items rarely mentioned and not fitting into any of these categories were left out. The results are given in the table below.

Data

Table showing the categorised causes of teachers' worries in the order of frequency of listing. (The values represent percentage of teachers giving three or less responses in each category. The percentage was rounded off to the nearest single unit).

Causes	Percentage of Mention by					
	Single Teachers		Married Teachers not living with wives/ husbands		Married Teachers living with wives/ husbands	
	Men	Women	Men	Women	Men	Women
Financial difficulties	34	45	40	48	29	41
Problems of own or relatives' health	32	42	36	46	26	40
Problems of self-improvement or personality difficulties	28	41	30	42	20	35
Home or family problems including lack of normal family relationships	26	39	24	38	18	30
Poor progress of pupils	16	34	15	34	12	26
Bad report of a boss, authoritarian boss	10	20	14	22	7	16
Disciplinary problems of class	6	18	10	20	4	14
Dissatisfaction with occupation	6	17	8	18	3	14
Unhappy marriage	–	–	3	7	2	4
Religious or moral issues	2	–	4	4	1	4

Results

1. Almost all the worries are more frequently mentioned by women than by the men. Women teachers, it appears, tend to worry more than men teachers, owing to one cause or another. This is true of all the three categories of teachers.
2. Women teachers who are not living with their husbands (causes for so living were not ascertained) seem to have

more worries than men teachers of their own category and then men or women teachers who are either single or are living with their wives or husbands.

3. Men teachers who are not living with their wives (causes for so living were not ascertained) have more worries in all matters (except in case of home and family problems and poor progress of pupils) than men teachers who are either single or are living with their wives.

   In case of Home and family problems and Poor progress of pupils these men teachers seem to worry a little less than single men teachers but considerably more than men teachers living with their wives.

4. Married teachers living with their wives/husbands have lesser worries than teachers who are either single or are not living with their wives/husbands.

5. Single teachers, both men and women, have more worries than married teachers living with their wives/husbands.

6. 'Financial difficulties', 'problems of own or relatives' health', 'problems of self-improvement or personality difficulties,' and 'home and family problems' cause most worries. 'Poor progress of pupils,' 'bad report by a boss,' 'disciplinary problems of class' and 'dissatisfaction with occupation' produce comparatively less worries.

   This leads to the *conclusion that the teacher's nervousness and tension may arise more often from his/her personal life than from his/her professional life.*

7. 'Unhappy marriage' has been mentioned less by teachers who are living with their wives/husbands than those who are not so living, though women in each of these two categories of teachers seem to worry more than men because of unhappy marriage.

8. Religious or moral issues seem to be the least concern or worry of most teachers, though this cause, as all others, has been mentioned most by teachers who are not living with their wives/husbands.

Discussion

1. It is not known how the number of worries in case of teachers compares with the number in other occupations. But it is a well-known fact that these worries end in inefficiency in

teaching. Teachers who become emotionally unstable as a result of these or other worries are prone to have emotionally unstable pupils or children, because tension is contagious. It is therefore worthwhile for administrators and teachers themselves to look into the causes of such worries with a view to ameliorating their own lot and indirectly improving that of the taught.

2. As at present women teachers tend to worry more than men teachers, it is likely this may affect their home life especially in relation to their own children. Hence all the more need to remove women-teachers' causes of worries.
3. When married teachers who are living with their wives/husbands have lesser worries than single teachers or teachers not living with their wives/husbands, the question arises: "Does 'to be married' improve a teacher's work"? If the answer is yes, reasons may be that marriage gives them experience with children or with family which is a very great humanizing agency.
4. When however married teachers who are not living with their wives/husbands are afflicted by more worries than those who are single or are living singly, it becomes obvious that happy personal life, no matter whether the teacher is married or single, is what makes all the difference.
5. Since worries arise more from teacher's personal life than his professional life, teachers would do well to reorient their private world of men and materials with a view to living a more satisfying life. At the same time, better emoluments, more amenities and facilities of work, good and sympathetic bosses, congenial environments and the like, which form part of the teacher's professional life, would go a long way in making his personal life happier and free from many worries. Hence the need to improve upon his professional life and to make teaching an adequately satisfying occupation.
6. That moral issues cause the least concern to teachers indicates that material values predominate the teachers' as others' lives, and this itself may have caused worries or unrest in their personal lives. Moral values in this material universe, which continuously creates more and more needs, with comparatively lesser means to satisfy those needs,

need to be upheld and sustained. Upon these values will be built the whole edifice of a true and full life devoid of dissatisfaction and grouse.

References

1. Peters, D.W., The status of the married women teacher, N.Y. Teachers' College C.U., 1934.
2. Pressey, S.L. Janney, J.E., and Kuhlen, R.G., Life: A Psychological Survey, N.Y. Harper, 1939.
3. Bills, A.G., The Psychology of Efficiency, N.Y. Harper, 1943.

68. PROFESSOR QUALITIES AS VIEWED BY STUDENTS

Gadzella (1) asked students to indicate the most important and least important criteria of an ideal professor. Of the five criteria selected as least important were those of researcher and writer. In studies by Quick and Wolfe (4), Pogue (3), students rated participation in research the least important characteristic of an ideal professor. Yamamoto and Disney (7) in a study aimed at findings students' preference for professors' roles showed that their order of preference was teacher, researcher, socialite, and administrator. In a study by Kelley and Hart (2), liberal arts students rated the teaching role as most important and the research role as least important, while parents assigned equally high ratings to the teaching and character-building roles and lower ratings to the research role.

The present study was aimed at determining the preferences of college students for certain qualities of college professors. The qualities employed were personality, character and principles, mastery of modern teaching methods, interest in teaching, mastery of subject, effective speech, effective teaching, punctuality and discipline, friendliness and love, and ability to understand students. These ten qualities had been earlier culled out of a host of such qualities that 1025 liberal arts students, which was almost the entire strength of three local colleges, had suggested when they were asked to write five qualities or characteristics each that college professors should possess. The qualities mentioned by 60 per cent or more of the group formed the basis of this study.

Method

Sample. The Ss consisted of 350 students, male and female in equal numbers, chosen at random from the final classes of the degree course in three liberal arts colleges. They represented identical population in the state in respect of socio-economic status, age, curricula taught, type of teachers they had, teacher-pupil relations and the general atmosphere they were exposed tc.

The Ss were required to indicate the importance of the ten qualities using a five-point rating scale. The ends of the continuum were designed as "extremely important" and "least important", while the midpoint of the continuum was designated as "moderately important." A score value of 5 was given to the highest rating and 1 to the lowest rating, while score values of 4, 3 and 2 were given to very important, moderately important, and not so important ratings respectively. The students completed the ratings during six group testing sessions conducted just before their final passing out.

Results

The mean ratings of the ten professor qualities by students are shown in Table 1. The quality 'ability to Understand students' was rated, highest, closely followed by the qualities 'effective teaching', 'subject mastery', 'methods mastery' and 'personality' in this order; quality 'friendliness, sympathy and love' was rated lowest, with 'interest in teaching' reaching almost similar rating.

To determine if the quality hierarchy was statistically significant a series of critical ratios was prepared (Table 2).

The numerical advantage held by effective teaching over all other qualities except 'mastery of subject,' and 'effective speech', is significant at .01 level of confidence. 'Ability to understand students,' 'mastery of subject,' and 'mastery of modern teaching methods' shares the second position in terms of exceeding some other qualities in terms of student preference. It is interesting to note that although 'ability to understand students,' 'effective teaching,' and 'mastery of subject' were not found to be significantly preferred over 'effective speech', 'effective speech' was found to be more desirable than 'interest in teaching and 'friendliness, sympathy and love'.

Table 1
Mean Ratings by Students of College Teacher Qualities

Serial No.	Quality	Mean Ratings
1.	Ability to understand students	3.40
2.	Effective teaching	3.27
3.	Mastery of subject	3.25
4.	Mastery of modern teaching methods	3.19
5.	Personality	3.16
6.	Character and principles	3.05
7.	Regularity, punctuality and discipline	3.04
8.	Effective speech	2.71
9.	Interest in teaching	2.62
10.	Friendliness, sympathy and love	2.60

'Personality' and 'character and principles' seem to occupy an intermediate position whereas 'regularity, punctuality and discipline,' 'effective speech,' 'interest in teaching,' and 'friendliness, sympathy and love' are, beyond question, the least preferred in this study. All qualities (except 'personality' and 'regularity, punctuality and discipline') are preferred over 'friendliness, sympathy and love'.

Table 2
Critical Ratios Between Selected Qualities

Serial qualities	Serial number of quality									
No. of Quality	1	2	3	4	5	6	7	8	9	10
1.		1.44	0.30	5.88*	0.90	4.88*	1.22	1.33	5.60*	2.66*
2.			1.60	4.44*	2.20**	3.44*	2.66*	0.11	4.30*	4.11
3.				6.22*	0.60	5.22*	0.88	1.66	5.36*	2.10**
4.					6.20*	1.00	7.11*	4.55*	0.30	8.55*
5.						5.88*	0.22	2.33**	6.50*	1.50
6.							6.87*	4.00*	1.33	8.50*
7.								2.87*	7.44*	1.62
8.									4.88*	4.50*
9.										8.00*

* Significant at .01 level of confidence.
** Significant at .05 level of confidence.

Analysis of variance of these data (6) indicated (Table 3) that the Quality main effect was highly significant (F = 4.42, df = 9/36, P < .01). The Rater main effect was also highly significant (F = 21.75, df = 4/36, P < .01).

Table 3 shows that the null/hypothesis with respect to preferences is untenable. The evidence is strong that real differences exist among the five preferences of each quality. Again, it is obvious that some qualities were consistently rated higher than others without regard to preference. Further analysis of variance (last F) may make us feel quite sure that preference differences were significantly greater than quality

Table 3
Analysis of Variance

Source of variation	df	Sums of squares	variance	SD
Between preference	4	476369	119092.25	
Among qualities	9	218007	24223.00	
Interaction	36	197112	5475.30	73.96
F preferences	= 21.75	df = 4/36	P< .01	
F qualities	= 4.42	df = 9/36	P< .01	
F pref-qual.	$= \frac{119092.25}{24223.00}$	= 4.91	df = 4/9 < P	.05

differences. Since the reverse is usually true, the implication to be drawn is that the differences in the rating of the different qualities, though significant, might not have been as high as they could be.

Discussion

The present findings indicate that liberal arts students attribute greatest importance to the teaching role of the professor and feel that his friendliness, love and sympathy, towards them are of least significance. An interesting finding was the high value the students placed on such qualities as 'ability to understand students', 'mastery of subject,' and 'mastery of modern teaching methods' and the low value they placed on 'regularity, punctuality and discipline,' 'effective speech', and 'interest in teaching'.

The findings concerning the professor qualities may be interpreted as further evidence to suggest that some basic conflicts with respect to the qualities of the college professor are developing within the society. On the one hand, the professor is subjected to pressure from the faculty or the college to be friendly and sympathetic to students and to take interest in teaching. 'Effective teaching,' 'subject mastery,' and 'mastery of modern teaching methods' does not receive a great deal of attention within the institutional setting. The students, on the other hand, attribute less importance to the professor's 'friendliness, sympathy and love', and his 'interest in teaching', and are considerably concerned with his teaching role and all that (effective teaching, subject mastery and mastery of modern teaching methods) it implies. The fact that institutions and students place different emphasis on what professor qualities are important obviously implies that these groups have different role expectancies for the college professor. The conflicts in role expectancies can possibly contribute to personal conflicts within the members of college teaching profession. Besides, these role conflicts may produce disorganisation within the institutional structure (5).

Further research into the qualities of the college professor is warranted. It would be worthwhile to determine the qualities and expectancies of student and parent groups for different types of institutions. In addition, it would be of particular interest to study more systematically the professor quality preferences of professors themselves, administrators and the general public.

References

1. Gadzella, B.M. "Student View of an Ideal Professor." *Teaching of Psychology Newsletter* (November 1967), pp, 10-11.
2. Kelly, Richard and Hart, B. Derrel. "Professor Role Preferences of Entering College Students and Their Parents." *The Journal of Educational Research*, Vol. 63, No. 4, December 1969, pp. 150-151.
3. Pogue, F.G. "Students' Ratings of the Ideal Teacher." *Improving College and University Teaching*, XV (Spring 1967), pp. 133-136.
4. Quick, A.F. and Wolfe, A.D. "The Ideal Professor," *Improving College and University Teaching*, XIII (Summer 1965), pp. 133-134.
5. Sarbin, T.R. "Role Theory," in G. Lindzey (ed.). *Handbook of Social Psychology*, Cambridge, Massachusetts: Addison-Wesley, 1954.
6. Winer, B.J. *Statistical Principles in Experimental Design*, New York: McGraw Hill Book Company, 1962.
7. Yamamoto, K., and Disney, H.F. "Eight Professors. A Study on College Students' Preferences Among Their Teachers," *Journal of Educational Psychology*, LVII (1966), pp. 146-150.

69. EXUBERANCE FOR TEACHING

Hundreds of graduate boys and girls throng the state's teacher training colleges every year in a bid, not always with a decision, to become teachers. Those who have taken the decision may have taken it lightly or hastily. Others might have entered the profession for lack of other things to do. Still others are those who have taken no decision except that of joining the training college the way they had been joining colleges before. The writer, intrigued by this seemingly blind exuberance of the youth for teaching, attempted to diagnose whether they really wanted to adopt the teaching career and if so, the reasons for wanting so.

It was assumed that not many of them really wanted to teach, that if many wanted to teach or to get into the teaching profession, their reasons for wanting so were fake, inadequate or based on high sounding cliches, stereotypes, abstract ideas of do-good-to-other type, and that some of them did not want to teach at all.

Method and Procedure

The student teachers of the State College of Education, Patiala (session 1967-68) formed the sample. They were a well-proportioned group of individuals belonging to below-average to above-average socio-economic strata of both rural and urban parts of Patiala District, and could legitimately represent identical population of the Punjab State. 258 subjects (123 males and 135 females out of an aggregate of 130 and 150 respectively) participated in the study.

The subjects were asked to answer a blanket question: Do you want to become a teacher? If yes, why? If no, why not? The study was personally made by the writer, taking a group of about 40 student teachers at one time. No time limit was placed, though no group took more than 15 minutes to hand over their responses. It took three days to complete the study. No identifying data, except putting B or G to indicate whether boy or girl respectively, was sought so as to lure them to give free and unfettered responses, without any fear of being identified. There were no particular instructions, except asking them to be relevant, precise and true in their responses. They were told to write in any language, to make them escape the hazards of expression in English which happened to be the medium of their instruction and examination. Necessary rapport was established to ensure their willing co-operation and faith in the task.

After the answers were collected, these were put into two heaps *i.e.* 'yes' and 'no'. Insignificant sex differences in the number of those saying 'yes', and that of those saying 'no' (as yielded by chi square test), warranted treating the 'yes' groups, as also 'no' groups, of males and females as a single group.

The reasons for 'yes' and 'no' were then sifted from the subjects' papers and their frequencies recorded. Again chi square test revealed that there were no significant sex differences in the reasons supporting 'yes' and in those supporting 'no'. As such the male and female subjects were treated as one group, also for the purpose of explaining reasons supporting 'yes' or 'no'. The differences between those saying 'yes' and the ones saying 'no', both in the case of males and females, were, however, found highly significant, even alarming.

The range of reasons given to support 'yes' *i.e.*, 'wanting to become a teacher', was 1 to 6, while that of those for 'no' *i.e.* 'not wanting to become a teacher', was 1 to 3. Reasons which were mentioned by 5 per cent or less of the subjects were discarded in the case of 'yes' answers, while no reasons, howsoever low in the frequency of their mention, were discarded in the case of 'no' answers.

Reasons, when examined, fell in eight categories *i.e.* altruistic, moralistic, economic, instinctive, academic, hedonistic, compulsive and egotistical, in the case of 'yes' answers; and in five categories *i.e.* economic, moralistic, egotistical, compulsive, and expedient in the case of 'no' answers.

Findings

A significantly large majority of student teachers, male and female, favoured teaching. The number of those who disfavoured teaching is notably small. More females than males wanted to become teachers, while more males than females did not want to go in for teaching. (See Table 1).

Table 1
Percentages of student teachers giving responses in 'Yes' or 'No' when asked "Do you want to become a teacher?"

Sex	"Yes" (Those wanting to become teachers)	"No" (Those not wanting to become teachers)	Total
Males	85.3	14.7	100
Females	88.9	11.1	100

Analysis of reasons given by those answering "yes" to the given question revealed that altruistic reasons predominated all other reasons for wanting to become a teacher. They ranged from the concrete requirement of improving school education to the abstract ideal of building the nation, morality and humanity. The frequency of mention varied from low to high as the reasons mentioned progressed from concrete to abstract.

Economic reasons, though with about half the frequency of the altruistic ones, were found to be supporting the proposition at (b) below (Table 2). They ranged from minor benefits like long vocations–which attracted lesser mention–to very substantial gains like the recently got skyrocketing pay grades (as compared to previous grades) which were mentioned by a greater number of subjects.

Third and fourth in the descending order of frequency of mention come instinctive and academic reasons in favour of teaching; inherent urge for and interest in teaching and a desire to enhance academic potential were mentioned by an appreciable number of the student teachers. Moralistic reasons in support of teaching were put forth by a number next only to that for academic reasons. Such reasons ranged from the statement that teaching profession develops moral values to the one that it is sacrosanct and soul-raising.

Sixth in the same order are the hedonistic reasons which, though mentioned by less than one-sixth of the "yes" group, herald pleasure principle which teaching satisfies by giving peace, contentment, satisfaction and active life. Least in the frequency of mention are the compulsive reasons which left certain teachers with no choice other than that of teaching. A few reasons, motivated by a desire to grind one's own axe or to make petty self-seeking, though classified as egoistical, were too few to be taken note of. (See Table 2).

Table 2
Reasons to support "Yes"

Category of reason	Reasons	Percentage of mention (out of those who want to become teachers)
(a) Altruistic	(1) To be a nation-builder; to develop nation's ideals and civilisation; to build ideals and morality; to be a guide and philosopher to the young; to build character of the youth; to be educator to all	36.2

		(2) To serve children; to understand their nature and help in their development	13.6
		(3) To make India prosperous; to make future generation of my dreams; to bring change	13.4
		(4) For service to humanity; for the welfare of society; for raising the level of humanity.	8.4
		(5) To solve problems of orthodoxy, corruption, frustrations, ill-will, hatred, communalism, mutual bickering	6.3
		(6) To improve school education	6.2
		(7) To produce leaders, generals, scientists, and good people	6.1
(b)	Economic	(1) For revised and attractive grades; for tuition-income.	29.3
		(2) It provides lot of leisure, ample spare time, long vocations, not much work	9.0
		(3) For its greater market value, much demand, easy to get job	8.7
(c)	Instinctive	(1) For love of it; taste for it; inherent interest in it; it is aim of life; to love children	23.0
		(2) It is an inborn urge; it satisfies the mind; it is an inner drive	15.6
		(3) To enjoy working with boys and girls	5.1
(d)	Academic	(1) To learn; to increase knowledge; to read literature; to be in touch with the learned; to develop literary taste' to become a write or poet.	16.1
		(2) To continue further studies; to improve qualifications	15.6
		(3) To be able to argue and discuss; to be able to speak to others and impress them	5.8

		(4)	Promoting culture	5.1
(e)	Moralistic	(1)	Teaching profession is the noblest, sacred, vital, sacrosanct, loftiest, honest, free from corruption, moral, best.	9.7
		(2)	It is ideal, soul-raising, inspiring, strategic, ennobling, virtuous, character-building.	7.4
		(3)	It is respectable; it has prestige value; it raises moral stature; it enhances social value	7.3
		(4)	It develops religious, moral and spiritual values	5.8
		(5)	It is setting worthwhile example	5.1
(f)	Hedonistic	(1)	To have easy and comfortable living; to enjoy peaceful, calm and quiet life; to enjoy peace of mind, goodness of nature and amusement	9.0
		(2)	To remain young and active in the company of the young; to be full of pleasure, excitement and life.	8.5
		(3)	Its pleasure-giving aspects	5.1
(g)	Compulsive	(1)	Being a teacher (JBT/OT) already	8.0
		(2)	Being unable to get any other job	6.1
(h)	Egoistical		(These being too few were discarded) To improve contacts with very high families and with people of high social status; to be able to go on tours with the young; to be able to stay at home or with parents since one can teach in one's own home-town; to avail of the chances of going abroad available in this profession	3.2

An examination of the reasons supporting "no" showed that as against 30.2 per cent who favour teaching on the plea that this profession is virtuous and moral, as many as 50.7 per cent of the student teachers disfavour it on the ground that it suffers from such immoral practices as greed, disparity between theory and practice, timidity, injustice and the like. Less than half of the number of those who are opposed to teaching on moralistic grounds are those who are so egotistical that they say "never" when asked "Do you want to become a teacher."

Whereas about one half of the student teachers want teaching for its high economic value, about one-eighth of them do not want it for its low (comparing it with other professions) economic benefits.

Fourth in the descending order of the frequency of mention come the student teachers who have joined teacher-training not for the love of it, but for expediency, especially with a view to securing themselves against adversity, so that a degree in education could help them in getting a teaching job after all other doors are slammed on them.

About one-third of the number of those who are inclined to teach owing to compulsive reasons are the ones who, though influenced by similar reasons, are disinclined to teach. Even the factors which compelled them to join teacher-training fail to make them want to go in for teaching after training. (See Table 3).

Table 3
Reasons to support "No"

Category of reason	Reasons	Percentage of mention (out of those who want to become teachers)
Compulsive	Nothing else to do; being unemployed	5.0
Economic	Low Salary; can earn more from business or other jobs; technical line is better both economically and socially	13.2
Egotistical	Have joined just to pass time; to get training for a rainy day; just to find some job; as a security against distress	10.3
Moralistic	Would never become a teacher even if I pass B.Ed.; would leave it when better employed; would not become a teacher even in dream; shall leave for something better after doing B.Ed.	20.4

Category of reason	Reasons	Percentage of mention (out of those who want to become teachers)
	Corruption in it; no respect, recognition or status; tyranny, partiality and injustice in it; because teachers don't practise what they preach; contact with teachers reveals that they are idlers, shirkers, gossipers, etc.; because there is not much of work to do. Our teachers have made the profession cheap; one can't do real service because there is stress on results; because teachers can't use the knowledge got in for lack of courage. Bitter experience with my own teachers who blocked my career; was guided wrongly by some teachers; greed for money in this profession	50.7

Discussion

Most of the student teachers, females more than males, seem to have joined teacher-training for the purpose of becoming teachers. This is a good augury for the teaching profession, especially because heretofore not many of the trainees, who got teacher training, actually became teachers. This finding runs counter to the investigator's aforesaid assumption that not many of the trainees really wanted to teach.

Though most of the young graduates do want to go in for teaching after completing the training they are undergoing, it is doubtful whether all of them can be groomed to be teachers simply by giving teacher training. The writer's observation over a long period of working in training colleges is that the teacher, like many students, does not learn the material taught or grasp teacher education well enough to cross the barriers from learning to thinking, from theory to practice and from complacency to adventure. Most of the teachers in our set-up seem to be wanting in educational and cultural advancement. They are found inadequate in the content they teach, and sometimes in the method with which they teach, though courses on method which is about all that their training *alma maters* give them cannot replace or make up for the absent content. This is in line with Bruner's (10) observation.

The writer's hypothesis regarding the student-teachers' reasons for intending to join teaching profession gets only partial support from the findings in that altruistic reasons, not stereotyped or abstract ones, reign supreme amongst the various arguments propounded in support of their affirmative answers.

Altruistic reasons, if genuine and true which this study does not attempt to determine, portend excellently well both for teachers and the teaching profession. They imply dedication to a great cause which aims at building the nation through serving the children, catering to their (children's) needs of growth and development, improving education and selflessly doing all else for the welfare of others. They also imply devotion with a promise of rich dividends in terms of helping others to grow and develop a healthy view of life and to acquire the necessary tools and skills that solve the problems lying ahead. Albert Schweitzer (1) also said that a teacher must show more than average devotion. He (2) again said that teaching is a 'giving' profession, requiring that the teacher give himself as a human to other human beings, "losing" himself in the destinies of his students.

Seventy-five per cent of the student teachers who gave these altruistic reasons, when asked to say something regarding their first excitement of teaching after they had completed their professional requirements for the teaching degree, reported that their greatest rewards were working with their students and seeing them grow and mature. These are wholesome rewards which may lead them to prepare well and improve their chances for success in teaching. Phelps (32,33) reported similar observations.

If teachers enjoy children and young people and are willing to work hard for them, they are most likely to enjoy life too. Karl Menninger (19) expressed similar ideas when he said that a teacher genuinely enjoys working with boys and girls, that he stimulates the love of learning and that he enjoys helping them regardless of their personal responses to him. Again Madame Mazurenko (31) said, "a good teacher teaches with her heart more than with her head; the head harvests too many things which wither and die; but the heart harvests only love, which is the greatest and which is deathless. You will always receive more from the children than you can give them. Plant the seed of love within them and they will teach you the meaning of life."

Closely associated with, though lesser (in the frequency of mention) than altruistic reasons in support of a teaching career, are the reasons heralded on grounds of nobility, sacredness, moral-building and inspirational qualities, and of loftiness of this profession, as also for its quality of developing religious and spiritual values. In fact, learning and religion have since ancient times been closely associated in the mind of an average Indian, even though constitutionally we have a secular state in which a clear-cut separation of religion and state is apparent. Ancient gurus (teachers) used to teach as well as conduct religious services. Our early school architecture reflected a close association of learning and religion. Most of the school buildings used temple-like architecture as a natural expression of a place of learning. These external forms of expressing the close identification of learning and religion have mostly disappeared from our modern state; but the hopes which our people hold have not. Majority of our people, following constitutional separation of religion and state, do not want the schools to teach sectarian religion; but they do expect the school teacher to protect and develop those moral and spiritual values which undergird our society.

That most of the parents expect good teachers to teach moral and spiritual values has been demonstrated in the studies by Grace Langdon and Irving W. Stout (21,13). The ennobling, inspiring and educational qualities of teaching have also been thus highlighted by The Prophet (18), Socrates (34), Erasmus (40), Whitehead (39), Cicero (41), Quintilian (41), Mathew Arnold (22), and William Lyon Phelps (33). Teaching is the art of: "awakening that which already lies half asleep in the dawning of your own knowledge (18)"; "stinging students to new thoughts and deeds through adroit questions" (34); "stimulating the love of learning" (40); "leading the student to experience the joy of discovery now" (39); "filling the mind with great thoughts" (41); "getting students to acquire knowledge with ease, and retain it with accuracy" (41); "introducing knowledge in such a way as to call forth a sense of pleasurable activity" (22); "providing leadership with a capital 'L' " (33). "Setting worthwhile example" which is a reason given by the subjects under study was an ideal for a teacher according to Becker (5). "Free from corruption," another reason given by subjects in this study, was considered worthwhile by Quintilian (41) too when he pointed out that the teacher must have no vices in himself and he should tolerate none in his pupils.

About half of those (an alarming number indeed) disfavouring a teaching career showed moralistic reasons for so doing. Injustice, shirking duty, lack of objectivity, diffidence, dishonesty, greed and the like, according to them, render the teaching profession as not worthwhile, not moral, not noble, not sacred, not virtuous as it used to be or as they would like it to be.

Lack of status, of respect, recognition, appreciation, and absence of rewards for effort and effectiveness seem to have made teaching, at least for some persons, a thankless job, leading to general discontent, low morale and lack of adjustment to teaching as a career. Similar findings were reported by Mouly (24). A redeeming feature, however, is that there is a much larger number of subjects, whom these reasons, which are rather transitory and are bound to go when the society gives due status to teaching profession (which in fact it has since started giving), do not stop from entering the profession and whose love for teaching and for the moral values good teaching can invariably produce is real and undiminishable.

Recent dramatic increases in the teacher's salaries and the continuing upward trend explain the economic reasons in favour of teaching. Nearly half of the student teachers, saying 'yes' in this study, closely scrutinizing their standard of living and aspirations, think that they can now live within the teacher's income. Ninety-five per cent of the teachers subscribing to this viewpoint, when interviewed, said that, compared with salaries in any other occupation for which they stand eligible, a teacher's salary is more attractive. Best (6), Blum (8), and NEA research (25, 27) also demonstrate teacher's satisfaction with salary schedules. That teachers' salaries have risen up and will maintain this rise as teachers continue to provide competent professional service and that this fact keeps up the teacher's mental health have been shown by Blos (7), Frank (15) and Kline (20). NEA (26) research have reported "Gains in average salaries of teachers have exceeded increases in the cost of living each year since 1951. Over the past ten years, gains in teachers' salaries in excess of cost-of-living increases amounted to 41 per cent." These researches have also demonstrated that increasing teachers' salaries is the starting place to increase the holding power, although most educators are agreed that this factor alone is not the answer. The position in our country, though much better than before, is likely to start becoming as optimistic as in America in the very near future, as the need for paying the teacher a good wage is now recognised by our society.

Benefits like long vacation, lots of leisure and market value (ample demand) form some of the other economic reasons favourable to teaching, as mentioned by some of the subjects. Stiles, NEA researches (27, 30), Barrup (4), Chandler (11), Cressman and Benda (12), Smiley (36), Van Dalen (38), and Wynn (44) have emphasized as a result of their studies the need of extending such and other benefits to teachers. That non-wage benefits are essential to a satisfactory climate in which teachers can perform services at professional levels has been emphasized in the NEA researches (28, 29).

A wide variety of fringe benefits like high salary, retirement-benefit plans, sick leave, insurance plans, etc., may be there, but the student whose major target in choosing a teaching career is extrinsic rewards centred on money and other benefits will not be overly attracted to teaching for his life's work. The intrinsic satisfactions must be weighed along with the monetary dividends. The rewards from teaching are substantial for those sworn to learning and teaching.

About one-eighth of the respondents saying 'no' disfavour teaching for its low salaries as compared to better returns in business, industry and other professions. These people reject this profession for its being 'low' on the economic side. Harris (17), Wilson (42), Mouly (24) and others have reported frustration, dissatisfaction and lack of interest in teaching owing to poor salaries.

The feeling that he is under-paid is likely to lead the teacher to disgust, to a lack of enthusiasm and initiative which may do serious harm if transmitted to children and, by preventing the teacher from doing his best, engenders endless difficulties and frustrations. For that reason an under-paid teacher, or for that matter a teacher who feels he is under-paid, is rarely worth what he is getting, and for the good of all including himself he should look for a job elsewhere. Teaching has certain attractions and certain repulsions. It needs a particular type of people who are content to operate within a particular framework. One who is not ready to work within that framework is morally obligated to all concerned to get out because the welfare of children is at stake.

Next to economic reasons in the descending order of the frequency of mention, were the instinctive reasons, though there is no such thing as teaching instinct. An inborn urge or a natural drive for teaching or inherent interest in teaching, love of children and the like were described in support of the wish to become teachers. Perhaps none of the difficulties and drawbacks experienced by an average teacher can bar the way to teaching of an individual having an innate drive to teach and love children. Teaching that is spontaneously given because the teacher inherently loves his work will always be more powerful than that which is given from a sense of duty. Karl Menninger (19) demonstrated how such a teacher stimulates the love of learning.

If certain prospective teachers, as perhaps the ones (43.7 per cent) of this study [see (c) Table 2], who have certain personality characteristics, be given training along lines that will enable them to make more efficacious use of their capacities of dealing effectively with children, they will promote the maximum development of the child. Similar findings have been reported by Barr (3), McAulay (23) and Witty (43).

Teachers are born as well as made. Such prospective teachers as have high ability, sound personality adjustment, and interest in children should be selected. They should then be provided, through curriculum and practice, with a knowledge of subject matter, an understanding of children and of the methods by which they can be helped to achieve the highest degree of self-realization.

Learning and enhancing academic interests and assets also seem to have motivated about one-seventh of the would-be teachers to choose this profession.

Teacher's academic self-improvement, though selfish from a strictly moral viewpoint, is bound to benefit the child ultimately, provided the teacher is interested in teaching too. It is the child who is to reap the harvest which the teacher will sow with toil and sweat. Personal and professional advancement are not irrevocably fixed; they change and the teacher himself can influence the direction of change. The cause of education, the welfare of children, understanding of the role of school in community and the teacher's own welfare are promoted when teachers keep up their academic pursuits, gain new knowledge, develop insights in teaching and improve skills in the profession. Association with knowledge, excitement in teaching and learning therefrom, excitement in helping others learn, and promoting cultural ideas have been reported as the important rewards of teaching by Kahlil-Jibran (18), Sharp (35) and Zeran (45). Research, studies and the use of mind on valuable subjects are the greatest rewards of teaching according to Gilbert Highet (16).

Pleasure principle, to be served through working with the young, enjoying active life and excitement and easy living, happened to be one of the reasons put up by a small proportion (18.4 per cent) of those who chose to favour teaching. If pleasure is a concomitant of the subjects' love for children and for teaching, it is worthy of being a motive to teaching. But if it is to be sought in isolation from the real requisites to teaching, it is nothing but a camouflage hiding sinister motives such as shirking, poor sense of work and self-seeking. Some teachers, as also reported by Brembeck (9), who find teaching easier and more pleasurable than they had expected, are quite realistic in their appraisal of it. They apprehended certain problems. Whey they began to teach, they either found, to their relief, that the problems were not as great as they had expected or that their ability to handle them was adequate. They were not found unawares by what they found in teaching.

A small number of student teachers, who felt compelled to join teacher training with the object of making a career of it, were matched by those who, though in a lesser number, also felt so compelled but without the object of becoming teachers after training. Both these types of teachers, though former lesser than the latter, may not find teaching worthwhile.

The decision to teach should not be taken for the lack of other things to do, as in the case of some student teachers in this study. Teaching, as opined by Brembeck (9), and Albert Schweitzer (2), is an exciting and demanding profession, a way of life for those who are suited to it and prepared for it. But unhappiness is the lot of those who are not suited to it.

Egotistical reasons showing self-interest and greed for petty advantages were given by a very few of the subjects opting for a teaching career. Such are the teachers who are a loss to the profession. They are not service-motivated. They do not have the welfare of children in mind. They cannot perform the vital function of teaching.

About one-fifth of those who do not want to become teachers are found too egotistical to be least inclined to take up teaching after training. They seem to condemn teaching profession in spite of having joined teacher-training. They must justify this utter dislike for teaching by taking up other jobs, as otherwise they may prove great liabilities in education.

Another small number of those who do not intend becoming teachers seem to have entered the training college for expediency, with a view to satisfying a distant and selfish motive and securing themselves against the onslaughts of destiny in the unforeseeable future. The profession is bound to suffer and the educands likely to develop warped views on education and on life if these clever individuals turn to teaching later. The study confirms the assumption that some of the student teachers did not want to teach at all.

Recommendations

Most of the student teachers seem to have taken the decision to become teachers lightly and even wrongly, as is evident from the multiple and in some cases inadequate, unreal or fake reasons. Some of them have taken no decision, as is reflected in their mutually divergent and conflicting reasons, while a few of them are almost determined not to go in for teaching. This suggests the imperative need of taking correct decision regarding whether to become a teacher.

Each graduate who knocks the door of a teacher training institution must decide firmly whether he has the necessary drive to become a teacher dedicated to the education of children. While deciding, he should keep in view, besides this drive, the present-day challenges to education which come from the changes in cultural conditions and from such factors as mobility, technological advances, suburbia, militarism and the space age. His decision should be based upon reasoned values, goals and the variety and extent of human relationships he is capable of building up. He should realize that the society has high expectations from teachers and that these expectations are both a challenge and an accolade. He should know that the rewards from a career in teaching are both extrinsic and intrinsic and that, though forward strides in teachers' salaries are already being made, the most estimable reward lies in the personal gratification that comes from being intimately associated with the learning process and its variety. He is to know about himself and how he got that way. Since much of his work is based on inter-personal relationships, he has to visualize many ethical responsibilities that confront him. "Service above personal gain" should be his motto.

To be able to meet the challenge of a rapidly changing world, the future teacher has to be: a liberally educated person with a blend of the past, knowledge of the present, and an awareness of the future; capable of teaching for the flexible use of knowledge, of performing more and different tasks, and of being alert to new developments in his own and related fields; knowledgeable in problems of the scientific age; a quality teacher who is adventurous in technique and confident enough to discard old techniques in favour of the new; sympathetic, with a sense of mission; and spiritually alert.

The teacher now has not just to teach, but to direct pupil growth. He has not just to promote academic growth, but to help in all-round growth. This makes the teacher's role more complex and more crucial than ever before. He should be emotionally stable. He should understand and respect children, and be democratic in his approach. Hence the need for care in the choice of a teaching career. The prospective teacher must evaluate himself before he plunges into a teaching career which, realistically thinking, is not everyone's cup of tea.

References

1. Albert Schweitzer. "Out of My Life and Thought." New York, Henry Holt and Co., 1949, p. 156.
2. Albert Schweitzer. "The Philosophy of Civilization," New York, The Macmillan Co., 1959, pp. 321, 322-325,156.
3. Barr,A.S., et. al. "Teaching Competencies," in W.S. Monroe, Encyclopedic. of Edu. Res. N.Y., Macmillan, 1950, pp. 1446-1454.
4. Barrup, Percy. "The Teacher and the Public School System," Chapters 12, 44, N.Y., Harper & Bros., I960.
5. Becker, Carl L. "Wisconsion Historian," in American Masters of Social Sciences, ed. Howard W. Odum, N.Y., Holt Rinehart and Winston, INC, 1927.
6. Best, John Wesley. "A Study of Certain Selected Factors Underlying the Choice of Teaching as a Profession," Journal of Exp. Educ. Vol. 17,1948, pp. 201-58.
7. Blos, P. "Aspects of Mental Health in Teaching and Learning," Mental Hygiene, 37,1953, pp. 555-569.

8. Blum, Lawrence, P. "A Comparative Study of Students Preparing for Five Selected Professions Including Teaching," Journal of Exp. Educ. Vol. 16,1947, pp. 31-65.
9. Brembeck, Cole, S. "The Discovery of Teaching," Prentice-Hall, INC, 1962, pp. 12-14, p. 297.
10. Bruner, Jerome S. "Learning and Thinking," Harvard Educational Review, 1959, 29,184-192.
11. Chandler, J.B. "Education and the Teacher," Chapters 10, 14, 15, N.Y., Dodd, Meed and Co., 1961.
12. Cressmen, George R., and Harold W. Benda. "Public Education in America," Chapters 7, 8. N.Y.; Appleton-Century Crofts, INC, 1961.
13. Cunningham, Earl C. "My Child's Teachers and I," Phi Delta Kappan, March, 1956, pp. 254-58.
14. Evans, Eva Knox. "So You're Going to Teach," Danvilla: III, The Inter-State Printers and Publishers, 1951.
15. Frank, L.K. "The Reorientation of Education to the Promotion of Mental Hygiene," Mental Hygiene, 23,1939, pp. 529-543.
16. Gilbert Highet. "The Art of Teaching," University Paperbacks, Matheun: London, 1963, pp. 66-68.
17. Harris, W.S. "Why Teachers Leave the Profession," Ohio, Schs, 36, No. 8,1958, pp. 26-27.
18. Kahil Gibran. "The Prophet", New York, Alfred A. Knoff, INC, 1923,1951, pp. 55-65; p. 18.
19. Karl Menninger. "Love Against Hate", "New York: Hercourt Brace and World 1942, pp. 77-89.
20. Kline, F.F. "Satisfactions and Annoyances in Teaching", Journal of Expr. Edu., 18,1949, pp.77-89.
21. Langdon, Grace., and Stout, Irving V. "Helping Parents Understand Their Child's Schools", Englewood Cliffs, N.J. Prentice-Hall, INC, 1957.
22. Mathew Arnold. "Reports on Elementary Schools", 1852-82, London: Wyman and Son, Ltd., 1908, pp.226-229.
23. McAulay, J.D. "Why a Teacher", Peabody J. of Educ. 36, 1959, pp.220-228.
24. Mouly, George J. "Psychology for Effective Teaching", Holt, Rinehart and Winston, N.Y., pp. 474-475.
25. NEA, Research Division. "Economic Status of Teachers in 1960-61", "Research Report", 1961, R-4, Wash. D.C., 1961, p. 42, Table 32.
26. NEA, Research Division. "The Financial Rewards of — Teaching", Research Bulletin, 38, No. 2, May, I960, p. 49.
27. NEA, Research Division. "Bulletin", Vol. 29, No. 2, May, 1961, pp. 52-57, "Ten Years of Change in Teacher's Salary Schedules".

28. NEA, Research Division. "Teacher Personnel Practices — Urban Sch. Distts., 1955-56, Spl. Memo. Wash. D.C., 1956, pp. 34.
29. NEA, Research Division. "Sabbatical Leave", Practices of Representative Educ. Agencies", Research, Memo. 1960-62, Wash. D.C., p. 53.
30. NEA, Research Division. "Economic Status of Teacher in 1958-59" Washington, D.C., 1959.
31. Oksana Kasenkina. "Leap to Freedom", Philadelphia: J.B. Lippincott Co., 1949, pp.24-26.
32. Phelps, William Lyon. "The Excitement of Teaching", NewYork, Liveright Publ. Corp. 1931, pp. 60-71.
33. Phelps, William Lyon. "Teaching in School and College" (New York: The Macmillian Co., 1918), pp. 12-14.
34. Plato. "Apology", William Chase Green, ed. The Dialogues of Plato, "Benjamin Jowett, Trans, (New York: Bone and Liveright, 1935).
35. Sharp, D. Louise (ed.). "Why Teach", New York: Henry Holt and Co., 1957, pp. 23-25, "All Professions in one" by Marjorie L. Carleson.
36. Smiley, Marjorie B., and John S. Diekhoff. "Prologue to Teaching," "Pt. I, The Vocation of Teaching, N.Y., Oxford University Press, 1959.
37. Stiles, Lindley J. "Security isn't Enough", The Nation's Schools, Vol. 58, Dec., 1936, pp. 43-44.
38. Van Dalen, De-obold B., and Robert W. Brittell. "Looking Ahead to Teaching", Chapters 2,3., Boston Allyn and Bacon, INC, 1959.
39. Whitehead, Alfred North. "The Aims of Education, pp. 1-4, 8-9.
40. William Harrison Woodward, "Desiderius Eramus, Concerning the Aim and, Method of Education", (New York Cambridge University Press, 1904), pp. 193-194, 204, 211-212.
41. William Smail. "Quintilian on Education", New York: Oxford University Press, INC, 1938, pp. 11, 30,73-74,101.
42. Wilson, J.P. "Appropriate Education and Eleven-Months Contracts," Ohio Schs. 39, 3,1961, pp. 12-13,40,41.
43. Witty, P.A. "Some Characteristics of the Effective Teacher," Educ. Admn. Superv, 36,1950, pp. 193-208.
44. Wynn, Richard. "Careers in Education", Chapters 1, 6, 7, N.Y.: McGraw-Hill Book Co., INC, 1960.
45. Zeran, Franklin R. (Edu). "The High School Teacher and His Job," New York: Chartwell House, INC, 1953.

70. PROBLEMS OF TEACHER TRAINEES

That teacher trainees have wide and varied problems which cause them worry and anxiety bordering on maladjustment is a fact too widely admitted needing any elaboration. While undergoing the stresses and strains of a formidable curriculum comprising the theory and practice of teaching, their new love, the trainees often seem to be bothered by several avoidable and unavoidable attributes of their own which invariably affect their performance and their ability to wriggle out of the training chores. Certain problems handicap their social adjustment, some reduce their academic output, others their capacity for good teachership, and still other problems tend to render them ill-adjusted to the course.

It was to identify such problems that the writer asked his group of 75 pupils' teachers (40 men and 35 women) of Govt. Training College, Jullundur to list on scraps of paper five problems which often worry them, no matter to which area a particular problem belongs, without mentioning any identifying particulars except their sex, so that they felt free enough to make a mention of any problem howsoever private or personal. When asked as to what purpose this study would serve, they were told that a general survey of the problems faced by teacher trainees was under way. The sample consisted of a well-represented and well-shuffled community of below average and average socio-economic strata of the urban part of Jullundur district. After the scraps were collected, the problems (419 in number, *i.e.*, 203 mentioned by girls and 216 by boys) were categorized under ten broad areas sex-wise as in Table 1. In Table 2, the problems were listed area-wise in the descending order of their frequencies. Problems mentioned by very few respondents were ignored.

Findings

(1) The total number of problems is nearly the same in either sex.

(2) Women trainees as compared to men trainees experience more problems in the areas of Emotions, Personality, Academic, Dissatisfaction with the present training course, Health and Social.

(3) Men trainees, as compared to women trainees, experience more problems in areas of family, sex and marriage, economic, concern for social ills, and vocational.

(4) Problems belonging to the areas of Emotions and personality, Academic, and family are as imperious to men as to women teacher trainees. These problems have been mentioned most by both the sexes.
(5) Concern for social ills has been shown least of all by the trainees whether men or women.
(6) Vocational problems are experienced least by women trainees.
(7) The correlation between problems of men and women trainees is about .50.
(8) Emotional and Personality problems are experienced most by both men and women trainees.

Discussion

Since Emotional and Personality problems are experienced most of all by most trainees, whether men or women, there is an urgent need of guidance in these problems and of training the child's emotions and personality during early stages of student trainees about the growth of development.

Sex may not cause much differences in the total number of problems experienced by the teacher trainees, but it does seem to matter in the matter of differences in the frequencies of different problems.

Girl child as compared to boy child is much less wanted or welcomed and consequently much less cared for in most of our homes.

She is not so much looked after in her growth and development. This may short weight the full development of her personality, which in turn may make her academic, health and social sides suffer as compared to boys. This explains the personality problems shown by woman trainees. Academic inadequacy may, at least partly, cause dissatisfaction with the training course.

Family, economic, and vocational problems are more frequently experienced by men than by women because of the place of women in our society. Men still are the wage-earners and heads of families, though this position is now gradually changing owing to industrialization. Marriage in case of women is still the concern of their parents, though this position is also changing owing to more education in women. Again, the place of women in society makes them less sophisticated in sex development and much less verbose in sex difficulties. Hence men mention more problems of sex and marriage than women.

Increasing educational and employment opportunities available to women in our society tend to make the women trainees' concern for academic work and family equal to that of men trainees. But women, by and large, are still the home makers, vocation being man's concern. Hence the vocational problem is experienced least by women.

Social ills in the India of today seem to be nobody's concern. Most individuals are hacking out their existence in their own individual or family set-up, experiencing social ills but not doing their little bit to eradicate them, thinking that these would be remedied by some transcendental powers at a predetermined time. Staunch believers in destiny and fate, we seem to ignore the necessity of moving our little finger in attending to social ills with a view to ending them.

Dissatisfaction with the present training course calls for improving the processes and programmes of teacher training, reforming the teaching techniques and curricula, getting better and mature teacher trainers and providing suitable equipment and material.

The aim of this small study is not to solve the problems revealed by it as that is the legitimate concern of experts, but to spell out boldly all such problems which educationists and psychologists need to keep in view while imparting teacher education.

Table 1
Percentage Frequency of Problems Area-wise

Area	Problem	Per cent Frequency of mention by	
		Women	Men
1	2		
1. Academic	Difficulty with studies; poor study habits; cannot concentrate; tend to sleep when studying; blank in some subjects; less time to study; anxiety of being poor in studies; inadequate intelligence; less interest; don't know what and when to study; wanting to go in for higher education; can't master English; anxiety to get more marks; too many tests.	19.6	12.9

2. Concern for	Deploring selfishness, bribery, suffering, vice; wanting social reforms, freedom from slavery and prejudice; ideas of ultimate reality.	4.4	4.6
3. Dissatisfaction	Teachers' reluctance to answer questions; hasty methods of completing the courses; teachers trying to discourage students; too many vacant periods; not enough staff for all subjects; poor building and equipment; not wanting to be a teacher; rude behaviour of professors; no interest in classes; difficulties in discussion lessons; not satisfied with progress; no hostel for girls; less freedom to girls than to boys; no games; suitable books not available; poor discipline; not satisfied with courses; partialities in awards.	10.8	6.0
4. Economic	Can't maintain good standards of life, can't finance studies; no independent sources of income; no money to keep up friendly relations; can't entertain anyone.	5.4	12.4
5. Emotional and personality	Emotional difficulty; inability to adjust; habit of worrying over trivialities; inertia; fickle-minded; can't stick to a thing; mentally upset; no peace of mind; pessimistic; can't break some habits; sad; finding life not worth living; inferiority complex; no guts; lack of self-confidence; hate artificiality; enemies undermining my success; worry over past incidents; brooding over fear of darkness; forgetfulness; reveries; oversleeping; mental conflicts; can't decide things quickly; nervous; can't judge people; intolerance; talk too little; very sensitive; wanting elderly affection & protection; hatred towards those in close contact; can't live without parents; shy of wearing spectacles; unable to execute what I want to or to achieve some goals; unable to realise ambitions such as going abroad; adding to qualifications; marrying to my choice; becoming great; poor memory.	24.0	16.5

6. Family	Family atmosphere not good; too many household chores; family responsibilities; illiterate parents; bad health of parents; brother doesn't study; poor financial state of family; father drinks and misbehaves; brother after marriage doesn't help family; can't help old parents; how to maintain family after father's death; family worries; cooking for the family leaves no time to study; parents not agreeing to my ideas of higher education or of travel or of visits to friends.	11.3	14.7
7. Health	Indigestion; infirmity; illness; deteriorating health; constant headache; diseases; less sleep; poor food; wanting to be slim; can't get up early morning; grey hair.	10.3	7.4
8. Sex and Marriage	Dissatisfaction; love affair; whether to marry a particular person; not wanting to many; how to marry the one I love; how to find a good marriage partner; parents compelling me for marriage; parties wanting to see me before saying 'yes'; economic and other factors hampering marriage; unable to talk to opposite sex; sensitive to boys asking me anything.	5.4	8.7
9. Social	Shyness; unable to speak before a group; unable to mix up with others; poor social status; no bosom friend; worry over friends; annoyance; can't make friends easily; doubting friends' sincerity; inability to understand others' natures; sick of friends.	6.4	5.1
10. Vocational	Unable to get proper job; wanting to be well-settled; no vocational guidance; ill-adjusted in job; tuitions not so lucrative.	2.0	1.06

Table 2
Percentage Frequency of Problem Areas

Women		Men	
Area	Frequency	Area	Frequency
1. Emotional and personality	24.0	Emotional and Personality	16.5

2.	Academic	19.6	Family	14.7
3.	Family	11.3	Academic	12.9
4.	Dissatisfaction with the present training course	10.8	Economic	12.4
5.	Health	10.3	Vocational	10.6
6.	Social	6.4	Sex and Marriage	8.7
7.	Sex and Marriage	5.4	Health	7.4
8.	Economic	5.4	Dissatisfaction with the present training course	6.0
9.	Concern for social ills.	4.4	Social	5.1
10.	Vocational	2.0	Concern for social ills	4.6

71. TEACHER BEHAVIOUR AND STUDENT CHARACTERISTICS

Teachers' behaviour tends to create quite different psychological environments for different students within the same classroom. A cross-section of this behaviour is the ways teachers dispense praise and reproof among their students. This paper attempts to identify, with the help of a scale developed earlier, students who receive praise and those who are reproved and to determine some of the psychological characteristics of such students. That a few students receive most of the praise showered by teachers and a few receive most of the reproof and that the students living in a praise-dominated environment and those living in a predominantly reproof-ridden atmosphere show significant differences in certain characteristics are the results, yielded by this study. Whereas these results may raise many eyebrows among teachers, that teachers might well examine their own behaviour is inevitably warranted.

Students work up to their ability in one school but not in another. A student is more effective, with respect to one set of goals or another, in one school setting *versus* another. A great deal, of course, depends on the interaction of learner, task, method and teacher variables. But the explanation of such differences, in fact, is to be found in the different psychological atmospheres that characterise the several educational environments. Psychological dimensions of educational environments have been examined by different researchers. Pace and Stern (1958) probe the general milieu provided by an educational setting. They, illustrating a number of efforts made to measure college environments in terms of their potential for satisfying the psychological needs of different types of students, find vast differences among colleges and within colleges. Gnagey (1960), dealing with another dimension, that of the power structure within a class group, demonstrates its effect on teacher, disciplinary action outcomes as well as upon learning. Medley and Mitzel (1958), investigating some general dimensions of classroom environments imposed by teachers and measurable by observational techniques, identified three important dimensions, *i.e.* emotional climate, verbal emphasis, and social structure. deGroat and Thompson (1949) illustrate that cold and hostile environment or warm and friendly environment, that the teachers might create, may lead to make a child less or more mature, knowledgeable and adjustive.

The environment, more precisely the social incentive climate, that teachers create, while distributing praise and reproof among their pupils, has been explored in the present study. This dimension of environment is built up by such behaviour of the teacher as is shown while commending or blaming a student. Firstly, this environment has been measured by spotting out children living under more or less clear-cut patterns of teacher praise and reproof. Prior to it, a scale for the purpose had been constructed and pretested. Secondly, an attempt has been made to determine some of the psychological characteristics of children living under the two different climates.

Any relationship that may exist between patterns of teacher praise-reproof and the psychological characteristics of students cannot be considered as a cause-effect paradigm. Thus the question as to whether students have developed certain characteristics partially or wholly as a result of teacher praise-reproof, or whether teachers show different evaluative attitudes toward students already having particular psychological characteristics, has been left unanswered. This interesting problem may be unraveled by future researchers involving a longitudinal approach.

Hypotheses

This experimental study was designed to test the following hypotheses: (i) Bright students receive more praise than reproof, whereas dull children receive more reproof than praise, from their teachers. (ii) High achievers receive more praise than reproof, whereas low achievers receive more reproof than praise. (iii) Those who show greater personality adjustment are more self-adjusted and more socially adjusted, receive more praise than reproof and those who show poor adjustment in the said aspects receive more reproof than praise. (iv) Those who receive little, if any, praise, or reproof, may be unsocial and withdrawn.

Construction and Pretesting of Teacher Praise and Reproof Scales

The author sampled a fairly large number of commonly occurring situations in which children are commended or blamed by teachers for different types of behaviour. He selected those on the basis of controlled observation of teacher-child interactions in nine classrooms (one each of Class V, VI and VII in each of the three urban schools that are 30 years old, well-established, known for their fairly high educational standard and manned by well-qualified and experienced teachers). "The child who is praised by the teacher for doing his/her homework regularly," and "the child who is rebuked by the teacher for being inattentive in class" are the two examples of the behaviour descriptions (first for teacher praise and the second for teacher reproof) thus chosen. Students were to nominate classmates for praise or reproof situations. Of the 46 behaviour descriptions originally collected (25 for teacher praise and 21 for teacher reproof), only 20 (ten each for teacher praise and teacher reproof) were finally retained, because the rest of the descriptions could not withstand the shock of a try-out test, that was administered to 30 Class VII students, as they were found either vague or liable to be responded to on the basis of a general 'halo' effect. The behaviour descriptions finally selected constituted the author's teacher praise and reproof scales. These behaviour descriptions, it is considered, are fairly representative of the types of situations in which students typically receive praise or reproof from their teachers.

Procedure

The teacher praise and reproof scales were administered, on two different occasions separated by a four-week interval, to two classrooms of Class VII in a suburban school (a 25-year-old school of recognised standing in the state's educational set-up). The data obtained from the first administration of the scales are presented graphically on this page. These data show a very small number of students receiving a high percentage of teacher praise nominations, a few receiving most of the teacher reproof nominations, and the majority receiving few, if any, nominations for either teacher praise or reproof.

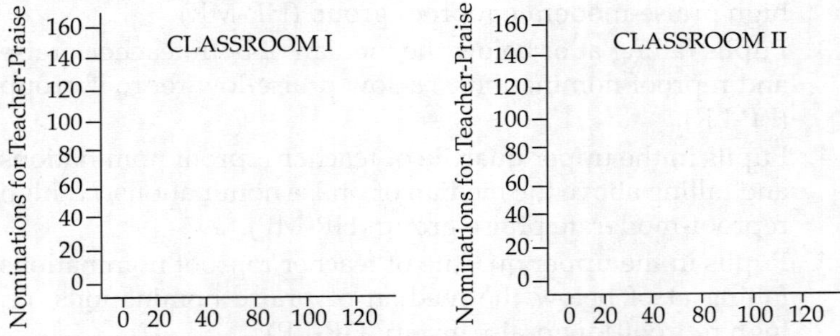

The stability of student rankings on teacher praise and reproof over the four-week interval is shown in Table 1. The consistency of the teacher reproof scales seems to exceed that of the teacher praise-scale.

The rank-order correlation coefficients indicate a fairly high amount of pupil consistency in nominating their classmates to fit teacher praise and reproof descriptions. Again, these correlation coefficients are fairly high for tests separated by a four-week interval, since it is likely that some real changes in rank, which the so-called 'perfect' measuring instrument may reveal, occurred during the four-week interval.

Table 1
Rank-order correlation coefficients between Test-Retest* Scores on Teacher Praise and Reproof Scales

Class**	Number of Students	The Scale	
		Praise	Reproof
I	52	.74	.85
II	45	.78	.82

* Test and retest occasions were separated by a four-week interval.
** Both were Class VII of an urban school.

Some of the psychological characteristics of students experiencing the following patterns of teacher praise-reproof were then studied:

1. Pupils in the upper quartile of teacher praise nominations and falling at or below the median of reproof nominations, *i.e.* high praise-low reproof group (HP-LR).
2. Pupils in the upper quartile of teacher praise nominations and falling above the median of reproof nominations, *i.e.* high praise-moderate reproof group (HP-MR)
3. Pupils falling at or below the median of both teacher praise and reproof nominations, *i.e.* low praise-low reproof group (LP-LR).
4. Pupils in the upper quartile of teacher reproof nominations and falling above the median of praise nominations, *i.e.* high reproof-moderate praise group (HR-MP).
5. Pupils in the upper quartile of teacher reproof nominations falling at of below the median of praise nominations, *i.e.* high reproof-low praise group (HR-LP).

These patterns of teacher praise-reproof may serve as adjoining areas in a two-dimensional plane of teacher praise-reproof, so that these five patterns constitute a two-dimensional 'area-continuum'. An individual student's scores on both teacher praise and reproof would determine his inclusion in one of the five patterns. As the above procedure is merely an approximation adopted for experimental analysis, a number of students may not be included in any of the five patterns.

The psychological characteristics to be studied were academic achievement, intelligence, and personality adjustment of students falling under fairly clear-cut categories of teacher praise and teacher reproof. Three classrooms of Class VII in an educationally meritorious school situated in an urban area were chosen for this phase of the study. The tests administered to the 154 pupils in these classrooms were: (i) Teacher-made objective type tests in the subjects of English, mathematics, science and social studies, each test carrying 100 marks. A student's aggregate marks in the four subjects formed his academic achievement. (ii) Lorge-Thorndike intelligence test level 4, Form A-nonverbal (1959) to determine IQ which was termed as intelligence level, (iii) California test of personality (1953) to get personality adjustment scores. The means and standard deviations of the scores of all the tests for each of the five praise-reproof groups are presented in Table 2. The data were analysed by Fisher's t test which yielded the results discussed below.

Table 2

Mean and SD's of Academic performance, Mental maturity and Personality scores of the Five teacher praise-reproof groups

		Patterns of Teacher Praise-Reproof				
		HP-LR	HP-MR	LP-LR	HR-MP	HR-LP
Academic performance	M	194.48	200.45	165.35	167.48	154.82
	SD	17.32	15.36	18.62	17.56	32.21
Intelligence level	M	95.84	103.92	84.15	85.65	78.72
	SD	13.91	10.42	12.02	10.92	16.05
Total personality	M	122.05	133.82	114.82	102.02	105.72
	SD	13.92	12.84	19.95	15.75	16.96
Personality 'self-score'	M	49.72	57.95	46.65	42.74	44.86
	SD	7.85	7.62	9.96	8.16	7.73
Personality 'social score'	M	64.02	59.75	52.82	45.55	48.64
	SD	3.46	3.34	6.72	6.02	8.95

Results

1. In academic achievement, the HP-LR group scores significantly higher than the HR-MP or the HR-LP group. The HP-MR group obtains a mean score significantly higher than the LP-LR and the HR-MP groups. This indicates that the children having more subject knowledge receive greater teacher approval, at least as judged by their classmates. This verifies hypothesis 1.
2. In intelligence, the HP-LR group is significantly higher than the HR-MP or the HR-LP group, while the HP-MR group scores significantly higher than the LP-LR and HR-MP groups. This supports hypothesis 2 that the more intelligent students in a typical classroom receive a significantly larger amount of teacher praise, as seen by their classmates, while the less intelligent pupils receive large amounts of teacher reproof.
3. The means of the total scores on personality follow a similar trend. The HP-LR is significantly better adjusted than the HR-MP or the HR-LP group, while the HP-MR group shows adjustment superior to the HR-MP and the HR-LP groups. As total score on California test of personality represents the pupil's 'adjustment' as he sees it, the result that those who

are better adjusted receive great teacher praise implies that the traditional teacher has a great deal of knowledge of, or is significantly influenced by, the student's valuation of his own adjustment, which appears to be unlikely, unless the student's valuation of his adjustment is true enough to be so manifest that the teacher has long known it, which seems to be the most probable explanation of the total score in the present study. The direction and nature of cause-effect relationship, if any, between personality adjustment and teacher praise-reproof is uncalled for in this limited study. A departmental study, longitudinal in design, may throw some light on whether pupils who are given large doses of praise by teachers or who are living in a predominantly teacher-praise atmosphere become more 'well-adjusted', while pupils who are reproved by teachers day in and day out or who are living in a predominantly reproof-ridden environment become progressively more 'poor-adjusted'.

4. The mean self-scores which form part of the total scores may be interpreted in a similar way. The HP-LR group is superior in self-adjustment to the HR-LP and HR-MP groups, while the HP-MR is significantly more self-adjusted than the LP-LR and HR-LP groups. The HP-MR group, besides, shows significantly better self-adjustment than any of the other four groups. But it is intriguing to find that the group (HP-MR), which is highly praised but which also receives a moderate doze of reproof from teachers, shows significantly better 'self-adjustment' than the group (HP-LR) which receives high praise and little reproof. A guess that may be hazarded is that pupils who receive large amounts of praise and no reproof may be operating under such intense pressure to conform to social demands as to be handicapped in areas of 'self-adjustment'. This is a provocative hypothesis that the present data do not support, as is evident in the fact that the HP-LR group has a higher mean score in social adjustment than the HP-MR group (result No. 5 below). Future studies need to examine this hypothesis more critically. It may, however, be concluded with a high degree of confidence that students who receive high amount of teacher praise show better 'self-adjustment' than those who face excessive teacher reproof.

5. Means of social scores decline regularly with progression from the teacher praise to the teacher reproof end of the 'continuum', which shows that the greater the social adjustment the greater the teacher praise and the lesser the social adjustment lesser the teacher praise. This interpretation, however, is somewhat difficult to accept because of the apparent lack of homogeneity of variance among the five praise-reproof groups. Had the groups shown homogeneous variability, the obtained t's could be interpreted as showing that the groups which receive greater teacher praise show superior 'social adjustment'. The high-praise groups, on the other hand, have higher mean scores in 'social adjustment', but significantly less variability in 'social adjustment' scores. Thus the third hypothesis that those who receive more praise than reproof are better adjusted (at least so far as they see it), are more self-adjusted and more socially adjusted also stands verified. Again, low mean score of LP-LR group supports the fourth hypothesis that those who receive, little, if any, praise or reproof, may be withdrawn and unsocial.

The study illustrates that being bright, high achieving, or more well-adjusted brings forth or creates a fund of admiration for and retards the flow of reprimand to a student, but the possibility that praise brings forth or creates brightness, high achievement, and greater personality adjustment–both self and social–cannot be ruled out. This possibility may be explored by future researches involving stricter controls and protracted over long periods of time so that on the one hand, the graduated development of the said characteristics and, on the other, retardation in the development of these, as causated by experimental doses of praise and of reproof, respectively, can be delineated.

The findings reported in this paper demonstrate that many 'unseen' or 'unperceived' but psychologically significant variables like praise and reproof may be operating in the educational context in which teachers instruct. These variables may accelerate or hinder the teacher's endeavours, depending upon a variety of complex interactions among students, teachers, and environment. Awareness that such dimensions of educational environment exist may help the teacher to forestall problems or to use these dimensions to instructional advantage. Awareness that some of the significant classroom dimensions are a direct product of the teacher's own behaviour (as personality maladjustment of a pupil may be the doing of a nagging teacher and a high achievement of a child that of an optimistic and encouraging teacher) may make him more sensitive to the ramifications of what he does in the classroom, and may even stimulate him to make constructive modifications in his behaviour.

References

deGroat, Albert F., and Thompson, George G. A study of the distribution of teacher approval and disapproval among sixth grade pupils. *The Journal of Experimental Education*, 18, 57-75, 1949.

Gnagey, William J. Effects on classmates of a deviant student's power and response to a teacher exerted control technique. *Journal of Educational Psychology*, 51, 1-8, 1960.

Lorge, Irving and Thorndike, Robert L. *The Large-Thorndike intelligence tests*, Houghton Mifflin Company, 1959.

Medley, Donald M. and Mitzel, Harold E. A technique for measuring classroom behaviour, *Journal of Educational Psychology*, 49, 86-92, 1958.

Pace, C. Robert., and Stem, George G. An approach to the measurement of psychological characteristics of college environments. *Journal of Educational Psychology*, 49, 269-277,1958.

Thorpe, L.P., Clark, W.W., and Tiegs, E.W. California test of personality. Monterey, *Calif. Test Bur.*, 1953.

72. WORRIES OF TEACHER TRAINEES

While the teacher trainees struggle through the rigorous course of training, they betray many problems which seem to pressurize them and to worry them to the extent of making their task of imbibing training considerably difficult. These problems are varied and in several areas. They have academic problems which may chiefly emerge from the institution, nature of schedules and of courses, and the requirements of a training project–all of which are quite different from their counterparts in the educational ladder they had been hitherto climbing. They have personality and social problems that may spring from their sudden convergence into adulthood which is for them not yet ripe and from their old adolescence which, in spite of their reluctance to leave, they are called upon to shed. Economic, occupational, marriage and family problems stare them in the face in anticipation of the era in which they would land soon after training. No less striking are the problems, moral and philosophic, which tend to confuse the growing minds rendered ill-at-ease in this intensely-material universe. Worries caused by such problems affect the trainees' learning and development as also the teachers' teaching. It was with this view that the writer took up a survey of the trainees' problems so as to clarify such problems for teachers and parents who might like to help their wards in eliminating or at least reducing the impact on the latter of the problems that cause worry.

40 women and 30 men in the B.T. Class (session 1965-66) formed the sample population which was a well-shuffled group of students (age group 19-25 years) hailing from lower middle and upper middle income-groups of the industrial town, Jullundur. They were asked to write down in any language on a page five problems, falling in any area, which worry them most. They were told to give no particulars or identity marks (except sex and age), to enable them to state their problems without any fear of being identified. Having collected the pages, the problems were classified into these areas: Personality and emotional, marriage, home and family, economic, health, philosophic, occupational, aspirations, academic and social.

Findings and Discussion

A chi square test revealed no significant differences in the number of problems (mentioned in each category) by male and female teacher trainees. Consequently the two groups were treated as one homogeneous group.

1. Academic problems were mentioned most of all. One-fourth of the total problems were in fact academic problems. Most of these problems centre round the training course, its nature and complex and the difficulty of adjusting to it and of being able to get through it successfully.

   Perhaps there is a need to make the training programme more meaningful and interesting, and increasingly in accordance with the requirements of a teaching job. This is to enable the trainee to adjust to the programme and to do justice to it. This may also result in the erosion of such curricular items and practices which in no way help the teacher and which have overburdened the training schedules. Training, as other education, must be attractive and purposeful if it is to be fully utilized by all those who intend becoming teachers.

Some academic problems owe their occurrence to the trainees' personal difficulties which guidance-minded teachers can well solve. Others owe their origin to poor treatment at the hands of teachers and may well be remedied by teachers taking more interest in their work in a bid to raise the level of their teaching and by their sympathetic, though impersonal, care of the trainees' progress.

2. Personality and emotional problems which in number are one-seventh of the total problems occupy second position in frequency of mention. They include problem of adjusting to members of opposite sex, nervousness, day-dreaming, diffidence, shyness, indecision and other personal inadequacies.

   Cocurricular activities, general talks, and individual guidance can go a long way in meeting these problems, at least in part. Giving trainees an opportunity and help to succeed in things may round off many angularities and oddities which seem to disintegrate their personalities.

3. Economic problems, though one-tenth of the total problems, stand third in their frequency. Not much can be done by teachers or institutions to meet these problems, except giving financial support in terms of fee remissions or scholarships. Economic prosperity brought about by industry and development of resources may perhaps solve these problems in times to come.

4. Fourth in order of frequency are aspirations varying from 'self-improvement' to 'serving the country'. These aspirations may arise from the need to realise one's potentialities, to raise one's life status, and to be of service to mankind Whereas encouragement and concrete help in achieving the attainable aspirations are desirable, a re-education to drop or to modify the ambitions which are exaggerated, fantastic and unattainable is both necessary and useful. The trainee's potentialities, his strengths and weaknesses, his limitations, have of course to be kept in view while sorting out the aspirations.

5. Home and health problems come next. Naming such problems and listing them in some detail may draw parents' and teachers' attention to the problems with a view to solving them. Some of the health problems can be solved with

teachers' and medicos' assistance, and some of the family problems cured with improvement in parental behaviour. Nevertheless there are problems which are real and which are to be regarded as inevitable concomitants of life and its stark realities. Trainees need to be taught that such problems, as also many others, are to be boldly faced, accepted and dealt with through their own performance.

6. Philosophic and abstract problems concerning the 'how' and 'why' of life, destiny, religion, future, free-floating fears of the unknown, ideals and the like occupy the seventh position in order of frequency of mention. Well-meaning, thorough and expert discussion of such problems by teachers with the trainees would certainly put the latter wiser and more adjustive with regard to these questions. Trainees need to be taught that dogmatism and rigidity in holding certain views must give place to flexibility and rational conviction and that they must no longer entertain, if they want to be called mature, false beliefs of reforming the world overnight or of getting emancipation from God and His doing.
7. Impending stage of occupations which the trainees would soon enter forestalls the occupational problems. Indecision with regard to their future role in life and uncertainty of becoming a good teacher as also a good worker raises such problems. A reorientation of life values and a realistic acceptance of their assets and liabilities would do the trainees ample good in rising above these problems.
8. Ninth in order of frequency of mention are social problems which are by no means unrelated to their personalities. Sociability and the ability to stand in affirmative relationship to others may be facilitated by group activities, both curricular and cocurricular.
9. Lastly the question of marriage for which the young graduates are just ripe presents some problems. These problems are characteristic of the immaturity which the trainees would soon outgrow.

Such are the teacher trainees' problems which need to be tackled adroitly and sympathetically by teachers and parents alike. These problems may be prevalent among the teacher-trainees elsewhere. If training must lead to changes in the trainees' personality and behaviour, if it must lead to developing attitudes, if it should develop their teaching skill, and if it should make them nation-builders as they are often called, the above-mentioned problems, especially academic and personality problems, must be kept in view while framing and practising the training programme.

73. AN ANALYSIS OF SUBJECT PREFERENCES OF TEACHER EDUCATION STUDENTS

This study attempts to analyse the subject preferences of teacher education students with a view to finding the relative popularity of certain Subjects and the relationship that exists between the choices of students and variables of sex, achievement in the subject preferred and level of intelligence, on a sample of 225 B.Ed. students from three colleges of Education.

In a study of subject preferences of fourth to sixth grade pupils, Mosher (4) found little significant difference between the first choices of boys and girls. He found that arithmetic, art, social studies and spelling were among the high-ranking preferences. Dean (2) in a similar study revealed boys' strong preferences for arithmetic, spelling, and reading. Chase and Wilson (1) found reading, art, spelling and social studies ranking high in the preferences of fifth grade children. Boys' significantly stronger preference for social studies than girls' and a strong relationship between teacher preferences and student choices in the case of all subjects except art and spelling were also reported in this study. Greenblatt (3), examining relative popularity of school subjects among children of third, fourth and fifth grades, found that art, arithmetic and reading were the most preferred subjects, that a significant relationship existed between achievement of girls in arithmetic and their selection of the subject, and that there was a strong correspondence between subject preferences of boys and girls with IQ of 110 or higher.

This study attempts to analyse the subject preferences with a view to find the relative popularity of certain subjects and the relationship that exists between the choices of students and variables of sex, achievement in the subject preferred, and level of intelligence.

Procedure

Approximately 225 Teacher Education (B.Ed.) students chosen at random from three Government teacher training colleges of Punjab State (the three colleges together representing the total population in all respects) were asked to list, in order of preference, their favourite subject. Fifteen lists being incomplete were rejected. First choices were allocated 5 points; second four points; third, three points; fourth, two points, and fifth, one point. The study was confined to the five subjects which were common to all the students. In this manner a total point accumulation (value scores) was calculated for each of the subjects.

Data related to level of intelligence and subject achievement were secured from the Lorge Thorndike intelligence test level 5 form A Non-Verbal and college achievement tests in each subject.

Findings

Insignificant differences in the mean preferences of boys and girls showed lack of relationship between the choices of students and sex variable. Consequently the boys and girls were treated as a single group for further treatment of data. On the basis of subject preferences (Table 1) total value scores, ranks and normal curve scores (Tables 1 and 2) were derived. Differences at extremes of the preference score imply the assumption of normality in the distribution of such scores. Educational Psychology enjoys a substantial degree of preference.

Table 1
Subject Preferences N=210
Number of Students who show preferences ranging from first to fifth against each subject

Subject	I	II	III	IV	V
Principles of Education	14	14	35	35	112
Educational Psychology	133	63	7	7	0
Indian Education	7	7	14	35	147
Guidance and Evaluation	21	21	56	63	49
Methods and School Organisation	0	28	21	56	105

Table 2
Total value scores, ranks, per cent positions and normal curve scores of different subjects

Subject	Total Value Scores	Rank	Per cent position	Normal Curve score
Educational Psychology	952	1	.24	98
Principles of Education	413	3	1.20	92
Indian Education	332	5	2.16	88
Guidance and Evaluation	532	2	.72	94
Methods and School Organization	392	4	1.68	90

Table 3
Subject preference derived by method of rank order

Subject	Mean Rank	Standard Deviation
Educational Psychology	1.94	.86
Principles of Education	4.03	1.25
Indian Education	4.46	.99
Guidance and Evaluation	3.46	1.22
Methods and School Organisation	4.13	1.08

Table 4
Per cent Rank of Subjects as Derived by Rank Order Method

Subject	Rank as in Table 1	Per cent Ranks
Educational Psychology	1	90
Guidance and Evaluation	2	0
Principles of Education	3	50
Methods and School Organisation	4	30
Indian Education	5	10

Guidance and Evaluation, Principles of Education, Methods and School Organization, and Indian Education in this very order come next on the preference scale. This position gets further confirmed from the mean ranks (Tables 3, 4). To determine if the subject hierarchy obtained was statistically significant a series of critical ratios was prepared (Table 5).

Table 5
Critical Ratios Between Preferred Subjects

	Educational Psychology	Guidance Evaluation	Principles of Education	Methods and School organisation	Indian Education
Educational Psychology		15.20	14.93	7.06	9.00
Guidance and Evaluation			5.70	6.70	10.00
Principles of Education				1.00*	3.07
Methods and School Organisation					10.00

* Not significant. All other CR's are significant at .01 level of confidence.

The numerical advantage held by Educational Psychology over all subjects is significant at .01 level of confidence. Guidance-and-Evaluation shares the position of Educational Psychology, exceeding others in terms of pupil preference. Principles of Education was found to be significantly preferred over Indian Education only. Though it was not found to be significantly preferred over Methods and School Organisation, it was found to be more desirable than any of the subjects except Indian Education.

Principles of Education, and Methods and School Organisation seem to occupy an intermediate position whereas Indian Education is, beyond question, the least preferred in this study.

Table 6
Chi Square tests of significance between subject preference and subject achievement

Subject	Chi Square
Educational Psychology	15.285*
Guidance and Evaluation	9.821**
Principles of Education	3.326
Methods and School Organisation	2.107
Indian Education	1.168

* Significant at .01 level of confidence.
** Significant at .05 level of confidence.

Chi square tests of significance between achievement in the subjects and preference of these subjects were computed.

In so far as Principles of Education, Methods and School Organisation, and Indian Education are concerned, no relationship was discovered between achievement of the students and the degree to which they preferred it. Students, however, appear to choose Educational Psychology and Guidance-and-Evaluation in terms of their achievement in the subject. This finding was significant at .01 and .05 levels of confidence.

To know if relationship exists between preferences of students and level of intelligence, two groups were formed. Group 1 consisted of students with an IQ of 110 or above, Group II of those with an IQ of 90 or below. Rank order correlations between the choices of students in each group and those between the choice of a group and the choice of the total sample were computed.

Table 7
Rank order correlations between subject preferences of students in each intelligence group

Items correlated	Rho
Choices of Group 1 students with those of Group II students	.26
Choices of Group 1 students with those of total group	.82*
Choices of Group II students with those of total group	.61**

* Significant at .01 level of confidence.
** Significant at .05 level of confidence.

Whereas wide divergence of opinion exists between the choices of students in Group 1 and students in Group II, there is a marked similarity in subject preferences between the students in Group I or Group II and the students in total group.

In the matter of subject preference, Group I students rank Educational Psychology first; Guidance and Evaluation, second; Principles of Education, third; Methods and School Organisation and Indian Education, fourth and fifth respectively. Group II students list in order of preference Educational Psychology, Guidance and Evaluation, Methods and School Organisation, Principles of Education, and Indian Education.

References

1. Chase, L.W., and Wilson, G.M. "Preference Studies in Elementary School Social Studies," Journal of Education, 140:1-28.

2. Dean, S.E. "Relation of Children's Subject Preferences to Their Achievement," Elementary School Journal, 51:89-92.
3. Greenblatt, E.L. "An Analysis of School Subject Preference of Elementary School Children of the Middle Grades." The Journal of Educational Research. Vol. 55, No. 10, August 1962, 554-62.
4. Mosher, H.H. "Subject Preferences of Girls and Boys." School Review, 60:34-38.

74. INFLUENCE OF TEACHER TRAINING ON TRAINEES' ATTITUDES

The study reported here was undertaken to determine the influence of teacher training upon the attitudes of undergraduate students towards children. The Minnesota Teacher Attitude Inventory was administered to 160 teacher trainees at the beginning and at the end of a teacher training programme (for elementary school teachers), and the pre-test and post-test scores compared. Nineteen trainees who showed the greatest change in scores were interviewed, and a change in the direction of more liberal attitude towards children at the end of the teacher training programme was noticed.

Newly trained teachers have here and there been found to be in no way better than their untrained counterparts. Their performance, beliefs and attitudes seem to have undergone little, if any, change as a consequence of teacher training. They give an unbridled impression of being unoriented to the profession of teaching. Teacher training is alleged to be too superficial to cause any fundamental change in the make-up of trainees. Such observations, perhaps partly real and mostly imagined, have led to build up the canard that teacher training is ineffective and hence unnecessary. Teacher trainers, when exposed to react to this charge, are unable to justify their programmes beyond mere cliches, hyperbole and affectations peculiar to teacher training, or at the most abstract impressions and estimates of their achievement in the unforeseeable future. The value of teacher education as an independent discipline has also been objected to by critics like Koerner (1963). Hence the need of studying the efficiency of teacher training programme, especially in the matter of influencing the trainees' attitudes (Doughlas, 1934; Lange, 1943; Stevens, 1954).

The present study was intended to assess the influence of an elementary teacher training programme on the trainees' attitudes toward children. More precisely, the problem was to find out the nature, and if possible, the determinants, of change in the trainees' attitudes toward children at the close of the teacher training programme.

Method

The Minnesota Teacher Attitude Inventory (MTAI), which measures teachers' attitudes toward children and which has been successfully used for studies of this kind (Callis, 1950; Doughlas, 1934; Leeds, 1950) was administered to 160 elementary teacher trainees (J.B.T. students) undergoing teacher training programme in the State College of Education, Patiala, and a local school during the session 1967-68. This was done during the initial days of their entry in the training programme. The scores obtained were named as pre-test scores.

The trainees were either matriculates or had passed higher secondary examination (in both cases possessed school-leaving certificates). They were in the age range of 16-18 years. The number of males and females were 60 and 100 respectively. The proportion of persons belonging to different socio-economic strata, *i.e.* below average to above average, in the sample under study was almost identical to that in the State's total population of such teacher trainees.

The inventory was again administered to the same students 20 weeks later during the closing period of the first phase of training. The scores obtained were named as post-test scores for the first phase of training and pre-test scores for the final phase which was to start after a two-month summer vacation. The inventory was finally administered during the closing days of the final phase of training. The scores now obtained were post-test scores for the final phase of training. These scores represented change in attitude caused by the whole period of training.

Comparisons were made between pre-test and post-test scores for each phase of training, assuming that differences between pre-test and post-test scores were attributable to change (in attitude toward children) caused by the training schedule. Differences were tested for significance by the use of t-test (Good, Barr and Scates, 1954). Nineteen subjects who showed the greatest difference between pre-test and post-test scores were interviewed so as to find causes of change in attitude toward children.

The J.B.T. professional course in the State is a two-year course taken after completion of high/higher secondary school education. It begins in the first year (first phase) with an introduction to elementary education, its content and subject courses. It is taken in a sequence that extends through the next year (final phase) which is the period of the professional teacher education programme and which includes introductory courses in Educational Psychology, Principles of Education, School Organisation, and Methods of Teaching, besides 60 hours of observing and teaching in schools under the close supervision of a classroom teacher and their supervisor (a college teacher).

Findings

1. The population of 160 students in the total teacher training programme underwent a definite change in attitude mean scores and variances during the whole period of training. Seen individually, the direction of change varied from person to person, but there was a considerably significant overall change to a high attitude mean on the MTAI. This is evident of an increasingly favourable attitude toward children. Significant increase in variance also emerged as shown in Table 1. Changes observed in the scores during the teacher training course may represent what students have actually learnt from their tutors about desirable attitudes to children. The gains in scores reported by Herbert and Turnbull (1963) and those reported by Evans (1967) are of much the same magnitude as those found in this study.

Table 1
Change in Raw Score means and S.D.'s of the Group, Pre-test to Post-test (For the whole Period of Training)

N	Test	Mean	Difference of Means	Level of Significance	S.D.
	Pre-test	59.6			26.2
160			17.9	.01	
	Post-test	77.5			32.6

2. Statistically significant changes to a higher MTAI mean score occurred at both the stages of training. But greater degree of change seemed to be manifest in the later than that in the earlier phase of the programme, as indicated in Table 2.

Table 2
Change in Raw Score means and S.D.'s of the group, Pre-test to Post-test, for each phase of Training

Phase of Training	N	Test	Mean	S.D.	Difference of Means	Level of Significance
First	160	Pre-test	59.6	26.2		
		Post-test	65.7	29.8	6.1	.01
Final	160	Pre-test	65.7	29.8		
		Post-test	77.5	32.6	11.8	.01

3. Interviews with nineteen students revealed causes which could be classified into two broad categories (mentioned in the order of importance), *viz*. (i) Experiences in the teacher training programme, (ii) Experiences outside the teacher training programme. Table 3 reveals the detailed causes of the change.

Table 3
Causes of Change in Attitudes Towards Children as Revealed in Nineteen Interviews

S. No.	Cause of Change		No. of Students giving this Cause	Percentage
Experiences in the Teacher Training Programme				
1.	Contents of lectures	..	7	36.82
2.	Discussions in the class	..	5	26.30
3.	Reading books, journals	..	6	31.56
4.	Teacher's methods	..	11	57.86
5.	Demonstration lessons by subject experts and other trainees	..	4	21.04
6.	Writing assignments	..	4	21.04
7.	Observing children in classroom and playgrounds	..	14	73.64
8.	Observing supervising teacher interacting with children	..	12	63.12
9.	Teaching children	..	16	84.16
10.	Informal meetings with teacher	..	2	10.52
11.	Observing other teachers teaching children	..	3	15.78
12.	Observing principal-child interaction	..	1	5.26

S. No.	Cause of Change		No. of Students giving this Cause	Percentage
Experiences Outside the Teacher Training Programme				
1.	Interaction with own children	..	2	10.52
2.	Experiences of own childhood recalled during training	..	1	5.26
3.	Fellow-students' experiences with children	..	1	5.26
4.	Informal meetings with children	..	1	5.26

(i) *Attitude changes owing to Experiences in the Teacher Training Programme.* The interviews revealed that experiences within the teacher training programme were more conducive to change of attitudes towards children than experiences outside the teacher training programme. Of the experiences within the teacher training programme, the most characteristic reasons for changing attitudes towards children were based on observation of and personal interaction with children.

Fourteen subjects (73.84 per cent) stated that the kinds of encounter within the teacher training programme which produced the change were observation of children in action in the classroom and on the playground. Three subjects indicated that they found opportunities to observe in classrooms other than the one to which they were assigned. In both cases this was believed to have been instrumental in producing attitude change.

Twelve subjects (63.12 per cent) said that their attitudes toward children were changed by having observed the supervising teacher's interaction with children. One student said that attitude change was caused by having observed the principal interacting with children. Such interaction involved teaching disciplining giving assignments, discussing and directing playground activities.

More than 80 per cent of the subjects stated that their attitudes were altered by direct interactions with children, which occurred when they assumed actual teaching duties. These teaching duties included teaching reading spelling, arithmetic, social studies and other subjects besides directing playground activities and paying individual attention. Two students stated that their attitudes changed as a result of informal meetings with teachers other than their supervising teacher. These meetings led to exchange of thought, about teaching and children, that caused the change.

The subjects were very positive and emphatic in their observations about the value of their in-training experiences. Even those persons who scored low on the MTAI (indicating their not-so-favourable, even negative, attitudes towards children and teaching) felt that the in-training experiences were worthwhile.

Besides observation of and personal interaction with children, the teacher training programme included experiences connected with curricular work. About 58 per cent of the students interviewed stated that the teachers' methods led to change their attitudes toward children. That the methods did so was perhaps owing to the fact that the methods reflected broad philosophical creeds which had a definite bearing upon student-thought. The methods particularly mentioned by the students, in this behalf, were posing provocative questions, giving typical examples to illustrate pithy points, presenting controversial ideas and view-points, strengthening or reinforcing pupils' responses, showing love for and interest in children as such, creating permissive classroom environment to encourage pupil initiative, giving pupils freedom and stimulation to draw their own conclusions, quoting profusely from textbooks to substantiate their lectures, and showing their love for teaching.

About 38 per cent of the subjects were of the belief that, besides the method of the teacher, the content of his lectures also produced change in attitudes toward children. More than 26 per cent of the students believed that discussions in the class had been effective in bringing the change. These discussions included exchange of experiences among students. Writing assignments on such topics as "who is a good teacher", "student unrest", "self-evaluation", "teacher-pupil relationship", "punishment in schools", and "self-concept of a teacher" were mentioned by 21 per cent of those interviewed as having been valuable in changing their attitudes.

As many as 31.56 per cent of the interviewees attribute the change is attitudes to the reading of books and journals which motivated them through research studies and interesting examples in support of concepts and theories. The illustrations of such materials were Coghill's *Anatomy and the Problems of Behaviour*, Gasell's *The First Five Years of Life*, *Piaget's The Moral Judgement of the Child, Shirley's The First Two Years.* Quite a few of those who said that books were effective in producing attitude changes toward children referred to the works of Garrison, John Dewey, Goodenough, Hurlock, Bayley, Smith, Lewin, and Margaret Mead. The subjects felt that these works were effective mostly because of their controversial nature. The journals particularly mentioned as having been effective in changing their attitudes were the *Journal of Educational Psychology*, and the *Journal of Child Development.* Four of the subjects believed that teaching demonstration by subject lecturers and other trainees led to change their attitudes. In this class both subject-lecturers and trainees taught lessons to the college class as though they were elementary pupils.

(ii) *Attitude Changes Owing to Experiences Outside the Teacher Training Programme.* More than 26 per cent of the students interviewed indicated that they had experiences outside the teacher training programme which changed their attitudes toward children. Two students said that experiences with their own children between pre-testing and post-testing led to the change. Experiences of own childhood recalled when reading about or talked about child development, fellow-students' experiences with children, and informal meetings with children were the other causes of attitude change stated by one student each. It was evident that these experiences were not different from those which the teacher training programme provided. In conclusion, it may be justifiably emphasized that actual experience with children, whether such experience is encountered within the teacher training programme or outside it, seems to be more effective than any other factor for producing change in attitudes toward children.

Conclusions

1. The attitudes of teacher trainees, when considered as one group, did change while in undergraduate teacher training programme at the State College of Education, Patiala. This change was in terms of a more liberal attitude toward children.

   Thus attitude toward children, or whatever MTAI really represents, seems to be susceptible to training. The MTAI is concerned with human relationships, and these are the subject of much of the work in a teacher training programme. Hence the increase in scores on the MTAI which represents liberalization of student's opinions about pupil-teacher relations. The MTAI being a much longer test, gives adequate scope for changes that the training programme may produce. Its use for measuring attitude change may, therefore, be appropriate.

2. Trainees' means on the MTAI were higher with each phase of training, which reflected that the amount of change is directly proportional to the amount of training. The trainees showed a much higher mean MTAI score on completion of the training programme than they did on entering the programme; similarly, they showed a higher mean score on entering the final phase of training than they did on entering the first phase. The change in each case was, of course, to a more liberal position in attitude toward children.
3. Increased variance in the post-training scores, for the whole period of training as also for each phase of training viewed separately, showed that the change was directed toward less attitudinal uniformity in the group.
4. Actual teaching was perceived to be most conducive to changes in attitudes. Observing children and observing teachers interacting with children in the classroom, the former more than the latter, was found to be considerably significant for causing the changes. The teachers' method and the contents of their lectures, followed by books and class discussions, occupy the next position, as mentioned by the trainees. Other experiences within and outside the teacher training programme were perceived to be either fairly or somewhat effective in effecting changes in attitudes toward children, though actual experience with children was found to be supreme in the matter of producing the change.

References

Callis, Robert. Change in teacher-pupil attitudes related to training and experience. *Educl. and Psychol. Measurement*, 1950,10: 718-727.

Doughlas, Lois. The pre-training selection of teachers. *J. Educl. Res.*, 1934, 28: 92-117.

Evans, K.M. Teacher-training courses and students' personal qualities. *Educl. Research, Nov.* 1967,10 (1): 72-77.

Good, Barr, Scates. *Methodology of Educational Research,* New York: Appleton Century-Crofts, 1954, 800-831.

Herbert, N., and Turnbull, G.H. Personality factors and effective progress in teaching. *Educ. Rev.*, 1963,16: 24-31.

Koerner, James D. *The Mis-Education of American Teachers.* Boston: Houghton-Mifflin, 1963.

Lange, Phil C. A study of concepts developed by students in an undergraduate course in the psychology and practice of teaching. *J. Educ. Res.*, 1943, 36: 641-661.

Leeds, Carroll H. A scale for measuring teacher-pupil attitudes and teacher-pupil rapport. *Psychological Monographs,* 1950, 64: 312.

Stevens, Leila. *The Attitude of High School Seniors Toward Teaching as a Career*. Madison: University of Wisconsin, 1954.

75. A SURVEY OF TEACHER-TRAINEES' SUCCESSES AND FAILURES

"Do teacher-trainees and class teachers in Secondary education agree on the trainees' areas of most and least success, and if so to what extent"? This problem has been investigated as shown in this study.

Upon completion of a four-week practice-teaching that the teacher-trainees in this college usually do in local secondary schools, at the end of their year-long training in the theory and practice-teaching, 154 trainees were asked to list five areas in which they felt they had achieved most success and five areas in which they felt they could get least success. On the top of a sheet, on which they were to list the areas, examples of areas given were lesson planning, classroom discipline, understanding children, educing response, good pupil-teacher relations, and teaching methods. The trainees were cautioned not to limit themselves to these areas alone.

From these lists, about 33 per cent (50) were picked out at random. Each of the class teachers who had worked with these 50 teacher-trainees were then asked to list the individual trainee's five areas of most success and five areas of least success. Results are tabulated at the end.

Findings:

1. Complete or 100 per cent agreement was found in no cases.
2. The highest percentage of agreement was in areas of least success rather than in those of most success. However, there was only one such case.

3. It is significant, though not altogether unexpected, that success or failure regarding the handling of discipline problems in the classroom was most frequently agreed upon by trainees and teachers.
4. Agreement involving the trainees' failure in discipline problems was fairly less than that involving their success, nine in the case of failure or least success as against fourteen in the success category. Problems of discipline are obviously a major concern in the secondary school teaching and a teacher-trainees' success or failure in dealing with them can be determined most readily.
5. Though planning lessons and other activities are of equal, if not of greater, importance in teaching, yet only 12 cases of agreement were found: 6 involving success and 6 involving failure.
6. In 5 cases, trainees and teachers agreed with respect to the students' success in teaching "intensive reading" lessons. In one case, there was agreement regarding trainees' failure.
7. In all, cases of agreement total 105 out of a possible 500.
8. The findings given in Table 2 indicate that trainees and teachers agree more frequently in areas of greatest success than in those of least success, though the difference when compared to areas of least success (Less than four per cent) seems negligible.

   The percentage of agreement so found betrays poor communication between the teacher-trainees and the class-teachers.
9. It is very much significant that little or no attention was given to the trainees' success or failure in teaching content. How well a trainee teaches Mathematics, Social Studies, General Sciences etc. needs to be looked into.

In an ideal atmosphere of teacher training, trainees and class teachers who work together can and should communicate most frequently and effectively. What a class teacher says is too frequently understood in a different way by a trainee and *vice versa.* Interpretations differ leading to misunderstandings. Good communication between the two, immensely helps the would-be teacher in his professional growth.

Table 1
Areas of Agreement between Teacher-Trainees & Classroom Teachers

Areas of Greatest Success	No. of Cases	Areas of Least Success	No. of Cases
Classroom discipline	14	Classroom discipline	9
Good teacher-pupil relations	12	Lesson Plans	6
Lesson plans	6	Good Voice	6
Teaching "intensive reading" lessons	5	General Interestingness	6
Educing response	4	Originality of teaching aids Model reading	5
Use of audio-visual aids	4	Use of proper Methods	4
Effective expression	3	Teaching of Art	4
Understanding Children	3	Teaching usage of words	3
Black-board writing	2	Teaching map-reading	2
Paying individual attention	2	Teaching "Intensive reading" Lessons	1
Total	55	Total	50

Table 2
Agreement between Teacher-Trainees and Class Teachers

	No. of Cases	Percentage of Agreement
Areas of Greatest Success		
No Agreement between trainee & teacher	7	0
Agreement between trainee & teacher in one area	18	20
Agreement between trainee & teacher in two areas	15	40
Agreement between trainee & teacher in three areas	10	60
Mean percentage of Agreement		31.58
Areas of Least Success		
No Agreement between trainee & teacher	5	0
Agreement between trainee & teacher in one area	28	20
Agreement between trainee & teacher in two areas	12	40
Agreement between trainee & teacher in three areas	4	60

Agreement between trainee & teacher in four areas	1	80
Mean percentage of Agreement		27.2

76. TEACHER TRAINEES' ATTITUDE TO THE USE OF CORPORAL PUNISHMENT

Whereas many schools, influenced by modern trends in education, bade good-bye to corporal punishment, many others retained it for reasons best known to them. Denmark, Switzerland and Ireland have completely abolished it, while some more countries are mobilizing public opinion with a view to ending it. That corporal punishment is bad and it tends to vitiate education and its processes is the growing belief which leads schools to abolish it. But that it is necessary to maintain good order and discipline and to make pupils work is the lingering obsession which makes school cling to it. The matter is discussed at length as a corollary to instructional programme in many seminars and conferences in this country, without of course reaching any decisive conclusion. In fact the school education is still bedeviled by the controversy over the question of corporal punishment in school.

Highfield and Pincent (1) found that 89.2% of the teachers in state schools in England and Wales thought that corporal punishment, as a last resort, should be retained; while only 5.6 favoured abolishing it. Starr's (4) investigation reveals that 71% of his sample of graduate student teachers favour retention of this punishment as a last resort and 64% opine that corporal punishment has not yet outlived its usefulness as a means of checking serious offences. 51% of his sample think that more harm than good is caused by the retention of corporal punishment, 24% agree that all corporal punishment should be abandoned in schools and 14% favour legal interdiction. Educational Institute of Scotland (3) in a memorandum favour the use of corporal punishment as an ultimate sanction until an effective alternative can be found.

All in all, a majority of teachers and educators have not been able to scotch the idea of corporal punishment in schools, notwithstanding an appreciable minority holding strong views against this idea. Perhaps decades have sped by in this wrangling and decades may still pass by until the whole educational machine is so revamped that the sordid pastime of corporal punishment be banished lock, stock and barrel. Education, more than anything else, would ultimately discover media which can serve the ends that the corporal punishment solely claims to serve. Education would rediscover education that can concomitantly perform the task of developing virtues and annihilating vices – the task that corporal punishment is contended to do.

The present study is intended to know the attitudes of teacher trainees (B.Ed. students) to the use of corporal punishment in schools.

Method

Attitudes to the use of corporal punishment in schools were assessed by administering an attitude inventory to 756 teacher trainees, men and women in equal numbers, undergoing a one-year course of professional training at the following training colleges of the Punjab State:

1.	Government Training College for Teachers, Jullundur	1966-67	N=156
2.	M.G.N. Khalsa Training College, Jullundur	1966-67	N=170
3.	State College of Education, Patiala	1966-67	N=280
		1967-68	N=150

The sample at each college consisted of equal number of male and female teacher trainees. This sample formed 84% of an aggregate of 900 trainees who represented a random choice of the State's graduates who came from average to above-average socio-economic and academic strata. Their age range was 19 to 31 years.

The inventory used consisted of 20 statements —10 favouring and 10 disfavouring the use of corporal punishment in schools. The subjects were required to tick either 'yes' or 'no', both of which were placed against each statement. From their responses to the inventory a numerical score representing the strength of each trainee to the use of corporal punishment was calculated. The higher the score the less favourable is the obtained attitude to the use of corporal punishment.

Other variables for which measures were obtained for each subject were sex, age, experience of corporal punishment at the primary school and that at the secondary school at which the trainee was a pupil, type of high school attended, academic achievement, and teaching skill. Information on the first four items was obtained through the questions placed on top of the Inventory, while that for the remaining two was obtained from the college records. Average scores on the Inventory between different groups of trainees were compared.

Results

Estimated attitudes to the use of corporal punishment on score of differences in the variables mentioned above are analysed below:

Sex and the Attitude

Women teacher trainees, as a group, have a less favourable attitude to the use of corporal punishment, as is evident from the finding that their mean inventory score is higher than that for their male counterparts (Table 1), though the difference is not significant.

The women's less favourable attitude to corporal punishment is also reflected from the finding that a greater percentage of men trainees and a lesser percentage of women trainees answered "yes" to all the ten statements favouring the use of corporal punishment, while a greater percentage of women trainees and a lesser percentage of men trainees answered "yes" to all except three of the statements disfavouring the proposition (Table 2). The differences between the proportions of men and women trainees answering "yes" to each statement of the inventory, barring two, are however not significant.

Table 1
Mean Inventory Scores

	Men	Women	Whole Sample
N	378	378	756
Mean Inventory Score	6.74	7.26	7.07
Standard Deviation	2.10	2.22	2.17
Sex Difference between Mean Inventory Scores	0.52		
Whether significant	n.s.		

Table 2
Percentage of students giving positive answers ('yes') to the statements of the Inventory

	Men	Women	Total
N	378	378	756
Sl. No. of Statements*	Sex-wise percentage answering 'yes'		Percentage of total sample answering 'yes'
	Men	Women	
Favouring			
1	80.2	70.6	75.0
2	79.6	69.0	74.0
3	78.0	62.0	70.0
4	66.0	58.0	62.0
5	67.6**	38.6**	53.0
6	56.4**	33.7**	45.0
7	40.0	38.0	39.0
8	12.9	11.0	12.0
9	11.5	10.6	11.0
10	10.8	9.3	10.0
Disfavouring			
11	46.6	58.0	52.0
12	29.3	37.2	33.0
13	29.2	28.9	29.0
14	22.0	22.2	22.0
15	18.2	19.8	19.0
16	15.9	13.9	15.0
17	12.1	11.0	11.0
18	10.2	10.0	10.0
19	9.4	9.0	9.0
20	4.3	5.3	5.0

* Placed in diminishing order of percentage agreement in the sample.
** Difference significant at .01 level.

Age and the Attitude

Older teacher trainees, when compared to the younger lot in the matter of attitude to corporal punishment, showed a significantly less favourable attitude. Those who were over 22 years were classified as the "older" and the rest as the "younger." The proportions of teacher trainees in the "older" and "younger" groups answering "yes" to each of the statements were compared. For all the statements except two, a higher proportion of trainees in the younger group gave the response favouring the use of corporal punishment, though the differences were in no case significant (Table 3).

Table 3
Mean Inventory Scores and Age

	Age	N	Mean Inventory Score	Significance Level of difference between Mean Values
Men	<22	240	6.62	n.s.
	>22	138	7.80	
Women	<22	325	7.41	n.s.
	>22	53	8.64	
Whole Sample	<22	565	6.97	n.s.
	>22	191	8.20	

Experience of corporal punishment at the primary school level and attitude

When asked to state whether corporal punishment was used 'often', 'sometimes', or 'not at all', at the primary schools at which they had been pupils, 340 trainees (180 men and 160 women) said 'often', 378 (170 men and 208 women) said 'sometimes,' and 38 (10 men and 28 women) said 'not at all.' Differences in attitude to the use of corporal punishment were found not significant, when the mean scores of the 'often' and 'sometimes' groups were compared.

Experience of corporal punishment at the secondary school level and attitude

378 teacher trainees (146 men and 232 women), in whose secondary schools corporal punishment was used occasionally, showed most favourable attitudes to corporal punishment. 128 of them (73 men and 53 women), who attended schools making frequent use of corporal punishment, showed less favourable attitude; and 250 (49 men and 201 women) trainees, whose schools never used corporal punishment, had a significantly less favourable attitude to its use.

Type of high school attended and the attitude

The differences between the mean scores of men/women trainees who had attended boys' schools/girls' schools and those who had attended co-educational schools were found 'not significant.'

Perhaps the type of school attended is not related to one's attitude to corporal punishment.

Academic achievement and the attitude

Considering the average achievement score in the theory papers of the B.Ed. Examination as an index of academic achievement, trainees getting 65 per cent or more marks were classified as 'superior' and the remainder as 'ordinary.' The mean scores of the two were compared. The 'superior' in academic achievement showed a slightly less favourable attitude to corporal punishment than the 'ordinary' in academic achievement (Table 4).

Table 4
Mean Inventory Scores and Academic Achievement

	Achievement	N	Mean Score	Level of significance of difference in mean scores
Men	Superior	38	8.20	n.s.
	Ordinary	340	6.80	
Women	Superior	77	8.30	n.s.
	Ordinary	301	6.96	
Whole sample	Superior	115	8.26	n.s.
	Ordinary	641	6.86	

Teaching skill and the attitude

The teacher trainees getting 65 per cent or more marks (superior) in their practical skill in teaching examination showed a less favourable attitude to corporal punishment than those getting below 65 per cent marks (ordinary), but the differences were not significant (Table 5).

Table 5
Mean Inventory Scores and Teaching Skill

	Teaching Skill	N	Mean Score	Level of Significance of difference in Mean Scores
Men	Superior	58	7.41	n.s.
	Ordinary	320	6.84	
Women	Superior	97	8.08	n.s.
	Ordinary	281	6.68	
Whole sample	Superior	155	7.80	n.s.
	Ordinary	601	6.76	

Discussion

As many as 75% of the teacher trainees favour the use of corporal punishment as an essential expedient and 74% favour its use saying that it is the only deterrent against child's lapses. Again 70% want corporal punishment to stay for its usefulness as a means of getting students to work, and 62% for providing fear without which, they say, many students don't work at all. 53% say that it should be there but to be used with prudence. Other reasons in favour of corporal punishment have not attracted many exponents.

52% of the trainees opine that corporal punishment harms the child's personality, 33% think that it antagonises the educands, 29% aver that it humiliates the child, and 20% assert that it has no place in the modern school set-up. 19% of the group under study favour its abolition forthwith, while lesser numbers vote against it for other reasons.

Though the teacher trainees who are 'for' the use of corporal punishment are in a majority, those who are 'against' it are in a notable minority. Moreover, the latter express great resentment against the use of corporal punishment.

Perhaps corporal punishment is an institution too old and too deep-rooted to be snapped so soon. In spite of so much publicity made against it by psychology and neo-educationists as also by modern reformers, corporal punishment refuses to go. Or perhaps most of the teachers, in spite of their training which profusely preaches against corporal punishment, find themselves too helpless or too ill-equipped to be able to deal with the taught without bringing in the element of physical cruelty. Those responsible for training teachers perhaps need to make their programmes more effective so that change of attitude (toward corporal punishment) coupled with suitable equipage for managing their work without it is fostered in the teacher trainees.

Men trainees, as a whole, were a little more inclined to the use of corporal punishment than women, though the differences were only suggestive and small. Women being the weaker sex are perhaps tempted less often than men to lay violent hands upon an offending pupil. They are too tender-minded, contrary to men who are tough-minded, to welcome chastisement or to dispense this punishment.

Older trainees were less favourable to the use of corporal punishment than the younger group. The younger element being less mature may be regarding corporal punishment as a remedy to problems of indiscipline experienced during teaching practice. They, more often than older trainees, may be provoked to anger which is caused by an offended self-esteem (2). They may be furious, possibly more often than their matured counterparts, at the thought that a pupil should have the courage to defy them or flout their authority. Again, women, whether young or old, seem to be less favourable than men to corporal punishment which, as already suggested, does not appeal to them so much.

Primary school (at which the trainees were pupils), whether it inflicts corporal punishment or not, does not seem to have made any appreciable difference in the trainees' attitude to corporal punishment. Probably the subjects are too grown up to recall their experiences at the primary schools which they had attended several years ago.

Teacher trainees educated in secondary schools, where corporal punishment was in vogue, expressed a more favourable attitude to it than those educated in schools in which this punishment was never used. The number favouring corporal punishment was considerably higher from the former group than that from the latter, while the number disfavouring it was pretty less from the former group than that from the latter. However, those coming from the schools making frequent use of corporal punishment were found less favourable to it than those coming from the schools making only an occasional use of it.

Perhaps experience of corporal punishment at secondary schools tends not only to take away the fear of it, but tends also to determine tolerance or even inclination for it. But if the frequency of this experience has been higher, the degree of favourableness to corporal punishment seems to have diminished proportionately. A judicious use of corporal punishment, used once in a while and coming as a natural and inevitable consequence of wrong-doing, is more readily accepted and regarded as right and just than frequent flogging which carries traditional associations of vindictive chastisement and repression. When children are exposed to violent treatment day in and day out without sufficient rhyme and reason or without being made aware of the connection between the offence and the consequent punishment, they tend to become anti-punishment and even punishment-proof.

Teacher trainees showing higher academic proficiency and greater teaching skill were less inclined to corporal punishment than those who were lower in the two abilities. As academic achievement and teaching skill are believed to be positively correlated, these differences may both reflect experience during their long teaching practice. The trainees who are poor in teaching skill may be handicapped in making students learn or work, or in controlling the class, and consequently be disposed to favour the use of corporal punishment. Ability whether academic or practical, especially the latter, develops confidence, even equipment, to make the mare go without the use of corporal punishment.

The findings of this study though suggestive confirm most of the facts revealed by Starr's (4) investigation, showing thereby that British and Indian teachers are considerably alike in their attitude to corporal punishment.

Summary

Teacher trainees' attitudes to the use of corporal punishment were assessed by administering an attitude inventory (containing 10 each of 'pro' and 'anti' statements) to 756 trainees, men and women in equal numbers, of the Punjab's three Training Colleges for Teachers. The subjects were to express their agreement or disagreement with the statements by saying 'yes' or 'no' respectively. Variables against which measures of attitudes were weighed were age, sex, experience of corporal punishment at the primary and secondary schools, the type of secondary school attended, and the academic and practical ability. Teacher trainees who favoured corporal punishment were many more in number than those who disfavoured it. Favourable attitude to corporal punishment was found in men more than women, in younger more than older, in those coming from schools using this punishment more than those from schools not using it, and in the inferior in theoretical and practical ability more than those superior in the same.

References

1. Highfield, M.E., and Pincent, A. (1952). "A Survey of Rewards and Punishments in Schools," N.F.E.R. (Newnes).
2. Pincent, A. "The Principles of Teaching Method." George G. Harrap & Co. Ltd., London, pp. 381-82.
3. "Punishment in Schools." A Memorandum of the Educational Institute of Scotland, Scottish Ed. J. XLVIII, 42.
4. Starr, J.W. "The Attitudes of a Group of Student Teachers to the Use of Corporal Punishment in Schools." Educational Review. Inst. of Educ. University of Birmingham, Vol. 19. No. 3, June 67. pp. 214-24.

77. ATTITUDES OF STUDENT TEACHERS TOWARD INCREASING PARTICIPATION OF WOMEN IN ECONOMIC, POLITICAL AND SOCIAL SPHERES

Abstract

How do student teachers view demands of women for greater opportunities to participate in the economic, political and social spheres? To find an answer to this question, a questionnaire was administered to 360 student teachers, males and females in equal number. Except for some increments in the males' egalitarian response, differences in responses were almost exclusively a function of the sex of the respondent. Female teachers saw women more optimistically and positively than did male teachers.

The time has come when women should have full and equal participation in all spheres: social, economic and political. The international women's year, that has followed the women's rights movement, has rightly focused attention on the need to promote this cause. Traditionalists disfavour increasing participation of women in the hitherto world of men for such reasons as biological and social characteristics of females. Again, they argue that both women and men prefer to retain the *status quo* which enjoins women's interest in home, children and family and men's interest in the larger economic, political and social spheres.

Sample and Methodology

The aim of this study was to surface attitudes toward women's increased participation in fields typically thought of as male. Greenberg (1) and earlier Storrs (2) studied such attitudes of elementary and secondary students when they found systematic and significant differences in responses between boys and girls. Both of them used one and the same questionnaire. The present investigator also adapted that very questionnaire though he used it on a different population. He chose a random sample of 360 student teachers (males and females in equal numbers) from a population of 1080 on the rolls of four teacher training colleges of Punjab State, so that the sample chosen was representative of the state's total population of student teachers. Since the population of student teachers broadly represented two social class groups (an upper and a lower), 180 students (males and females in equal numbers) in each of the two classes were sampled.

The adaptation of the questionnaire implied scrutinisation of each of its 20 items with a view to ensuring its (item's) intelligibility by the Ss and its orientation to Indian social, economic and political culture. To accomplish the former, 6 items (serial Nos. 1,13,14,15,17,18) were slightly modified, to do the latter 11 items (serial Nos. 2,3,4,5,7,8,10,11,12,16,19) were retouched and to do both 1 item (serial No. 6) was modified; 2 items (serial Nos. 9,20) were retained as they were.

Results

The answers to items 1-19 were converted into an egalitarian score and an interval score calculated for each subject. Answers to item 20 were excluded from the egalitarian score. The meanings of the responses were difficult to evaluate in terms of their egalitarian dimension, even though the patterns of male/female responses were quite different. Thus, answering "yes" to items 1–12,16–19 and "no" to items 13,14,15 were all scored as positive on the egalitarian score. A three-way analysis of variance was then drawn on the data to examine the variable of social class. No difference emerged between numbers of the two classes. This finding argues against the notion of a more liberal posture towards social change among more privileged males (at least on this issue) and also against the notion that the women's rights movement reflects only the perceived interests of more privileged females. Again, no significant differences were revealed in analysing the answers by sex. Males and females had almost equal egalitarian scores.

An item analysis of the questionnaire was performed and percentages of female and male answers calculated as shown in Table 1.

Table 1

Percentage of Male/Female Questionnaire Responses

Items	Female response		Male response	
	Yes	No	Yes	No
1. Do you think a woman should have the same chance as a man to go in for any job she wants if she is qualified?	100	00	82	18
2. Do you feel that a female engineer would be as good as a male?	40	60	30	70
3. Should radio station employ more female announcers?	97	3	79	21
4. Should there be more female rickshaw drivers?	0	100	15	85
5. Are Women athletes as smart as men athletes?	75	25	45	55
6. Would a trained female mechanic be as good as male if your scooter needed repair?	38	62	21	79
7. Should we have female pilots?	75	25	30	70
8. Should more women be encouraged to become legislators, and magistrates?	100	0	58	42
9. Do you think that we shall ever have a woman President?	100	0	79	21
10. Are women as intellectual as men?	90	10	67	33
11. Do you think most female doctors are as good as most male doctors?	90	10	76	24
12. Do you feel that a female would be as good a college Principal as a male?	83	17	70	30
13. Do women get perturbed more easily than men?	78	22	88	12
14. Would you mind working under a female boss?	17	83	36	64
15. Is it fair that men should be expected to usher in and stand up for women if women have equal jobs?	65	35	30	70

16. Do you think men should be allowed to go in for jobs that women usually do, such as male nurses and telephone operators?	30	70	55	45
17. Do you think women in all countries of the world should have the same rights as men?	100	0	79	21
18. Should women in all countries be allowed to vote for women leaders if men do?	48	52	30	70
19. Do you feel women are as talented as men in fine arts and dramatics?	90	10	91	9
20. Is it better to be a man or a woman in India today?	Female response:	Man		55%
		Woman		45%
	Male response:	Man		97%
		Women		3%

Item 18, "Should women in all countries be allowed to vote for women leaders if men do"?–was the one item which was answered in more egalitarian form by female than by males.

Item 19, "Do you feel women are as talented as men in fine arts and dramatics"?–was the one question in which agreement of males and females was almost perfect with 90 per cent of the females saying "yes" and 91 per cent of the males saying "yes".

Discussion and Conclusions

The male's tendency, significant or slight, towards more egalitarian responses to such items as 16,5,8,14,10 and even others, as compared to females', may be due to greater sophistication and understanding of social issues or a better ability to understand the language and thrust of the questions themselves in our man-dominated set-up.

Significant differences between responses of male and female teachers on questions concerning knowledge of objective fact or the ability to analyse objective reality was interesting. Thus item 10, "Are women as intellectual as men?" and item 9, "Do you think that we shall ever have a woman President?" are not questions which tap personal preference or belief in quite the same way as "Should we have female pilots (item 7)?" Yet the former questions were responded to in the same pattern as the latter, *i.e.* females said "yes" more often than males.

More females than males saying "yes" to a large number of items (Nos. 1, 2, 3, 5, 6, 7, 8, 9, 10, 11, 12, 15, 17, 18), more males than females saying "yes" to a few items (Nos. 4,13,14,16), more males than females wanting to be men rather than women (item 20)– all these demonstrate that systematic differences exist between responses of the two groups. These differences of responses are primarily a function of the sex of the respondent.

Agreement between males and females in the nature, not magnitude, of responses to as many as 16 (80 per cent) of the 20 items show males' increasing liberal and accommodative attitude towards social change favouring women's participation in spheres which were hitherto men's. It also significantly reflects women's awareness of their rights and to an extent the fact that men have started recognizing women's rights, as also their ability to do things which for long have been considered to be men's domain.

Disagreement between males and females in the nature as well as magnitude of responses to the remaining 4 items was revealing though surprising, More men saying "no" and more women saying "yes" to, "Are women athletes as smart as men (item 5)?" and to, "Should we have female pilots (item 7)?" show females' forceful plea for and assertive claim to positions that were traditionally men's and that men still fear to yield to their female counterparts. More women saying "yes" and more men saying "no" to "Is it fair that men should be expected to usher in and stand for women if women have equal jobs (item 15)?" reflects women's reaction formation to the subordinate role they had been playing for ages and their deliberate endeavour to capture their turn for standing superior to men. More women saying "no" and more men saying "yes" to "Do you think men should be allowed to go in for jobs that women usually do such as male nurses and telephone operators (item 16)?" betray women's rigid stance and their refusal to allow their male counterparts to participate in spheres that have been traditionally females'.

Thus, female teachers see women more optimistically than do males. Also they are more favourable to the concept of social change which promises greater participation of women in the economic, political and social spheres.

Limitations

In spite of the adaptation of the questionnaire to Indian conditions, such items as "Are women as intellectual as men (item 10)" and "Would you mind working under a female boss (item 14)" suffer from the unconscious anti-woman bias which can seriously affect responses of an individual, no matter whether one is male or female. But the fact, that the present study has yielded results congruent with Ms. Storrs' (2) and Greenberg's (1) (except that in these studies females and in this study, males tended to give egalitarian responses), shows that the questionnaire used is reliable and capable of revealing attitudinal differences. It may, however, be appropriate to test the value of this instrument and the replication of the findings by testing larger and different population groups.

References

1. Greenberg, Selma S. "Attitudes of elementary and secondary students toward increased social, economic and political participation by women." *J. of Educ. Res.:* Vol. 67, No. 4, 1973.
2. Storrs, Sally. "Attitudes of sixth grade students towards increased social, economic and political participation by women." Unpublished study mentioned in 1 above.

78. ATTITUDE OF TEACHER TRAINEES AND THEIR PARENTS TOWARDS TEACHING

Similarities of teaching attitudes of 120 teacher-trainees and their parents were studied by means of Minnesota Teacher Attitude Inventory. The results suggest that (a) parents are relatively similar in their attitudes towards teaching, (b) a fair, positive relationship exists between the attitudes of trainees and those of their parents, (c) trainees tend to identify themselves with the attitudes of the parent of the same sex, (d) sons are most permissive in their concept of teacher-pupil relationships while daughters are less so, and (e) fathers and mothers tend to be more authoritarian than do their children of either sex. The study confirms that parents do have a role in helping form the professional attitudes of those of their children who become teachers.

Introduction

Factors that build attitudes towards teaching and pupil-teacher relationship are somewhat difficult to identify. Riccio (1959), in a survey of the studies on teacher attitudes, identified such related variables as personality traits, values, experiences and academic attitudes. A variable often overlooked is the role of parents in helping form the professional attitudes of those of their children who go in for teaching. The present study is an attempt in this direction. The author investigates into the possible relationships between professional attitudes of teacher trainees (teacher education students) and their parents. The points examined were: the degree of similarity, if any, between the attitudes of trainees and their parents; whether the trainee tends to identify more with one parent than with the other; the degree of relationship, if any, between a student's parents.

Procedure

B.Ed. teacher trainees, 120 in number (75 girls and 45 boys), of State College of Education, Patiala were administered Minnesota Teacher Attitude Inventory (MTAI-1952) in a classroom session at the close of their course. The subjects were postgraduate in Arts or Science in the age-range 21-24 years. A month later, inventories and a forwarding note (stating that we were interested in parental attitudes towards education) were sent to parents of the subjects. Both parents of a trainee were required to answer the inventory. They were required to avoid showing their answers to each other.

Results and Discussion

The data in Table 1, showing the relationship between the MTAI scores of trainees and those of their parents, suggest three trends: significant similarity between parents' attitudes; significantly similar attitudes of students and their parents; and, though tenuously, the students' attitudinal identification with the parent of the same sex. Daughters and mothers show a higher relationship (.43) than do daughters and fathers (.19). Similarly the son-father correlation (.35) is higher than the son-mother correlation (.21). Although these differences were not statistically reliable, these were not unexpected in view of similar results reported in studies made in other areas of parent-child identification. Father-son and mother-daughter identifications were shown in a study of values (1956) and again in a study of interests (1958).

Table 2, showing the means and standard deviations, indicates that the variance is homogeneous for all groups, though the means are significantly different.

Table 1
Product-Moment correlations between students' and parents' MTAI scores

Group	*r*	N
Trainees-fathers	.32**	120
Trainees-mothers	.36**	120
Mothers-fathers	.52**	120
Sons-fathers	.35**	45
Sons-mothers	.21*	45
Daughters-fathers	.19*	75
Daughters-mothers	.43**	75

* Significant at .05 level of significance.
** Significant at .01 level of significance.

As the MTAI reflects on an authoritarianism-permissiveness continuum (higher positive scores represent permissiveness in teacher-pupil relationships whereas low positive or negative scores indicate authoritarian attitudes), it may be possible to rank sons as most permissive with daughters, mothers and fathers following in that order. Perhaps an age as well as a sex variable is operating here.

Table 2
Means and Standard Deviations of MTAI scores for students and parents

Group	N	M	SD
All trainees	120	32.3	24.9
Sons	45	37.2	25.2
Daughters	75	22.4	22.3
Mothers	120	4.7	28.7
Fathers	120	2.9	25.4

References

Cook, W.W., Leeds, C.H., & Callis, R. "Minnesota Teacher Attitude Inventory Manual", New York: Psychological Corporation, 1952.

Gray, S.W. & Klaus, R. "Assessment of parental identification." Genet Psychol. Mong, 1956, 54, 87-100.

Hendersan, H.L. "The relationship between interests of fathers and sons and sons' identification with fathers." Unpublished Doctoral Dissertation, Columbia University, 1958.

Riccio, A.C. "The relationship of selected variables to attitudes towards teaching." Unpublished Doctoral Dissertation, Ohio State University, 1959.

XI. Teaching Skill and Techniques

79. A CRITIQUE OF TEACHING TECHNIQUES

A vital problem in the field of teacher education is the method or technique of teaching. Whereas the mastery of the subject may enable the teacher to put the knowledge across, it is the technique of teaching which can achieve such learning products as understandings, appreciations, predispositions, skills, creative insight and originality. The subject-matter, when transmitted to the learner, must lead to certain changes–cognitive, affective or conative–in the learner who in turn will adopt, retain and then use these changes in his day-to-day behaviour; the learner must get the thrill, the adventure and the joy of learning, of grappling with ideas, of realizing the essential purposes which are implicit in the different subjects of study. The desired changes in the learner represent the purposes or ends of instruction, while the learning experiences spearheaded by a teaching technique are the instruments or means related to these ends. A teaching method is not good or appropriate unless it helps to bring about the kinds of changes which are regarded as the goals of instruction. Thus the high school curriculum, based on the respective subject areas, will provide the ingredients of a good education only if the subjects are taught skillfully, if they are maneuvered at the behest of a suitable teaching method, or if they are negotiated with an effective teaching technique.

Teaching Methods: An Overview

When we turn to teaching anything, identification of learning units becomes our primary concern, and the formulation of unit objectives our vital task. The next problem is the technique of pedagogical attack. Teacher training institutions often raise furor over the methods used for the teaching of reading, writing, mathematics, or science. These methods sometimes cross the writer's mind in terms of such vaguely worded phrases as sentence method, phonetic method, direct method, natural method, heuristic method, recitation method etc. The pedagogical history is full of ephemeral methods associated with the names of authors, or of places where they have flourished or of textbooks that have swept the country. A method used in a foreign land, which has somehow stood superior, may be just politically, in our scheme of thought, appeals to us. If an educational expert or a prestigious educator names a method, we tend to be convinced that this is the best method. This general attitude towards the problem of teaching may be quite remote from a sound educational viewpoint.

A right method of teaching makes learning easy and economical and a wrong one makes learning difficult and uneconomical. One method tends to yield a given learning product and another tends, other things being equal, to yield a different product. For instance, nobody would today contend that the alphabet method of teaching reading will ever develop reading ability in the most direct, effective and economical manner. The grammatical method of teaching a foreign language produces one kind of learning product, and the direct method quite another. Heuristic teaching of mathematics or science tends to cause mental confusion in the pupil, while direct expository teaching tends to lead to vivid understanding. Again, a good teacher will get better result with a method which itself has a wrong tendency than will a poor teacher with a method which has a right tendency. In fact, there has emerged a body of verified principles touching the application and results of teaching methods which we may designate as the methodology of teaching (Beauchamp, 1925). However, it does not follow that a method, howsoever well-established in principle, can *ipso facto* be applied to any situation. On the other hand, an effective teaching procedure involves much more than a method. Success depends upon the teacher and his skill in applying an elaborate fund of special knowledge to the solution of teaching problems. In direct teaching, method bulks large, but the teacher's personality, vigour and control technique bulk larger. No method has ever been evolved, nor in the nature of the case is it likely that it ever will be evolved, which will enable anybody to follow a routine or set course with the belief that certain results must follow, nor will the mere routine operate by itself.

The Crux of a Teaching Technique

It is not enough to teach; it is necessary to know whether or not our teaching has registered. And our teaching does not get registered if our pupils are not in need of teaching. Corrective teaching thus presents itself as the most important factor conducive to thoroughness of teaching. Again, teaching method in the ordinary sense gives place to skill in studying the individual pupil, and to acumen in criticising the teaching that we have administered in the particular situation.

Teaching is only the handmaid of study. In time, teaching should become unnecessary and the learning process should become henceforth wholly a study process. Hence the teacher's energy, thought and time should largely be devoted to the selection of study material, to the focusing of such material on the learning unit, to directing the study of pupils, and to developing in them methods of study. Here, the teacher is again a student of the individual pupil and, above all, a student of the subject being taught and studied. The teacher cannot teach that which he himself does not know. The teacher does need to get training in education as his technological subject, but this in no way can minimise the importance of a rich and continual competency in the academic aspect of the subject he teaches. The latter is especially imperative in the selection of units to be taught and in organising study material The teacher cannot organise units unless his mind can sweep over the whole expanse of his subject and judge between what constitutes the significant and comprehensive material of intelligent attitudes and what is merely detail which contributes little. He cannot organise and focus study material unless he has at his command intellectual resources that enable him to apply to the unit being studied the desired wealth of material which illuminates and makes significant the understanding sought. Lastly, the teacher must provide hot only opportunity for genuine and adequate pupil reaction but a constraint which compels the immature pupil to react to and thus make this own attitude which the unit implies.

All these requirements of teaching must be weaved into a systematic technique of teaching which, for success, will of course depend upon the personality, intelligence, professional insight and skill, learning and perseverance of the teacher.

The technique to be followed begins with the preliminary appraisal of the present experiential background of the pupils with respect to the unit to be taught. The appraisal determines the procedure to be followed thereafter. A written test, an oral quiz, or a class discussion may be employed to do this appraisal. This orients the teacher with reference to the presentation of the new unit and orients the class with reference to the new learning.

Then in the pupil's mind normal learning curiosity is to be awakened. It is this curiosity which is the chief constraint the teacher has to rely upon for pedagogical purposes. If we ensure the connection between the new unit and what the pupil already knows, motivation based upon curiosity will be established. The normal curiosity will, however, operate only if the whole spirit of the school is focused upon convincing the pupils that they must learn and that learning depends upon themselves. The secondary school pupils from well-to-do homes and the young hoodlums of the city streets, as also the vast majority of normal children, have somehow failed to develop until now the learning attitude and the conviction that learning effort is a serious matter. As such, a fairly vigorous remedial treatment is required before their blunted curiosity is re-aroused.

The habit of total dependence in the primary school tends to keep the secondary school pupil more or less dependent upon direct teaching at the hands of the instructor. Learning self-dependence has yet to be achieved. So after normal curiosity has been generated, the essential understanding must be established in broad terms by direct expository teaching. It is here that the teacher can make effective direct teaching and develop understandings implied in the unit. When presentation is completed, motivation gets registered and the new unit 'sold' to the class. An intelligent attitude toward the new unit is built, and the new understanding by the process of direct learning occurs. The teacher must learn to concentrate his material and throw into his presentation his whole personality.

Soon after the presentation, the teacher must test the pupils to ensure that the presentation has registered. This test also serves to develop study ability, because making the pupil conscious, during the process of presentation, that he is immediately afterwards to be tested, tends to train him in the ability to listen attentively and to assimilate the content of what is taught. Then comes the step of developing a student who is started on his way to self-dependence through the process of supervised and guided assimilative study. Here is the valuable opportunity for break with the meagre textbook assignment. Direct learning again occurs through this type of teaching. The pupil works over, in a long study period, an adequate body of assimilative material focused upon the unit and achieves, in the most thorough-going and economical manner, the change in the attitude which is the essence of learning. The teacher's function becomes that of a persistent and industrious seeker after new and better material. The pupil is so engrossed in learning and study that the teacher is just to sit quietly or to walk quietly about the room, keeping order. Lastly, for every unit of learning is provided a period in which the pupil is led to react as effectively as possible to the content of his learning. This reaction in turn seems to accomplish the final establishment of the new attitude. Here the pupil assembles his thought content and focuses it upon a clear expression of his understanding of the unit. He is now not absorbing but giving forth. He expresses the new attitude.

Success in establishing the learning attitude mainly depends upon the teacher. The teacher who unremittingly requires satisfactory performance gets the desired results, while the one who lets poor work slide and uncritically consoles himself with the thought that the work done by the pupil is the best of which he is capable gets poor results. Here lies the teacher's chief opportunity for training the pupil into intellectual coherence and integrity.

By the time the pupil has reached this stage in the study of a unit, he has acquired genuine insight into the subject, assimilated a large part of material and has organised therefrom the content of his understanding. The class is now held for the purpose of giving expression to the individual understandings of the pupils. Oral presentations set in, in which each pupil attacks the unit as did the teacher in his presentation to the class. This step may serve as a test of understanding, but actually it is a part of the learning process. In it, he reacts to his understanding in language forms which provokes class discussion. He thus progresses in the development of the power of setting forth an actual intellectual content which may be the final expression of intellectual integrity and coherence sought in a learning unit.

Experimental Evidence Favouring the Above Technique

An experiment was conducted by the author to teach an intensive reading lesson in English to four seventh-grade classes. The classes were matched for intelligence, age, achievement in English in the two previous examinations, socio-economic status and language (English) ability. The classes were randomly assigned to the two experimental treatment groups and the two control groups. The former two groups were taught by teachers trained in the technique envisaged above, while the latter two groups was taught by teachers using classroom discourse, an age-old traditional method. One immediate and one delayed post-test were given to determine achievement in reading. Analysis of variance procedures used to analyse the results showed significant differences in favour of the technique suggested. Whereas the significant differences emerged when each experimental group was compared to each of the two control groups, no significant difference was found when the two experimental groups, as also the two control groups, were mutually compared.

Experience as well as instructional theory reveal that the best method of bringing about improvement in reading skill is that in which students are given frequent opportunities to perform (or practise) under the critical and analytic guidance of a teacher (Bloom, 1953), as in the case of the technique under study. The students taught by this technique were more often relevant to the subject-matter and possessed more favourable attitude towards the subject-matter as a whole than those taught by the other method.

Again, an experiment conducted by the author to teach the conquests of Akbar, a history lesson, to the tenth-grade students revealed significant differences in favour of the said technique. The control group here was taught by Herbart's traditional five-step method by teachers using this method in a routine, mechanical way. The factors controlled in the said experiment on teaching reading lesson were controlled here as well.

Whether the technique outlined above is accomplished in Johann Herbart's five formal steps, or in Morrison's (1956) unit organisation–which includes exploration, presentation, assimilation, organisation and recitation–it, if adapted to varying conditions in the school, may achieve the essential purposes that are implied in teaching and may lead to what may be legitimately called effective education.

This technique does not guarantee success to all teachers nor to any teacher for all pupils; but it does furnish a method by which real progress may be made and on the basis of which may be developed individual independence.

Role of Teacher Training Colleges

While a technique of teaching is propounded, we should not assume that all fields of knowledge are established, rather than in flux. Secondary education presents complex problems which warrant some flexibility, adaptation, or growth in the techniques, as they do in other aspects like curricula. Hence the need of avoiding rigidity in approach. Again, any technique at best caters to the learning needs of the general run of students and not to the needs of the sophisticated or the retarded pupils. For the latter, a given technique has to be modified here and there, in form if not in spirit. This fact must be brought home to the student teachers at the time of their training, as otherwise they get frustrated when they find that the teaching techniques taught to them by the colleges of education do not work in the schools. The teachers must know that the techniques learned by them need to be adapted to the students, the school, the subject and the requirements they are destined to reckon with. Orientation of teachers to the essentials of a teaching technique, not so much to the formal steps that the colleges of education tend to prescribe, is a matter of prime importance. Teachers are prone to take specific preparation for a given learning unit or course for granted. It thus often happens that while the section is in general ready for the unit, there are details which, if left untaught, will cause wasteful and fatal inhibitions. This is particularly true of the technical vocabulary of a science lesson. Such are the modifications that the teachers should be trained to make, whenever necessary.

The teacher training colleges, while building a theory of teaching, must take into account the fact that the psychology of the learning process, the nature of the essential objectives sought (Gage, 1968, 1963), and consequently the teaching process itself, all differ in important details as we go from one subject to another in the secondary school. For instance, in subjects like mathematics, physical and social sciences, grammars of most languages, home economics, and the like, the objectives are adaptations which are in firm understanding of principles or processes in the relation of cause and effect; the method of learning is a process of reflection and rationalization, and the product is an intelligent attitude towards the environment or the science. In fine arts, religion and literature are found learnings which are expressed in attitudes toward conduct, which psychologically are concerned with affective side of man's nature, and the adaptations may imply enjoyment or some sort of suffering (though all this in a spirit of willing devotion). Mechanical arts, household arts like cooking, sewing, and courses like drawing and painting envisage objectives that lead to intelligent manipulation of appliances and moulding of materials. In languages, arise adaptations through which access is had to most of the materials of learning and through which the use of spoken and written discourse is learned. In typewriting, fundamental operations in arithmetic, spelling and some aspects of physical education the objectives are in the form of automatic facility and the learning process is pure repetition until the adaptation sought becomes established (Morrison, 1926).

Each subject stands for a form of learning and consequently for a form of teaching technique that is appropriate to certain specific objectives. When the teachers do not master teaching techniques appropriate to a subject, the factor generally responsible for it is the persistent attempts to achieve a given learning product under the wrong type of technique. Failure to note the significance of difference in types of learning and teaching often leads to assembling incongruous elements in the same course or sequence. In the teaching of English alone, there are at least four different types of teaching. Grammar is to be taught like science, literature like an appreciation lesson, composition like language, and spelling like some aspects of arithmetic. The result of herding all these subjects together without discrimination is non-mastery and waste. It is precisely in this area, the area of teaching techniques, that the teacher training colleges must specialise, conduct action research and evolve a theory as well as a practice of teaching which the student-teachers will imbibe with a view to becoming masters in the teaching of different subjects or aspects of subjects.

References

Beauchamp, W.L. *Studies in Secondary Education*, Vol. II, "Supplementary Educational Monographies", Chicago, The University of Chicago Press, 1925.

Bloom, Benjamin S. "Thought Process in Lectures and Discussions", J. *Gen. Ed.* 7, 160-9,1953.

Gage, N.L. "Can Science Contribute to the Art of Teaching?", *Phil Delta Kappan*, 49, 399-403,1968.

— (Ed.). *Handbook of Research on Teaching*, Rand McNally, 1218,1963. Monroe, Walter, S., and Marks Arlyn. "General Methods of Teaching," Ed. Adm. Sup. 24,497-512,1938.

Morrison, Henry C. *The Practice of Teaching in the Secondary School*, Chicago, The University of Chicago Press, 79-99, 220-231, 1926.

80. TEACHING PERFORMANCE OF MEN AND WOMEN TEACHERS

Abstract

An experiment aimed at knowing the performances of men and women college teachers in their academic roles, using autonomous competition (process itself measuring success i.e. the teacher whose students learn most is, ipso facto *the best teacher), revealed that the women mathematics teachers were neither as good as the best men teachers nor as bad as the worst; they tended to be mediocre. Another interesting finding was that the women teachers tended to be relatively more effective with the poorer students them they were with the superior ones, suggesting that they were patient rather than stimulating in instruction.*

Thomas (6), after observing men and women at Bryn Mawr for thirty-seven years, was convinced that women make exceptionally successful teachers. MacCracken (3) illustrated how bad the teaching by women could be. In an experiment in the teaching of English, the contribution of women teachers was at least average in success. It was, incidentally, judged better by colleagues than by students (4). An experiment in the field of sociology offered the most illuminating insights into the role-related handicaps of women in teaching students, especially in areas of knowledge which do not have the weight of established tradition behind them (5). Jessie, Bernard (2) observed that the success of any role performance, no matter whether it is man's or woman's, depends as much on Alter's performance of the complementary role as it does on Ego's performance of his role. In an experiment on Speech Study, it transpired that it was the personal confrontation between teacher and individual student which many of the women-taught students found so valuable and that the academic women seemed to be especially effective in this situation (1).

The present experiment was in the field of mathematics.

Method

The evaluation process was autonomous: the criterion for evaluating teaching performance was the amount that students learned as measured on final examination. Thirteen classes of the three-year degree course (Part II) were subjected to the experiment. Since 5 of these classes were taught by women, the general results provided a comparison of the relative success of men and women teachers. 103 students were taught by women and 319 by men teachers.

Eighty per cent of the subjects were boys; sex was controlled by random assignments to the classes constituting mathematics groups. All were given a common examination at the end of the term, and the answer books graded by a common committee. An aptitude test score for mathematics, of each subject, was obtained earlier. Thus effort was made to make the controls as tight as possible, but there could be several other variables, such as those which intervene between the time the students are taught and the time they are examined, that were left uncontrolled.

Results and Discussion

The average mathematics grade for the 5 classes taught by women was 51.3 while that for the 8 classes taught by men was 55.8. A similar result was found when grades were compared on an individual rather than on a grouped or class basis. The average grade for the students taught by women was 51.6 and of the 319 students taught by men teachers, 54.2. These differences, though statistically significant because of the large numbers involved, were fairly small.

There was greater variance among the classes taught by men than among those taught by women – 40.71 as compared with 16.29. The classes taught by women tended to approach the average. None of their classes did as well as that of the best male teacher (64.6) nor, on the other hand, as poorly as that of the worst male teacher (40.2). The position of the women teachers is somewhat less favourable, however, if student aptitude is considered. The average aptitude score of the students taught by the women teachers was 18.4, of the students taught by the men teachers, 17.2. On the average, the students of the women teachers had done slightly better on the aptitude test than had the students of the men teachers. For all the classes, the rank difference correlation between aptitude scores and achievement scores was 0.19. This figure, however, concealed the occurrence of two contradictory relationships. For the 8 classes taught by men, the correlation between aptitude and achievement was 0.47, for the 5 classes taught by women, it was—.39. Whereas the relationship for classes taught by men was in the expected direction in that the classes with good aptitude scores did better than those with poor scores, that for classes taught by women was in the reverse direction because the classes with poor aptitude scores did better than those with good predicted scores. If appears that the women teachers worked harder with the poorer classes (as shown by the aptitude score) than they did with the better classes. They were probably patient, persevering and practical rather than stimulating and superior in teaching.

Again, if aptitude score is held constant, the good students of the women teachers (aptitude scores of 18 and above) showed lower achievement than the good students of the men teachers (aptitude scores of 17 and above), but the ordinary and the below average students of the women teachers (aptitude scores less than 18) tended to average higher (median 55.8) than such students of the men teachers (median 51.8). These results are shown in Table 1.

Table 1
Average Achievement Scores of Classes in Mathematics Taught by Men and Women Teachers

Aptitude Score	Average achievement scores of classes taught by women	Average achievement scores of classes taught by men
20.0-20.4	41.7	64.6
19.5-19.9		
19.0-19.4		59.4
18.5-18.9	49.5	63.1
18.0-18.4		59.3

17.5-17.9	55.8, 59.7	
17.00-17.4		52.1
16.5-16.9	50.0	
16.0-16.4		56.6
15.5-15.9		
15.0-15.4		40.2
14.5-14.9		51.3

The chief conclusion is that, as measured by student achievement in tests, the women teachers were about as good on the average as the men teachers; their classes tended to show less variance than those of the men, more closely approaching the average. The women were not as good as the best nor as poor as the worst of the men teachers. Also the women teachers tended to be relatively more effective with the less able students (as measured by aptitude tests) than with the more able ones. They were relatively better than the men teachers with students of average aptitude, but not as good with the superior students.

Limitations of the Study

The picture drawn by the experiment is not one of two discrete universes, one for each sex, nor even one of overlapping universes but rather of a less variable universe within the limits of a more variable one. It would not be prudent therefore to make any generalization whatsoever on the basis of this not-so-strictly controlled and a limited observation.

The evidence yielded by the experiment, which tends to render the position of women teachers less favourable, may be inconclusive and for want of more scientific data even less accurate. Replication, using more rigid controls and better techniques as well as larger samples and sharper instruments, is very much needed before the said evidence can be generalised. The results are at best only suggestive.

References

1. Brilhert, John K., and Richard Spencer. "The Speech Study" — Department of Speech and University Division of International Services. Pennsylvania, State University, 1963.
2. Jessie Bernard. "Academic Women". The Pennsylvania State University Press, 1964, p. 130.
3. MacCracken, Henry Noble. "The Hickory Limb. " New York: Scribner's, 1950, p. 25.

4. Otis, E. Lancaster. "The English Study"—How to Recognise Good Teachers and Measure Teaching Ability. Pennsylvania State University, 1958.
5. Otis, E. Lancaster. "The Sociology Study"—How to Recognise Good Teachers and Measure Teaching Ability. Pennsylvania State University, 1958.
6. Thomas, M. Carey. "Address, Bryn, Mawr College Fiftieth Anniversary (Bryn Mawr: Bryn Mawr College, 1935), p. 55.

81. INFLUENCE OF EDUCATIONAL PSYCHOLOGY ON TEACHING SKILL

That to acquire knowledge of Educational Psychology is a 'must' for professional competence and growth of a teacher is generally accepted. Educational Psychology builds up a background for understanding and meeting a wide variety of classroom problems; it, together with other basic courses especially the Philosophical and Sociological bases of Education, goes a long way towards the making of a good teacher. Although it is in no way an embodiment of teaching techniques, yet it helps the teacher to grasp general principles–principles which help him perform all the tasks entrusted to him. The ideas imbibed through a knowledge of educational psychology are keys to an integrated conception of the school. A course in Educational Psychology leads to the teacher's continuing development; it has a considerable bearing on matters – educational and professional. As distinct from other teachers, the teacher teaching Educational Psychology is teaching about teaching. Hence he becomes self-conscious of whether his own teaching conforms to the principles he commends to his students. All the same, the investigator feels that the understanding of the principles of educational Psychology influences teaching skill. It was with this assumption that he took up the present experiment.

Procedure

(i) The marks in Educational Psychology secured by 153 teacher- trainees of Government Training College, Jullundur in the First Essay-type examination were compared to their marks in their first teaching skill examination held a little before their theory examination. The syllabus covered in Educational Psychology before the first examination was 50%.

(ii) Their second achievement in Educational Psychology after they had covered 100% syllabus was compared with their second achievement in teaching skill examination held subsequently.

(iii) The two achievements in Educational Psychology were mutually compared as were the two in teaching skill.

(iv) The average of the two achievements in Educational Psychology was compared with the average of the two achievements in teaching skill.

(v) The achievement in Educational Psychology of those showing a difference of 4 or less marks in the two evaluations was compared to their corresponding achievement in teaching skill.

(vi) The achievement in Educational Psychology of those showing a difference of 15 or more marks in the two evaluations was compared to their corresponding achievement in teaching skill.

The answer books of Educational Psychology each time were marked by different examiners. The practical skill of each candidate was assessed by different examiners each time.

Statistical analysis of the data, up to correlation coefficient derived through Pearson Product-moment method, was attempted.

Data in Brief:

Averages:- Mean of the 1st evaluation in Educational Psychology = 34

Mean of the 2nd evaluation in Educational Psychology = 40

Mean of the 1st evaluation in Teaching Skill = 51

Mean of the 2nd evaluation in Teaching Skill = 52

Correlation Coefficients – Achievement of 153 students

1. 'r' between 1st Evaluation in Educational Psychology and 1st Evaluation in Teaching Skill = .61
2. 'r' between 2nd Evaluation in Educational Psychology and 2nd Evaluation in Teaching Skill = .68
3. 'r' between 1st and 2nd Evaluation in Educational Psychology = .71
4. 'r' between 1st and 2nd Evaluation in Teaching skill = .73

5. 'r' between Evaluation in Educational Psychology and that in teaching skill (taking average of the two evaluations in each case) = .62

Achievement of 45 students who show a difference of 4 or less marks in their two evaluations in Educational Psychology

6. 'r' between 1st and 2nd Evaluation in Educational Psychology = .95
7. 'r' between 1st and 2nd evaluation of Teaching Skill = .74
8. 'r' between 1st Evaluation in Educational Psychology and 1st achievement in Teaching Skill = .72
9. 'r' between 2nd Evaluation in Educational Psychology and 2nd Achievement in Teaching Skill = .66

Achievement of 19 students who show a difference of 15 or more marks in their two achievements in Educational Psychology.

10. 'r' between 1st and 2nd Evaluation in Educational Psychology = .87
11. 'r' between 1st and 2nd Evaluation in Teaching Skill = .61
12. 'r' between 1st Evaluation in Educational Psychology and 1st Evaluation in Teaching Skill = .62
13. 'r' between 2nd Evaluation in Educational Psychology and 2nd Evaluation in Teaching Skill. = .65

Findings with reference to the above data:

(a) 'r's at 1, 2, 5, 8,9,12 & 13 vary from .61 to .72. The 'r's being considerably high and fairly consistent indicate that the knowledge of Educational Psychology may positively influence Teaching Skill.

(b) 'r's at 1, & 2 show increasing correlation between Educational Psychology and Teaching Skill. So do the 'r's at 12 & 13. It may indicate that greater the knowledge of Educational Psychology greater becomes the Teaching Skill.

(c) 'r' at 3, 6 & 10 show that Essay Type examinations so often decried, in Educational Psychology, may not be so bad. The correlations between 2 of such evaluations seem to be fairly high and the students' achievements in the two examinations fairly consistent.

(d) 'r's at 4,7 & 11 show that the two evaluations of Teaching Skill are fairly correlated and the students' achievement in Teaching Skill quite consistent.

(e) Findings at (c) & (d) above indicate that those whose achievement in Educational Psychology is consistent may be equally consistent in their achievement in Teaching Skill.

(f) 'r's at 8 and 9 show that these 45 students when equipped with greater knowledge of Educational Psychology did not gain as much in their Teaching Skill as others did.

Limitations

1. The tests in Educational Psychology, being ordinary essay-type, are not standardised nor are the evaluations in teaching skill so. Both the examinations may not satisfy the technical criteria of a test though these are very well-tried examinations.
2. The gain in the knowledge of Educational Psychology may not be exclusively due to covering more syllabus in the subject, but it may partly be due to many other factors (like experience, transfer of learning from other subjects etc.) none of which was controlled in the experiment.
3. The gain in teaching skill may not be wholly due to the increased knowledge of Educational Psychology; it may partly be owing to the added knowledge of Educational Philosophy and/or other subjects and other factors which were not controlled.
4. The experiment yields findings which need further verification through similar and/or improved techniques.

82. SOME CORRELATES OF N-ACHIEVEMENT

Abstract

Relationship of n-achievement with academic achievement, bureaucratic orientation, intelligence and interest in teaching in respect of 90 graduate teacher trainees belonging to average socio-economic and cultural strata was explored. The study concluded that n-achievement may be related to intelligence and academic achievement but not too bureaucratic orientation or interest in teaching. Again, it appeared that intelligence tends to enhance the relation between n-achievement and academic achievement and that n-achievement tends to enhance the relation between intelligence and academic achievement.

McClelland (1949) observed that achievement motivation is anticipatory or forward looking. Earlier Hull (1931) had reached a similar conclusion that fractional anticipatory goal responses are the key to understanding purposeful and motivational phenomenon. Using thematic apperception as the measure of achievement motive, McClelland (1953) found that urge for achievement is the major factor in human motivation and behaviour and that this urge affects the performance of an individual to a large extent. He (1963) also found that progressive societies have high n-achievement [need achievement, the word originally used by Murray (1943)], as compared to backward societies.

Again McClelland (1963) observed that individual, with high n-achievement tend to be on the positive side of these characteristics: risk taking, energetic and novel instrumental activity, individual responsibility, knowledge of results, anticipation of future possibilities, and organisational skills. McClelland (1963), Atkinson (1958) and others found that cultural and environmental factors affect the need to achieve. Katz (1967) found that persons from low socio-economic groups have a lower estimate of their n-achievement and that poor people develop an avoidance reaction.

French (1955) found close relationship between performance and n-achievement. Lowel (1952) concluded that students with high n-achievement score, though starting with about the same level of performance as the subjects with low n-achievement score, do progressively better as they proceed with the rather complex task of unscrambling words. Wintarbottom (1953) found that early training in independence and mastery contributes to strong achievement motivation. Martire's (1956) general finding was that subjects who obtained high n-achievement scores under both neutral and achievement-oriented conditions showed significantly greater discrepancy between their self-ideal and self-ratings. McClelland (1955) observed that individuals with high n-achievement tended to take moderate risks, while subjects with low n-achievement preferred significantly more often very safe or speculative enterprises. Raphelson's (1957) study revealed a significant negative relationship between anxiety and n-achievement. Knap (1959) found significant correlation between n-achievement and aesthetic preference. Atkinson (1958) and others observed that difference between subjects having high and low n-achievement scores in recognition thresholds for success and failure words would be greater in motive aroused than in the neutral perceptual conditions. McClelland (1963) found that stories from a given country appear to be consistently high or low in n-achievement. The study of Atkinson and others (1966) demonstrated that motivational level in learning is determined by the life space (Lewin's Concept) of individual.

Prayag Mehta's (1966-68) study yields low positive correlation between n-achievement and examination results of high school boys, but the correlation seems to be favourably comparable with the correlation of intelligence tests and school marks. He also contemplated the possibility of raising teachers' level of n-achievement by adequate methods and that of its effect on students' motivation. Shanthamaain and Hofeez (1968) found significant differences between Engineering, Arts and Commerce students in n-achievement. Also they noted a low negative correlation between n-achievement and neuroticism. Birney's (1969) study suggested that persons motivated by stronger n-achievement set high goals of life. Muthaya and Rajeshwari (1969) found no significant difference between personal aspiration and achievement motive. Siddiqi and Akhtar (1969) found that the basic difference between disciplined and undisciplined groups is that the former group has a higher achievement motive and the latter has higher affiliation and power motives. Chamanlal (1970) verified the hypothesis that students taking professional courses have higher n-achievement level than those taking academic courses and that achievement motive and academic performance are related.

The present study is meant to estimate the relationship between n- achievement and each of the four variables *i.e.* academic Achievement, Bureaucratic Orientation, Intelligence, Interest in

Teaching, in respect of 90 graduate teacher trainees (age range 19-22) chosen randomly from a population of 300 in the State College of Education, Patiala. The study rests on the hypothesis that need achievement of teacher trainees may be related, more or less, to each of the above variables.

Methods and Procedure

The instrument used for measuring need achievement was Need Achievement Inventory, adapted to Indian situations from McClelland's Achievement Imagery by Chamanlal. It is a 50 item likert type form. Twenty-five items reflect positive and twenty-five negative motive. Positive items reflect achievement-oriented behaviour, and negative items depict fear of failure. The split half reliability and validity with a rating scale (devised on the basis of McClelland's seven characteristics of achievement-oriented behaviour) were found to be .96 and .67 (significant at .01 level) respectively. Percentage of a trainee's aggregate marks in the university graduate examination was taken as a measure of his academic achievement. The mean reliability of this measure, as found by correlating the trainees' marks used here with their marks in the previous three comparable examinations held during the graduation course, was .78. Bureaucratic Orientation was measured by Gordon's (1968) Work Environment Preference Schedule (WEPS), the test retest reliability and criterion validity of which stand established at .65 and .59 (1971) respectively. The Lorge-Thorndike Intelligence Test Form A, non-verbal, level 5, having a minimum validity of .65 was used to gather scores of intelligences (1957). Scores for interest in teaching were obtained by using KTAT (1968), the split-half reliability and predictive validity of which are known to be .53 and .69 respectively.

The tests were administered to the sample group a month after admission in the teacher training course. The admission took place two weeks after they passed their graduate examination.

Results and Discussion

As observed by McClelland (1953) and verified by French (1955), Lowell (1952), Prayag Mehta (1966-68) and Chamanalal (1970) significant and positive correlation of n-achievement with academic achievement is a finding yielded by this study as well (Table 1). This correlation may be expected, because the achievement motive spurs one on to performance consistent with the strength of the motive. Stronger motive leads to setting higher goals, as also suggested by Birney (1969). In a bid to reach these goals, the individual starts off on activity making adequate achievement.

Table 1
Intercorrelational r's of n-achievement and other Variables

n-achievement	Academic achievement	Bureaucratic orientation	Intelligence	Interest in teaching
n-achievement	.39*	–.10	.67*	.15
Academic achievement		–.009	.35*	–.10
Bureaucratic orientation			–.06	.09
Intelligence				.20**

* Significant at .01 level.
** Significant at .05 level.

A high correlation between n-achievement and intelligence, not hitherto revealed by any of the studies reviewed by the author, tends to indicate that intelligence may be conducive to need achievement, though it would not be fair to contemplate such cause-effect relationships in the absence of positive evidence in this behalf. A high IQ is too often used to keep its owner keenly aware of his own discontent in the matter of his need to achieve and hence perhaps the high relationship of this need with intelligence. A university of California research group have made an unexpected discovery that at any age a person is happier if he is not too bright. The happiness referred to here may be due to the discontent the greater brightness fosters in terms of higher n-achievement.

Positive relationship between intelligence and academic achievement and that between intelligence and interest in teaching are what may be expected and what several studies have already shown. The former relationship may be owing to the fact that a high IQ tends to keep its possessor on tenterhooks until he manages to manage adequate achievement.

The correlations between n-achievement and academic achievement may be due to the effect of intelligence and that between intelligence and academic achievement may be due to the effect of n-achievement. To rule out the effect of the third variable in each case, partial correlations were drawn. (Table 2).

When intelligence was partialled out, the correlation between n-achievement and academic achievement came to .22 instead of .39. This means that when all the 90 trainees possess the same degree of intelligence, there is dearly a much lesser relation between n-achievement and academic achievement than there is when intelligence varies. Intelligence obviously is a variable that affects the relation between n-achievement and actual achievement.

When n-achievement was held constant, the correlation between intelligence and academic achievement came to .12 instead of .35. This means that when all our trainees show the same amount of n-achievement, there is a far less relation between intelligence and academic achievement, than there is when n-achievement varies. This finding tends to make suspect the relation between intelligence and academic achievement which all too often is positive and highly significant. The influence of need achievement on the relation between intelligence; and academic achievement is obviously too vital to be ruled out. N-achievement is, therefore, a variable to be reckoned with in all studies involving intelligence and achievement.

When academic achievement was partialled out, the correlation between n-achievement and intelligence remained almost the same as it was when academic achievement kept varying. This is what may be expected because academic achievement does not seem to affect either intelligence or n-achievement though each of the two latter variables may affect academic achievement.

Table 2
Partial correlations between N-achievement[1], Academic achievement[2] and Intelligence[3]

r when third is not partialled out	r when third variable is partialled out
r_{12} = .39	$r_{12.3}$ = .22
r_{23} = .35	$r_{23.1}$ = .12
r_{13} = .67	$r_{13.2}$ = .64

The study concludes that need achievement of teacher trainees may be related to intelligence and academic achievement but not to bureaucratic orientation or interest in teaching.

References

1. Atkinson, J.W. "Motives in Fantasy, Action, and Society" D. Von Nostrand Coy, INC., N.J. 1958,64-82.
2. Atkinson J.W., and Norman, T. Feather. "A theory of achievement motive." John Willy and Sons, Inc. N.Y., 1966.
3. Chamanlal. "A Comparative study of the need achievement of college students taking professional and academic courses." MED Dissertation 1970. Punjab University, Patiala.
4. French, Elizabeth G. "Some characteristics of Achievement motivation." J. exp Psychol, 1955, 50, 232-236. pp. 34, 401, 402.
5. Gordon, L.V. Work Environment Preference Schedule—WEPS. Albany: 1968 (1).
6. Gordon, L.V., "Preliminary Manual, Work Environment Preference Schedule" - WEPS. Albany: 1971.
7. Hull, C.H. Goal attraction and directing ideas conceived as habit phenomena. Psychol. Rev., 1931, 38, 487-509.
8. Kakkar, S.B. "Teacher Trainees' Interest in the Teaching Profession." S.I.E. Chandigarh Publ. 52,1968.
9. Knapp, R., and Green H. "Time judgement, aesthetic preference and need for achievement". J. abnor. Soc Psychol. 58,140-142.
10. Lowell, E.L., "The effect of need for achievement on learning and speed of performance." J. Psychol., 1952,33,31-0. pp. 252,260,267, 278,284,374,416.
11. Martire, J.G., "Relationships between the self-concept and differences in the strength and generality of achievement motivation. J. Pers., 1956, 24, 364-375.
12. McClelland, D.C., and others "The Achievement Motive." New York: Appleton. Century Crofts. 1953.
13. McClelland, D.C. "The Achieving Society" Princeton N.J.: D. Van Nostrand Co., Inc. 1963.
14. McClelland, D.C. "Some social consequences of achievement motivation." In M.R. Jones (Ed.), Nebraska symposium on motivation, 1955, Lincoln: University of Nebraska Press, 1955, p. 649.
15. Murray, H.A., Thematic Apperception Test Manual. Cambridge. Harvard University Press, 1943. pp. 1, 673, 694.
16. McClelland, D.C., Atkinson, J.W., and Clark, R.A. The projective expression of needs. III. The effect of ego involvement, success and failure on perception. J. Psychol., 1949, 27, 311-330, pp. 68,77,78, 79.
17. Muthayya, B.C., and Rajeshwari, S. (1969). "Personal aspiration and its relationship to achievement motive." J. Psych. Res. 1969,13,1, 52-55.

18. Prayag Mehta. "The Achievement Motive in High School Boys." N.C.E.R.T. New Delhi, 1966-68.
19. Rephelson, A.C. "The relationship between imaginative, direct verbal, and physiological measures of anxiety in an achievement situation." J. Abnorm. Soc. Psychol, 1957, 54,13-18.
20. Shanthamani, U.S., and Hafeez, A. "Need for achievement among Engineering, Arts and Commerce students." Manas J. Scient. Psy. 1968, 15, 2,67-69.
21. Siddiqui, M.M., and Sultan Akhtar, S. "Quantitative study of n-achievement, n-affiliation and n-power among disciplined and undisciplined students." J. Psychol. Res. 1969,13, 2,85-89.
22. Thorndike, Robert L., and Irving Lorge "The Lorge-Thorndike Intelligence Tests, Level 5." The Houghton Mifflin Coy. Boston (1957).
23. Winverbottom, Marian R. "The relation of childhood training in independence to achievement motivation." Unpublished doctoral dissertation, University of Michigan, 1953, pp.453,462,472.

83. TEACHER EDUCATION IN INDIA: AMERICAN INFLUENCE*

India inherited from the British a fairly well-established, though not national, productive, appropriate or adequate educational system, which tends to persist even today. As this system, since its inception by the foreign rulers, was neither linked to Indian needs and aspirations nor aimed at producing the right individuals for a free democratic social order that India chose to adopt, the education in India and, consequently, India's growth and development continue to suffer. Nevertheless, some changes made in the recent past and some that are in the offing may be the foreboding of a reasonably suitable educational system and of a bright future for the country.

The belief that India had virtually no educational system before independence from the English rule is a travesty of truth and is derogatory to the Indians and disparaging to the British. Indians on their own had established and maintained an indigenous system of education, and in addition the British rulers gave India an educational system, often called Western education. Thus, when the British rulers left in the late forties, India had a fairly organised and functional educational system, though it was neither widespread nor modern.

* Dr. H. Dhand (Sask Univ., Canada) was the co-author.

American Influence

If India's teacher education programmes have a pattern of courses that strongly resembles those in North America, it may not be due to the influence of the American Agency for International Development, as claimed by American teacher educators (1). Instead, the influence may be that of the British programme of teacher education of which Indian system is still more or less a replica, and to which the North American programme might have been similar. By and large, teacher education programmes in India, apart from a few unsubstantial changes, are still the same that India had in the pre-independence era.

American influence in certain areas of teacher education, however, has been very much there, though in a limited number of institutions. For instance, the four-to-five-year programme for secondary teachers and the two-year programme for primary teachers are based on the North American pattern. The four-year programme for secondary teachers is confined to the four Regional Colleges of Education which are run under the aegis of the National Council of Educational Research and Training (NCERT). In almost all the other colleges of education in the country the pattern for the training of secondary teachers is one-year teacher education following one or more university degree, which the British rulers had introduced before independence in 1947.

A typical programme of teacher education in India in the after-degree teacher education colleges would include courses in Philosophical and Social Foundations of Education, Educational Psychology, Indian Education, School Organization, and Methodology of Teaching and a student teaching. This represents a bequeathal from the British tradition. The fact that the courses in teacher education in India are similar to those in North America does not mean that they have been imported from the USA or brought to India by the American experts. It may mean that the British courses on teacher education are similar to the corresponding American courses. A remarkable difference between the courses on teacher education in India and the USA is that the textbooks used in India are shorter and their style is akin to that of the College Outline Series. It might be argued that if the courses in India followed the North American pattern, Indian teacher education would be better.

Courses on curriculum and instruction do not teach, much less do they emphasize the importance of behavioural objectives and taxonomies, though these would, certainly, improve teacher education and, concomitantly, raise the quality of teachers. In the fifties, educators in India had the good fortune of learning a great deal in this regard from Dr. Benjamin Bloom of Chicago University who introduced to the colleges of education the taxonomy of educational objectives. He held several workshops at various places in the country to train educators regarding the intrinsic interdependence of the trinity—educational purposes, learning experiences and evaluation techniques–without which no abiding reform in education can be made. Dr. Bloom did spearhead a countrywide programme to reorient the examination system with a view to making it an important ally in the creative reconstruction of the Indian educational system. A remarkably effective teacher, he made many teacher educators, school heads and all those who were in a position to enforce his movement in education, fully conversant with the ways evaluation and, consequently, instruction could be completely reformed.

Although Bloom's movement continued, mainly through the follow-up maintained by the All India Council for Secondary Education and the NCERT, and his concepts registered their indelible impact on certain institutions, *status quo* and orthodoxy stood in the way of its absorption in education. The inescapable result of resistance to change is that Indian education stands deprived of the educational reforms that Bloom's teachings could have yielded.

Student teaching in the teacher education programme in India is akin to that in North America probably because student teaching in North America resembles that in Britain, while the Indians continue to practise the student teaching pattern that the British gave them. Among the typical characteristics of the age-old Indian teacher education programme are the practices of teacher education faculty supervising all the lessons taught by student teachers, classes strictly observing the syllabi and textbooks, recitation method dominating in teacher education, and content being examination oriented. These practices symbolise major differences between Indian and North American programmes.

There is no denying the fact that the content taught in Indian schools and colleges is tied tightly to an unforgiving system of evaluation. In fact, the Indian educational system gives an unbridled impression that learning or education is nothing but rote memory which external examinations must test. It was this flaw in the examination system and, consequently, in the educational programmes that Bloom's campaign sought to remove.

It is true that the present quality of teachers is, by and large, not as good as it needs to be, though the fault does not lie merely with the fact that teacher education does not attract its share of good candidates. That a few of the better students enter teaching, that women enter teaching to ensure against the death or loss of earning power of the spouse, that monetary or status reasons make persons attain any job except teaching, that they enter teaching as a last resort–were old, hackneyed arguments offered several years ago when teaching was not a lucrative or status profession. Today, teaching is comparable to any other employment that brings reasonable pay and good status. Some urban graduates, upon completion of teacher training, prefer other equally good jobs to teaching for fear of being posted to far-flung villages where status, mobility and material quality of living are lacking, though those who love teaching do not do so.

To a small extent, teacher education does miss its share of good candidates for the reason that some high achievers are tempted to go in for administrative services, which in India are at the top from the viewpoint of monetary and social status.

The major reason, however, for not having good quality teachers is the faulty recruitment of teacher candidates. The criteria of selecting teacher trainees in most colleges of education include conditions other than the results of teaching aptitude tests; the most popular criterion is the scholastic score in the final graduation examination. Those who are seen to have aptitude for teaching are expected to profit most from their training, they will make good teachers, and they will accept teaching positions upon graduation and will permanently stick to the profession.

The quality of teacher education too is seen to matter in the making of a good teacher; it may frustrate a budding teacher or chisel out one who can make a nation builder. Teacher candidates selected on the basis of a sharp teaching aptitude instrument and provided with an enriching comprehensive teacher education experience can turn into teachers and a profession, of which the country can legitimately be proud.

Inservice education of teachers is not neglected in India as has been misconstrued by some scholars in North America. Besides the extension services departments in colleges of education, independent in-service education centres are also providing inservice education, both academic and pedagogical, to employed teachers. Inservice educational development of teachers gets further impetus from the university correspondence and continuing education courses as well as from such agencies as the National Council of Educational Research and Training (NCERT), similar councils at state levels, state institutes of science, the National Institute of Educational Administration and the like. Inservice as well as continuing education of teachers is, thus, amply looked after in India.

Research in Teacher Education in India

Educational research is no longer a new activity; there has been an increasing upsurge in the last two decades. Substantial research in teacher education has been conducted by teacher educators and research scholars at M.Ed., M.Phil., and Ph.D. levels. Quite a few of the research studies completed in India compare favourably to similar research studies in the USA and Canada. Some of the research is funded or subsidized by the University Grants Commission (UGC), the NCERT and the universities, while many of them are financed by the scholars themselves. Here lies a major difference with North America where research budgets and support, as well as incentives for research, appear to be larger than those available in India.

Some of the Indian research studies take the form of evaluation of innovations in teacher education. But what causes consternation is that many of the research studies, after completion, are relegated to the "educational utopia", never to be resurrected. Some innovations are North American imports. Investigations of interaction analysis, micro-teaching, simulative teaching, teaching strategies and programmed instruction have become targets of research only recently. The introduction of these areas in teacher education curriculum and their attendant research have, of course, initially resulted from individual interest and experiments by teacher educators who became interested in the new approaches to teaching through American research literature. A few professors in a college of education or a university department of education or at the NCERT would stimulate interest in others by conducting their own research, assigning research problems to their M.Ed., M. Phil, and Ph.D. students, and holding conferences with, and training the staff of teacher education colleges on problems related to these topics. Whether the size and contribution of the research exceeds that in the USA is a question that could be answered only after a comparative survey of the research completed in the two countries.

A very pertinent question that many educators in colleges of education are likely to raise is whether the results of research studies in education or teacher education are utilised to reform education or the relevant aspect of education, and whether the innovations found successful or useful as a result of research studies are actually introduced or assimilated into the educational system. There is usually a gap between what research has revealed and what is actually translated into practice. It seems that this "gap" is larger in India than in North America.

Many of the innovations, like micro-teaching, simulative teaching, and programming of different varieties, imported from the USA, are being successfully tried in the teacher education system of India, and several trials have shown that they are equally useful and effective in the Indian cultural setting. In fact, a concept or innovative procedure that is theoretically sound, or based on certain psychological principles governing human behaviour, can be transplanted anywhere. Educational researchers, proceeding from such assumption, have gone ahead with introducing imported innovations in India and have invariably found their evaluations of these almost similar to the findings of American researchers. Whereas numerous studies on the transplanted innovations have been completed and several others are in the process, the educational leaders have still to make these innovations a part and parcel of the teacher education system. So far it has not been done, the reason being that the size and rapid development of the country and its vastness and diversity do not easily permit uniformity of the system. At the same time, indigenous innovations, that come handy in promoting education and teacher education and that are particularly convenient and suitable to Indian conditions of work and to Indian education keep on attracting educators, who sometimes, however, tend to resist anything new, American or Indian.

Teacher Education – A Critique

It is a fact that Indian teacher education is still far from achieving national goals, that it continues to be largely unchanged, that it stands isolated from the mainstream of national life, from the academic life of the university, from school and even from the community it is meant to serve, that the quality of its faculty is too low to raise the image of education as a discipline, and that changes in the areas of "the teacher as a citizen, education as a discipline and the theory-to-practice gap" are still hanging fire, as has been reported by the NCERT (2). It is evident that Indian education has neither absorbed the imported innovations of the West which could raise the level of teacher education, nor has it achieved complete riddance from the British system of teacher education, which was a prerequisite to orientating education so that it could play the role of transforming India into a truly democratic, socialist, and secular society.

Fortunately, however, educators, political leaders, social reformers, and the establishment are increasingly getting intensely concerned about education. Here and there many educators have voiced the urgent need of value education so as to develop Gandhian values of non-violence, dignity of labour, truthfulness, self-discipline and self-reliance. Need for vocational and social education both at school and university levels is also being discussed.

Recently the Prime Minister of India has presented to the nation the *Challenge of Education-A Policy Perspective* (3), a very vital and key document on education where the shortcomings of the present education, including teacher education, have been delineated. It also provides a blue-print for future educational plans, and it emphasises the necessity of overhauling the system so as to make education strictly national, effective and appropriate. Commitment of society to education and the sense of purpose, dedication and integrity in all those who are destined to implement educational policy have been particularly emphasised in the document. The document has aroused considerable interest in both educators and the general public all over the country, giving rise to the holding of numerous seminars, discussion groups and conferences. All this augurs well for future education of the country.

The major criticisms of Indian teacher education such as its academic weakness, isolation from academic community, lack of disciplined structure and irrelevance to social conditions, are universal in nature, as identical criticisms are reported in the UNESCO reports (1976-1978) and the US report (Joyce and Clift, 1984) (4) Is, then, teacher education a commonly much-maligned system in most countries? Is there something in the very nature of this system which prevents it from steering clear of its flaws? Is teacher education the weakest link in the education system of most countries? If the answers to these questions are positive, as it appears they are, these would raise many eyebrows and impel us to dig deep into the system of teacher education with a view to removing the snags, and making it an effective vehicle for the training and education of future teacher.

Problems in Innovation

Even though the suitability of some imported innovations on India's soil has been demonstrated by educational researchers and teacher educators, resistance to assimilating universally those ideas in their teacher education system crops up. Inter-cultural differences in educational and social settings, even intra-cultural differences in settings, in the vastly diverse society of India, tend to cause such resistance, the fear being that the innovations tested in one setting will not be applicable or suitable to another setting. Demographic, linguistic, economic or other variations do make the settings different, but these differences do not supplant the essential similarities which exist within different settings in the same country and which essentially insure against any desperate finding. Assertions and apprehensions that different settings in the same country will not yield similar effects of an innovation have been proven false by several studies in India. But such apprehensions are an obsession with most teacher educators that restricts them from going ahead with the adoption of imported ideas. They insist that they must test the innovation in their own setting before adopting it, and, since testing means organising and executing a research for which they do not have the time and wherewithal, they desist from adopting the innovation.

Nevertheless, there is need to undertake research to determine the extent to which educational procedures in the United States or Canada may fit the Indian cultural setting. Similarly, there is need to conduct studies dealing with Inter-cultural differences and intracultural differences in Indian settings. Till then, apprehensions regarding the applicability of American ideas to Indian cultural settings, or that of Indian ideas tested in one setting to another setting, are bound to linger on.

Such problems of introducing innovations in the teacher education programme as finding time for them in an already full-time curriculum, integrating them with the predominantly theoretical and verbalistic courses, including them in the subjects of examination (without which no subject is really learnt in the examination-oriented educational system), and achieving a place for them in the certification and accreditation system do crop up at the initial stages, but these would not be a hurdle once teacher educators get convinced of the efficacy and suitability of the imported ideas in their setting.

As in North America, linking courses to student teaching, which is essentially warranted when we adopt the innovations in teacher education, is possible only if the school setting is tightly linked to the university and if school and college of education teachers work in close collaboration with each other while they study and use the same or parallel procedures. Most college faculty members have very little contact with schools, apart from direct supervision of student teaching. Thus, as the introduction of innovations must be preceded by certain administrative and functional changes, developing procedures and training faculty members, which no college of education can do on its own, Indian educators fail to proceed beyond conducting research studies on innovations.

It is not surprising to note that there are parallels between the problems of innovation in the cultures of India and the USA, and that similar difficulties arise in the two countries in the way of inducting innovations in teacher education. The parallels are especially striking when we consider that American students and teachers cherish values that render them prone to adopting innovation, as against Indian students and teachers who are tradition-oriented and thus resistant to innovations. These differences in values were revealed in a study by Kakkar and Gordon (5), in which Indian teachers and students scored significantly higher in conformity (doing what is traditionally done) and lower in independence (having freedom to do what one wants) than their American counterparts, and again in another study by Gordon (6), in which American students scored significantly higher than their Indian counterparts in practical-mindedness (to do things that pay off) and variety (to do new and different things).

The ability to generate and implement an innovation in teacher education is not invested in the executive in India. What happens is that faculty members in a college of education generate an idea, study it, experiment with it and discuss it with other faculty members. If the idea is accepted by the faculty, the college principal sends it to the dean of education in the university where it is discussed by the board of studies in education, the faculty of education and the academic council – in this order, each body, if it accepts it, passing if to the next. If the academic council accepts the idea, it becomes a part of the syllabus or curriculum of a college of education; and it, then, has to be executed or implemented by all the colleges of education affiliated to that university. The new material (*i.e.* innovation) then has a firm niche in the curriculum of an institution, and has achieved the requisite priority in the examination, which is the only guarantee that the innovation will be learnt and practised by all those who undergo the course. Sometimes the innovation comes to a college of education from the NCERT (via a university) which has already discussed it threadbare in several workshops or conferences in which professors of colleges of education also participate. The NCERT passes on the new idea to the university where it has to pass through the three above-mentioned bodies before it forms part of a course-schedule of a college of education.

The overseas originators, as it is well known, enjoy greater freedom and autonomy and should be able to achieve a greater depth of implementation. In India, there are many teachers, professors and directors who are very receptive to innovations, and earnestly cooperate to test and implement them, but they alone cannot achieve implementation.

It is true that Indians are rapidly adopting foreign, modern and advanced artifacts, ideas, and technology and that tremendous social change is going on. But, Indians stand for change as much as for stability, while retaining their typical Indianness. Their speed of change may be great simply because they need to change in a big way in a relatively shorter span of time for achieving prosperity, removing age-old poverty, raising the standard of living of their people and becoming adequately self-sufficient in every aspect of living.

The magnitude and the speed of change, however, have been infinitesimal in Indian education, more so in teacher education, as compared to the social and technological changes that are taking place there. Amidst a massive cultural reorientation, and advanced technology from the West, the dimension of change in teacher education has been rather small, though Indian teacher educators wish it were much more! The need for such change has been intense and that is why the Indian teacher educators are always itching to try and implement the Western innovations. Perhaps the English education system had been rooted so deeply that early attempts to uproot it proved futile, or perhaps conformity with what is already there, which is a dominant value nourished by the Indian tradition and culture, has been keeping

India back from seeking an overhaul of the existing education system.

Indian educators have still to build mechanisms to promote experimentation and research into the structure of teacher education, even education as such, which would go a long way towards the adopting of innovations that can improve and raise the level of teacher education.

Here and there in institutions of India there are committed researchers, teacher educators, and educational leaders who are really interested in introducing new ideas and making bold ventures into education with a view to bringing it in line with any modern system on which the nation could safely depend.

Joyce and Showers (7), while making interesting and incisive observations on the structure of Indian teacher education and while comparing it with theirs, have found several parallels that tend to comfort the Indian educators amidst scores of problems that keep on worrying them. Smug with the belief that the USA and Canada, the technologically and educationally advanced countries, face difficulties, similar to theirs, in the matter of introducing educational innovations, Indian educators feel contented with whatever they have achieved in this behalf, though their achievements leave much to be desired.

References

1. Joyce, Bruce and Beverly Showers. (1985), "Teacher Education in India: Observation on American Innovations Abroad". *Educational Researcher, 14 (8), 3-9.*
2. National Council of Educational Research and Training. (1978), *Teacher Education Curriculum: A Framework.* New Delhi: Author.
3. Ministry of Education, Government of India (August 1985). *Challenge of Education-4 Policy Perspective.* New Delhi: Author.
4. Joyce, Bruce and Beverly Showers, op. cit., 5-6.
5. Kakkar, S.B., and Gordon, L.V. (1966), "The Interpersonal Values of Teacher Trainees", *Journal of Social Psychology, 69,341-42.*
6. Gordon, L.V. (1966), *Survey of Personal Values, Manual.* Chicago: Science Research Associates, Inc.
7. Joyce, Bruce and Beverly Showers, *op. cit.*, 3-9.